## Sadlier-Oxford

**NEW**

# PHONICS AND WORD STUDY

## GRADES 4-6

biologist

explorer

astronomer

# Developing the Skills to Become

## SENIOR AUTHORS

**Richard T. Vacca**
Professor of Education
Kent State University

**Lesley Mandel Morrow**
Professor of Literacy
Rutgers University

## Introducing
# Sadlier Word Study

Current reading research suggests that children need to gain automaticity in decoding to become successful at comprehending text. An emphasis on word study at the middle grades builds upon the powerful relationship that exists between accurate, quick decoding and reading comprehension.

*Sadlier Word Study, Levels D–F,* provides students with the skills and strategies necessary to decode unfamiliar words by extending the development of phonics instruction into the middle grades. The program helps students apply decoding skills and develop word-meaning strategies as they read content-area materials.

The systematic sequence of skills and strategies in *Sadlier Word Study* provides students with a ready knowledge of word parts and the ability to use context clues, leading to better comprehension.

**Introduction**

# Successful Readers

## CONTENT OVERVIEW

| Unit Theme | Literature Selection | Skill Focus |
|---|---|---|
| 1. Athletes | *Beach Volleyball* by Martin Lee and Marcia Miller | Consonant Blends and Consonant Digraphs |
| 2. Explorers | *Meet an Underwater Explorer* by Luise Woelflein | Short, Long, and *r*-controlled Vowels; Vowel Pairs, Vowel Digraphs, Diphthongs, and Phonograms |
| 3. Artists and Composers | *Twisted Trails* from *Time for Kids* | Word Endings, Contractions, Plurals, Possessives, and Compound Words |
| 4. Making a Difference | *It's Our World, Too!* by Phillip Hoose | Prefixes, Roots, and Syllables |
| 5. Scientists | *Your Future in Space* by Alan L. Bean | Suffixes and Syllables |
| 6. People and Government | *Everybody's Uncle Sam* by Lester David | Dictionary and Thesaurus Skills; Synonyms, Antonyms, Homonyms; Clipped, Blended, and Borrowed Words; Idioms and Analogies |
| 1. The Northeast | *Native Peoples of the Northeast* by Trudie Lamb Richmond | Consonant Blends, Consonant Digraphs, and Double Consonant Sounds |
| 2. The Southeast | *Saving the Everglades* from *Time for Kids* | Vowel Pairs, Vowel Digraphs, Diphthongs, and Phonograms |
| 3. The Middle West | *How to Grow a Painting* by Gail Skroback Hennessey | Word Endings, Contractions, Plurals, Possessives, and Compound Words |
| 4. The Southwest | *Deep in the Heart of...Big Bend* by Bud McDonald | Prefixes, Roots, Base Words, and Suffixes |
| 5. The West | *Catching Up with Lewis and Clark* from *Time for Kids* | Context Clues |
| 6. The Northwest and Hawaii | *Hawaii: Then and Now* by Marcie and Rick Carroll | Dictionary and Thesaurus Skills; Synonyms, Antonyms, and Homonyms; Word Origin and Language Development |
| 1. World Regions | *Thinking Big* by Scott Wallace | Consonant Blends and Consonant Digraphs; Vowel Pairs, Vowel Digraphs, Diphthongs, and Phonograms |
| 2. Africa and the Middle East | *Cleopatra's Lost Palace* from *Time for Kids* | Word Endings, Contractions, Plurals, Possessives, and Compound Words |
| 3. India and the Far East | *Science in Ancient China* by George Beshore | Prefixes, Roots, Base Words, and Suffixes |
| 4. Ancient Greece to the Renaissance | *When Clothes Told a Story* by Linda Honan | More Prefixes, Roots, Base Words, and Suffixes |
| 5. The Americas | *Coyote and the Stars* by Tsonakwa | Context Clues |
| 6. The Modern World | *Can We Rescue the Reefs?* from *Time for Kids* | Dictionary and Thesaurus Skills; Synonyms, Antonyms, and Homonyms; Word Origin and Language Development |

**Level D**

**Level E**

**Level F**

# Using Word Study Skills to

As students move into the middle grades, they are expected to read and respond to a wide variety of content-area reading materials. *Sadlier Word Study* provides students with the word study skills and strategies necessary to tackle challenging texts.

Abundant instructional activities provide the practice and reinforcement students need, developing their confidence as they read to learn. With the systematic instruction provided in *Sadlier Word Study*, students learn to pronounce words and unlock their meanings more quickly and more accurately, leading to better reading comprehension.

## Student Texts

## Word Study in Context

Nonfiction photo-essays apply word study strategies to reading comprehension and critical thinking skills.

## Structural Analysis

Lessons provide students with a clear map to help analyze structural and meaning clues in parts of words.

## Critical Thinking

*Critical Thinking* questions encourage use of higher-order thinking skills.

## Home Connection

A *Family Page* encourages family members to become partners in helping children become better readers.

## "Chunking" Strategies

The use of phonograms, consonant blends and digraphs, and word endings help students apply their knowledge of phonics to decode difficult words.

# Build Comprehension

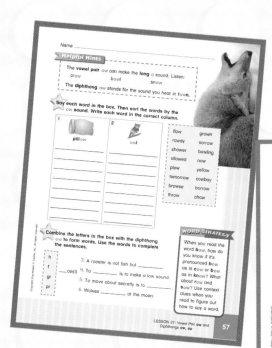

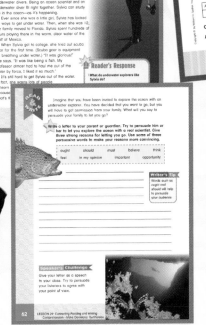

## Context Clues

The *Word Strategy* feature shows students how to use specific context clues to unlock the meaning of unfamiliar words.

## Dictionary Usage

Practical lessons help students learn to use dictionaries and thesauruses as tools for word study.

## Reading and Writing

Engaging thematic lessons help students apply word study strategies in order to better comprehend content-area reading materials.

"Students at the middle grades need to maximize their ability to analyze chunks or letters within words; analyze the structure of words for morphemic or meaning-bearing clues; use context clues not only to pronounce unfamiliar words, but also to figure out their meanings; and use dictionaries and thesauruses as tools for word study. Students develop knowledge and control over these strategies through explicit instructional activities."

(Vacca, 2000)

# Featuring a Complete

The *Sadlier Word Study* Teacher's Edition provides all of the resources necessary to meet today's challenging standards. Lesson features include systematic, explicit instruction and a wide variety of activities and strategies to meet the needs of all learners.

## Teacher's Edition

### Objectives
Clearly stated objectives correlate to national reading standards shown on the *Planning Resource* pages.

### Warm Up
Each lesson begins with a review of a previously taught skill.

### Explicit Instruction
Explicit and systematic instruction helps students master word study skills and strategies.

### Supporting All Learners
Activities cater to all students' learning styles and language needs.

---

**LESSON 49 • UNIT 4**
### Student Pages 101–102

## Prefixes
### un-, re-, dis-

#### Objectives
- To identify the prefixes **un-, re-,** and **dis-**
- To identify the meanings of words with these prefixes
- To write words with these prefixes

### Warming Up

- Write this rhyme on the board.

  Suppose you were a word,
  And a prefix came along,
  It would change your very meaning.
  All you know might now be wrong.
  Would you feel glad or **unhappy?**
  Would you smile or feel **unkind?**
  Would you make it feel **unwelcome?**
  Would you mind?

- Read the rhyme aloud with students. Have a volunteer underline the words that contain a prefix (shown in bold type). Ask students to define these words.

- Ask students what these words have in common. (They begin with the letters **un**, and they mean the opposite of the word that follows the letters **un.**)

### Teaching the Lesson

- Explain that many words begin with letter combinations called prefixes. Tell students that prefixes are not words by themselves, but they do have meaning. Point out that adding a prefix changes the meaning of the word they are added to.

- Read aloud the Helpful Hints on page 101 as students follow along silently.

---

Name _____

#### Helpful Hints

A **prefix** is a word part added to the **beginning** of a base word. Adding a prefix to a word can change the meaning of the word. It can also make a new word.

The prefix un means "not", as in un**afraid.**
The prefix dis means "not" or "opposite of," as in dis**like.**
The prefix re means "again," as in re**write**, or "back," as in re**turn.**

Watch out for words that seem to have prefixes but really do not. When you remove the un from **uncle**, no base word remains.

Add un, re, or dis to each of these base words. Write the new word on the line.

1. not **kind**
   unkind
2. **pay** back
   repay
3. the opposite of **agree**
   disagree
4. **fill** again
   refill
5. not **known**
   unknown
6. not **important**
   unimportant

Read the base word at the left of each sentence. Add the prefix un, re, or dis to the base word. Write the new word on the line.

welcome 7. The members of the cleanup crew were greeted by a(n) ___unwelcome___ sight.

safe 8. The amount of trash left over from the parade made the street ___unsafe___.

appear 9. The volunteers quickly went to work to make the garbage ___disappear___.

store 10. They worked long and hard to ___restore___ the street to its original condition.

pleasant 11. We are sorry their task was so ___unpleasant___.

#### CHALLENGE
Some words have *two* prefixes. Underline the two prefixes in each of these words. Then tell what each word means.

unresolved
rediscovered

LESSON 49: Prefixes un-, re-, dis-  **101**

---

### UNIVERSAL ACCESS
## Meeting Individual Needs

#### Visual Learners
Write these base words and definitions on the board.

_____ **lucky** (not lucky)
_____ **obey** (not obey)
_____ **pay** (pay back)
_____ **view** (view again)
_____ **cover** (cover again)
_____ **agree** (not agree)

Have students use a different color chalk to write the prefix **un-, re-,** or **dis-** before each base word to make a new word.

#### Kinesthetic Learners
Write these words on index cards: **use, place, fill, comfort, obey, attach, new, healthy, fold, clog,** and **paid.** Place the cards around the classroom. Make another set of cards with the words **reuse, replace, refill, discomfort, disobey, reattach, renew, unhealthy, unfold, unclog,** and **unpaid.** Place these cards in a pile. Have students select a card from the pile and find its "match." Have students say a sentence for each word.

# Teacher Support System

*Level D Teacher's Edition*

---

**Add the prefixes in red to the base words in the box. Write the new words on the lines.**

| 1 | un | 2 | re | 3 | dis |
|---|---|---|---|---|---|
| familiar | unfamiliar | place | replace | connect | disconnect |
| opened | unopened | turn | return | honest | dishonest |
| able | unable | view | review | color | discolor |
| happy | unhappy | solve | resolve | loyal | disloyal |
| checked | unchecked | think | rethink | like | dislike |
| tie | untie | live | relive | approve | disapprove |

**Use the best word from above to complete each sentence correctly.**

4. Some people feel they are _____unable_____ to solve community problems.

5. If people are _____unfamiliar_____ with the problems in their community, they can do nothing to help solve them.

6. A community must _____resolve_____ its problems by finding solutions.

7. If pollution goes _____unchecked_____, it can make people and animals sick.

8. Waste in rivers and streams can _____discolor_____ the water, turning it from blue to muddy gray.

9. Yet rivers and streams can _____return_____ to their original state with just a little help.

10. Scientists must _____review_____ all the facts before choosing a plan of action.

11. Sometimes, scientists must _____rethink_____ their solutions to problems.

12. Their solutions must not make people sad or _____unhappy_____.

102    LESSON 49: Prefixes un-, re-, dis-

Home Involvement Activity *Return of the Jedi* is a movie with a prefix in its title. Underline the prefix in the title of these videos your whole family can enjoy. *Egypt Uncovered   Discovering Canada by Rail*

---

## Practicing the Skill

- Read aloud the direction lines on pages 101 and 102. Guide students as needed. You may want to complete the first item in each set together.

- For exercises 4–12 on page 102, have students consider the context in order to choose the most appropriate word.

## Curriculum Connections

### Spelling Link

Write these scrambled words and sentences on the board. Have students unscramble the words and write them in the blanks to complete each sentence.

**plercea**
**(replace)**
It is time to _____ some old library books with new copies.

**skildei**
**(dislike)**
I _____ it when book pages are torn or missing.

**blenua**
**(unable)**
People are _____ to use very worn books.

**weivre**
**(review)**
Please _____ our plan to raise money.

**voleser**
**(resolve)**
It should _____ the problem.

### Science Link

- Have groups of students do research to find out more about the effects of water pollution and what people can do to help clean up polluted areas. Suggest that students go to the library to find nonfiction books about the subject. Encyclopedias and students' science textbooks may also be useful resources.

- Have group members discuss their findings and prepare a brief written report. Photocopy the report for other students to read. Ask students to circle the words in the report that contain the prefixes **un-**, **re-**, or **dis-** added to a base word.

### Observational Assessment

*Note how readily students are able to determine which prefix to add to a base word.*

102

---

### Practice
Clear instruction, including modeling and guided practice, enables students to experience success as they practice each new skill in the Student Text.

### Curriculum Connections
Cross-curricular activities extend word study skills and strategies into other subject areas, such as Social Studies, Science, and Math.

### Assessment
Strategies for observing, recording, and monitoring student progress are frequently highlighted in the Lesson Plans.

---

**English-Language Learners/ESL**

Write these sentences on the board and underline as shown.

I am not happy with my garden. I do not like all the weeds. I will again plant the flowers.

Write the words **replant**, **dislike**, and **unhappy** on cards and display them. Have a volunteer read a sentence and find the card that matches the meaning of the underlined words.

**Gifted Learners**

Display the following list:
**dismal, distant, disband, reread, reason, restart, relish, unless, unseen, untitled, under,** and **unwise.** Have students circle each word that has been formed by adding a prefix to a base word. **(disband, reread, restart, unseen, untitled, unwise)**

**Learners With Special Needs**

Additional strategies for supporting learners with special needs can be found on page 99L.

# SADLIER READING

**Getting Ready to Read
with Mother Goose**
Level PreK/K

**Sadlier Phonics**
Levels K, A, B, and C

**Sadlier Word Study**
Levels D, E, and F

# TEACHER'S EDITION

## Sadlier WORD STUDY Reading

**Level E**

### Senior Authors

Richard T. Vacca
Lesley Mandel Morrow

### Contributing Authors

Charles T. Mangrum II, Ed.D.
Professor of Reading Education
University of Miami

Stephen S. Strichart, Ph.D.
Professor of Education
Florida International University

### Program Consultants

Raymond P. Kettel, Ed.D.
Associate Professor of Education
University of Michigan-Dearborn
Dearborn, Michigan

Sylvia A. Rendón, Ph.D.
Coordinator for English Language Arts
Cypress-Fairbanks I.S.D.
Houston, Texas

Lisbeth Ceaser, Ph.D.
Dir., Precollegiate Academic Development
California Polytechnic State University
San Luis Obispo, California

Susan Stempleski, M.Ed., M.A.
Lecturer in TESOL
Teachers College, Columbia University
New York, New York

**Sadlier-Oxford**
A Division of William H. Sadlier, Inc.

## Advisors

The publisher wishes to thank the following teachers and administrators who read portions of the series prior to publication for their comments and suggestions.

Rubbie D. Baker
Fifth Grade Teacher
Decatur, Georgia

Margarite K. Beniaris
Assistant Principal
Chicago, Illinois

Trish Bresch
Elementary School Teacher
Westmont, New Jersey

Carmen Talavera
Fourth Grade Teacher
Long Beach, California

Margaret Clifford
Principal
Michigan City, Indiana

Veronica Durden
Counselor
Beaumont, Texas

Christine Henschell
Sixth Grade Teacher
Grand Rapids, Michigan

Malini Horiuchi
Fifth Grade Teacher
Hollis Hills, New York

Amy T. Kwock
Principal
Honolulu, Hawaii

Connie Sartori
Sixth Grade L.A. Teacher
Seminole, Florida

Shaun R. Burke
Fourth Grade Teacher
Rancho Santa Margarita, California

## Acknowledgments

William H. Sadlier, Inc., gratefully acknowledges the following for the use of copyrighted materials:

"Catching Up with Lewis and Clark" (text only). Reprinted from the October 10, 1997, issue of TIME FOR KIDS magazine, with the permission of the publisher, Time Inc. Copyright © 1997 Time Inc.

"Deep in the Heart of . . . Big Bend" (text only) by Bud McDonald. By permission of the author. Reprinted from FALCON magazine (March/April 1995), published by Falcon Press Publishing.

Dictionary pronunciation keys (text only). Reprinted from Macmillan School Dictionary 1, with the permission of the publisher, The McGraw-Hill Companies, Inc. Copyright © 1990 by Macmillan Publishing Company, a division of Macmillan, Inc.

"Digging Up the Past" (text only). Reprinted from the October 12, 1992, issue of TIME FOR KIDS magazine, with the permission of the publisher, Time Inc. Copyright © 1992 Time Inc.

"Fire in the Sky" (text only) by David Foster. By permission of the author. Reprinted from BOYS' LIFE magazine (February 1996), published by the Boy Scouts of America.

Adapted from "Hawaii: Then and Now" (text only) by Marcie Carroll. Copyright © 1995 with permission from OWL magazine, Bayard Presse Canada Inc.

"How to Grow a Painting" (text only) by Gail Skroback. Reprinted from 3*2*1 CONTACT, May 1996, © Sesame Workshop. All rights reserved.

"Native Peoples of the Northeast" (text only) by Trudie Lamb Richmond. Excerpted from COBBLESTONE's November 1994 issue: Indians of the Northeast Coast, © 1994, Cobblestone Publishing Company, 30 Grove Street, Suite C, Peterborough, NH 03458. All Rights Reserved. Reprinted by permission of the publisher.

"Rough, Tough Pecos Bill" (text only) by Lester David. By permission of Maggie Rosen. Reprinted from BOYS' LIFE magazine (October 1995), published by the Boy Scouts of America.

"Saving the Everglades" (text only). Reprinted from the October 1, 1999, issue of TIME FOR KIDS magazine, with the permission of the publisher, Time Inc. Copyright © 1999 Time Inc.

"Snowmobile Safari!" (text only) by W. E. Butterworth IV. By permission of the author and BOYS' LIFE magazine. Reprinted from BOYS' LIFE magazine (December 1995), published by the Boy Scouts of America.

**Photo Credits:** Aileen Ah-Tye: 168; Animals Animals/Gary Griffen: 77; Art Resource: 102; Artville/Burke & Triolo: 16 left & bottom right; California State Railroad Museum: 99; CORBIS/BETTMANN: The Mariners' Museum: 5 top; Peter Finger: 5 bottom center; Robert Holmes: 8, 189 background; Galen Rowell: 18; Richard T. Nowitz: 22, 113; Richard A. Cooke: 24, 91 top right, 191; Michael S. Yamashita: 25 inset, David J. & Janice L. Frent Collection: 28; BETTMANN: 29 top, 64, 65, 72 bottom right, 72 left, 73 top right, 81 inset, 131, 133 background, 134, 172, 166, 196, 216 left; Dave Bartruff: 29 bottom right; Richard Cummins: 29 right, 160; Kevin R. Morris: 32, 90, 139 bottom, 158; Bob Krist: 33, 211; CORBIS: 36 top left, 45, 86, 192 bottom right; David Muench: 39 background, 80, 91 bottom right, 108, 138, 198, 187, 194; Robert Landau: 43; Buddy Mays: 44, 93, 157, 197; Kevin Fleming: 48, 68; Terry Whittaker/Frank Lane Picture Agency: 50 top left; George McCarthy: 50 bottom right; Dave G. Houser: 58, 59 bottom right, 71 inset, 100, 122, 170 bottom right; Roger Ressmeyer: 59 top, 95, 96, 118, 139 top, 184; Craig Aurness: 59 bottom, 202; Tom Bean: 62, 91 top, 135, 136 left, 136 bottom right, 173 top, 185; Tim Thompson: 63, 105 inset; Jim Zuckerman: 67; Paul A. Souders: 71 background, 112; Philip Gould: 73 bottom right, 87, 139 bottom right; Layne Kennedy: 74, 110; Charles E. Rotkin: 75; Reuters NewMedia Inc.: 78; Phil Schermeister: 79, 167 inset, 173 bottom right; Ted Spiegel: 83; Joseph Sohn/ChromoSohn Inc.: 59 right, 85, 105 background, 117, 125, 183; Scott T. Smith: 91 bottom; Dewitt Jones: 97; Mark Gibson: 114; D. Boone: 115; Danny Lehman: 116, 133 inset; Catherine Karnow: 120; Marc Muench: 121; Morton Beebe, S.F.: 123; Andrew Brown/Ecoscene: 124; Jim Sugar Photography: 126; Liz Hymans: 128; Ansel Adams Publishing Rights Trust: 139 top right; Philip James Corwin: 141; Lowell Georgia: 143, 154; Ric Ergenbright: 146; Wolfgang Kaehler: 147, 179, 195; James Marshall: 148; James L. Amos: 155; Mark Garanger: 156; AFP: 163, 214; Roy Parkes/Eye Ubiquitous: 167 background; Raymond Gehman: 169; Neil Rabinowitz: 170 top left; Galen Rowell: 173 top center, 221; Rick Doyle: 173 top right, 181; Kelly-Mooney Photography: 173 bottom; Chase Swift: 176; Joel W. Rogers: 180; Steve Kaufman: 186, 215 background; Karl Weatherly: 188; Nik Wheeler: 189 inset, 216 bottom right; Roy Corral: 204; Nick Gunderson: 206; Owen Franken: 209; Kennan Ward: 215 inset; Bjorn Backe/Papilio: 222; B. Daemmrich/The Image Works: 82; Bob Daemmrich: 103; Eyewire: 36 bottom right; Michael Geissinger: 38; H. Armstrong Roberts, Inc./M. Berman: 13; H. Armstrong Roberts, Inc./ H. Armstrong Roberts: 25 background; Index Stock Imagery/Mark Hunt/PictureQuest: 52; Lady-Hawke Images/Dusty L. Perin: 27; Minden Pictures/Flip Nicklin: 177; National Gallery of Art/Alexander Calder: 88; National Park Service/Colonial National Historical Park: 55; Phil Degginger: 153; Photo Researchers, Inc./Steve Maslowski: 16 top right; Photo Resource Hawaii/Sal Moiraghi: 192 left; Photo Resource Hawaii/Joe Solem: 199; PhotoDisc: 56 bottom right; Photofest/RKO Radio Pictures, Inc.: 159; PICTUREQUEST: Michael W. Nelson/Stock South: 14; DigitalVision: 26 left, top left & bottom left; Jeff Greenberg/eStock Photography: 29 top right; Phyllis Picardi/Stock South: 35; Michael Newman/PhotoEdit: 37; Archive Photos: 39 inset; Lee Snider: 40; Ann Purcell/ Carl Purcell/Words & Pictures: 46; Canstock Images Inc./eStock Photography: 47; Erwin Bauer/Peggy Bauer/Bruce Coleman, Inc.: 49; Stockbyte: 56 top left; Siede Preis PhotoDisc: 81 background; David Burdett/Contact Press Images: 106; David Young-Wolf PhotoEdit: 161; Robert Fried/Stock, Boston: 178; Robert Schoen/Index Stock Imagery: 190; Alan Oddie/PhotoEdit: 213; Mark Kelly/Stock, Boston: 224; Richard L. Stack: 20; Robert Weldon: 149; Ron Kimball Photography, Inc.: 130; The Granger Collection: 152, 165; The Image Bank/Michael John O'Neill: 5; The Stock Market: 12; Bancroft Library, UC Berkeley: 145; Wayne Arnst/Great Falls Tribune: 162; Western Folklife Center: 150; © Wolfgang Kaehler 2000 www.wkaehlerphoto.com: 210.

**Illustrators:** Dirk Wunderlich: Cover; Cobblestone Magazine: 15; C. F. Payne: 119; Merle Nacht: 151; Mary Powers: 59m, 91m; Function Thru Form: 16, 36, 49, 135, 144, 208, 217; Functional Art: Diane Ali, Batelman Illustration, Moffit Cecil, Adam Gordon, Susumu Kawabe, Larry Lee, John Quinn, Zina Saunders, Sintora Regina Vanderhorst, Michael Woo

ISBN: 0-8215-1043-6

123456789 /05 04 03 02 01

# Dear Teacher,

As students enter the middle grades, their need to become strategic readers increases as they encounter unfamiliar words in content-area reading materials. The instructional core of the Sadlier Word Study program promotes strategic reading by guiding students through a logical sequence of skills and strategies that will enable them to decode difficult words quickly and accurately and will increase their reading comprehension.

Sadlier Word Study reflects current approaches to using word study strategies to improve reading comprehension in grades 4 through 6. Most notably, the program is built upon the following sound principles:

- **Chunking Strategies** extend the use of phonics while helping students develop a knowledge of word parts, such as consonant blends, phonograms, prefixes, suffixes, and roots, that will enable them to decode unfamiliar words.

- **Context Clues** help students build meaning by decoding words in context.

- **Word Study in Context** enables students to contextualize word study strategies by applying them to quality nonfiction photo-essays in content-area reading.

- **Integrated Language Arts** connect speaking, listening, reading, writing, and viewing, and tie nonfiction reading selections to numerous research and inquiry activities, while fostering communication skills.

- **Review and Assessment** provide frequent opportunities to monitor students' knowledge of word study strategies and adapt instruction to student performance.

As educators, we are proud to present a research-based, integrated approach to word study instruction. We are confident that your students will enjoy the content-area literature and the theme-based lessons, both of which provide an exciting context for learning and applying word study strategies.

We hope that you and your class will enjoy using *Sadlier Word Study*.

Sincerely,

*Richard T. Vacca*

**Richard T. Vacca, Ph. D.**

*Lesley M. Morrow*

**Lesley Mandel Morrow, Ph. D.**

# Contents

# Sadlier Word Study Reading

# A Research-Based Program

**S**adlier Word Study, Levels D–F, comprises a research-based program for intermediate reading instruction. Today, a growing body of research confirms that a balanced approach to reading instruction is in students' best interests (Morrow, 2001). One way in which teachers achieve balance is to "scaffold" instruction explicitly so that students become competent in the use of skills and strategies of effective readers (Vacca and Vacca, 1999). Sadlier Word Study provides a framework for explicit instruction necessary for developing students' ability to unlock the meaning of words (Vacca, 2000). Based on the program goals listed below you can see that an integrated language arts approach to the teaching of skills is employed.

## Program Goals

Sadlier Word Study provides middle-grade students with a solid foundation of word study skills and strategies. The program is designed to extend the development of phonics, while emphasizing strategies that students need to construct meaning for unfamiliar or difficult words. In this way, the relationship between necessary decoding skills and reading comprehension is strengthened. To do this successfully, Sadlier Word Study focuses on the following program goals that are key components in balanced literacy instruction:

- ▶ Use of Word Study Strategies
- ▶ **Spelling Instruction**
- ▶ Reading Comprehension
- ▶ **Writing Practice**

- ▶ Explicit Instruction
- ▶ **Modified Instruction for ELL/ESL**
- ▶ Thematic Instruction
- ▶ **Mulitple Assessment Strategies**

## Use of Word Study Strategies

### The Research

Research suggests that word knowledge is a key factor in comprehension (Hennings, 2000). The greater a student's knowledge of word meanings, the better his or her chances of figuring out new or unfamiliar words on a page. For students to be strategic as they to learn new words, they should:

- ▶ Analyze chunks of letters within words

- ▶ Analyze the structure of words for morphemic or meaning-bearing clues

- ▶ Use context clues to pronounce and figure out the meaning of new words

- ▶ Use dictionaries and thesauruses as word study tools (Vacca, 2000)

**S**adlier Word Study follows through on this research by offering activities designed to help students become proficient in their use of word study strategies. Students build words and divide them into parts. They sort words according to spelling patterns, word parts, or other features. They do cloze exercises, create word walls, and use dictionaries and thesauruses to learn word histories, definitions, and synonyms. Repeated practice enables students to build a strong base of word study strategies.

# Spelling Instruction

## The Research

The ability to spell well enhances students' writing and vocabulary development (Adams, Treiman, & Pressley, 1996). Spelling instruction supports students as they learn about and confirm their knowledge of the structure of English. Students benefit from the following:

▶ learning the spelling and the meanings of prefixes, suffixes, base words, and roots

▶ recognizing spelling patterns

**A**s suggested by this research, *Sadlier Word Study* offers one or more *Spell and Write* lessons in each unit. In these lessons, students are asked to spell words from the unit and are given instruction in recognizing spelling patterns through sorting activities and word building exercises. Students are then given a writing prompt and are asked to write an original piece using the words in context. In addition, a *Spelling Link* is featured in every lesson. Words and sentences are suggested for dictation to provide additional spelling practice.

# Reading Comprehension

## The Research

For students to receive the greatest benefit and enjoyment from their reading, they must receive comprehension strategy instruction that builds on their knowledge of the world and of language (Pressley, 1998). *The Report of the National Reading Panel* (National Institute of Child Health and Human Development, 2000) points out that reading comprehension can be improved by teaching students to use specific cognitive strategies or to reason strategically when they encounter problems in understanding what they are reading.

The research on the importance of teaching reading comprehension is clear. To understand what is being read is a primary goal of reading instruction. To this end, *Sadlier Word Study* builds a student's ability to comprehend text through a systematic and focused emphasis on the skills and strategies necessary to unlock meaning. The *Read and Write* lessons in each unit help students develop key comprehension skills such as comparing and contrasting, making inferences, distinguishing between fact and nonfact, identifying main idea and supporting details, summarizing, and synthesizing information. As students read the authentic nonfiction literature selections, their attention is focused on one or more of these comprehension strategies. Through specific questioning and repeated practice, students become more skillful in their ability to comprehend non-fiction literature.

## The Research

Many researchers today view reading and writing as skills that build upon each other; when they are cultivated concurrently, each adds to the proficiency in the other (Morrow, 2001). According to Pearson et al. (1992), "Good [reading] instruction includes an environment conducive to learning where the usefulness of reading is constantly seen. Students who interact daily with print, read what others have written, and write to and for others develop conceptual understandings about the value of reading. Writing practice allows students to make this important connection between reading and writing.

The *Sadlier Word Study* program offers both *Read and Write* and *Spell and Write* lessons designed to give students writing practice as suggested by research. Students are asked to use their experiential knowledge as they write letters, descriptions, explanations, directions, journal entries, and creative expressions. The writing activities lead students step-by-step through the writing process and at the end they are asked to add each new piece to their writing portfolios. By the end of the year, students' portfolios will reflect their knowledge of newly learned reading and writing skills.

# Explicit Instruction

## The Research

Explicit instruction reflects the dynamic interaction between the teacher and the student. The concept of explicit instruction has evolved from research on cognitive and metacognitive processes in reading (Vacca, 2000). When students are taught analytical procedures for learning words, instead of expecting them to figure out the procedures on their own, the efficiency of word-learning is improved (Gaskins & Ehri et al., 1996/1997). Explicit instruction of word study strategies ensures that students are aware of the strategies, and understand how and when to use them.

The *Sadlier Word Study* program has been designed to address the research that calls for explicit instruction. Students develop knowledge and control over skills and strategies through explicit instructional activities. The lesson plans provide for the four major components of explicit instruction: *explanation, demonstration, practice,* and *application.* During *explanation,* teachers direct attention to the *Helpful Hints* that allow students to learn the rules and procedures behind the use of the strategy. Once students understand the rules and procedures, teachers *demonstrate* their use through a "think-aloud" method, allowing them to model the thinking processes used in applying the skill or strategy. Students are then given *practice* activities to develop expertise in the use of the skill or strategy. Finally, students are asked to *apply* the skills and strategies they've learned through regular, ongoing class activities.

# ELL/ESL Modified Instruction

## The Research

When English is a second language for students, a firm foundation in their first language will support academic achievement in the second language (Cummins, 1979). Teachers encounter students from diverse cultural and language backgrounds. Good teaching strategies that adapt to these differences are those that work best. (Morrow, 1997)

The *Sadlier Word Study* program includes activities specifically designed for English-language learners and ESL students. The activities provide students with opportunities to attach meaning to unfamiliar vocabulary through the use of concrete objects, pictures, photographs, and pantomimed gestures. The lessons allow students whose first language is not English to participate fully in the lessons as they develop their competency in both the language and in cross-curricular content.

# Thematic Instruction

## The Research

Current research supports thematic instruction. Content-area themes provide a "context" for learning and by their very nature allow for curricular as well as language-arts integration. Students hone their reading skills as they "read to learn" (Vacca, Vacca & Gove, 2000).

*Sadlier Word Study* teaches strategies and skills in the context of high-interest, motivating themes that integrate all of the language arts, as well as the content areas. As students read about their world, they explore topics through authentic and challenging projects. The convenient two-page thematic lessons provide flexibility for teaching skills based on the needs of the students.

# Multiple Assessment Strategies

## The Research

Monitoring learners' progress calls for a variety of assessment strategies. Teachers must use keen observation of student development to inform instruction (Braunger and Lewis, 1997). The following types of assessment are recommended: screening assessments, checklists, writing rubrics, tests, comprehensive assessments, and portfolios.

*Sadlier Word Study* provides many opportunities for both formal and informal assessment. Each unit includes *Review and Assess* lessons. In addition, the Teacher's Edition contains Pretests, Post Tests, writing rubrics, checklists, as well as observational, performance-based, and portfolio assessments. The multiple assessment strategies allow for early detection of difficulties and give a solid determination of what each student has learned.

## One Final Note

The *Sadlier Word Study* program reflects the most current research available and supports balanced literacy instruction. We wish you success in helping each and every student continue to become a proficient reader.

*Richard T. Vacca*     *Lesley M. Morrow*

# Word Study Workshop

## What Is Word Study?

Word study as a discipline includes phonics and goes beyond it. Whereas phonics focuses on letters and their sounds, word study focuses on words. Word study picks up where phonics leaves off, teaching readers how to use their phonological knowledge to figure out what words mean. *Sadlier Word Study,* a program developed to meet the needs of students in grades 4–6, includes elements of phonics, vocabulary, spelling, and study skills.

The program asks students to study words up close (dissecting them and analyzing their parts) and from a distance (looking at context and determining how it affects meaning). *Sadlier Word Study's* combination of "micro" and "macro" approaches offers a unique support system to teach middle-grade readers strategies for unlocking word meaning.

Richard T. Vacca, Professor of Education at Kent State University identifies the following basic strategies regularly used by competent readers:

▶ using the structure of words, the meaning-bearing clues provided by word parts, to construct meaning

▶ using *context clues* to figure out the meanings of unfamiliar words

▶ knowing how and when to use a dictionary when other strategies fail

These strategies are word-study strategies, and they all have to do with word meaning. So, how does word study bridge the gap between knowing how to pronounce words (where phonics leaves off) to figuring out what they mean? The answer to this question is virtually the explanation of how people learn to read.

# Word Study Mirrors Reading Development

Recent studies have isolated four developmental phases in the acquisition of reading. They are *prealphabetic, partial alphabetic, full alphabetic,* and *consolidated alphabetic.* Identifying this sequence has helped educators recognize both the need for and the role of word study.

## Prealphabetic

Children in this phase can recognize some words by using nonalphabetic visual cues. For example, a child seeing the octagonal shape of a stop sign might say, "stop," or a child recognizing the label on a box of cereal might say the cereal's name.

## Partial Alphabetic

In this phase children know some letters and their sounds and notice these letters and sounds within words. A child at this stage might recognize his or her written name but not necessarily know all the letter-sound relationships within it.

## Full Alphabetic

Children who are fully alphabetic know all the letters of the alphabet. They can figure out how to pronounce unfamiliar words by sounding out letters.

## Consolidated Alphabetic

Children in the consolidated alphabetic phase approach words by looking at more than one letter—or chunks of words at a time.

## Chunks: Bridging Letters and Meaning

Looking at word chunks, or "chunking," is a hallmark word study strategy. The chunks readers recognize are usually predictable letter patterns that contain meaning clues. Prefixes, suffixes, and roots are good examples.

Encountering the word *unimaginable,* a student could look at the chunks *un + imagin + able* and put together their meanings to figure out that the word means, roughly, "not able to be imagined." Other examples of word chunks that contain meaning clues are inflectional endings, comparatives, and superlatives.

## Word Study in the Middle Grades

Many middle graders are on the brink of the fourth phase of reading development. Vacca explains that some students may need help sounding out and blending letters. He believes that the challenge of word study programs in the middle grades is to extend instruction in increasingly sophisticated ways into the consolidated alphabetic phase of development.

# Explicit Instruction

**M**iddle-grade students need to learn how to use the following word study strategies presented and taught in *Sadlier Word Study:*

▶ analyze chunks of letters within words

▶ analyze the structure of words for morphemic, or meaning-bearing clues

▶ use context clues to pronounce and figure out the meaning of unfamiliar words

▶ use dictionaries and thesauruses as tools for word study

Students practice and develop their ability to use these strategies through explicit instruction.

The goal of explicit instruction is to help students develop strategies for self-regulated, independent use—to cope with the kinds of problems they must solve as they are reading. Explicit instruction includes *explanation, demonstration, practice,* and *application.*

**Explanation** Through direct explanation of the strategy, students become more aware of *what* the strategy is and *how* and *when* to use it. Explanations help students learn the strategy and develop a rationale for its use.

**Demonstration** The teacher models the use of the strategy using a *think-aloud,* mirroring the thinking required to use the strategy effectively.

**Practice** The teacher provides students with practice activities to develop expertise in using the strategy and to discuss students' use of it.

**Application** Once students have had some practice with the use of a strategy, regular, on-going class activities encourage its application.

# Thematic Instruction

Each *Sadlier Word Study* Student Edition is organized by theme. An engaging piece of nonfiction presents each unit's word study strategies within the context of a different theme. The thematic connection is maintained throughout the unit, with individual lessons using theme-related vocabulary, excerpts, and activities to teach word study strategies.

# Curriculum Integration

Each unit of *Sadlier Word Study* begins with a nonfiction selection from a content area such as science, social studies, math, health, music, or art. The *Read and Write* lessons also provide selections about subjects appropriate to the students' age and interests.

The support material in both the Student Edition and Teacher's Edition offers opportunities for students to apply word study strategies in their pursuit of knowledge in the content areas. The program's cross-curricular features and follow-up activities give students a relevant context in which to practice the skills they are learning.

# Integrating Word Study and Language Arts

*Sadlier Word Study* integrates the language arts so that students gain practice applying word study strategies to various language experiences.

**Listening and Speaking** The Teacher's Edition often prompts students to read aloud, listen to oral presentations, and to take part in informal discussions. Features in the Student Edition specifically designed to encourage discussion include the *Critical Thinking* and the *Reader's Response* questions.

**Reading** The program provides opportunities for students to read authentic literature in the *Unit Openers* and the *Read and Write* lessons. The Student Edition and the Teacher's Edition also offer lists of theme-related books for students to read on their own.

**Writing** Writing is an integral part of both the *Read and Write* and *Spell and Write* features, which often appear twice in each unit. In addition, the Teacher's Edition includes activities asking students to express themselves through expository and creative writing.

**Spelling** The *Spell and Write* features in every unit offer word sort activities that help students recognize predictable spelling patterns that often contain clues to meaning. These features also require students to write a composition using the spelling words in context.

## Assessment

To help teachers evaluate students' work, each unit in the *Sadlier Word Study* Teacher's Edition contains an overview of strategies for assessment, including blackline masters. In it, unit-specific suggestions are given for how to use each of the assessment tools below.

**Pretests and Post Tests** Provided in each unit, these two tests are similar in content and can be used in various ways. One may be given as a pretest—a diagnostic tool to identify a starting point for instruction—and the other as a post test—a formal end-of-unit assessment of students' mastery of the unit skills.

**Observational Assessment** It is important to observe and record students' performance in the classroom frequently. Try to set aside 5–15 minutes a day to observe two or three students, so that you observe each class member about every two to

three weeks. Specific instances for doing so are highlighted in the lesson plans.

**Review and Assess** Appearing in the Student Edition often twice in each unit, these lessons help the teacher ascertain whether students have mastered the unit content. If students need more instruction, the teacher can use the Reteaching activities found in the lesson plans.

**Performance** Classroom-based projects and activities help teachers determine whether students have correctly assimilated specific word study strategies. Suggestions for such activities can be found in the *Assessment* overview for each unit.

**Portfolio** Have students keep a portfolio of writing samples and other pieces of work that demonstrate their reading and writing skills. Such samples show how students have improved and where they may still have difficulty.

## Universal Access

*Sadlier Word Study* offers lesson-specific methods for teaching students with a wide range of abilities, including those whose first language is not English, students struggling below grade level, gifted learners, and those with special needs. The pre-unit section labeled *Universal Access: Students* with *Special Needs* particularly addresses students who have learning deficits, attention-deficit disorder, or problems with sensory discrimination. This section suggests ways of tailoring the more challenging lessons to meet the needs of these students.

## Teaching ELL/ESL Students

Because students for whom English is not the primary language can be at any level of fluency, it is important to select teaching strategies and materials appropriate to the individual. Following are listed the stages, or levels, of second-language acquisition.

**Pre-Production** This stage of proficiency applies to those who are new to English. Shared-reading activities are appropriate for this level.

**Early Production** Students at this level are trying out the new language, responding with one- or two-word answers. Errors in grammar and pronunciation are to be expected.

**Speech Emergence** Learners at this level of proficiency use the new language to engage in conversation. Provide opportunities for these students to work in groups, encouraging communication between group members.

**Intermediate Fluency** Intermediate-level students may demonstrate fluency in social settings. However, academic language is still limited. Teachers can focus on continuing to build the vocabulary of these students and developing higher levels of language use.

**Advanced Fluency** Once English learners reach advanced fluency, they understand and speak English almost as well as native speakers. At this point, continue to build literacy skills, broadening vocabulary and developing more sophisticated levels of language use.

The English-Language Learners/ESL activities in the *Sadlier Word Study* Teacher's Edition have been designed with the above five stages in mind. The goal is to help students develop both receptive (listening, reading, viewing) and expressive (speaking, writing) abilities.

## Intervention

Early reading failure can be a powerful force in shaping students' visions of themselves. The relationship between reading skills and success in all subject areas is a compelling reason for timely intervention activities.

**Determine When to Intervene** When a new concept is introduced, students must demonstrate understanding of this concept before moving on to the next step in the process.

**Target Students for Intervention** Activities that are playful in nature can help you identify students who are having difficulty. Such activities do not single out a student to the rest of the class, but they do provide you with an opportunity for informal evaluation.

**Use Intervention Strategies** Lesson-specific intervention strategies are recommended on the *Intervention* page in each pre-unit section of the Teacher's Edition.

# Consonant Sounds

## Theme: Northeast

### STANDARDS

- ✪ Read expository text with grade-appropriate fluency and understand its content
- ✪ Develop and strengthen vocabulary by reading and studying words in context
- ✪ Recognize letter-sound correspondence in consonant blends, consonant digraphs, and double consonants

### OBJECTIVES

- ▶ To appreciate nonfiction works about the Northeast
- ▶ To identify and pronounce consonant sounds
- ▶ To decode and write words with consonant blends, consonant digraphs, and double consonants

### LESSONS

## Assessment Strategies

An overview of assessment strategies appears on page **5C**. It offers multiple suggestions for ways in which teachers can use a variety of unit-specific assessment tools, including **Pretests** and **Post Tests** (pages **5D–5G**), the **Activity Master** (page **5M**), and the **Assessment Checklist** (page **5H**).

## Thematic Teaching

In Unit 1 students will learn about consonant blends, consonant digraphs, and double consonants. Students encounter words with these letter combinations in the context of nonfiction selections and exercises related to the theme the *Northeast.*

Students begin their investigation of the Northeast by creating a historic time line of the region. The resource list below provides titles of books, videos, and other materials that can help students focus their study of the northeastern part of the country. Many of the Teacher's Edition lessons in this unit open with poems, riddles, or passages related to one or more of the states in this region. The openers act as "hooks," piquing students' interest in the theme and in the play of words.

## Curriculum Integration

### Writing
Students list and define words on page **14** and write about gnomes on page **24.**

### Science
Students describe their state's climate on page **8.**

### Social Studies
Students make a map on page **6,** identify cities on page **10,** and learn about natural resources on page **20.**

## Optional Learning Activities

### Meeting Individual Needs
Most of the Teacher's Edition lessons offer activities for students with distinct learning styles or particular intellectual or sensory strengths. The activities are labeled for learners with the following "styles": **Visual, Kinesthetic, Auditory, Musical,** and **Tactile.**

### Multicultural Connections
Students learn about the Iroquois peoples on page **6,** research the names of cities and states on page **12,** and research differences between British and American English on page **22.**

### Word Study Strategies
Pages **5I–5J** offer an array of activities that give students practice with word study strategies. Students sort words, build words, and define words in context.

### Universal Access
Exercises tailored to meet the needs of **English-Language Learners** and **Gifted Learners** can be found in almost every Teacher's Edition lesson. Strategies designed to help **Learners with Special Needs,** such as students with Memory Deficits, can be found on page **5L.**

### Intervention
Page **5K** offers **Intervention Strategies** designed to help students performing below grade level understand the concepts taught in **Lessons 3, 4,** and **5.**

### Reteaching
On page **18** students identify and build words with consonant blends and consonant digraphs, and on page **28** students match and write words with consonant blends, consonant digraphs, and double consonants.

### Technology
Page **5N** offers activities for students who enjoy working with computers or audio/video equipment. In addition, **Computer Connections**—tips for students who use a word processor—can be found on pages **16** and **26.**

### RESOURCES

**Books**
Freedman, Russell. *Immigrant Kids,* NY: Puffin, 1995.
Levine, Ellen. *If Your Name Was Changed at Ellis Island,* NY: Scholastic, 1994.

**CDs**
*The Days Gone By: Songs of the American Poets,* Rhino Records. 2000.

**Videos**
*Inside the White House,* National Geographic, 1995.
*New York,* PBS Home Video, 1999.
*Native Americans, The Nations of the Northeast,* Turner Home Entertainment, 1998.

In Unit 1 students study consonant blends, consonant digraphs, and double consonant sounds. To evaluate students' mastery of these skills, use any or all of the assessment methods suggested below.

## Pretests and Post Tests

The tests on pages **5D–5G** objectively assess how well students understand consonant blends, consonant digraphs, and double consonant sounds. These tests may be used at the beginning of the unit as an informal diagnostic tool or at the end of the unit as a more formal measure of students' progress.

## Observational Assessment

Each lesson includes a reminder to observe students as they apply lesson-specific skills. Check students' written work on a regular basis to see whether they continue to apply what they learn successfully.

## Using Technology

The Technology activities on page **5N** may also help evaluate students whose language skills are best shown when using computers or audio/video equipment.

## Performance Assessment

Have students copy the following headings on a sheet of paper: **Consonant Blends, Consonant Digraphs,** and **Double Consonants.** Then have students sort these words under the correct headings: **rang, pepper, skate, brook, giggle, rush.** For each word, have students circle the consonant blend, consonant digraph, or double consonant.

## Portfolio Assessment

The portfolio icon in the lesson plans indicates an opportunity for students to add to the growing body of work in their portfolios. Each student's portfolio will be unique and should contain pieces that the student feels represents his or her best work. You may wish to give students additional opportunities to add to their portfolios.

## Rubric for Writing

| | Always | Sometimes | Never |
|---|---|---|---|
| Uses capitalization, punctuation, spelling, and grammar appropriately | | | |
| Creates a variety of sentences containing words with consonant blends, consonant digraphs, and double consonant sounds | | | |
| Uses rhyming pairs of words appropriate for intended purpose | | | |
| Uses letter parts correctly | | | |
| Conveys purpose and meaning through writing | | | |

## Answer Key

**Page 5D**
1. plush
2. grass
3. sort
4. treasure
5. silk
6. class
7. blade
8. trophy
9. group
10. pleasure
11. final
12. initial
13. medial
14. medial
15. final
16. school
17. string
18. scramble
19. splinter
20. thrifty
21. cattle
22. pepper
23. write
24. glass
25. lamb

**Page 5E**
1. dresser I
2. field F
3. stump B
4. triple I
5. melt F
6. pretend B
7. pulp F
8. slipper I
9. blossom I
10. swift I
11. whale I

12. wish F
13. cough F
14. graph F
15. machine M
16. tooth F
17. weather M
18. photo I
19. shape I
20. teacher M
21. comb
22. wrap
23. knob
24. kettle
25. mammal
26. bell
27. cuff
28. pepper
29. calm
30. mess

**Page 5F**
1. belt
2. clever
3. frog
4. crow
5. swoop
6. pint
7. cold
8. scale
9. send
10. coast
11. medial
12. initial
13. final
14. initial
15. medial
16. chrome
17. shriek
18. spring

19. thrash
20. scheme
21. bubble
22. fiddle
23. giggle
24. knot
25. sign

**Page 5G**
1. flock I
2. swamp B
3. sway I
4. climate I
5. draft B
6. sand F
7. colt F
8. grasp B
9. slant B
10. left F
11. trophy
12. reach F
13. finish F
14. wheel I
15. farther M
16. shoulder I
17. pheasant I
18. north F
19. much F
20. chute I
21. known
22. common
23. button
24. gnat
25. different
26. palm
27. less
28. crumb
29. scenery
30. wrist

**Fill in the circle of the word that contains a consonant blend.**

| | | |
|---|---|---|
| **1.** ○ pillow | ○ pupil | ○ plush |
| **2.** ○ garage | ○ grass | ○ gear |
| **3.** ○ sort | ○ some | ○ shore |
| **4.** ○ tear | ○ treasure | ○ tease |
| **5.** ○ silk | ○ shine | ○ silly |
| **6.** ○ class | ○ case | ○ chase |
| **7.** ○ baker | ○ blade | ○ because |
| **8.** ○ those | ○ token | ○ trophy |
| **9.** ○ goal | ○ group | ○ goose |
| **10.** ○ pear | ○ peace | ○ pleasure |

**Say the word. Fill in the circle for the consonant digraph's position.**

| | | | |
|---|---|---|---|
| **11. graph** | ○ initial | ○ medial | ○ final |
| **12. whisper** | ○ initial | ○ medial | ○ final |
| **13. bleacher** | ○ initial | ○ medial | ○ final |
| **14. author** | ○ initial | ○ medial | ○ final |
| **15. tough** | ○ initial | ○ medial | ○ final |

**Fill in the circle of the word that contains a three-letter consonant blend.**

| | | |
|---|---|---|
| **16.** ○ school | ○ soccer | ○ score |
| **17.** ○ sting | ○ string | ○ sticker |
| **18.** ○ scamper | ○ scare | ○ scramble |
| **19.** ○ splinter | ○ spill | ○ simple |
| **20.** ○ thirty | ○ thrifty | ○ thirsty |

**Fill in the circle of the word in which two consonants make one sound.**

| | | |
|---|---|---|
| **21.** ○ camper | ○ cattle | ○ capital |
| **22.** ○ pepper | ○ person | ○ peel |
| **23.** ○ write | ○ wire | ○ wise |
| **24.** ○ gram | ○ glass | ○ grasp |
| **25.** ○ lamb | ○ lamp | ○ land |

Possible score on Unit 1 Pretest 1 is 25. Score _____

## Pretest 2

Name _____

**Circle the consonant blend(s) in each word. On the line write "I" for initial, "F" for final, or "B" for both.**

1. dresser ____
2. field ____
3. stump ____
4. triple ____
5. melt ____
6. pretend ____
7. pulp ____
8. slipper ____
9. blossom ____
10. swift ____

**Circle the consonant digraph in each word. On the line write "I" for initial, "M" for medial, or "F" for final.**

11. whale ____
12. wish ____
13. cough ____
14. graph ____
15. machine ____
16. tooth ____
17. weather ____
18. photo ____
19. shape ____
20. teacher ____

**Circle the double consonant blend in each word that stands for one sound.**

21. comb
22. wrap
23. knob
24. kettle
25. mammal
26. bell
27. cuff
28. pepper
29. calm
30. mess

Possible score on Unit 1 Pretest 2 is 30. Score _____

**Fill in the circle of the word that contains a consonant blend.**

| | | | |
|---|---|---|---|
| 1. | ○ bath | ○ beat | ○ belt |
| 2. | ○ celery | ○ cheese | ○ clever |
| 3. | ○ foggy | ○ frog | ○ furry |
| 4. | ○ crow | ○ choir | ○ cover |
| 5. | ○ soup | ○ swoop | ○ super |
| 6. | ○ pint | ○ piece | ○ pier |
| 7. | ○ coral | ○ cold | ○ cool |
| 8. | ○ scale | ○ seam | ○ sheer |
| 9. | ○ shell | ○ send | ○ seller |
| 10. | ○ coal | ○ coat | ○ coast |

**Say the word. Fill in the circle for the consonant digraph's position.**

| | | | |
|---|---|---|---|
| 11. **alphabet** | ○ initial | ○ medial | ○ final |
| 12. **shallow** | ○ initial | ○ medial | ○ final |
| 13. **cough** | ○ initial | ○ medial | ○ final |
| 14. **thimble** | ○ initial | ○ medial | ○ final |
| 15. **merchant** | ○ initial | ○ medial | ○ final |

**Fill in the circle of the word that contains a three-letter consonant blend.**

| | | | |
|---|---|---|---|
| 16. | ○ chord | ○ chrome | ○ choice |
| 17. | ○ shield | ○ shelf | ○ shriek |
| 18. | ○ spring | ○ spin | ○ spider |
| 19. | ○ trash | ○ that | ○ thrash |
| 20. | ○ scene | ○ scheme | ○ seem |

**Fill in the circle of the word in which two consonants make one sound.**

| | | | |
|---|---|---|---|
| 21. | ○ bundle | ○ bubble | ○ bulb |
| 22. | ○ fiddle | ○ finger | ○ find |
| 23. | ○ giggle | ○ gift | ○ give |
| 24. | ○ knot | ○ note | ○ monkey |
| 25. | ○ sing | ○ sign | ○ sift |

Possible score on Unit I Post Test I is 25. Score _____

**Circle the consonant blend(s) in each word. On the line write "I" for initial, "F" for final, or "B" for both.**

| | |
|---|---|
| 1. flock ____ | 2. swamp ____ |
| 3. sway ____ | 4. climate ____ |
| 5. draft ____ | 6. sand ____ |
| 7. colt ____ | 8. grasp ____ |
| 9. slant ____ | 10. left ____ |

**Circle the consonant digraph in each word. On the line write "I" for initial, "M" for medial, or "F" for final.**

| | |
|---|---|
| 11. trophy ____ | 12. reach ____ |
| 13. finish ____ | 14. wheel ____ |
| 15. farther ____ | 16. shoulder ____ |
| 17. pheasant ____ | 18. north ____ |
| 19. much ____ | 20. chute ____ |

**Circle the double consonant blend in each word that stands for one sound.**

| | |
|---|---|
| 21. known | 22. common |
| 23. button | 24. gnat |
| 25. different | 26. palm |
| 27. less | 28. crumb |
| 29. scenery | 30. wrist |

Possible score on Unit 1 Post Test 2 is 30. Score _____

**Student Name** _____

## UNIT ONE
## STUDENT SKILLS ASSESSMENT CHECKLIST

☑ Assessed    ☒ Retaught    ▣ Mastered

- ❏ Initial **l**-blends
- ❏ Initial **r**- and **s**-blends
- ❏ Final **t**-, **d**-, and **p**-blends
- ❏ Consonant Digraphs
- ❏ Three-letter Cosonant Blends
- ❏ Double Consonant Sounds
- ❏ Irregular Double Consonant Sounds

## TEACHER COMMENTS

# WORD STUDY STRATEGIES

In Unit 1 students study consonant blends, consonant digraphs, and double consonant sounds. To give students opportunities to master word study strategies, use any or all of the activities suggested below.

## Word Building

Add the consonant blend to the phonograms to build new words. Write an additional word using the same blend but a different phonogram.

1. cl ___ip ___ay _____

2. st ___ick ___and _____

3. fr ___ame ___ight _____

4. sw ___ing ___eet _____

## Word Meaning

Circle the final consonant blend in each word. Then use the words to answer the questions below.

| belt | cold | grasp | gift | scalp |
|------|------|-------|------|-------|
| plant | start | found | stamp | fast |

1. Which word means **swift**? _____

2. Which word means **begin**? _____

3. Which word means a **present**? _____

4. Which word is the opposite of **hot**? _____

5. Which word is the opposite of **lost**? _____

6. Which word means something worn around the waist? _____

7. Which word means part of your head? _____

8. Which word means something that grows in soil? _____

9. Which word means something you stick on an envelope? _____

10. Which word means to hold firmly? _____

## Digraph Search

Circle the consonant digraph in each word. Sort the words according to the heads in the chart below.

| blush | birthday | merchant |
|-------|----------|----------|
| shift | physical | overwhelm |
| graph | alphabet | south |
| though | touch | exchange |
| chord | smooth | chain |
| bother | arch | thimble |

| Initial Digraph | Medial Digraph | Final Digraph |
|-----------------|----------------|---------------|
| _____ | _____ | _____ |
| _____ | _____ | _____ |
| _____ | _____ | _____ |
| _____ | _____ | _____ |
| _____ | _____ | _____ |
| _____ | _____ | _____ |

## Word Selection

Cross out the word in each row that does not have the same sound as the underlined consonants.

1. **st̲atue**  stomach  slate  coast
2. **me̲lt**  milk  tilt  colt
3. **si̲ngle**  cling  ringer  sign
4. **wh̲ale**  whole  whistle  wharf
5. **roug̲h̲**  eight  physical  famous
6. **c̲h̲ore**  chef  chapter  chief
7. **cras̲h̲**  spinach  chiffon  shoulders
8. **s̲c̲h̲ool**  telescope  skeleton  chair
9. **th̲rifty**  throb  thrive  treaty
10. **spl̲ash**  slap  splinter  splendid
11. **p̲hysical**  feet  photo  plant
12. **c̲h̲orus**  chirp  choir  character

## Word Sort

Underlined the double consonants that make one sound in each word. Then sort the words under the correct heading below.

| wrench | wreck | calm |
| thumb | gnat | design |
| knit | lamb | wrap |
| sign | knot | write |
| climb | wring | palm |
| wrinkle | limb | gnome |

| Sound of **m** | Sound of **n** | Sound of **r** |
| --- | --- | --- |
| | | |
| | | |
| | | |
| | | |
| | | |
| | | |

## Word Building

Circle the double consonants to complete each word. Then write on the line a new word that contains the same double consonants.

1. ca ___ le  _____
   **bb  tt  pp**

2. bu ___ le  _____
   **bb  gg  dd**

3. fi ___ le  _____
   **pp  tt  dd**

4. pi ___ ow  _____
   **dd  ll  rr**

5. la ___ o  _____
   **rr  mm  ss**

6. a ___ ord  _____
   **gg  ff  pp**

7. pe ___ er  _____
   **ff  pp  ll**

8. su ___ er  _____
   **gg  bb  mm**

9. a ___ ounce  _____
   **mm  nn  pp**

10. gi ___ le  _____
    **gg  ff  pp**

11. ba ___ el  _____
    **pp  rr  nn**

12. da ___ le  _____
    **zz  ff  rr**

| LESSONS | **3** Initial **r**-blends | **4** Final **t**-, **d**-, and **p**-blends | **5** Consonant Digraphs |
|---|---|---|---|
| **Problem** | Student does not pronounce the **r** in words with initial **r**-blends. | Student does not pronounce the final consonant in words with final **t**-, **d**-, and **p**-blends. | Student has trouble spelling words in which the consonant digraph **ch** is pronounced as **k** or **sh**. |
| **Intervention Strategies** | • Tell the student that the sound of the letter **r** makes a vibration in the back of the throat. List the following word pairs on the board: **fright/fight, brought/bought, crash/cash, drive/dive.**<br><br>• As the student reads the word pairs aloud, have them emphasize the initial sounds in each word and encourage them to place a finger on their throats to feel the vibration made when they read the words with initial **r**-blends. | • Write the following sentences on the board: *We bought a (**plan, plant**) at the florist. Did you (**fin, find**) the remote control for the VCR? The exit (**ram, ramp**) on the highway was icy.* Have the student choose the correct word to complete each of the sentences.<br><br>• Have the student read the word choices aloud and emphasize the two different endings. Then have him or her place a hand in front of the mouth. Encourage the student to repeat the word choices and note which final blends cause air to be released on his or her hand. | • Encourage the student to make a word-study notebook that can be used as students complete exercises in this book.<br><br>• The consonant digraph **ch** can be pronounced as **ch** (**chair**), as **k** (**chaos**), or as **sh** (**chute**). Have the student use these words as heads under which he or she can list similar words encountered in the lesson.<br><br>• A mnemonic sentence may help students with the sounds of **ch**: A *ship's sails aren't made of **ch**iffon. A **ch**orus shouldn't sing off-**k**ey.* |

he following activities offer strategies for helping students with special needs to participate in selected exercises in Unit 1.

## Auditory Perceptual Deficits
### Consonant Digraphs
Students with auditory perceptual deficits may be confused by consonants that do not sound the same in combinations as when each stands alone. Help students make the connection between consonant digraphs and the sounds they stand for by doing the following exercise.

- On the board, write the words **camping, hamper,** and **champion.** Read the words aloud, emphasizing the initial sounds. Ask students to identify the word that begins with the same sound as the word **chimpanzee.** Have a volunteer underline the word **(champion)** and circle the consonant digraph. Then ask the student to find an object in the room whose name begins with that sound. Possible objects include **chalk** and **chair.**

- For the consonant digraph **sh,** write the words **shouting, surrounded,** and **hounds** on the board and read them aloud. Ask students to identify the word that begins like **shower.** Invite a student to underline the word **(shouting)** and circle the **sh.** Then have him or her find an item in the room whose name begins with the same sound. Possibilities include **shoes, shirts,** and **shelves.**

- Continue in a similar manner with the consonant digraphs **th** and **ph.** You may wish to use the following words: **thunder, thumb, thinker** and **pharmacy, photo, phonics book.**

## Visual Perceptual Deficits
### Unscrambling Words
Students who reverse letters in reading and writing may have difficulty unscrambling the words in the exercise on page **19.**

- Give students magnetic letters and a metal board. Have them sound out the name of the object pictured in each example. Then help students choose the magnetic letters that represent those sounds. You may need to review the lesson on three-letter consonant blends.

- Have students place the letters in the order in which they are pronounced. Ask students to look at the scrambled version of the word to find the letters for the sounds they used when pronouncing the word. Have them form the word using the magnetic letters while repeating the picture's name, emphasizing each letter's sound. Encourage students to check each word in a dictionary.

## Memory Deficits
### Double Consonant Sounds
Students who have difficulty remembering that two consonants can stand for one sound may misspell words with double consonants.

- Help students focus on the correct spelling of words with double consonants by creating word-study notebook.

- Make columns on the pages and label them as follows: **dd, tt, ll, mm, nn, pp, gg, bb, ss, ff, cc, mb, lm, wr, gn, dg,** and **kn.** As students encounter words in the lessons of Unit 1 encourage them to list the words in the correct section of their word-study notebook. Then have them highlight the double consonants that make one sound.

- Encourage students to use their word-study notebooks as a source of words for writing activities or for checking the spelling of words. Remind students from time to time to add new words to their notebooks as they work through the unit.

**GAMES**

## Across

1. This "Keystone State" has the double consonant **nn** in its name.

3. This "Ocean State" has the final consonant blend **nd** in its name.

5. This "Green Mountain State" has the final consonant blend **nt** in its name.

7. This capital city of Massachusetts has the consonant blend **st** in its name.

9. This "Granite State" has the consonant blend **mp** and the consonant digraph **sh** in its name.

11. This "Old Line State" has the consonant blend **nd** in its name.

13. This capital city of New Hampshire has the phonogram **ord** in its name.

## Down

2. This capital city of Rhode Island starts with the consonant blend **pr**.

4. This capital city of Vermont contains the consonant blend **nt**.

6. This capital city of New Jersey starts with the consonant blend **tr**.

8. This capital city of Maine contains the consonant blend **st**.

10. This "Bay State" has the consonant digraph **ch** and the double consonants **ss** and **tt** in its name.

12. This capital city of Maryland contains the double consonant **nn**.

14. This "Constitution State" has the double consonant **nn** in its name.

15. This "Empire State" has the phonogram **ork** in its title.

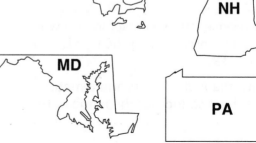

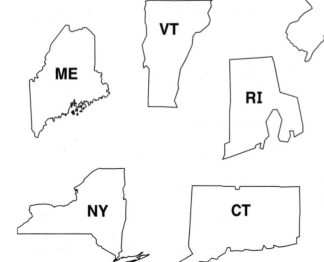

## Ellis Island Skits

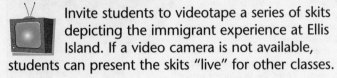

Invite students to videotape a series of skits depicting the immigrant experience at Ellis Island. If a video camera is not available, students can present the skits "live" for other classes.

- Have students make a list of tasks involved in creating a skit—researching the topic, writing the script, designing costumes, and making scenery.

- Help students research the immigration experience by compiling a list of reference materials, including firsthand accounts of immigrants who entered the country through Ellis Island. The following web sites are good sources of information about immigration and related topics: www.historychannel.com and www.ellisisland.com.

- Encourage students to include words with consonant blends, consonant digraphs, and double consonant sounds in the dialogue. Examples include: **freedom, prosperity, dream, shelter, ship, flag, statue, pride, school, strive, scholar, settle, official, currency, country, ancestors, shortage, choice, explore, opportunity,** and **property.**

## Design an Iroquois Web Site

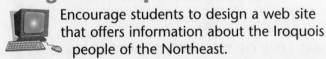

Encourage students to design a web site that offers information about the Iroquois people of the Northeast.

- If needed, students may use various sources on the Internet for instructions and assistance on designing web pages.

- Divide the project's task among small groups to research information about the Iroquois people. Topics might include: government, economy, environment, culture, and belief systems. Suggest that students use these terms as hyperlinks to the researched information for each topic. Encourage students to create maps and drawings.

- Have students include words with consonant blends, consonant digraphs, and double consonant sounds in their text, such as **land, plant, hunt, depend, environment, agreement, treaty, east, government, battle, village,** **attack, settlers, tobacco, moccasin, community, history, country, harvest, tribes, northeast,** and **crops.**

## WELCOME TO AN IROQUOIS VILLAGE

- Learn about the Iroquois government by attending a conference.

- Visit a longhouse and enjoy a typical Iroquois meal.

- Celebrate the harvest at the Green Corn festival.

## Create a Regional Cookbook

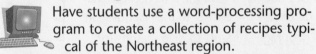

Have students use a word-processing program to create a collection of recipes typical of the Northeast region.

- Encourage students to brainstorm and compile recipes associated with northeastern states, such as Boston baked beans, Manhattan clam chowder, New England clam chowder, Maryland crab cakes, and so on. Discuss how local resources and concentrations of ethnic groups can affect an area's cuisine.

- Provide students with cookbooks to use as models. Point out that cooks need to know the amount of ingredients, oven temperature, and time needed in order to obtain the intended results.

- Students can organize and combine the recipes by state or by food type—soup, entrée, desert, etc. Then have them search through the contents of the cookbook and list words from the recipes that contain consonant blends, consonant digraphs, and double consonants.

- Print the recipes and organize them into a bound book. Encourage students to experiment at home with the recipes. Share the cookbook with other classes by adding it to the school library.

## Introduction to
### Consonant Sounds

#### Objectives

- **To enjoy a nonfiction selection related to the theme the *Northeast***
- **To study consonant blends, consonant digraphs, and double consonant sounds**

## Starting with Literature

- Ask a student to read "A Symbol of Freedom" aloud for the class.
- Write the following words from the selection on the board:

| | | |
|---|---|---|
| **glimpse** | **crown** | **climb** |
| **stop** | **shines** | **project** |

- Have students say the words aloud and emphasize the initial consonant sounds.

### Critical Thinking

- Ask students to read the selection carefully to determine the answer to the first question.
- Encourage students to give reasons for their answers to questions two and three.

## Introducing the Skill

- Write these consonant pairs on the board: **gr, pr, fr, st, th**. Have students scan the selection for words that begin with these pairs. (For example: **grand, present, France, steps, there**) Write the words on the board.
- Have volunteers say the words aloud and circle the initial consonant pairs.

## Practicing the Skill

Have students work in groups. Assign each group a specific consonant pair to find in the selection. Ask each group to suggest additional words with the same consonant pair. Tell students to include words with more than one syllable.

---

# A Symbol of Freedom

Every year millions of people take to the air or the road to visit the American land. Often, their first stop is one of the big cities in the Northeast. Sometimes, the Statue of Liberty is the first sight tourists see. This "mighty woman with a torch" stands in New York City as a symbol of freedom to the whole world.

Years ago, most immigrants to the United States got their first glimpse of the country when they sailed into New York Harbor. There, the best-known woman in the world welcomed them.

The Statue of Liberty was a present to the United States from the people of France. It marked the one hundredth birthday of our country. The project to build the statue took almost ten years to complete. At last, there was a grand ceremony on October 28, 1886. President Grover Cleveland was there. He said, "We will not forget that Liberty has here made her home...."

Millions of people visit the Statue of Liberty each year. Some choose to climb the 354 steps to her crown. At the top they can gaze at New York Harbor. From anywhere around the harbor, people can see the green statue and its golden torch. The torch stays lit all day and all night. It is a symbol of the light of liberty that shines on the American land.

### Critical Thinking

1. What does the Statue of Liberty stand for?
2. How do you think immigrants felt when they first saw the Statue of Liberty?
3. How would you have felt? Explain to a partner.

1. The Statue of Liberty is a symbol of freedom for the whole world.
2. Answers will vary.
3. Answers will vary.

LESSON 1: Introduction to Consonant Blends, Consonant Digraphs, and Double Consonant Sounds

**5**

---

# Theme Activity

**HISTORIC TIME LINE OF THE NORTHEAST** Ask students to create a time line showing significant events in the history of the Northeast. Students may illustrate their time lines with captioned pictures relating to the original thirteen colonies and later the Northeast states in the region.

Students should also include information about the Native American peoples who were living in the Northeast before the Europeans arrived. Encourage students to include detailed drawings showing aspects of the Native Americans' way of life.

Have students label items on their time line with "Unit 1" words—words with consonant blends, consonant digraphs, or double consonant sounds. Invite students to add to their "Historic Time Line of the Northeast" throughout the unit.

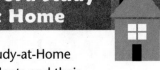

# Dear Family,

Welcome to Sadlier's *Word Study* program. Each unit presents strategies and exercises to help your child become a better reader. In Unit 1, your child will review and explore consonant blends, consonant digraphs, and double consonant sounds. The focus of Level E is the *American Land—Its People and History*. The unit theme is the *Northeast*.

A **consonant blend** is two or three consonants sounded together so that each letter is heard (**gl**ass, fie**ld**, **spl**inter).

A **consonant digraph** is two consonants that together stand for one sound (**ch**arm, wea**th**er, sa**sh**). The word digra**ph** itself ends with the digraph **ph,** which makes the sound of **f.**

The sound that **double consonants** make is usually the sound of just one of the consonants, as in ke**tt**le and ra**bb**it.

## Family Focus

- Read together the nonfiction selection on page 5. Talk about it with your child. Discuss the meaning of a national symbol. What other symbols can your child identify? How do these symbols convey their meaning?

- Brainstorm places of national interest, such as Independence Hall, Plymouth Rock, or the White House. What historic places have you seen? Which historic landmarks do you hope to visit? Make a list of these places.

## LINKS TO LEARNING

To extend learning together, you might explore:

**Web Sites**
www.nps.gov/stli/mainmenu.htm
www.libertystatepark.com/
statueof.htm

**Video**
*The Statue of Liberty,* a film by Ken Burns, PBS Home Video.

**Literature**
*Indians of the Northeast*
by Colin G. Calloway, ©1991.

**Places to Visit**
Plimoth Plantation, Plymouth, MA
The Statue of Liberty, New York, NY

# Word Study at Home

- The Word-Study-at-Home page gives students and their families an opportunity to work together as students develop their language skills.

- On the Word-Study-at-Home page for Unit 1, students and their families will find activities that relate to the theme the *Northeast* and focus on words with consonant blends, consonant digraphs, and double consonants.

- Have students remove page 6 from their books. Direct them to take the page home so that their families may share in the Word-Study-at-Home activities.

- Encourage students to talk about familiar symbols and how these symbols came to have meaning. Discuss how symbols represent abstract qualities, such as peace, courage, and brotherhood.

- Invite students to describe places of national interest that they have visited. Encourage students to learn more about historic landmarks they would like to visit. You may also want to have students research which U.S. historic sites draw the most visitors each year. Discuss why so many of these sites are popular with visitors from other nations.

## Theme-Related Resources

### Books
*The Statue of Liberty Encyclopedia,* by Barry Moreno, Simon & Schuster, 2000
*Liberty,* by Lynn Curlee, Atheneum, 2000

### Web Sites
www.nyctourist.com/liberty1.html
www.greatbuildings.com/buildings/
Statue_of_Liberty.html

## Multicultural Connection

The Iroquois was a confederation of Native American peoples formed in the 16th century in what is now New York State. The Iroquois originally included five tribes: the Mohawk, Onondaga, Cayuga, Oneida, and Seneca. Have students research the history of the Iroquois peoples and their relationships with the Europeans who settled the Northeast.

## Social Studies Link

Have students make a map of the Northeast region. Direct students to label the states and principal cities. Have them identify and label major geographic features, such as the Hudson River and the Appalachian Mountains.

# Initial l-blends

## Objectives

- **To recognize the sounds of initial l-blends**
- **To associate these sounds with the letters that stand for them**
- **To read, form, and write words with initial l-blends**

## Warming Up

- Write the following paragraph on the board. Ask a volunteer to read it aloud.

  The Northeast is a colorful **bl**end of people and **pl**aces. There are quiet towns, where **gl**istening streams **fl**ow and children **pl**ay. There are also noisy cities, **cl**ogged with **sl**ow-moving cars.

- Have students identify all the words with initial l-blends. Underline the words as students say them and circle the l-blend.

## Teaching the Lesson

- Write the words **slope, fling, blond,** and **plank** on the board and read them aloud. Ask students how they are alike. Explain that each word begins with a consonant plus the letter **l**.

- Write **blend** and **phonogram** on the board. Then have volunteers read aloud the Helpful Hints on pages 7 and 8. Explain that initial l-blends combine with phonograms to form words, such as **sl** + **ide** and **fl** + **ock**. Ask students to suggest additional examples of words formed by combining initial l-blends with phonograms.

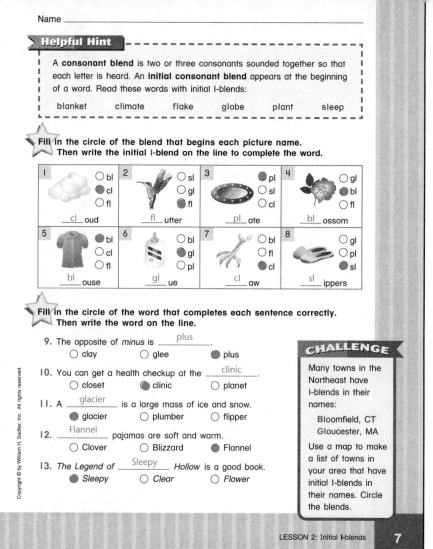

Name _____

**Helpful Hint**

A **consonant blend** is two or three consonants sounded together so that each letter is heard. An **initial consonant blend** appears at the beginning of a word. Read these words with initial l-blends:

blanket    climate    flake    globe    plant    sleep

★ Fill in the circle of the blend that begins each picture name. Then write the initial l-blend on the line to complete the word.

1. ○ bl  ● cl  ○ fl — _cl_ oud
2. ○ sl  ○ gl  ● fl — _fl_ utter
3. ● pl  ○ sl  ○ cl — _pl_ ate
4. ○ gl  ● bl  ○ fl — _bl_ ossom
5. ● bl  ○ cl  ○ fl — _bl_ ouse
6. ○ bl  ● gl  ○ pl — _gl_ ue
7. ○ bl  ○ fl  ● cl — _cl_ aw
8. ○ gl  ○ pl  ● sl — _sl_ ippers

★ Fill in the circle of the word that completes each sentence correctly. Then write the word on the line.

9. The opposite of *minus* is ___plus___.
   ○ clay    ○ glee    ● plus

10. You can get a health checkup at the ___clinic___.
    ○ closet    ● clinic    ○ planet

11. A ___glacier___ is a large mass of ice and snow.
    ● glacier    ○ plumber    ○ flipper

12. ___Flannel___ pajamas are soft and warm.
    ○ Clover    ○ Blizzard    ● Flannel

13. *The Legend of* ___Sleepy___ *Hollow* is a good book.
    ● Sleepy    ○ Clear    ○ Flower

**CHALLENGE**

Many towns in the Northeast have l-blends in their names:

Bloomfield, CT
Gloucester, MA

Use a map to make a list of towns in your area that have initial l-blends in their names. Circle the blends.

**U N I V E R S A L   A C C E S S**
# Meeting Individual Needs

### Visual Learners

Draw the chart below on the board for students to copy. Ask students to combine the initial l-blends with the phonograms. Challenge students to add other phonograms that can be combined with one or more of the initial l-blends to form words.

|      | pl    | cl    | sl    |
|------|-------|-------|-------|
| ump  | plump | clump | slump |
| ay   | play  | clay  | slay  |

### Kinesthetic Learners

Write the following words with initial l-blends on separate index cards. Have volunteers pantomime each word as the class tries to guess it. As each word is identified, have a volunteer write it on the board and circle the initial blend.

**climb    glue    slide**
**plate    flag    flutter**
**flip    slip    blanket**

A **phonogram** is a syllable that has a vowel and any letters that follow. Usually, a phonogram has a vowel followed by one or more consonants. Some phonograms have two vowels, but only one vowel sound.

Here are some phonograms:

ack   ance   ant   are   aw   ay   ide   ing   ink   ock   ug   ump

⭐ Each box has three initial l-blends and three phonograms. Match the blends and the phonograms in each box to build three words. Write the words on the lines.

**1**
gl ⟍ ⟋ ay
bl ⤬ ink
pl ⟋ ⟍ ide

glide

blink

play

**2**
pl ⟍ ⟋ ing
cl ⤬ are
gl ⟋ ⟍ ug

plug

cling

glare

**3**
bl ⟍ ⟋ ock
gl ⤬ ump
sl ⟋ ⟍ ance

block

glance

slump

⭐ Write a word from the box below to complete each sentence about Gloucester, Massachusetts. This old town has a long history of fishing.

block    claw    plant    play    black    glance

4. You can pick up a map of Gloucester at the tourist office, just one __block__ from the port.

5. Sailors in __black__ rubber boots slosh in water all day.

6. The largest docks lead to a major fish-processing __plant__.

7. The meat from a lobster __claw__ is very tasty.

8. A quick __glance__ toward the horizon shows that a storm is coming.

9. Actors performed a __play__ about this fishing village.

8    LESSON 2: Initial l-blends

 **Home Involvement Activity** Find Gloucester, Massachusetts, on a map. Brainstorm ocean-related words that begin with an l-blend. **Fl**ounder is one. How many others can you name? Make a list.

## English-Language Learners/ESL

Find pictures of easily identifiable words with initial l-blends, such as **cloud**, **plate**, **blouse**, **planet**, and **sled**. Paste each picture on a large index card. Help students identify each object and correctly say the word. Then help them write the word on the card. Finally, have students sort the cards according to their initial l-blend.

## Gifted Learners

Challenge students to make up silly sentences using three or more initial l-blend words, each with a different initial consonant. For example: The **cl**owns **sl**ipped and **fl**ipped on the wet **gl**ue.

## Learners with Special Needs

Additional strategies for supporting learners with special needs can be found on page 5L.

● Read aloud the direction lines on pages 7 and 8. Complete the first item in each exercise with students.

● Encourage students to use the process of elimination to help them complete the exercises on page 8.

## Curriculum Connections

### Spelling Link

Have students listen as you read aloud the words and sentences below. Ask for volunteers to spell each word orally and to write it on the board.

**slump**   The team was in a batting **slump**.

**climate**   I want to live in a milder **climate.**

**blizzard**   The **blizzard** left ten inches of snow on the ground.

**glacier**   A **glacier** is a large mass of ice.

**plumber**   The **plumber** fixed the leaky pipe.

**cling**   Adam had to **cling** to the rope to keep from falling.

**blouse**   Her green **blouse** matched her skirt.

### Science Link

Distance from the equator affects climate. In the Northeast, for example, Maine has colder winters than Maryland because it is farther from the equator. Have students find their state on a map and see how far it is from the equator. Then have them write a paragraph describing their state's climate. Challenge them to use words with initial l-blends in their paragraph.

### Observational Assessment

*Check to see that students understand how initial blends combine with phonograms to form words.*

# Initial r- and s-blends

## Objectives

- To recognize the sounds of **r-** and **s-blends**
- To associate these sounds with the letters that stand for them
- To read, form, and write words with initial **r-** and **s-blends**

## Warming Up

- Write the following paragraph on the board and have a volunteer read it.

  Marian Anderson was born in Philadelphia. She **dr**eamed of becoming a **gr**eat singer. She **st**udied and **pr**acticed for years. Her **tr**aining paid off. She was the first African American singer to take the **st**age at the Metropolitan Opera House in New York City. The **cr**owd loved her.

- Ask volunteers to identify the words that begin with a consonant + **r**. Underline the words as students say them and circle the **r**-blends. Next, have students underline words that begin with **s** + a consonant. Ask them to say each word aloud and circle the **s**-blends.

## Teaching the Lesson

- Review the definition of a consonant blend on page 7. Then write **ground**, **truthful**, and **freckle** on the board. Have students read the words aloud. Ask students what these words have in common. (initial **r**-blends)
- Write **spoon**, **skid**, and **snarl** on the board. Have students read the words. Then elicit that the three start with an **s** + consonant blend.
- Review how initial blends and phonograms form words. Then have students look again at the text on the board and analyze the combinations of blends and phonograms.

9

---

Name _____

**Helpful Hint**

Many consonants blend with r. These words have initial r-blends:

bring   crumble   drain   frantic   ground   present   treat

Write an r-blend from the box below to complete each picture name.

| br | cr | dr | fr | gr | pr | tr |

| 1 | 2 | 3 | 4 |
|---|---|---|---|
| __fr__ eckles | __cr__ ib | __tr__ iangle | __gr__ oceries |

| 5 | 6 | 7 | 8 |
|---|---|---|---|
| __br__ occoli | __pr__ etzel | __tr__ apeze | __dr__ esser |

Fill in the circle of the word that completes each sentence correctly. Then write the word on the line.

9. Wheat flour and corn meal are used in making __bread__.
   ○ brooks   ○ braids   ● bread

10. A nightmare is a bad __dream__.
    ○ drain   ● dream   ○ drummer

11. The winner gets to wear a glittery __crown__.
    ○ crash   ● crown   ○ creature

12. The __traffic__ backs up whenever the drawbridge opens.
    ○ trickle   ● traffic   ○ trumpet

13. Get the __griddle__ good and hot before you make pancakes.
    ○ greenhouse   ● griddle   ○ gravy

**CHALLENGE**

Circle the r-blends in these words:

fresher
abroad
impress
grandfather

Then write a sentence for each word.

LESSON 3: Initial r- and s-blends    9

---

# UNIVERSAL ACCESS
## Meeting Individual Needs

### Visual Learners

Assign each student a text selection, such as a page from a magazine or book. Have students identify examples of words with initial **r**-blends and words with initial **s**-blends. Tell students to write their words on a sheet of paper, circling the consonant blends. Extend the activity by having the class make a master list that incorporates all of their words.

### Musical Learners

Challenge students to write songs using words that begin with **r**-blends or **s**-blends. Suggest that students make up a melody or borrow one from a familiar song. Encourage students to compile a list of words they can use when creating their songs. Have volunteers perform their finished songs for the class.

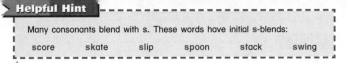

**Helpful Hint**

Many consonants blend with s. These words have initial s-blends:

score    skate    slip    spoon    stack    swing

Each word in the box below has an initial s-blend. Choose the word from the box that names each picture. Then write the word on the line.

scallop  skeleton  slicker  smile  snorkel  spinach  stamp  sweater

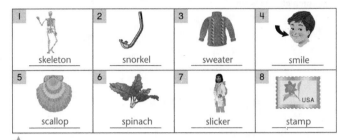

| 1 | 2 | 3 | 4 |
|---|---|---|---|
| skeleton | snorkel | sweater | smile |
| 5 | 6 | 7 | 8 |
| scallop | spinach | slicker | stamp |

Each box has three initial s-blends and three phonograms. Match the blends and phonograms to build words. Write the words on the lines.

| 9 | 10 | 11 |
|---|----|----|
| sc    unk | sn    and | sl    all |
| sk    ay  | st    ell | sm    in  |
| sw    ale | sp    ail | sk    ing |
| scale | snail | sling |
| skunk | stand | small |
| sway  | spell | skin  |

Use a word from the three boxes above to complete each silly rhyming question.

12. Does a ___skunk___ have spunk?    13. Can you get a whale on a ___scale___?

14. Can you ___stand___ on your hand?    15. Does a ___snail___ have a tail?

10    LESSON 3: Initial **r**- and s-blends

**Home Involvement Activity** Work together to list items in your home that begin with r-blends and s-blends, such as br**oom** and st**airs.** Circle the r- and s-blends in the words on your list.

---

**English-Language Learners/ESL**

Pair students with more fluent speakers and have them make up simple riddles for words with initial **r**-blends and **s**-blends. For example: *A king or queen wears one. It has five letters and an initial **r**-blend. What's the word?* **(crown)** Have students write their riddles on the board and read them aloud. As the class solves the riddles, have volunteers write the answers on the board.

**Gifted Learners**

Have students research and write a paragraph about a famous place in the Northeast. Encourage students to use words with initial **r**-blends or **s**-blends. For example, they might write about a well-known **br**idge or a **sp**orts **st**adium.

**Learners with Special Needs**

Additional strategies for supporting learners with special needs can be found on page 5L.

---

## Practicing the Skill

● Read aloud the direction lines on pages 9 and 10. Complete the first item in each exercise with students.

● Extend the last activity by challenging students to make up additional rhyming questions for words not already used in items 12–15.

Turn to page 5K for an Intervention Strategy designed to help students who need extra support with this lesson.

## Curriculum Connections

### Spelling Link

The following words contain initial **r**-blends and **s**-blends. Read each word aloud. Then have a volunteer spell the word, write it on the board, and use it in a sentence.

| | |
|---|---|
| **spinach** | **skeleton** |
| **sweater** | **groceries** |
| **pretzel** | **trapeze** |
| **snail** | **sway** |
| **snorkel** | **crumble** |
| **broccoli** | **creature** |

### Social Studies Link

Many cities in the Northeast have names that begin with **r**-blends and **s**-blends. Using a map of the region, have students identify as many such cities as they can. Possible answers include Brattleboro (Vermont), Providence (Rhode Island), Bridgeport and Stamford (Connecticut).

### Observational Assessment

*Check to see that students understand that the changing consonant comes before the **r** in **r**-blends but after the **s** in **s**-blends.*

# Final **t-**, **d-**, and **p-**blends

## Objectives

- To recognize the sounds of final **t-**, **d-**, and **p-** consonant blends
- To associate these sounds with the letters that stand for them
- To read, form, and write words with these blends

## Warming Up

- Write the following paragraph on the board. Have a student read the paragraph aloud.

  Pilgrims on the *Mayflower* le**ft** Engla**nd** a**nd** came to the Northea**st** coa**st** in 1620. The la**nd** on which they found-ed the settleme**nt** of Plymouth was the site of an o**ld** Native American village.

- Ask volunteers to underline the words that end with consonant blends and then circle the blends. Have students say the words aloud, emphasizing the consonant blend sounds.

## Teaching the Lesson

- Write the words **mast, field, dump, pound,** and **wilt** on the board. Have a volunteer read the words aloud. Ask students what the words have in common. (All the words end with a consonant blend.) Have students circle the blends.

- Ask volunteers to read aloud the Helpful Hints on pages 11–12. Point out that the letter pattern *initial consonant blend + vowel + final consonant blend* is common. Have students read the example words shown in the Helpful Hint on page 12 and suggest additional examples.

---

Name _____

### Helpful Hint

A **final consonant blend** appears at the end of a word.

belt   field   hint   jump   left   lisp   pulp   rest   sound

Say the name of each picture. Listen for the final blend. Then circle the blend that ends each picture name. Write that blend on the line to complete the word.

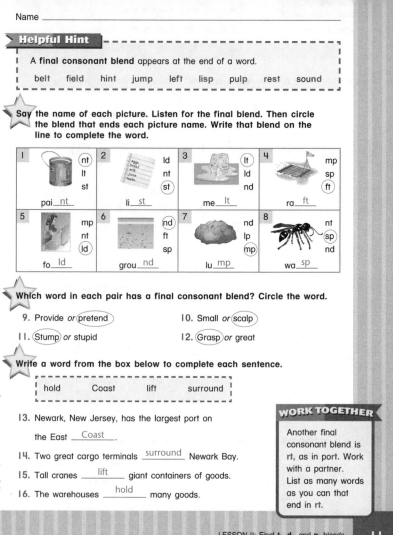

1. (nt) lt st — pai**nt**
2. ld nt (st) — li**st**
3. (lt) ld nd — me**lt**
4. mp sp (ft) — ra**ft**
5. mp nt (ld) — fo**ld**
6. (nd) ft sp — grou**nd**
7. nd lp (mp) — lu**mp**
8. nt (sp) nd — wa**sp**

Which word in each pair has a final consonant blend? Circle the word.

9. Provide *or* (pretend)
10. Small *or* (scalp)
11. (Stump) *or* stupid
12. (Grasp) *or* great

Write a word from the box below to complete each sentence.

hold     Coast     lift     surround

13. Newark, New Jersey, has the largest port on the East ___Coast___.
14. Two great cargo terminals ___surround___ Newark Bay.
15. Tall cranes ___lift___ giant containers of goods.
16. The warehouses ___hold___ many goods.

### WORK TOGETHER

Another final consonant blend is rt, as in port. Work with a partner. List as many words as you can that end in rt.

---

# UNIVERSAL ACCESS
## Meeting Individual Needs

### Visual Learners

Draw the following chart on the board for students to copy and complete. For each combination of initial consonant(s) and final blend, have students fill in at least one example. Sample answers are shown.

| Initial Consonant(s) | Final Blend | Example |
|---|---|---|
| b | ld | (bald) |
| g | sp | (gasp) |
| m | st | (most) |
| sp | nd | (spend) |
| gr | sp | (grasp) |

### Auditory Learners

Have students draw three boxes on a sheet of paper and label the boxes "final **t-** blend," "final **d-** blend," and "final **p-** blend." As you say each of the following words aloud have students write each word in the correct box.

| | | |
|---|---|---|
| **pump** | **wild** | **honest** |
| **absent** | **crust** | **tramp** |
| **intend** | **hint** | **stomp** |
| **ground** | **bold** | **shrimp** |

⭐ **Underline the initial and final consonant blends in each word in bold type.**

1. White-water rafting requires **swift** water.

2. The campers pounded in the stakes with a **blunt** rock.

3. The members of the hiking club have **trust** in their leader.

4. **Grasp** the handle and turn it to the right.

5. Hot milk can **scald** you.

6. The story is set in the **present** time.

7. That is a well-known **brand** of cranberry sauce.

8. To fold the table, you must loosen the **clamp.**

9. I can daydream for hours as the clouds **drift** by.

10. They started a fire with sparks from a piece of **flint.**

⭐ **Say each word in the list. Listen for initial and final consonant blends. On the line, write the letter of the word from the list that matches each clue. Then underline the initial and final consonant blends in each word in the list.**

| | | |
|---|---|---|
| _b_ | 11. the opposite of *back* | a. blond |
| _h_ | 12. the opposite of *stop* | b. front |
| _e_ | 13. to make believe | c. grand |
| _f_ | 14. a sharp pain in a muscle | d. plump |
| _c_ | 15. large or excellent | e. pretend |
| _d_ | 16. chubby, like a baby | f. cramp |
| _a_ | 17. light yellow hair | g. draft |
| _g_ | 18. a current of air | h. start |

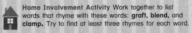

12   LESSON 4: Final **t-, d-,** and **p-** blends

🏠 **Home Involvement Activity** Work together to list words that rhyme with these words: **graft, blend,** and **clamp.** Try to find at least three rhymes for each word.

---

### English-Language Learners/ESL

Display pictures or objects named by words with final **t-, d-,** and **p-** blends, such as **tent, ground, nest, lamp, pump, toast, band.** Have students identify each object and correctly pronounce the word. Then have them use the word in a sentence. Finally, help students write their sentence on the board and underline the word.

### Gifted Learners

Challenge students to find examples of places in the Northeast named by words with final **t-** or **d-** blends. Make the activity into a contest by giving 1 point for state names (Vermo**nt**, Rhode Isla**nd**), 2 points for cities and towns (Portla**nd**, Springfie**ld**), and 3 points for other features (Piedmo**nt**).

### Learners with Special Needs

Additional strategies for supporting learners with special needs can be found on page 5L.

---

## Practicing the Skill

● Read aloud the direction lines on page 11. Suggest that students say the words aloud to identify the final consonant blends.

● Read aloud the direction lines on page 12. For the first exercise, remind students to underline both an initial and a final consonant blend in each word.

**Intervention Strategy**

Turn to page 5K for an Intervention Strategy designed to help students who need extra support with this lesson.

## Curriculum Connections

### Spelling Link

The pairs of words below contain final consonant blends. Read each word pair aloud. Then have volunteers spell each word and use each pair of words together in an imaginative sentence.

| | | |
|---|---|---|
| **trust** | and | **sport** |
| **surround** | and | **field** |
| **blond** | and | **scalp** |
| **grasp** | and | **swift** |
| **pretend** | and | **wasp** |

### Multicultural Connection

● The French explorer Samuel de Champlain first came to the place that would later become the state of Vermont in the early 1600s. In fact, the name of the state comes from two French words: *vert* and *mont*, meaning "green mountain."

● Have students research the names of other states or cities in the Northeast and determine which languages and cultures the names come from.

## Observational Assessment

*Check to see that students pronounce the last letter when saying words with consonant blends—especially words that end with **d** or **t**, such as **wand** and **trust**.*

# Consonant Digraphs

## Objectives

- **To identify initial, medial, and final consonant digraphs in words**
- **To associate letters and sounds for consonant digraphs**
- **To write words with consonant digraphs**

## Warming Up

- Write the following poem on the board. Have a student read it aloud.

    New England's villages have **ch**arm,

    And its coast is easy to rea**ch**.

    From **th**ere you can see boats and **sh**ips

    And enjoy **th**e suns**h**ine and bea**ch**.

- Explain that sometimes two consonants together make one sound. Write the digraphs **ch, sh,** and **th** on the board. Have students find examples of these digraphs in the poem. Point out that the digraphs may appear at the beginning, middle, or end of a word. Underline the examples as students identify them and circle the digraphs.

## Teaching the Lesson

- Ask a student to read aloud the Helpful Hints on page 13. Call attention to the digraphs in the examples. Ask students to suggest other words with the same digraphs. Write them on the board.

- Ask a volunteer to read aloud the Helpful Hints on page 14. Have students say **chirp, chiffon** (a kind of fabric), and **character** aloud, listening carefully to the different sounds of **ch**. Then have them say **physical** and **rough**, listening carefully for the **f** sound.

---

Name _____

**Helpful Hints**

A **consonant digraph** is two consonants that together stand for one sound.

**Initial digraphs** *begin* words.   charm   phone   shelf   thin   whale
**Medial digraphs** are *in the middle* of words.   merchant   telephone   author
**Final digraphs** *end* words.   touch   sing   graph   rush   path

Read each group of words. Circle the consonant digraph in the word in bold type. Then write **I** for Initial, **M** for Medial, or **F** for Final, depending on where the consonant digraph appears in the word.

1. ra**ng** the alarm _____ F
2. heard the **wh**istle _____ I
3. snapped a **ph**oto _____ I
4. establi**sh** the rules _____ F
5. sat in the blea**ch**ers _____ M
6. saw ano**th**er fire _____ M

PHILADELPHIA FIRE DEPT.

The towns below are all in the Northeast. Each town has one or more consonant digraphs in its name. Circle the letter **I** for Initial, **M** for Medial, or **F** for Final to show where in the name each digraph appears. Then add the number of digraphs in each name.

| Name of Town | Location of Diagraph(s) | | | Number of Diagraphs |
|---|---|---|---|---|
| 7. **Sh**arpsburg, MD | (I) | M | F | 1 |
| 8. **Ph**iladel**ph**ia, PA | (I) | (M) | F | 2 |
| 9. **Ch**epa**ch**et, RI | (I) | (M) | F | 2 |
| 10. Moona**ch**ie, NJ | I | (M) | F | 1 |
| 11. Portsmou**th**, NH | I | M | (F) | 1 |
| 12. **Ch**es**h**ire, MA | (I) | (M) | F | 2 |

LESSON 5: Consonant Digraphs   13

**CHALLENGE**

Choose a state in the Northeast. Use a map to list place names in the state that have one or more consonant digraphs. Add the total number of consonant digraphs in the names.

---

# UNIVERSAL ACCESS
## Meeting Individual Needs

### Auditory Learners

Have students write the following digraphs on separate index cards: **ch, ph, sh, th, wh, gh.** Say the following words aloud and have students hold up the card that shows the digraph they hear.

| | | |
|---|---|---|
| **tough** | **chemical** | **autograph** |
| **search** | **trophy** | **theme** |
| **fresh** | **anywhere** | **telephone** |
| **while** | **weather** | **shovel** |

### Visual Learners

Draw the chart below on the board for students to copy. Have students fill in words with digraphs in initial, medial, and final positions. The first line has been done as an example.

| Digraph | Initial | Medial | Final |
|---|---|---|---|
| ch | chart | orchestra | pouch |
| ph | | | |
| sh | | | |
| th | | | |
| gh | | | |
| wh | | | |

The **digraph** ch can make three different sounds. Usually, it makes the sound you hear in **chirp**, **preacher**, or **birch**. Sometimes, it makes the sound of sh, as in **chiffon**, or the sound of k, as in **character**.

The digraphs ph and gh can stand for the same sound. **Physical** and **rough** make the same sound of f.

★ **Each word in the box below has the consonant digraph ch, ph, or gh. Write the word on the line that best completes each sentence.**

| telephone | rough | Chesapeake |
|---|---|---|

1. Maryland's ___Chesapeake___ Bay is famous for its crabs.

2. There is a stretch of ___rough___ road near Woodstock, New York.

3. We used our cellular ___telephone___ to say we'd be arriving in Boston soon.

Catching crabs on Ch**esapeake** Bay

★ **Each of the scrambled words below has a consonant digraph. Use the clues in each sentence to unscramble the word. Then write the letters in the spaces. The boxes show where the digraphs belong.**

4. I got a **fwifh** of salt air crossing the bridge to Cape Cod.

w [h] i f f

5. Although there are snakes in the Northeast, there are no **tpynosh**.

p y [t] [h] o n s

6. We could smell that **meclhcai** spill on the road.

[c] [h] e m i c a l

7. Several **llfhsiyje** washed up on the beach after the storm.

j e l l y f i s [h]

8. It takes a lot of **scilyhap** effort to hike through Bear Mountain.

[p] [h] y s i c a l

9. Many houses in the Northeast are **tatahced** to each other.

a t t a [c] [h] e d

14    LESSON 5: Consonant Digraphs

**Home Involvement Activity** Together, look at a road atlas. Which main highways crisscross the Northeast? Which are north-south roads? Which roads go east-west? Which might you take to go up the coast?

---

## English-Language Learners/ESL

List words containing consonant digraphs, such as **telephone**, **whale**, and **bench**. Say each word aloud and have students repeat after you. Display pictures, and help students match each word with its corresponding picture. Say each word again slowly and point to the digraph. Have students repeat each word and circle the consonant digraphs.

## Gifted Learners

Have students research and write sentences about the history of the Northeast using words that contain consonant digraphs. Example: *Farmers in the nor**th**eastern colonies grew **wh**eat, vegetables, and other crops.*

## Learners with Special Needs

Additional strategies for supporting learners with special needs can be found on page 5L.

---

## Practicing the Skill

- Read aloud the directions on page 13. For items 7–12, tell students to look for more than one digraph in the names.

- For the exercises on page 14, tell students to use sentence context (the surrounding words) to help them fill in the blanks.

 **Intervention Strategy** Turn to page 5K for an Intervention Strategy designed to help students who need extra support with this lesson.

## Curriculum Connections

### Spelling Link

- Write the following words on the board, leave spaces for the missing consonant digraphs.

| | |
|---|---|
| tele_ _one | ele_ _ant |
| _ _elf | _ _ile |
| establi_ _ | ano_ _er |
| prea_ _er | _ _ysical |
| _ _aracter | _ _emical |
| _ _istle | mer_ _ant |

- Have students spell each word aloud, filling in the missing digraph. Then have them use the word in a sentence.

### Writing Link

The word part **-graph** means something that writes or records (**seismograph**) or something written or recorded (**autograph**). With the aid of a dictionary, have students list and define as many words as they can that contain the word part **-graph.**

## Observational Assessment

*Check to see that students can correctly spell and pronounce words with the digraphs ph and ch such as **nephew**, **pamphlet**, **dolphin**, **trophy**, **chorus**, **parachute**, **orchid**.*

# Connecting Reading and Writing

## Objectives

- **To read a nonfiction selection and respond to it in writing**
- **To make inferences and interpret information**
- **To write a poem**

## Warming Up

### Comprehension Skills

- Tell students that when they **make inferences,** they form ideas or make predictions based on facts, clues, or evidence. Making inferences as they read can help students understand and enjoy what they read more fully, whether it is an article, novel, book, poem, or textbook.

- **Interpreting** is another skill that can help students as they read. To interpret an article, story, or poem is to make sense of it or give it meaning.

## Teaching the Lesson

- Encourage students to read the article more than once and to think carefully about what they are reading.
- Remind students that to answer the Reader's Response questions they will have to combine their knowledge with ideas and information in the article.
- Tell students who need help answering the third question to reread the third paragraph of the article.

## Practicing the Skill

Read aloud the directions on page 16. Direct students' attention to the Writer's Tips. Discuss how making a list of rhyming pairs can be helpful.

**15**

---

Name _____

**Read about the native groups of the Northeast. Then answer the questions that follow.**

# Native Peoples of the Northeast
### by Trudie Lamb Richmond

The Northeast is often defined as the area stretching from the Great Lakes region east to the Atlantic coast and from southern Canada and Maine south through Pennsylvania to the Tidewater region of Virginia. It is a broad and diverse area in both landscape and climate. Seasons range from harsh winters and cool summers in the north to milder winters and hot, humid summers in the south.

Traditional Lands of the Northeast Indians

Five hundred years ago, when the first European explorers arrived, they discovered that the area was occupied by the Iroquois and the Algonquians. Within these two groups, there were many different tribes, bands, and villages, each with its own language and way of life. Most native groups in the Northeast grew some food and did not depend solely on hunting and gathering.

All the groups had a deep respect for the land and the plant and animal life they depended on. Hunting, for example, was never done for sport. Aside from food, animals were a valuable source of clothing, shelter, and tools.

There are an estimated 157,000 native people living in the Northeast of the United States today. Penobscots, Micmacs, Pequots, Wampanoags, Abenakis, Narragansetts, Mohawks, Mohegans, and others live in cities, towns, and rural areas, as well as on reservation lands set aside for their

### Reader's Response

1. Who are some of the native peoples of the Northeast?

2. What do you think life was like for these people before the European explorers arrived? After the explorers came?

3. Why do you think these native groups respect the land and its plants and animals? Give reasons.

1. Iroquois, Algonquians, Penobscots, Micmacs, Pequots, Wampanoags, Abenakis, Narragansetts, Mohawks, and Mohegans
2. Answers will vary.
3. Answers will vary.

LESSON 6: Connecting Reading and Writing
Comprehension—Make Inferences; Interpret

**15**

---

# UNIVERSAL ACCESS
# Meeting Individual Needs

### Auditory Learners

Read aloud several simple poems from a poetry anthology. Explore how poets communicate with readers. What descriptive techniques do poets use? How do they express emotions? How do they use language to convey point of view?

### Visual Learners

Show students photographs of environmental damage, such as lake pollution or rainforest destruction. If possible, include some before-and-after pictures of places that have suffered damage. Encourage students to consider the consequences of environmental destruction. Have students describe their feelings about what they see in the pictures using specific words.

### Learners with Special Needs

Additional strategies for supporting learners with special needs can be found on page 5L.

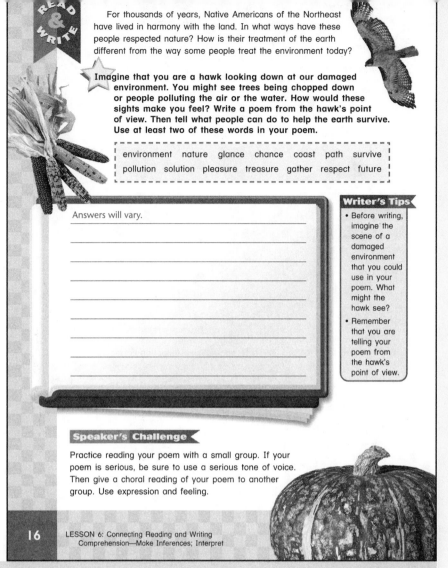

For thousands of years, Native Americans of the Northeast have lived in harmony with the land. In what ways have these people respected nature? How is their treatment of the earth different from the way some people treat the environment today?

⭐ Imagine that you are a hawk looking down at our damaged environment. You might see trees being chopped down or people polluting the air or the water. How would these sights make you feel? Write a poem from the hawk's point of view. Then tell what people can do to help the earth survive. Use at least two of these words in your poem.

| | | | | | | |
|---|---|---|---|---|---|---|
| environment | nature | glance | chance | coast | path | survive |
| pollution | solution | pleasure | treasure | gather | respect | future |

Answers will vary.

**Writer's Tips**

• Before writing, imagine the scene of a damaged environment that you could use in your poem. What might the hawk see?

• Remember that you are telling your poem from the hawk's point of view.

**Speaker's Challenge**

Practice reading your poem with a small group. If your poem is serious, be sure to use a serious tone of voice. Then give a choral reading of your poem to another group. Use expression and feeling.

16   LESSON 6: Connecting Reading and Writing
Comprehension—Make Inferences; Interpret

**English-Language Learners/ESL**

Help students read aloud the selection on page 15. Write challenging vocabulary words on the board, and discuss their meanings and pronunciations. Pause after each paragraph and encourage students to summarize the paragraph's important ideas.

**Gifted Learners**

Have students research and write a composition about native peoples of the Northeast. Direct them to include information about the peoples' history and way of life both before and after the arrival of Europeans. Have volunteers read their compositions aloud to the class.

## The Writing Process

Tell students that on page 16 they will write a poem. Discuss the directions to make sure students understand the writing task. Have students read the spelling words that they are to use.

**Prewrite** Tell students to visualize the damaged environment from the hawk's point of view. What would they see? How would they feel? Have them include specific words that capture their emotions.

**Write** Remind students to refer to the Writer's Tips on page 16. Also suggest that before beginning, students think about which spelling words might work best in their poem.

**Revise** Have students reread their poem and revise it as needed. Encourage them to share their poems with a partner and exchange constructive criticism.

**Proofread** Tell students to check for spelling, grammar, and punctuation errors.

**Publish** Have students copy their final drafts onto page 16 or onto separate paper. Volunteers may read their poems aloud.

Computer Connection

Share the following tip with students who use a word processor to do their writing.

● Most word-processing programs have a spelling checker. Tell students that it is a useful feature, but they should not become dependent on it. A spelling checker will not distinguish one homonym from another if the word is spelled correctly.

● Encourage students to pay attention to computer-detected spelling corrections so that they can learn from their errors.

Portfolio Suggest that students add their finished poems to their portfolios.

16

# Reviewing and Assessing
## Consonant Blends and Consonant Digraphs

### Objective
**To review and assess consonant blends and consonant digraphs**

## Warming Up

- Ask students: *What is the difference between a consonant blend and a consonant digraph?* (A blend is two or three consonants sounded together so that each letter is heard; a digraph is two consonants that together stand for one sound.) Have students give examples of each.

- List the following words on the board: **plaster, sling, claw, merchant, crisp, whistle, tough, pretend, flint, author, alphabet, coast**. Have students say each word and then circle the consonant blend(s) and/or consonant digraph(s).

## ★ Teaching the Lesson

- Using the words from the *Warming-Up* exercise as examples, review the fact that consonant blends and digraphs may appear at the beginning or end of words or within words. Have students suggest additional examples of words.

- Review the definition of a phonogram. Then make two lists on the board, one of initial consonant blends and digraphs, the other of phonograms. Have students create as many words as they can by combining word parts from the two lists.

- Review digraphs **ch**, **ph**, and **gh**. Ask for examples of words containing each. Then have students use their examples in sentences.

---

Name _____

Fill in the circle of the blend or digraph that completes each picture name. Then write the blend or digraph on the line to complete the word.

| # | | Choices | | # | | Choices | | # | | Choices |
|---|---|---|---|---|---|---|---|---|---|---|
| 1 | | ○ gl  ● fl  ○ cl | __fl__ utter | 2 | | ○ tw  ○ gr  ● cr | __cr__ own | 3 | | ● sn  ○ sm  ○ st | __sn__ ail |
| 4 | | ○ st  ○ lp  ● mp | stu __mp__ | 5 | | ○ tr  ● sc  ○ cr | __sc__ ale | 6 | | ● pr  ○ pl  ○ cr | __pr__ esent |
| 7 | | ○ sk  ● lt  ○ nd | me __lt__ | 8 | | ○ ph  ○ gh  ● th | wea __th__ er | 9 | | ○ th  ● sp  ○ st | __sp__ inach |
| 10 | | ○ ch  ○ sh  ● ph | tele __ph__ one | 11 | | ● sh  ○ ch  ○ th | __sh__ oulder | 12 | | ○ th  ○ ph  ● ch | bea __ch__ |

Write a word from the box below to answer each question correctly.

| chorus | block | telephone | crown | weather | spinach |
|---|---|---|---|---|---|

13. Which can be cloudy or sunny? _____ weather
14. Which is a group of singers? _____ chorus
15. Which do you speak into? _____ telephone
16. Which is worn by a king or a queen? _____ crown
17. Which is a vegetable? _____ spinach
18. Which is another name for *street*? _____ block

---

# UNIVERSAL ACCESS
## Meeting Individual Needs

### Kinesthetic Learners
Write the following words on separate index cards: **lift, jump, crash, skate, scale, wasp, plant, stamp, rest, twirl.** Have students take turns choosing a card from a box and acting out the word. As each word is identified, write it on the board and circle the consonant blend or digraph.

### Visual Learners
Have each student choose ten words from the lesson that contain consonant blends or digraphs. Tell students to list the words on a sheet of paper, mixing up the letters of each word. Then have students trade papers with a partner and unscramble each other's words. If students get stuck on a word, their partner should provide a clue.

### Learners with Special Needs
Additional strategies for supporting learners with special needs can be found on page 5L.

★ **Read the sentences. Fill in the circle of the word that correctly completes each sentence. Then write the word on the line.**

1. Have you heard of Lake Placid, in New York ___State___ ?
   ○ South    ○ Coast    ● State

2. In 1980, the Winter Olympic Games took place ___there___ .
   ○ first    ● there    ○ when

3. Visitors to Lake Placid can still see the ski ___jumps___ , the hockey stadium, and other places built for the Olympics.
   ● jumps    ○ pumps    ○ clumps

4. No one who saw the Olympic Games there can forget the ___triumph___ of the U.S. hockey team over the team from the Soviet Union.
   ○ touch    ● triumph    ○ physical

5. Athletes who live in cold ___climates___ take part in many winter sports.
   ○ crescents    ○ shoulders    ● climates

6. Some people like to play ice hockey or skate on a ___frozen___ pond in the winter.
   ● frozen    ○ shoulders    ○ stolen

7. Others put on snowshoes to ___trudge___ through wintry forests.
   ○ jump    ● trudge    ○ bump

8. Still others cross-country ski over open ___fields___ .
   ○ feasts    ○ plants    ● fields

9. The Northeast is famous for skiing. Ski centers have ___lifts___ to get skiers to the top of the runs.
   ● lifts    ○ gifts    ○ drifts

U.S. vs. the Soviet Union—1980
Winter Olympics, Lake Placid, NY

**Extend & Apply**

**Think of a different winter word for each clue. Write the word on the line.**
Answers will vary.

10. It has an initial blend. _____    11. It has a final blend. _____

12. It has an initial digraph. _____    13. It has a final digraph. _____

# Reteaching Activities

## Consonant Contest

Write several consonant blends and digraphs on the board. Ask small groups of students to identify objects in the room whose names contain the blends and digraphs. Tell students to keep a list of the objects they find, circling the digraph(s) or blend(s) in each word. Give one point for each blend or digraph. (Words that have more than one blend or digraph earn more than one point.) The group with the most points wins.

## Building Words

Write the letters **ea** on the board. Have students make as many words as they can using one or more consonant blends or digraphs. For example, students could write **teach, cheap, wheat, theater, preach, yeast**. Repeat the activity with the letters **ee**.

## Assessing the Skill

**Check Up** The exercises on pages 17–18 will help students review consonant blends and consonant digraphs and help you evaluate students' progress toward mastery.

Read aloud the directions for each exercise and have students complete them. Tell students to consider each possible answer to multiple-choice questions before choosing the best one. Encourage students to use context clues when completing items 13–18 on page 17 and items 1–9 on page 18.

**Observational Assessment** As students do the exercises, watch for hesitation or other signs of difficulty. Try to determine which items present the greatest challenge for students. Review observations or notes from earlier lessons to gain a clearer perspective on students' progress.

**Student Skills Assessment** Keep track of each student's progress in understanding consonant blends and digraphs using the checklist on page 5H.

**Writing Conference** Meet with each student to talk over written work they have done, such as their poem on page 16. Ask students to recall a favorite piece of writing in their Home Portfolios and suggest that they share it with the class. In their written work, help students identify words that have consonant blends and digraphs. Check that all words are spelled correctly.

Group together students who need further instruction in consonant blends and digraphs and have them complete the *Reteaching Activities*. Turn to page 5C for alternative assessment methods.

# Three-letter Consonant Blends

## Objectives

- **To recognize the sounds of three-letter consonant blends**

- **To associate these sounds with the letters that stand for them**

- **To read, form, and write words with three-letter consonant blends**

## Warming Up

- Write the following poem on the board. Ask a student to read it aloud.

New Jersey's woods are green with **shr**ubs and trees.

Sweet smells are **spr**ead by each gentle breeze.

Blooming flowers **thr**ive along every **str**eam.

A **spr**ing day like this is a time to dream!

- Have students identify the words that start with a blend of three consonants. Underline the words as students say them.

## Teaching the Lesson

- Explain that some consonant blends are made up of three letters sounded together so that each letter is heard. Focus attention on the words **spread**, **stream**, and **spring** in the poem on the board.

- Point out that a consonant digraph (two consonants that together stand for one sound) is sometimes blended with a third letter, as in the words **shrubs (sh + r)** and **thrive (th + r)** in the poem.

- Have a student read aloud the Helpful Hint on page 19. Ask volunteers to suggest additional examples of words with three-letter consonant blends.

19

---

Name _____

**Helpful Hint**

Some consonant blends or digraphs are made up of three letters. You will find **three-letter consonant blends** in words such as **scr**amble.

Here are some three-letter blends:

chr    sch    scr    shr    spl    spr    str    thr

Write one of the three-letter blends from the box above to complete each sentence.

1. The train whistle makes a high, __shr__ill sound.

2. The actors study the __scr__ipt to learn their lines.

3. Fenders on old cars used to be made of shiny ____chr__ome.

4. Founded in 1635, Boston Latin is the oldest __sch__ool in the United States.

5. The season between winter and summer is __spr__ing.

Unscramble the letters to name the picture. Then write the name of the picture on the line.

| 6 | 7 | 8 |
|---|---|---|
| **buhrs** | **norhet** | **cwers** |
| shrub | throne | screw |

| 9 | 10 | 11 |
|---|---|---|
| **sphals** | **inrestar** | **cloosh** |
| splash | strainer | school |

**WORK TOGETHER**

You know that u is not a consonant. Yet sometimes, squ is called a three-letter consonant blend.

Get together with a small group. List words, such as **squirrel**, that have the squ-blend.

# UNIVERSAL ACCESS
## Meeting Individual Needs

### Auditory Learners

Distribute pages from a newspaper or magazine. Have students work in pairs to find examples of words that begin with three-letter consonant blends. Have students list the words on paper, sorting them by consonant blend. Then have students write **3** next to blends that consist of three consonants sounded together so that each letter is heard and **D** next to blends that consist of a digraph plus a third letter.

### Visual Learners

Display several unusual photographs or drawings. Ask students to write descriptive or imaginative captions for each picture, including some words that begin with three-letter consonant blends. Have volunteers write their captions on the board. Then have students identify each consonant blend and suggest other words that start with the same three-letter blend.

**Use a word from the box to solve each clue. Write one letter in each space. Then read down the shaded column to answer the question below.**

| Christina | scheme | schooner | scrambled | scroll | shriek |
|-----------|--------|----------|-----------|--------|--------|
| shrug | splint | spread | straddle | straight | thrifty | throb |

1. a type of cooked eggs — s c r a m b l e d
2. a ship with many masts and sails — s c h o o n e r
3. once, a queen of Sweden — C h r i s t i n a
4. to pound, like a heart — t h r o b
5. a thin support to keep a broken bone in place — s p l i n t
6. a secret or dishonest plan — s c h e m e
7. the opposite of *crooked* — s t r a i g h t
8. being careful about spending money — t h r i f t y
9. a loud, sharp yell or scream — s h r i e k
10. to stand or sit with one leg or foot on either side — s t r a d d l e
11. to open or stretch out — s p r e a d
12. a long piece of paper you read by unrolling it — s c r o l l
13. shoulder motion that means you don't know or care — s h r u g

**Question:** Josh the Wonder Dog was a mutt who lived in Glen Burnie, Maryland. Before he died in 1977, 478,802 people helped him earn an amazing record. What was it?

**Answer:** Josh was the world's _____ most _____ petted dog

Josh the Wonder Dog

LESSON 8: Three-letter Consonant Blends

**Home Involvement Activity** Find out about these Northeastern cities that begin with three-letter consonant blends: Scranton, PA; Spring Lake, NJ; Stratford, CT. Write a brief fact sheet for each city.

## English-Language Learners/ESL

On index cards write ten words from the lesson that begin with three-letter consonant blends. Ask a volunteer to choose a card and give verbal or nonverbal clues to help the class guess the word. Have the first student who correctly guesses the word write it on the board and circle the consonant blend. That student may then choose the next card.

## Gifted Learners

Challenge students to identify pairs of rhyming words that use the three-letter consonant blends shown on page 19 in combination with the same phonogram. Some examples are **spread** and **thread**, **spring** and **string**. Students may use their words to write a poem.

### Learners with Special Needs

Additional strategies for supporting learners with special needs can be found on page 5L.

- Read aloud the direction lines on pages 19 and 20. Assist students as needed in completing the exercises.
- For items 1–5 on page 19, encourage students to use context clues to help them complete the sentences.
- Be sure students know the meaning and correct pronunciation of the word **chrome** on page 19 and the words **scheme** and **schooner** on page 20.

## Curriculum Connections

### Spelling Link

List the following consonant blends and phonograms on the board. Have students match each blend correctly with a phonogram. Have volunteers say the words aloud and spell each one.

| chr | ipt | (chrome) |
|-----|-----|----------|
| sch | ash | (school) |
| scr | ang | (script) |
| spl | aight | (splash) |
| spr | ool | (sprang) |
| str | one | (straight) |
| thr | ug | (throne) |
| shr | ome | (shrug) |

### Social Studies Link

Have students consult an encyclopedia or other reference source to learn more about the natural resources of one of the Northeast states. Challenge them to write a paragraph about the state of their choice, using words that start with three-letter consonant blends. Encourage students to include words other than those that appear in the lesson.

### Observational Assessment

*Check that students do not omit the **h** when writing words that begin with **sch**, such as **schedule**, **scheme**, **scholar**, and **schooner**.*

# Double Consonant Sounds

## Objectives

- **To identify and write words with double consonants**
- **To sort words by their double-consonant sounds**

## Warming Up

- Write the following on the board. Have a student read the paragraph aloud.

  English colonists se**tt**led in the Northeast in the 1600s. Some built fishing vi**ll**ages along the coast. Ships cro**ss**ing the sea ca**rr**ied both su**pp**lies and people.

- Have volunteers identify words that contain double consonants and circle the consonant pairs. Explain that in all of the words, the sound of the double consonant is the same as the sound of one of the consonants.

## Teaching the Lesson

- Write the words **giggle**, **babble**, and **grammar** on the board. Have students identify the sound of the double consonants.
- Discuss the Helpful Hints on pages 21 and 22. Point out that although there are exceptions to the rule, the sound that double consonants make is usually the sound of just one of the consonants.
- Write the words **soccer**, **moccasin**, and **success** on the board. Ask students how the words are alike and how they differ. Explain that all three words have a double **c**. In the first two words, the double **c** has a **k** sound; in **success**, the second **c** has the sound of **s**.

---

Name _____

> **Helpful Hint**
>
> **Double consonants** often make one sound. You hear only one sound of p in **ripple**. You hear only one sound of m in **grammar**. You hear only one sound of b in **bubble**.

Say the name of each picture. Then fill in the missing double consonant to complete the word.

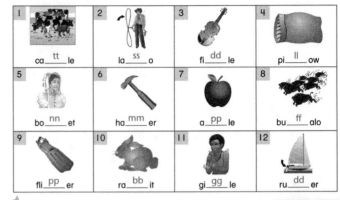

| | | | |
|---|---|---|---|
| 1   ca**tt**le | 2   la**ss**o | 3   fi**dd**le | 4   pi**ll**ow |
| 5   bo**nn**et | 6   ha**mm**er | 7   a**pp**le | 8   bu**ff**alo |
| 9   fli**pp**er | 10   ra**bb**it | 11   gi**gg**le | 12   ru**dd**er |

Each word in the box below has a double consonant. Write a word from the box to complete each sentence.

> waddle    fussy    pepper    gallop

13. A horse in a hurry will ___gallop___ to get where it's going.

14. If a duck had feet like ours, would it still ___waddle___?

15. If you don't like ___pepper___, you may not like chili.

16. My cat is ___fussy___ about her food.

> **WORD STRATEGY**
>
> When do you double a consonant? Listen to the vowel sound that comes before a double consonant. For example, the vowel i has a *long* sound in **diner** but a *short* sound in **dinner**. Write a spelling rule for double consonants.

LESSON 9: Double Consonant Sounds    **21**

---

# UNIVERSAL ACCESS
## Meeting Individual Needs

### Auditory Learners

Write the following words on the board: **cattle**, **dinner**, **mellow**. Have students suggest rhyming words for each one. List students' words on the board, pointing out that the double consonants in each set share the sound of just one consonant. Possible answers include **battle, rattle, winner, spinner; bellow, yellow**.

### Visual Learners

Down the left side of a sheet of chart paper, list all the consonants of the alphabet except for **h, j, k, q, v, w, x,** and **y**. Have students create a chart of words that contain double consonants by writing at least two examples for each letter. Encourage students to include both common and proper nouns. For **c** words, discuss whether the double **c** has a **k** sound or whether the second **c** has the sound of **s**.

There are some exceptions to the sound that double consonants make.

In some words spelled with a double c, the first c has the sound of k, as in **kite**, and the second c has the sound of s, as in **sail**.

**accept** = ak/sept          **accident** = ak/sident

Here is an exception for double g: In **suggest**, most Americans pronounce the first g as the g in **go** and the second g as j, as in **jet**.

**Read the sentences. Underline each word that has a double c. Then read each underlined word aloud. Sort the words by the sound that the double c makes. Write the words correctly in the chart below.**

1. Our class trip to Washington, DC, was a special <u>occasion</u>.

2. Two parents <u>accompanied</u> our class on the trip.

3. At one museum, we <u>accepted</u> free passes.

4. Our guide there was <u>eccentric</u>. He walked back and forth the whole time.

5. He was funny, too. He could speak with different <u>accents</u>.

6. The information he gave us was both interesting and <u>accurate</u>.

7. All the museums we visited had wheelchair <u>access</u>.

8. There was plenty to <u>occupy</u> us at the Air and Space Museum.

9. All in all, the trip was a great <u>success</u>.

10. We <u>accomplished</u> all we had set out to do.

| Double c as in *accordion* | Double c as in *accept* |
|---|---|
| occasion | accepted |
| accompanied | eccentric |
| accurate | accents |
| occupy | access |
| accomplished | success |

22    LESSON 9: Double Consonant Sounds

 **Home Involvement Activity** Look together at the words with double c in the chart. Add at least two more words to each column.

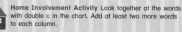

### English-Language Learners/ESL

On the board, list words that contain double consonants, leaving blank spaces for the two missing letters. Include some double **c** words in which the double **c** has a **k** sound and some in which the second **c** has the sound of **s**. Have students pronounce each word as they fill in the blanks. Then have students use each word correctly in a sentence.

### Gifted Learners

Have students work in pairs to write a four-line poem in which each line ends with a double-consonant word. Ask volunteers to read their poems aloud to the class.

### Learners with Special Needs

Additional strategies for supporting learners with special needs can be found on page 5L.

## Practicing the Skill

● Read aloud the directions on pages 21–22. Make sure students understand what they are to do for each exercise.

● Check to make sure that students know the meaning and correct pronunciation of the words **eccentric** and **access** on page 22. Also, you may want to take this opportunity to help students distinguish between the words **accept** and **except**.

## Curriculum Connections

### Spelling Link

Have students listen as you read aloud the words and sentences below. Ask volunteers to spell each word orally and write it on the board.

| | |
|---|---|
| **pillow** | I fell asleep as soon as my head hit the **pillow**. |
| **giggle** | A clown made us **giggle**. |
| **accompany** | Mr. Jackson will **accompany** you to the theater. |
| **rudder** | The **rudder** of a boat is used for steering. |
| **gallop** | A horse can **gallop**. |
| **accent** | Our new teacher has a Spanish **accent**. |
| **success** | The new restaurant proved to be a great **success**. |

### Multicultural Connection

American English and British English are not identical. Some American words have different or additional meanings in British English. For example, in England the word **bonnet** may mean the hood of a car. A **lift** is an elevator, and a **boot** is the trunk of a car. Have students find other examples of such language differences.

### Observational Assessment

*Check to see whether students confuse the spelling or pronunciation of similar single- and double-consonant words,* such as **bellow** and **below** and **dinner** and **diner**.

# Irregular Double Consonant Sounds

## Objectives

- **To recognize irregular double consonant sounds**
- **To associate these sounds with the letters that stand for them**
- **To read, form, and write words with irregular double consonant sounds**

## Warming Up

- Write the following paragraph on the board. Ask a volunteer to read it aloud.

  The Northeast is **kn**own for its natural beauty. The colorful fall **sc**enery attracts numerous visitors. Some cli**mb** mountains. Others hike through pine-**sc**ented woods, where there are few si**gn**s of civilization.

- Explain that in each of the underlined words, two letters together make one sound. Have students identify each double consonant sound: **n** for **kn** in **known**, **s** for **sc** in **scenery** and **scented**, **m** for **mb** in **climb**, and **n** for **gn** in **sign**.

## ⭐ Teaching the Lesson

- Write the words **knit**, **calm**, **limb**, **scene**, **write**, and **ridge** on the board. Explain that each word contains two consonants that together make one sound. Read each word aloud. Guide students in identifying the sound of each double consonant combination.

- Discuss the Helpful Hints on pages 23. Point out that an irregular double consonant combination may appear at the beginning of a word, as in **knit**, or at the end of a word, as in **design**. It may also appear in the middle of a word, as in **rewrite** or **judgment**.

23

---

Name _____

> **Helpful Hints**

Some words have **irregular double consonant sounds**. These are two different consonants that together make one sound. One letter in the pair is silent.

The consonants gn and kn sound like n, as in g**n**at, **kn**it, and desi**gn**.
lm sounds like m → ca**lm**        sc sounds like s → **sc**ene
mb sounds like m → cli**mb**       wr sounds like r → **wr**ite
The consonants dg together sound like j, as in bri**dg**e.

Say the name of each picture. Then fill in the two missing consonants to complete the word.

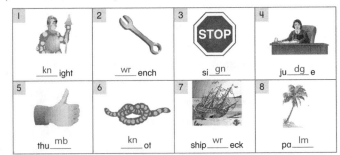

| 1 | 2 | 3 | 4 |
|---|---|---|---|
| __kn__ ight | __wr__ ench | si __gn__ | ju __dg__ e |

| 5 | 6 | 7 | 8 |
|---|---|---|---|
| thu __mb__ | __kn__ ot | ship __wr__ eck | pa __lm__ |

Write the word that completes each sentence.

9. One African antelope is called a ___gnu___ .
   lamb            gnome            gnu

10. A ___knickknack___ is a small object used as an ornament.
    knickknack        wrapper        monkey wrench

11. Large tree branches are called ___limbs___ .
    wreaths           limbs           wedges

12. Acts in a play are divided into ___scenes___ .
    scenes            psalms          knolls

> **CHALLENGE**
>
> Underline the irregular double consonant sound in these words. Then write a homonym for each word.
>
> gnu
> know
> scent
> wring

LESSON 10: Irregular Double Consonant Sounds    **23**

---

# UNIVERSAL ACCESS
## Meeting Individual Needs

### Visual Learners

Write the following chart headings on the board for students to copy:

| Consonants | Sound | Examples |
|---|---|---|
| gn | n | gnat, gnaw, sign |
|  |  |  |
|  |  |  |

Have students list examples of words containing the irregular double consonant combinations **gn, kn, lm, mb, sc, wr,** and **dg**. Encourage students to include some examples that do not have the double consonants at the beginning of the word.

### Kinesthetic Learners

Read aloud a series of words containing the sounds **n, m, s, r,** and **dg**. Include words with and without irregular double consonant sounds, such as **sign** and **pine**, **crumb** and **hum**, **scent** and **sense**, **wrench** and **ranch**, and **bridge** and **juice**. Ask students to raise their left hand if the word has an irregular double consonant sound, their right hand if it does not. Reinforce learning by listing and sorting the words on the board.

**Use a word from the box to solve each clue. Write one letter in each space. Then read down the shaded column to answer the question below.**

> thumb  wreath  rewrite  assign  fudge  hedge  wrinkle  align
> knoll  grudge  wriggle  crumb  knapsack  knob  lamb  scenery

1. a soft candy — f u d g e
2. to write something again — r e w r i t e
3. to put in a straight line — a l i g n
4. a small, rounded hill — k n o l l
5. a canvas bag — k n a p s a c k
6. a young sheep — l a m b
7. a small fold in paper — w r i n k l e
8. handle on a door — k n o b
9. backdrop on a stage — s c e n e r y
10. a long-held dislike or anger — g r u d g e
11. twist from side to side — w r i g g l e
12. a tiny piece of cake or bread — c r u m b
13. to give something as a task — a s s i g n
14. a row of shrubs or trees — h e d g e
15. flowers woven together — w r e a t h
16. your shortest digit — t h u m b

**Question:** The house in the photograph is called Fallingwater. It is in Pennsylvania. What famous architect built it?

**Answer:** ____Frank Lloyd Wright____.

24    LESSON 10: Irregular Double Consonant Sounds

**Home Involvement Activity** What are some interesting or unusual buildings in your city or town? Make a list together. Describe what makes them special. Pay a visit to one, if possible.

---

## Practicing the Skill

- Read the direction lines on pages 23 and 24. Help students as needed in completing the exercises.

- Students may find several words on pages 23–24 challenging. Check to see that students know the meaning, correct pronunciation, and spelling of **gnu, gnome,** and **knickknack** on page 23 and **align** and **knoll** on page 24.

## Curriculum Connections

### Spelling Link

- The following words contain irregular double consonant sounds. Read each word aloud. Have students spell the words, write them on the board, and circle the irregular double consonant combinations.

| | | |
|---|---|---|
| **wrench** | **thumb** | **palm** |
| **assign** | **grudge** | **knob** |
| **wriggle** | **shipwreck** | **scenery** |

- Challenge students to write sentences using two words per sentence. Have volunteers read their sentences aloud.

### Writing Link

The word **gnome** comes from a Greek word meaning "intelligence." Gnomes, dwarflike creatures that lived in the earth, were thought to have special knowledge of the earth and its underground treasures. Have students research and write a paragraph about these creatures of folklore and fairy tales.

### Observational Assessment

*Check to see whether students correctly pronounce and spell words with irregular double consonant combinations.*

---

### English-Language Learners/ESL

Discuss how different letter combinations can produce the same sounds in English. Write two columns of words: one in which words have irregular double consonant sounds and one in which they do not. For example, include such words pairs as **knight/night, knot/not, scene/seen, write/right, wring/ring,** and **scent/sent.** Show pictures or use pantomime to help students see the differences in meaning.

### Gifted Learners

Point out that the irregular double consonant combinations do not always work together to produce one sound. Sometimes the consonants retain both individual sounds, as in **chamber.** Challenge students to find other such words. Possible examples: **signal, clamber, clambake, hangnail, palmetto.**

### Learners with Special Needs

Additional strategies for supporting learners with special needs can be found on page 5L.

# Connecting Spelling and Writing

## Objectives

- **To say, spell, sort, and write words with initial consonant blends and digraphs**
- **To write a business letter**

## Warming Up

- Write the following poem on the board, and have a volunteer read it aloud.

  New York's a city **th**at never **sl**eeps.

  If **th**at's **tr**ue, I'm not **pr**epared to say.

  But **wh**en you go, I'll **pr**omise you **th**is:

  **Th**ere's so much to do, you'll want to **st**ay!

- Ask students to underline the words that begin with consonant blends and circle the blends. Have them draw a box around the words that start with consonant digraphs and circle the digraphs.

## Teaching the Lesson

- Write these words on the board: **glare, spinach, whale, script, skeleton, photo, clinic, whole, chemical, scold, flutter**. Have volunteers identify the initial consonant blend or digraph in each word and suggest other words with the same blend or digraph.
- Review the three sounds of the digraph **ch**, as in **ch**irp, **ch**andelier, **ch**aracter.

## Practicing the Skill

- Read aloud the directions on page 25. Call on students to read each phrase. Then have students complete the page.
- Point out that **thumbs** and **trudge** contain consonant pairs that make one sound; **graph** contains a digraph; and **schedule** begins with a three-letter blend.

---

Name _____

Read each group of words. Say and spell each word in bold type. Repeat the word. Then sort the words by their initial consonant blend or digraph. Write each word in the correct column below.

- a **cluster** of trees
- two **thumbs** up
- a pie **graph**
- **frequent** visitors
- cherry **blossoms**
- gave **specific** directions
- clouds **drifting** by
- at the **present** time
- **pleasing** scenery
- gave a **thorough** report
- **physical** fitness
- leafy **broccoli**
- **trudge** through snow
- fit into our **schedule**

- **flutter** its wings
- prize-winning **photographer**
- caught a quick **glimpse**
- a **splashing** sound

Niagara Falls, New York

| A–F | G–R | S–Z |
|---|---|---|
| cluster | graph | thumbs |
| frequent | present | specific |
| blossoms | pleasing | thorough |
| drifting | physical | trudge |
| broccoli | photographer | schedule |
| flutter | glimpse | splashing |

---

# UNIVERSAL ACCESS
## Meeting Individual Needs

### Auditory Learners

Read the following words aloud. Have volunteers spell the words, write them on the board, and identify the blend or digraph. Ask students to write sentences using two words per sentence.

| | | |
|---|---|---|
| **blanket** | **sweater** | **physical** |
| **dresser** | **climate** | **shrill** |
| **glide** | **whimper** | **chrome** |
| **crown** | **shiny** | **groceries** |

### Visual Learners

On the board, list initial consonant blends and digraphs. Ask a volunteer to think of a word that starts with one of the combinations listed. Have the student write the initial consonants on the board and add spaces after them to indicate the missing letters. The class may then guess the letters that go in the blanks. The first student to figure out the word puts up the next mystery word. Have students use each word in a sentence.

### Learners with Special Needs

Additional strategies for supporting learners with special needs can be found on page 5L.

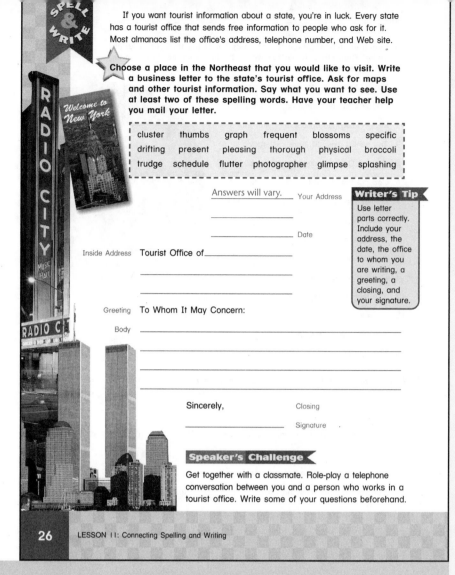

If you want tourist information about a state, you're in luck. Every state has a tourist office that sends free information to people who ask for it. Most almanacs list the office's address, telephone number, and Web site.

⭐ Choose a place in the Northeast that you would like to visit. Write a business letter to the state's tourist office. Ask for maps and other tourist information. Say what you want to see. Use at least two of these spelling words. Have your teacher help you mail your letter.

| cluster | thumbs | graph | frequent | blossoms | specific |
|---------|--------|-------|----------|----------|----------|
| drifting | present | pleasing | thorough | physical | broccoli |
| trudge | schedule | flutter | photographer | glimpse | splashing |

Answers will vary. _____ Your Address
_____
_____ Date

Inside Address  Tourist Office of_____
_____
_____

Greeting  To Whom It May Concern:

Body  _____
_____
_____
_____
_____

Sincerely,  Closing
_____  Signature .

**Writer's Tip**
Use letter parts correctly. Include your address, the date, the office to whom you are writing, a greeting, a closing, and your signature.

**Speaker's Challenge**
Get together with a classmate. Role-play a telephone conversation between you and a person who works in a tourist office. Write some of your questions beforehand.

26    LESSON 11: Connecting Spelling and Writing

---

**English-Language Learners/ESL**

Show the class pictures of well-known places in the Northeast. Have students write sentences on the board describing what they see in each picture. Then have them identify consonant blends and digraphs in their sentences.

**Gifted Learners**

Challenge students to make up silly riddles that can be answered by pairs of rhyming words, each of which has an initial consonant blend or digraph. Here are two examples: *What does a penguin wear around the house?* **(flipper slippers)** *What do you use to weigh a large marine mammal?* **(a whale scale)**

---

## The Writing Process

Tell students that on page 26 they will write a letter to the tourist office of a Northeast state. Read the directions and spelling words at the top of the page.

**Prewrite** Discuss the states that make up the Northeast region. What are the famous places to visit in each state? Which states are known for their seasonal activities, such as viewing fall foliage, apple-picking, or skiing?

**Write** Discuss with students the Writer's Tip on page 26. Encourage students to make their request for information as specific as possible. Also, remind them to use two or more spelling words.

**Revise** Tell students to reread their letter carefully. Ask *Have you used letter parts correctly? Have you made your request for information clear and specific? Have you included at least two spelling words?*

**Proofread** Have students check for errors in spelling, grammar, and punctuation.

**Publish** Direct students to copy their final drafts onto page 26 or a separate sheet of paper. Ask volunteers to read their letters to the class.

**Computer Connection**

Share the following tip with students who use a word processor to do their writing.

• The grammar checker feature in many word-processing programs can be helpful. Most grammar checkers can find passive constructions, which students may want to change to active.

• Grammar checkers will not spot all mistakes, however, and may suggest some changes that aren't needed. Students should use good judgment.

**Portfolio** Suggest that students add their finished letters to their portfolios.

# Reviewing and Assessing

## Consonant Blends, Consonant Digraphs, and Double Consonant Sounds

### Objective

To review and assess consonant blends, consonant digraphs, and double consonant sounds

## Warming Up

- Write the following paragraph on the board. Ask a student to read it aloud.

  Heavy **sn**ow in the Nor**th**east can sometimes **sh**ut down **sch**ools and **cl**ose roads. **Dr**ivers mu**st** use caution and remain ca**lm** to avoid a**cc**iden**ts**.

- Have students identify and circle words with consonant blends, consonant diagraphs, and double consonant sounds.

## ★ Teaching the Lesson

- Make four columns on the board, and label them **Initial Blends**, **Final Blends**, **Consonant Digraphs**, and **Double Consonant Sounds.**

- Have students take turns writing appropriate words in the columns. The first student writes a word with an initial blend, the next student writes a word with a final blend, and so on. Be sure students include some three-letter blends and both regular and irregular double consonant sounds.

- Underline the appropriate letter combinations and have students say each word aloud.

27

---

Name _____

★ Read each sentence. Listen for the sound that the underlined letters make. Then circle *two* other words in the sentence that contain the same sound.

1. Nathan knows not to race that horse.
2. Please sign your name on the dotted line.
3. Mr. Jackson had an accident with that axe.
4. The dentist was still there yesterday.
5. General Daley pledged justice for all.
6. Carl put the chemistry set in the kitchen.
7. Mother's locket fits into the palm of my hand.
8. Doing the dog paddle helps us to swim.
9. I may never have a name for my gnu!
10. It never occurred to me that Kent could ride.
11. Rob noticed a wrinkle in the title page of the report.
12. The telephone rang five times before nine o'clock.
13. Chris knows that Mr. Krauss likes chocolate ice cream.
14. A few rough games caused physical problems.
15. Marcy, don't put your thumb in your mouth!

**Write a word from the box to complete each sentence correctly.**

| calm | gallop | grudge | knob |
|------|--------|--------|------|

16. Listen to the rhythmic sound when horses ___gallop___ at top speed.
17. He tried to open the door, but the ___knob___ refused to budge.
18. I swim in the ocean only when the water is ___calm___.
19. Can your brother really hold a ___grudge___ for a whole week?

---

# UNIVERSAL ACCESS
## Meeting Individual Needs

### Tactile Learners

Have students work in pairs, using letter cards or tiles. Direct students to spell out words with initial blends, final blends, consonant digraphs, and double consonant sounds. Challenge them to include words that contain more than one blend or digraph, words with medial digraphs, words with three-letter blends, and words with irregular consonant sounds.

### Learners with Special Needs

Additional strategies for supporting learners with special needs can be found on page 5L.

### Visual Learners

Have students work with a map of the Northeast region. Direct students to find examples of proper nouns such as names of cities, rivers, mountains that contain initial or final consonant blends, consonant digraphs, or double consonant sounds. Have students list the words and circle the appropriate letter combinations. Extend the activity by having students sort their words by letter combination or by geographic feature.

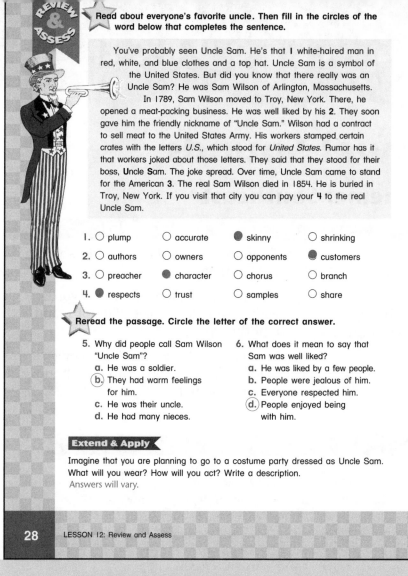

**Read about everyone's favorite uncle. Then fill in the circles of the word below that completes the sentence.**

You've probably seen Uncle Sam. He's that **1** white-haired man in red, white, and blue clothes and a top hat. Uncle Sam is a symbol of the United States. But did you know that there really was an Uncle Sam? He was Sam Wilson of Arlington, Massachusetts.

In 1789, Sam Wilson moved to Troy, New York. There, he opened a meat-packing business. He was well liked by his **2**. They soon gave him the friendly nickname of "Uncle Sam." Wilson had a contract to sell meat to the United States Army. His workers stamped certain crates with the letters *U.S.*, which stood for *United States*. Rumor has it that workers joked about those letters. They said that they stood for their boss, Uncle **S**am. The joke spread. Over time, Uncle Sam came to stand for the American **3**. The real Sam Wilson died in 1854. He is buried in Troy, New York. If you visit that city you can pay your **4** to the real Uncle Sam.

1. ○ plump    ○ accurate    ● skinny    ○ shrinking
2. ○ authors    ○ owners    ○ opponents    ● customers
3. ○ preacher    ● character    ○ chorus    ○ branch
4. ● respects    ○ trust    ○ samples    ○ share

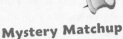 **Reread the passage. Circle the letter of the correct answer.**

5. Why did people call Sam Wilson "Uncle Sam"?
   a. He was a soldier.
   (b.) They had warm feelings for him.
   c. He was their uncle.
   d. He had many nieces.

6. What does it mean to say that Sam was well liked?
   a. He was liked by a few people.
   b. People were jealous of him.
   c. Everyone respected him.
   (d.) People enjoyed being with him.

**Extend & Apply**

Imagine that you are planning to go to a costume party dressed as Uncle Sam. What will you wear? How will you act? Write a description.
Answers will vary.

# Reteaching Activities

## Word Circle

Have students write consonant blends, consonant digraphs, and double consonants (regular and irregular sounds) on separate index cards. Then have them sit in a circle with the index cards face-down. Have a volunteer choose a card and say a word that contains the blend, digraph, or double consonant. Then have the next student choose a card and say a corresponding word, and so on, continuing around the circle.

## Mystery Matchup

Have students match each word in the first column with its corresponding clue in the second column.

| | |
|---|---|
| **chorus** | the **b** is silent |
| **script** | initial **f** sound |
| **pledge** | sound of **k + s** |
| **accent** | one **d** sound |
| **thumb** | three-letter blend |
| **draft** | initial **k** sound |
| **rudder** | sounds like a **j** |
| **physical** | two consonant blends |

**Check Up** The exercises on pages 27–28 will help students review consonant blends, consonant digraphs, and double consonant sounds. The exercises will also help you assess students' progress.

Discuss the directions on page 27. Be sure students understand that for items 1–14 they have to circle two words that have the same sound but not necessarily the same letters. Then have students complete the page. Next, discuss the directions on page 28. Tell students to consider all answer choices before choosing one. Encourage students to reread the passage as needed.

**Observational Assessment** Review your observational notes from earlier lessons to help you determine whether any previously noted weaknesses have improved. Watch for any reading difficulties as students complete page 28.

**Student Skills Assessment** Keep track of each student's progress in understanding consonant blends, digraphs, and double consonant sounds using the checklist on page 5H.

**Writing Conference** As you complete Unit 1, meet with students individually. Review portfolio samples and other writing, and offer encouragement. Suggest that students share with the class favorite written work from their Home Portfolios. In their writing, call students' attention to words with consonant blends and digraphs. Check for correct spelling.

Group together students who need further instruction in consonant blends, digraphs, and double consonant sounds and have them complete the *Reteaching Activities*. Turn to page 5C for alternative assessment methods.

# Vowel Sounds

## Theme: Southeast

### STANDARDS

- Read expository text with grade-appropriate fluency and understand its content

- Develop and strengthen vocabulary by reading and studying words in context

- Recognize letter-sound correspondence in vowel pairs, vowel digraphs, diphthongs, and phonograms

### OBJECTIVES

▶ To appreciate nonfiction works about the Southeast

▶ To identify, decode, and write words with vowel pairs, vowel digraphs, and diphthongs

▶ To build words by combining vowel pairs, vowel digraphs, and diphthongs with phonograms

### LESSONS

Lesson 13 . . . . . . . Introduction to Vowel Pairs, Vowel Digraphs, Diphthongs, and Phonograms
Lesson 14 . . . . . . . Vowel Pairs **ai, ay, ee, ei, ie, oa, oe, ow**
Lesson 15 . . . . . . . Vowel Digraphs **ea, ei, ey, ie, au, aw, oo**
Lesson 16 . . . . . . . Connecting Reading and Writing—Comprehension: Distinguish Between Fact and Nonfact, Interpret
Lesson 17 . . . . . . . Diphthongs **oi, oy, ou, ow, ew**
Lesson 18 . . . . . . . Connecting Spelling and Writing
Lesson 19 . . . . . . . Review and Assess
Lesson 20 . . . . . . . Combining Consonants with Phonograms
Lesson 21 . . . . . . . Combining Consonant Blends with Phonograms
Lesson 22 . . . . . . . Combining More Consonant Blends with Phonograms
Lesson 23 . . . . . . . Connecting Reading and Writing—Comprehension: Compare and Contrast, Synthesize
Lesson 24 . . . . . . . Combining Consonant Digraphs with Phonograms
Lesson 25 . . . . . . . Combining Consonants, Consonant Blends, and Consonant Digraphs with Phonograms
Lesson 26 . . . . . . . Connecting Reading and Writing—Comprehension: Main Idea and Details, Summarize
Lesson 27 . . . . . . . Review and Assess

## Assessment Strategies

An overview of assessment strategies appears on page **29C**. It offers multiple suggestions for using unit-specific assessment tools, including **Pretests** and **Post Tests** (pages **29D–29G**), the **Activity Master** (page **29M**), and the **Assessment Checklist** (page **29H**).

## Thematic Teaching

In Unit 2 students learn about vowel sounds and the letters that represent them. Students encounter words with these sounds and letters in the context of nonfiction selections and exercises related to the theme the *Southeast.*

Students begin their investigation of the Southeast by creating a travel guide, highlighting points of interest and historical events. The resource list below provides titles of books, videos, and other materials that can help students focus their study of the region. Many of the Teacher's Edition lessons in this unit open with poems, riddles, or tongue twisters related to the Southeast. These "hooks" can spark students' interest in the theme and in the play of words.

## Curriculum Integration

### Social Studies
Students investigate NASA on page **30,** research presidents on page **32,** practice map skills on page **44,** and contact a museum on page **52.**

### Writing
Students write about Williamsburg on page **38** and compose a story on page **48.**

### Science
Students research animals native to the Southeast on page **34.**

### Math
Students write word problems on page **54.**

## Optional Learning Activities

### Meeting Individual Needs
Most of the Teacher's Edition lessons offer activities for students with distinct learning styles or particular intellectual or sensory strengths. The activities are labeled for learners with the following "styles": **Visual, Kinesthetic, Auditory, Logical,** and **Tactile.**

### Multicultural Connections
Students learn about European influences in the Southeast on page **30** and research the life and work of Zora Neale Hurston on page **46.**

### Word Study Strategies
Pages **29I–29J** offer activities that give students practice with word study strategies. Students sort words, build words, and define words in context.

### Universal Access
Exercises tailored to meet the needs of **English-Language Learners** and **Gifted Learners** can be found in almost every Teacher's Edition lesson. Strategies designed to help **Learners with Special Needs,** such as students with Auditory/Oral Discrimination Deficits, can be found on page **29L.**

### Intervention
Page **29K** offers **Intervention Strategies** designed to help students performing below grade level understand the concepts taught in **Lessons 15, 17,** and **21.**

### Reteaching
On page **42** students identify letter-sound correspondences, and on page **58** students write poems and words with particular phonograms.

### Technology
Page **29N** offers activities for students who enjoy working with computers or audio/video equipment. In addition, **Computer Connections**—tips for students who use a word processor—can be found on pages **36, 40, 50,** and **56.**

### RESOURCES

**Books**
Fisher, Leonard Everett. *Monticello,* NY: Holiday House, 1998.
Knight, James E. *Jamestown: New World Adventure (Adventures in Colonial America),* NY: Troll Associates, 1998.

**Videos**
*America the Beautiful: The Natural Splendors of Florida,* V.I.E.W. Video, 1994.
*Thomas Jefferson: A Film by Ken Burns,* PBS Home Video, 1996.

**CDs**
*John Henry,* Rabbit Ears (series), Madacy Records, 1999.

In Unit 2 students study vowel pairs, vowel digraphs, diphthongs, and phonograms. To evaluate students' mastery of these skills, use any or all of the assessment methods suggested below.

## Pretests and Post Tests

The tests on pages **29D–29G** objectively assess how well students understand vowel pairs, vowel digraphs, diphthongs, and phonograms. These tests may be used at the beginning of the unit as an informal diagnostic tool or at the end of the unit as a more formal measure of students' progress.

## Observational Assessment

Each lesson includes a reminder to observe students as they apply lesson-specific skills. Check students' written work on a regular basis to see whether they continue to successfully apply what they learn.

## Using Technology

The activities on page **29N** may be used to evaluate students whose language skills are best shown when using computers or audio/video equipment.

## Performance Assessment

Have students make a chart to be used for sorting words that contain the same vowel sounds. Use the following words as headings for each column: **book, steak, hawk, chew, proud, boy, agree, follow.** Then have students use the chart to sort the following words: **row, allow, coin, new, chief, shook, sauce, sleigh**. Then ask students to complete the chart by adding two new words that contain the same vowel sound to each column.

## Portfolio Assessment

The portfolio icon in the lesson plans indicates an opportunity for students to add to the growing body of work in their portfolios. Each student's portfolio will be different and should contain pieces that the student feels represents his or her best work. You may wish to give students additional opportunities to add to their portfolios.

## Rubric for Writing

| | Always | Sometimes | Never |
|---|---|---|---|
| Uses capitalization, punctuation, spelling, and grammar appropriately | | | |
| Creates a variety of sentences containing words formed by combining vowel pairs, vowel digraphs, and diphthongs with phonograms | | | |
| Writes a story with a clearly defined beginning, middle, and end | | | |
| Incorporates details to convey meaning through writing | | | |
| Uses words to signal comparison and contrast | | | |

## Answer Key

**Page 29D**
1. rough
2. teeth
3. follow
4. clown
5. false
6. pleasure
7. known
8. couple
9. receive
10. cloud
11. weight
12. monkey
13. copy
14. freight
15. tries
16. believe
17. speed
18. double
19. hood
20. cape

**Page 29E**
1. remain, clay
2. niece, wreath
3. supply, pie
4. cruel, moose
5. motion, pillow
6. gnaw, faucet
7. realm, measure
8. coil, enjoy
9. oath, glow
10. screech, deceive

11. snowflake, tomorrow
12. caution, false
13. stew, tissue
14. defy, lie
15. pause, paws
16. ight
17. aint
18. ealth
19. ow
20. oat
21. ouch
22. ore
23. amp
24. erry
25. eck

**Page 29F**
1. honey
2. pliers
3. browse
4. tale
5. reign
6. blouse
7. moisture
8. foil
9. deaf
10. employ
11. loyal
12. counter
13. widow
14. fancy
15. raid
16. league
17. foreign
18. powder
19. chalk

20. sound

**Page 29G**
1. awkward, waltz
2. double, southern
3. teacher, sleeve
4. fee, piece
5. brew, issue
6. shower, hour
7. crayon, raisin
8. roam, doe
9. royal, annoy
10. league, relieve
11. sauce, salt
12. neighbor, stray
13. needle, cease
14. sailboat, window
15. cycle, tie
16. ape
17. ain
18. ash
19. oke
20. ice
21. ance
22. ink
23. est
24. inkle
25. are

Name _____

**Fill in the circle of the word that does *not* contain the same vowel sound as the word in bold type.**

| | | | |
|---|---|---|---|
| **1. oath** | ○ grow | ○ rough | ○ doe |
| **2. wealth** | ○ leather | ○ teeth | ○ check |
| **3. spoil** | ○ loyal | ○ follow | ○ boil |
| **4. mow** | ○ road | ○ woe | ○ clown |
| **5. faint** | ○ holiday | ○ maintain | ○ false |
| **6. squeak** | ○ cheese | ○ southeast | ○ pleasure |
| **7. joy** | ○ known | ○ oyster | ○ moist |
| **8. cow** | ○ couple | ○ proud | ○ eyebrow |
| **9. bay** | ○ grain | ○ eight | ○ receive |
| **10. should** | ○ wood | ○ could | ○ cloud |
| **11. seize** | ○ weight | ○ peanut | ○ street |
| **12. prey** | ○ monkey | ○ sleigh | ○ away |
| **13. toe** | ○ foam | ○ arrow | ○ copy |
| **14. chief** | ○ lease | ○ freeze | ○ freight |
| **15. three** | ○ hockey | ○ defeat | ○ tries |
| **16. pie** | ○ magnify | ○ believe | ○ lie |
| **17. stew** | ○ glue | ○ shoe | ○ speed |
| **18. loud** | ○ doubt | ○ double | ○ down |
| **19. boost** | ○ hood | ○ goose | ○ smooth |
| **20. law** | ○ cape | ○ cause | ○ chalk |

Possible score on Unit 2 Pretest 1 is 20. Score _____

Name _____

**Underline the two words in each row that contain the same vowel sound.**

| | | | |
|---|---|---|---|
| 1. remain | shallow | clay | salt |
| 2. niece | wreath | health | neighbor |
| 3. supply | chief | pie | grin |
| 4. cruel | faucet | moose | telephone |
| 5. look | flounder | motion | pillow |
| 6. shape | apple | gnaw | faucet |
| 7. realm | reality | measure | race |
| 8. coil | value | steady | enjoy |
| 9. oath | chair | appointment | glow |
| 10. screech | sweater | sleigh | deceive |
| 11. snowflake | proud | tomorrow | ointment |
| 12. caution | couch | false | maiden |
| 13. stew | steam | tissue | staple |
| 14. awning | destroy | defy | lie |
| 15. pause | camel | paws | pipe |

**Circle the phonogram in each word. Then write an additional word that contains the phonogram.**

16. fright _____  17. quaint _____

18. wealth _____  19. grow _____

20. throat _____  21. couch _____

22. shore _____  23. stamp _____

24. ferry _____  25. deck _____

Possible score on Unit 2 Pretest 2 is 25. Score _____

Name _____

**Fill in the circle of the word that does _not_ contain the same vowel sound as the word in bold type.**

| | | | |
|---|---|---|---|
| **1. vain** | ○ raisin | ○ survey | ○ honey |
| **2. fleet** | ○ shriek | ○ cease | ○ pliers |
| **3. tow** | ○ browse | ○ shallow | ○ narrow |
| **4. thaw** | ○ auto | ○ squall | ○ tale |
| **5. dread** | ○ jealous | ○ reign | ○ connect |
| **6. young** | ○ southern | ○ trouble | ○ blouse |
| **7. booth** | ○ moisture | ○ brew | ○ statue |
| **8. roam** | ○ elbow | ○ foe | ○ foil |
| **9. leash** | ○ proceed | ○ deaf | ○ diesel |
| **10. clue** | ○ steward | ○ moose | ○ employ |
| **11. tray** | ○ loyal | ○ reindeer | ○ crayon |
| **12. soy** | ○ avoid | ○ destroy | ○ counter |
| **13. foul** | ○ widow | ○ coward | ○ pound |
| **14. sly** | ○ tie | ○ apply | ○ fancy |
| **15. waltz** | ○ raid | ○ autumn | ○ awkward |
| **16. breath** | ○ league | ○ peasant | ○ sweater |
| **17. sleeve** | ○ deceive | ○ relief | ○ foreign |
| **18. woe** | ○ burrow | ○ powder | ○ tiptoe |
| **19. boil** | ○ loyal | ○ poison | ○ chalk |
| **20. drew** | ○ blueberry | ○ root | ○ sound |

Possible score on Unit 2 Post Test 1 is 20. Score _____

Name _____

**Underline the two words in each row that contain the same vowel sound.**

| | | | |
|---|---|---|---|
| 1. awkward | eight | waltz | weather |
| 2. double | shout | minnow | southern |
| 3. dread | teacher | reins | sleeve |
| 4. complain | fee | piece | avoid |
| 5. brew | auto | sour | issue |
| 6. shower | sparrow | point | hour |
| 7. jealous | succeed | crayon | raisin |
| 8. roam | money | doe | browse |
| 9. booth | royal | couch | annoy |
| 10. leather | league | clue | relieve |
| 11. south | sauce | salt | soybean |
| 12. neighbor | bald | diesel | stray |
| 13. needle | dew | cease | peasant |
| 14. trout | sailboat | window | employ |
| 15. cycle | system | handy | tie |

**Circle the phonogram in each word. Then write an additional word that contains the phonogram.**

16. shape _____     17. pain _____

18. trash _____     19. joke _____

20. spice _____     21. chance _____

22. blink _____     23. test _____

24. twinkle _____     25. flare _____

Possible score on Unit 2 Post Test 2 is 25. Score _____

**Student Name** _____

## UNIT TWO
## STUDENT SKILLS ASSESSMENT
## CHECKLIST

☑ Assessed     ☒ Retaught     ▣ Mastered

- ❑ Vowel Pairs **ai, ay, ee, ei, ie, oa, oe, ow**

- ❑ Vowel Digraphs **ea, ei, ey, ie, au, aw, oo**

- ❑ Diphthongs **oi, oy, ou, ow, ew**

- ❑ Combining Consonants with Phonograms

- ❑ Combining Consonant Blends with Phonograms

- ❑ Combining More Consonant Blends with Phonograms

- ❑ Combining Consonant Digraphs with Phonograms

- ❑ Combining Consonants, Consonant Blends, and Consonant Digraphs with Phonograms

## TEACHER COMMENTS

In Unit 2 students study vowel pairs, vowel digraphs, diphthongs, and phonograms. To give students opportunities to master word study strategies, use any or all of the activities suggested below.

## Vowel Sort

Underline the vowel pair or vowel digraph in each word. Then sort the words as directed below.

| | | |
|---|---|---|
| **easel** | **doe** | **willow** |
| **decay** | **mainland** | **proceed** |
| **coastal** | **neighbor** | **deceive** |

1. Write the words with the long **a** vowel sound.

   _____  _____  _____

2. Write the words with the long **e** vowel sound.

   _____  _____  _____

3. Write the words with the long **o** vowel sound.

   _____  _____  _____

## Word Selection

Underline the word in each pair that has the same vowel sound as the numbered word.

| | | |
|---|---|---|
| 1. **head** | weed/wealth | please/heavy |
| 2. **steak** | paste/thread | weather/break |
| 3. **sleigh** | receive/eight | week/weight |
| 4. **obey** | survey/seal | monkey/sway |
| 5. **brief** | pie/seize | thief/they |
| 6. **cheese** | treasure/treat | great/grief |
| 7. **coat** | snow/cow | touch/toes |
| 8. **cried** | afraid/ties | pie/deceive |
| 9. **jaw** | sauce/owl | foal/author |
| 10. **voice** | joy/yellow | coal/foil |

## Word Building

Build words that have the same vowel sound as each numbered word below. Write a vowel pair or vowel digraph to complete each word. Then write two words on the lines that contain the same vowel sound.

1. sauce   c __ se   _____  _____

2. hawk   cr __ l   _____  _____

3. bloom   sp __ n   _____  _____

4. weight   sl __ gh   _____  _____

5. grown   mell __   _____  _____

6. toast   l __ n   _____  _____

7. grief   d __ sel   _____  _____

8. clay   l __ er   _____  _____

9. weak   r __ ch   _____  _____

10. head   w __ ther   _____  _____

GREETINGS from HOT SPRINGS NATIONAL PARK ARKANSAS

# Word Meaning

Circle the word that completes each sentence. Then write the word on the line.

1. We _____ sugarless gum.

   **chalk**     **choice**     **chew**

2. We are _____ of our volunteers.

   **proud**     **pound**     **point**

3. The circus _____ wore funny hats.

   **clouds**     **clowns**     **crows**

4. There is a _____ of fruit on the table.

   **boil**     **book**     **bowl**

5. The store _____ five salesclerks.

   **employs**     **empties**     **elbows**

6. He covered the leftovers with _____ .

   **flow**     **foil**     **flounder**

# Building with Phonograms

Find a word from the box that contains the same phonogram as each numbered word and write it on the line. Then write an additional word that contains that phonogram.

| bumpy | define | pocket | block |
|-------|--------|--------|-------|
| chore | string | flap   | draw  |

1. clock     _____     _____

2. shore     _____     _____

3. grumpy     _____     _____

4. clap     _____     _____

5. rocket     _____     _____

6. spring     _____     _____

7. straw     _____     _____

8. refine     _____     _____

# Phonograms in Words

Underline the phonogram in each set of words. Then write two additional words that contain the same phonogram.

1. block     locket     rocker

   _____     _____

2. twist     sister     blister

   _____     _____

3. plank     ankle     tanker

   _____     _____

4. swing     single     finger

   _____     _____

5. stop     helicopter     chopstick

   _____     _____

6. crab     babble     tablet

   _____     _____

7. chance     dancer     cancel

   _____     _____

8. stay     layer     relay

   _____     _____

9. straw     fawn     lawyer

   _____     _____

10. wink     twinkle     trinket

    _____     _____

11. afford     cord     landlord

    _____     _____

12. invent     dental     cent

    _____     _____

| LESSONS | **15** Vowel Digraphs | **17** Diphthongs | **21** Consonant Blends with Phonograms |
|---|---|---|---|
| **Problem** | Student confuses the spelling of vowel digraphs that have the same pronunciation, such as, **aw, au,** and **al**. | Student has difficulty distinguishing between the different pronunciations of the diphthong **ow** and the vowel pair **ow**. | Student has difficulty distinguishing between phonograms and consonant blends. |
| **Intervention Strategies** | • Have the student label three columns in their word-study notebook as follows: **aw** as in **law, au** as in **sauce,** and **al** as in **salt**. As the student encounters words that contain these vowel digraphs, ask him or her to add the words to the appropriate column. Ask the student to look for the words in the Unit 2 lesson and in other reading material as well. | • Have the student write phrases in his or her word-study notebook using the difficult meanings of the words **bow** and **sow**. For example, **bow** to your partner, **bow** and arrow; **sow**, a female pig, **sow** seeds.<br><br>• Tell the student that some words that contain the diphthong **ow** are homographs. (words that are spelled the same but pronounced differently) Encourage the student to review the phrases when he or she encounters words with **ow**. | • Point out that a phonogram has at least one vowel combined with consonants while a consonant blend consists of two or three consonants.<br><br>• Have the student list the vowels in the alphabet. Then have him or her list the words from the lesson.<br><br>• Have the student use the list of vowels to identify the phonograms by highlighting the vowel(s), circling the consonant blends, and underlining the phonograms in each word. |

# UNIVERSAL ACCESS
## Students with Special Needs

The following activities offer strategies for helping students with special needs to participate in selected exercises in Unit 2.

## Auditory/Oral Discrimination Deficits

### Vowel Pairs

Students who have difficulty with pronunciation and/or sound discrimination may not distinguish between paired vowel sounds.

- Refer the students to the list of eight vowel pairs on page 31. Help the students read the list aloud to make sure that they pronounce each pair correctly. Remind the students of this rule regarding vowel pairs: *When two vowels go walking, the first vowel does the talking.*

- Have the students write the following words and highlight each vowel pair: **pain, sheet, follow, loan, Sunday, receive, thief,** and **toe.** Then have them read each word aloud, identify the vowel pair, and tell the sound that the vowel pair makes. Encourage the students to write an additional word for each vowel pair and repeat the activity.

## Visual Perceptual Deficits

Students who have difficulty locating positions and keeping their place as they work may experience difficulty with the exercises on pages 41 and 57.

For example, they may neglect to cross out three words on each line in the chart on page 41 and confuse the phonograms that are listed vertically and horizontally on page 57.

- Provide the students with a piece of construction paper or index card to be used a marker when working on pages 41 and 57. Encourage them to use the marker to block out the items that they are not currently working on. Guide the student to keep the marker straight while working and move the marker vertically to the next item when finished with a line horizontally.

- When students have completed an item, have them use a pen or crayon to "mark" the row so they know it is complete and should not revisit it when choosing answer choices.

## Memory Deficits

### Combining Consonants, Consonant Blends, and Consonant Digraphs with Phonograms

Students who have difficulty retaining or building vocabulary information may not see the relationship between the rhyming words in the exercise on page 54. For example, in item three if a student does not recognize **gymnast** or **vault,** he/she will not understand the phrase **standing landing.**

- Ask students who are having trouble with the exercise to look up the meanings of the sentences' key words and then write them down. Demonstrate how to use context clues to find the word that belongs in the blank. For example, if students have difficulty with item seven, they will learn (by using the dictionary) that the word **candidate** refers to someone who aspires to an office, and that most offices are filled by the election process. Therefore, **election** is the word that best completes the sentence.

- Have the students highlight the Helpful Hints on page 54 to remind them that when creating a hink-pink, hinky-pinky, or hinkity-pinkity they need to consider the number of syllables in each word of the pair. It may help them to write down the number of syllables they need to use as they write the word pairs.

Name _____

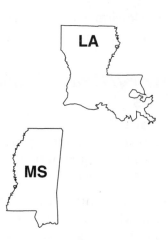

**GAMES**

**Fill in the blanks to complete the names in the sentences. Then circle the words in the puzzle.**

1. North Carolina is called the _ _ _ _ e e _ State.

2. _ _ _ _ _ _ _ e e is called the Volunteer State.

3. The capital of Florida is _ _ _ _ _ _ _ _ _ e e.

4. Kentucky is called the _ _ u e _ _ _ _ _ State.

5. Georgia is called the _ e a _ _ State.

6. Alabama's state bird is the _ _ _ _ o w _ _ _ _ _.

7. West Virginia is called the _ o u _ _ _ _ _ State.

8. Virginia's state flower is the _ _ _ _ o o d.

9. South Carolina's state flower is the _ _ _ _ o w jessamine.

10. The capital of Louisiana is _ _ _ _ _ _ o u _ _ .

11. Mississippi is known for its Gulf _ o a _ _ .

| S | D | E | U | B | P | E | A | C | H | E | O | S |
|---|---|---|---|---|---|---|---|---|---|---|---|---|
| S | O | Y | B | L | E | U | A | O | E | S | E | S |
| A | Y | E | L | L | O | W | H | A | M | M | E | R |
| R | U | L | U | O | D | A | L | S | M | O | S | E |
| G | E | L | E | O | W | S | S | T | A | U | S | N |
| E | D | O | G | W | O | O | D | R | E | N | E | S |
| U | O | W | R | T | A | L | E | H | A | T | N | E |
| L | S | T | A | R | H | E | E | L | S | A | N | E |
| B | A | T | O | N | R | O | U | G | E | I | E | E |
| T | A | L | L | A | H | A | S | S | E | N | T | T |
| E | A | T | A | L | L | A | H | A | S | S | E | E |

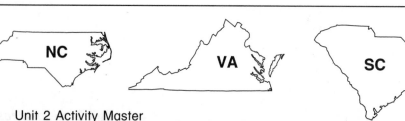

# Unit 2 TECHNOLOGY

## Life in Jamestown

Invite students to create a documentary video about the colony of Jamestown. Encourage them to show a typical day in the life of the colonists. If a video camera is not available students can use a camera to present the documentary as a photo essay.

- Tell students that the setting is Jamestown, Virginia, the first permanent English settlement in America. Provide reference books and have the class research the topic. Encourage students to use the Internet to find information about the colonists' daily life.

- Have students form groups and divide the tasks needed to create the documentary: script writing, designing costumes, creating scenery, directing, videotaping, and acting.

- Have students include in their scripts words with vowel pairs, vowel digraphs, and diphthongs. Explain that an actor must speak his or her lines clearly. Distribute the script and have students find the words in it that contain vowel pairs, vowel digraphs, and diphthongs. Have them read the script together to practice pronouncing the different vowel sounds. Students who do not wish to act can form a committee to audition those who do.

## Southeastern Mail Race

Help students discover features about the Southeast by using the computer to correspond with students who live in the southeastern states.

- Using the Internet, have students compile a list of elementary schools' names and addresses from different areas in the southeastern region. Suggest that students locate schools in urban, suburban, and rural areas of a given state.

- Brainstorm with students a list of topics for inquiry, such as geographical features, places of interest, climate, and so on.

- Have the students use a word-processing program to write their letters. Students may also include a class email address (if possible) for their "pen pal." Have partners proofread the letters and list words that contain vowel pairs, vowel digraphs, and diphthongs.

- Display a map of the United States and track incoming mail using pushpins.

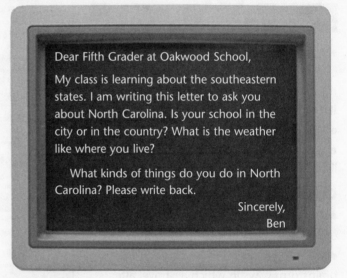

Dear Fifth Grader at Oakwood School,

My class is learning about the southeastern states. I am writing this letter to ask you about North Carolina. Is your school in the city or in the country? What is the weather like where you live?

What kinds of things do you do in North Carolina? Please write back.

Sincerely,
Ben

## Southeast Soundtrack

Encourage students to make an audiocassette of southeastern folk songs.

- Compile songbooks that contain southeastern folksongs such as *American Folk Songs for Children* by Ruth Crawford Seeger, *Gonna Sing my Head Off!* by Kathleen Krull, and *American Sampler (18 Ethnic and Regional American Folk Songs)* by Shirley McRae.

- Have students choose songs to perform. Help them play the songs on the piano or enlist the aid of singers and students who play instruments to accompany the singers. Have students take turns operating the audiocassette recorder. Share the tape with other classes and with the school library.

- Ask students to list words they find in the lyrics that contain vowel pairs, vowel digraphs, and diphthongs. Then ask them to highlight each of these features in the words on their lists.

## Introduction to
### Vowel Sounds

#### Objectives
- **To enjoy a nonfiction piece related to the theme the *Southeast***
- **To identify vowel pairs, vowel digraphs, and diphthongs**

### Starting with Literature

- Ask a student to read "Making History in the Southeast" aloud for the class. Write these words on the board: **Southeast** and **Kitty Hawk.**

- Point out the **ou** and the **ea** in **Southeast** and the **aw** in **Hawk.** Have students listen to the differences in their sounds.

#### Critical Thinking

- Ask students to review the selection in order to answer the first question.

- For the second question, have students brainstorm ways in which air travel affects people's lives today.

- Students may share their answers to the third question.

### Introducing the Skill

Write these words on the board: **Southeast, stayed, fields, Kitty Hawk,** and **taught.** Circle the letters **ou, ea, ay, ie, aw,** and **au** and ask students to say the sound of each combination.

### Practicing the Skill

Have students work in groups. Assign each group a different combination of letters to find in words within the selection. Then have students generate other words that share the same pair of letters and the same vowel sound.

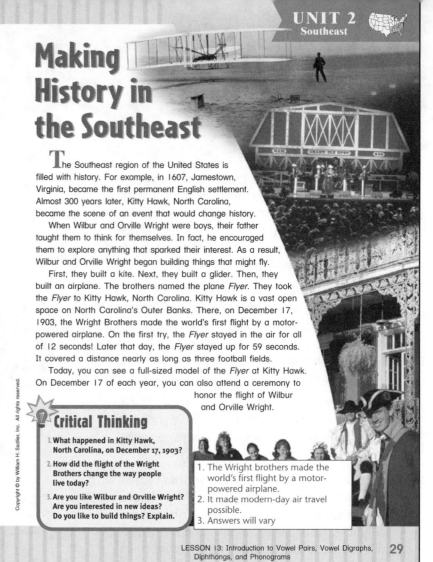

# Making History in the Southeast

The Southeast region of the United States is filled with history. For example, in 1607, Jamestown, Virginia, became the first permanent English settlement. Almost 300 years later, Kitty Hawk, North Carolina, became the scene of an event that would change history.

When Wilbur and Orville Wright were boys, their father taught them to think for themselves. In fact, he encouraged them to explore anything that sparked their interest. As a result, Wilbur and Orville Wright began building things that might fly.

First, they built a kite. Next, they built a glider. Then, they built an airplane. The brothers named the plane *Flyer.* They took the *Flyer* to Kitty Hawk, North Carolina. Kitty Hawk is a vast open space on North Carolina's Outer Banks. There, on December 17, 1903, the Wright Brothers made the world's first flight by a motor-powered airplane. On the first try, the *Flyer* stayed in the air for all of 12 seconds! Later that day, the *Flyer* stayed up for 59 seconds. It covered a distance nearly as long as three football fields.

Today, you can see a full-sized model of the *Flyer* at Kitty Hawk. On December 17 of each year, you can also attend a ceremony to honor the flight of Wilbur and Orville Wright.

### Critical Thinking

1. What happened in Kitty Hawk, North Carolina, on December 17, 1903?

2. How did the flight of the Wright Brothers change the way people live today?

3. Are you like Wilbur and Orville Wright? Are you interested in new ideas? Do you like to build things? Explain.

1. The Wright brothers made the world's first flight by a motor-powered airplane.
2. It made modern-day air travel possible.
3. Answers will vary

LESSON 13: Introduction to Vowel Pairs, Vowel Digraphs, Diphthongs, and Phonograms    29

# Theme Activity

**HISTORIC TRAVEL GUIDE TO THE SOUTHEAST** Discuss important features of a travel guide. Have several travel guides in the classroom for students to use as models. Ask students what type of information they would expect to see in a travel guide of a place they might wish to visit. (maps, points of interest, photographs, time line of historical events) Explain that the history of the Southeast is rich and that there are many areas to visit where tourists can learn more about America.

Suggest that students work in groups. One group may want to take a certain region in the Southeast, or the groups may wish to divide tasks by travel guide features. For example, one group could be gathering information for a section on points of interest, while another group works on the historical time line. As students work through this unit and learn more about the Southeast, they may continue to update and refine the travel guide.

## Dear Family,

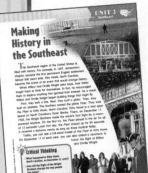

Your child is about to begin Unit 2 of Sadlier's *Word Study* program. In this unit, students will examine vowel pairs, vowel digraphs, diphthongs, and phonograms. The theme of this unit is the *Southeast,* including its people and history.

A **vowel pair** is two vowels sounded together to make one long vowel sound. The first vowel in the pair has the long sound of its name, and the second vowel is silent (br**ai**n, br**ee**ze).

A **vowel digraph** is two vowels sounded together to make a long or short sound (ch**ie**f, h**ea**d, sl**eigh**), or a special sound (s**au**ce, str**aw**, b**oo**k).

A **diphthong** is two vowels blended together as one sound. Examples include p**oi**nt, j**oy**; sh**ou**t, fr**own**; st**ew**.

### Family Focus

- Read together the passage on page 29. Discuss the impact of the Wright Brothers' achievement on modern life. Then reread the passage. Have your child identify words with vowel pairs, vowel digraphs, and diphthongs.

- Find Kitty Hawk, North Carolina, on a map. About how far is it from where you live? What route might your family take if you were to drive there? Make a plan together. List other places you might wish to see along the way.

### LINKS TO LEARNING

To extend learning together, you might explore:

**Web Sites**
www.nps.gov/wrbr/
http://fly.to/AviationHistory

**Videos**
*American Road Trips,* Discovery Channel Video, 4 videos.
*The Century: America's Time,* Discovery Channel Video, 6 videos.

**Literature**
*The Wright Brothers: How They Invented the Airplane* by Russell Freedman, ©1991.
*Outer Banks Mysteries and Seaside Stories* by Charles Harry Whedbee, ©1980.

## Multicultural Connection

England, Spain, and France all had land claims in the Southeast. Have students research the European influences in this region and write a composition describing some of them. Tell students to look for clues, such as names, that hint at the influence of a particular nation. (For example, New Orleans's French past is seen in its celebration of Mardi Gras.)

## Social Studies Link

Transportation has come a long way since the Wright Brothers' 1903 flight. Florida's Cape Canaveral has been the launch site for NASA's four decades of space exploration. Have students research NASA's plans for Mars exploration, which began in the late 1990s and is scheduled to continue in the coming decade.

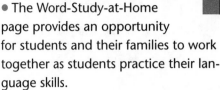

## Word Study at Home

- The Word-Study-at-Home page provides an opportunity for students and their families to work together as students practice their language skills.

- On the Word-Study-at-Home page for Unit 2, students and their families will find activities that relate to the theme, the *Southeast,* and focus on vowel pairs, vowel digraphs, and diphthongs.

- Have students remove page 30 from their books. Tell them to take the page home so that their families may share in the Word-Study-at-Home activities.

- Families may want to engage in a discussion about technological advances (even as recently as in the last decade) and how these advances have changed people's lives.

- Invite students to find out about other important sites in the Southeast having to do with travel, for example: Cape Canaveral in Florida. Students may want to research the workings of a modern airport, such as those in Raleigh, North Carolina; Atlanta, Georgia; or Dallas, Texas. Students may prepare a poster or an oral report about their subject.

### Theme-Related Resources

**Web Sites**

www.kennedyspacecenter.com/
html/exhibits.html

www.kidinfo.com/American_History/
Inventors_Inventions.html

www.thehistorynet.com/THNarchives/
AmericanHistory/

www.suite101.com/welcome.cfm/
history_for_children

### Audiotapes

*Follow the Drinking Gourd—A Story of the Underground Railroad* (Rabbit Ears Productions)

# Vowel Pairs
## ai, ay, ee, ei, ie, oa, oe, ow

### Objectives

- **To recognize the sounds of the vowel pairs ai, ay, ee, ei, ie, oa, oe, and ow**
- **To associate the sounds of the vowel pairs with their letters**
- **To form words by adding one or more consonants to a phonogram that contains a vowel pair**

## Warming Up

- Write this weather forecast on the board and read it aloud to students.

  **Rain** and **hail** in **today's** forecast, **followed** by **sleet** and **freezing snow.** Turn up the **heat** and **keep** your **toes toasty** and your wool scarf **tied.**

- Circle the vowel pairs **ai, ay (rain, hail, today's); ee, ea, (sleet, freezing, keep, heat); ie (tied);** and **oa, oe, ow (toasty, toes, followed, snow)**

- Ask students what each group of words has in common. (a long vowel sound)

## Teaching the Lesson

- Explain that there are many ways to combine vowels in order to make the same vowel sound. Two vowels that together make a long vowel sound are called a vowel pair.
- Write the vowel pairs **ai, ay, ee, ei, ie, oa, oe,** and **ow** on the board and read them aloud. Tell students that the second vowel in a vowel pair is silent.
- Write the words **rain** and **heat** on the board. Cover the first letter of each word and tell students that the part they see is a phonogram. Review the fact that a phonogram is a one-syllable word part with only one vowel sound.

---

Name _____

**Helpful Hint**

A **vowel pair** is two vowels sounded together to make one long vowel sound. Here are eight vowel pairs:

ai   ay   ee   ei   ie   oa   oe   ow

The first vowel in the pair has the sound of its name, and the second vowel is silent. Listen:

Don't **delay** the **train.**          Can I **receive** a free pass?
Will you have some **pie**?          **Joe** has a **row boat.**

Say each word in the box below. Then sort the words by the sound that each vowel pair makes. Write each word in the correct column.

| afraid agree approach toe deceive doe float holiday wait |
| mower playful free seize thirteen spray street moan rain |

| 1  Long a | 2  Long e | 3  Long o |
|-----------|-----------|-----------|
| afraid    | agree     | approach  |
| holiday   | deceive   | toe       |
| wait      | free      | doe       |
| playful   | seize     | float     |
| spray     | thirteen  | mower     |
| rain      | street    | moan      |

Underline the words in each sentence that have the *same* vowel sound as the sound given at the start of the row.

4. **Long a**   What an array of whole grains the market has!
5. **Long i**   She cried as she tried to peel the onion.
6. **Long o**   Joe bought a garden hoe and a bow tie.

**CHALLENGE**

Circle the vowel pairs in this word:

freeway

List other words with two vowel pairs.

LESSON 14: Vowel Pairs **ai, ay, ee, ei, ie, oa, oe, ow**

---

# UNIVERSAL ACCESS
## Meeting Individual Needs

### Visual Learners

Divide the class into two teams and make two sets of cards with the following words: **approach, doe, float, mower, moan, goat, goal, afraid, holiday, spray, playful, receive,** and **fifteen.**

Have each team write a sentence using as many word cards as possible. Award five points for each word card used and subtract one point for any other word used.

### Auditory Learners

Write the following words on the board: **holiday, playful, wait, agree, street, seize, mower, moan, oath, praise, deceive** and **decay.** Invite students to write a sentence combining two words and then read it aloud. Have a volunteer circle the vowel pair in each word.

## Helpful Hint

Many **vowel pairs** build words with phonograms. A **phonogram** is a syllable that has a vowel or vowels plus one or more consonants. Phonograms have only one vowel sound. Here are some phonograms:

**ain    ay    oal    oat**

Use each phonogram and the letters given in the boxes below to form words. Use the words to complete the sentences.

____oal    | c | f | g | sh |

1. This is a newborn horse. __foal__  2. This is your aim or purpose. __goal__
3. Water is shallow here. __shoal__  4. Burn this mineral for heat. __coal__

____ain    | pl | ch | tr | str |

5. This means "not fancy." __plain__  6. This is to stretch too far. __strain__
7. You make this with links. __chain__  8. Another name for *railroad*. __train__

Complete each sentence with a word from the box below.

| decay | deceive | oath | praise | screeched | woe |

9. The President takes a solemn __oath__ to defend the Constitution.
10. "__Woe__ is me!" cried the doomed prisoner.
11. Teachers __praise__ students who put forth their best efforts.
12. Brush and floss your teeth regularly to prevent tooth __decay__.
13. The car __screeched__ to a halt to avoid hitting the deer.
14. Did you __deceive__ them by pretending to be asleep?

32    LESSON 14: Vowel Pairs
ai, ay, ee, ei, ie, oa, oe, ow

**Home Involvement Activity** Have your child underline the vowel pairs in these words: **afloat** and **tiptoe.** Together, list examples of words with the same vowel pairs found on a page of your child's social studies book.

**Foal**

---

## English-Language Learners/ESL

Prepare separate word and picture cards for the following words: **paint, tray, pail, stain, green, grease, oats, coal, bowl, doe.** Have students choose a picture card and then find its matching word card. Ask the student to pronounce the word and use it in a sentence.

## Gifted Learners

Have students play a game in which they change the first letter(s) before or the last letter(s) after the vowel pairs: **ai, ea, ee,** or **oa.** Ask students to find ten words for each column.

| ai | ea | ee | oa |
|----|----|----|----|
| train | heal | sleet | goat |
| stain | heat | feet | goal |

## Learners with Special Needs

Additional strategies for supporting learners with special needs can be found on page 29L.

---

## Practicing the Skill

● Read aloud the direction lines on pages 31 and 32. Do the first item together in each exercise.

● For items 1–8 on page 32, students may check their answers by looking up the words in a dictionary.

## Curriculum Connections

### Spelling Link

Have students unscramble these words and write them to complete each sentence:
**aiafrd, esot, praapohc, deiveec, latof, neetrith.**

**(afraid)** Many animals are _____ of humans.

**(toes)** How many _____ does a sloth have?

**(approach)** You should _____ a porcupine carefully.

**(deceive)** The alligator can _____ its prey by camouflaging itself.

**(float)** A beaver can _____ or swim in the water.

**(thirteen)** I counted _____ flamingos at the park.

### Social Studies Link

Have students locate the states that make up the Southeast in an atlas or social studies textbook. Ask students to use reference books and almanacs to research which American presidents were born in these states. Have students make a map of the region and label it with the names and birth dates of the presidents in their home states.

### Observational Assessment

*Check to see whether students correctly pronounce words containing the vowel pairs **ai, ay, ee, ei, ie, oa, oe,** and **ow.***

32

# Vowel Digraphs
## ea, ei, ey, ie, au, aw, oo

### Objectives

- **To recognize the sounds of the vowel digraphs ea, ei, ey, ie, au, aw, and oo**

- **To understand that a vowel digraph can make a long or short vowel sound, or a special vowel sound**

## Warming Up

- Write this passage on the board and read it aloud to students:

  Yesterday I **read** a **good book**. It was about a **hawk** who became a **cook**. He made a **sauce** from the river **instead** of milk. He was no **fool**. He became very **wealthy**!

- Have students circle the words containing two vowels together.

- Review the fact that a vowel pair is two vowels that have the long sound of the first vowel. Ask if the circled words follow that rule. (no) Ask students to describe the vowel sounds of the circled words. (The letters **ea** have the short **e** sound. The letters **oo** have the vowel sounds heard in **good** and **fool**. The letters **au** and **aw** make the same sound.)

## Teaching the Lesson

- Have students sort vowel digraphs by their sounds and add words to this chart:

| Digraphs with long vowel sounds | Digraphs with short vowel sounds | Digraphs with special vowel sounds |
|---|---|---|
| ei, ey, ie | ea | au, aw, oo |

- Read aloud the Helpful Hints. Have students explain how a vowel digraph is different than a vowel pair. Point out that more than one vowel digraph may make the same vowel sound.

**33**

---

Name _____

### Helpful Hints

Like a vowel pair, a **vowel digraph** is two vowels sounded together. Yet vowel digraphs do not follow the long vowel rule. A vowel digraph can make a **long** sound, a **short** sound, or a very **special** sound. Here are four vowel digraphs: ea ei ey ie.

head    sleigh    obey    field    thief

When ea has the **long** e sound, as in **neat** or **reach**, it is a **vowel pair**.

Street band playing in
New Orleans' French Quarter

 Read aloud the words in bold type. Sort the words by the sound that each vowel digraph makes. Write each word in the correct column below.

| | | |
|---|---|---|
| three-**piece** band | bird of **prey** | good **neighbor** |
| **steady** beat | take a **survey** | **eight** days |
| strong **beliefs** | cotton **sweater** | amazing **wealth** |
| under **siege** | **instead** of milk | **grey** day |
| silver **shield** | **achieve** a goal | **leather** wallet |

| 1   Short e | 2   Long a | 3   Long e |
|---|---|---|
| steady | prey | piece |
| sweater | neighbor | beliefs |
| wealth | survey | siege |
| instead | eight | shield |
| leather | grey | achieve |

### WORK TOGETHER

Get together with a partner. Write sentences that use words with the vowel digraphs ea, ei, ey, and ie. Sort the words according to short e, long a, or long e.

---

# UNIVERSAL ACCESS
## Meeting Individual Needs

### Visual Learners

Have students work with a partner to list as many words as they can with the vowel digraphs **ea, ei, ey, ie, au, aw,** and **oo.** Have students put the words into a word search puzzle. Suggest that students set up the puzzle on a sheet of graph paper and then have partners trade puzzles with another set of partners.

### Auditory Learners

Make cards for the words **boot, good, fool, book, root, foot, hood, look, pool,** and **stool,** and place them on the board. Students must find two word cards with the same digraph, but the digraphs have to make different vowel sounds. Encourage students to say a sentence that contains both of the words they chose.

These **vowel digraphs** blend sounds together: au aw oo.

These two vowel digraphs stand for the aw sound. Listen:

**Paul draws.**

Now listen for two different sounds of oo:

The **cook shook** the **spoon** to make it **cool.**

Write the vowel digraph au, aw, or oo to complete each word.

| | | | |
|---|---|---|---|
| 1 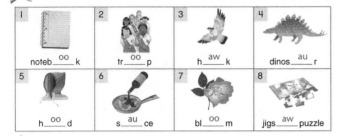 noteb__oo__k | 2 tr__oo__p | 3 h__aw__k | 4 dinos__au__r |
| 5 h__oo__d | 6 s__au__ce | 7 bl__oo__m | 8 jigs__aw__puzzle |

Complete each sentence with a word from the box below. Then circle the *spoon* or the *foot* to show the oo sound in the word you wrote.

baboon  barefoot  childhood  overlooks  seafood  teaspoon  good

9. The cabin ___overlooks___ the Shenandoah Valley.

10. A trip to Savannah will give you a ___good___ history lesson.

11. One of my earliest ___childhood___ memories is of a trip to Florida.

12. The ___baboon___ is a kind of ape.

13. The recipe calls for one ___teaspoon___ of salt.

14. I love to walk ___barefoot___ along a soft, sandy beach.

15. The North Carolina coast has great ___seafood___ restaurants.

**34**   LESSON 15: Vowel Digraphs
ea, ei, ey, ie, au, aw, oo

**Home Involvement Activity** Find words in a newspaper with the vowel digraphs ea, ei, ey, ie, au, aw, and oo. Listen for the sounds of the digraphs. Make a chart to sort the words by their vowel sounds.

## English-Language Learners/ESL

Have students look in a magazine or make illustrations of food for a restaurant menu. Dishes might include: **noodles, mushrooms, sausages, seafood, bread,** and **cookies.** Students should label the menu and read it aloud. Encourage students to include words that have a digraph from this lesson. Then have one student read the menu and the other take the order.

## Gifted Learners

Encourage students to look in the dictionary for information about the word **digraph.** They should break it down into its prefix, **di-** (two), and its root, **graph** (writing), and analyze the word's history and the meaning of the word. Have students report their findings to their classmates.

## Learners with Special Needs

Additional strategies for supporting learners with special needs can be found on page 29L.

## Practicing the Skill

• Read aloud the directions on pages 33–34. Make sure students understand what the phrase "bold type" means.

• On page 34, make sure students can identify the different vowel sounds in **spoon** and **foot** before they start the exercise.

Turn to page 29K for an Intervention Strategy designed to help students who need extra support with this lesson.

## Curriculum Connections

### Spelling Link

• Make a set of word cards for the following words: **steady, neighbor, jigsaw, leather, draw, dinosaur, sauce, bloom, head, notebook, spoon,** and **seafood.** Place the cards in a bag and give to a pair of students.

• One student chooses a word card and then gives clues to the second student so that he or she can guess the word. The student who guesses the word must spell the word aloud or write it on a sheet of paper. The bag is then passed on to another pair of students who repeat the activity. Continue play until all words have been guessed and spelled.

### Science Link

• Have students research one of these animals that is native to the Southeast: brown pelican, flamingo, alligator, armadillo, or sea cow (manatee).

• Have them prepare a chart or a written report that answers these questions: *Where is this animal found? Describe its physical characteristics. How does it make its home? What does it eat? Is it endangered?*

## Observational Assessment

*Note whether students can identify which pronunciation to use in words that contain the vowel digraph **oo**.*

**34**

# Connecting Reading and Writing

## Objectives

- **To read a story and respond to it in writing**

- **To interpret story events and distinguish between fact and nonfact**

## Warming Up

### Comprehension Skills

- Tell students that in this lesson they will practice the reading skill of **distinguishing between fact and nonfact**.

- Explain that the picture on page 35 shows a stage in Nashville, Tennessee. Say: *Nashville is a city in Tennessee.* Tell them that this is a fact that can be proven. Say: *Everyone in Tennessee is a country music performer.* Ask students if they believe this is a fact. (no) Explain that this is a nonfact because it can not be proven true.

- Explain that readers must **interpret** events in a story to determine its overall meaning.

## Teaching the Lesson

- Suggest that students reread the selection to find the answers to the Reader's Response questions.

- Point out that some events seem unrealistic and might not be facts. Ask students at what point in the story they began to realize that the narrator was only dreaming.

## Practicing the Skill

Read the directions on page 36 together. Encourage students to imagine ways in which they might reach their career goals. Remind them that they may use both fact and nonfact in their stories.

35

---

Name _____

 **Read about a young girl's "dream" to be a country-music star. Then answer the questions that follow.**

## In Music City, U.S.A.

**H**ere I am in Nashville, Tennessee, the country music capital of the world. It's where the biggest country stars perform, and where I've always wanted to be.

Look at me, here on Music Row! Over here is the Country Music Hall of Fame. There is Ryman Auditorium. That's where the *Grand Ole Opry* used to be broadcast. My folks always listen to the live performances on the radio. They say that it's the nation's longest-running radio show. Nowadays, the show is broadcast from Music Valley on Opryland Drive. I'll just hop on the trolley that goes there. I hope it's not too late to get a ticket for today's show.

Well, I do get a ticket. It's right in the front row. I'm so excited! I've loved to sing ever since I was old enough to carry a tune. Some people say I'm pretty good, maybe even good enough to see my name in lights one day. No one stops me as I make my way up onto the stage and begin to wail. The star performer steps aside from the microphone and smiles.

The audience loves me. I can hardly believe it! I am making my singing debut at the *Grand Ole Opry!* Now the star is saying something. She's telling me…what? To wake up? Why is she…?

"Wake up, Ashley. It's late! The school bus will be here soon! Don't forget you have glee-club practice today."

"I know, Mom." Oh well, my adoring fans will just have to wait another night.

1. No one stops the narrator from going up to the stage. The narrator is told to wake up.
2. Visiting the Grand Ole Opry could happen. Going on stage and singing probably could not happen.
3. Answers will vary.

 **Reader's Response**

1. What clues let you know that the story is a dream?

2. Which parts of the story could be true? Which parts probably could not happen in real life?

3. Have you ever had a dream that you hoped would come true? Explain.

**LESSON 16: Connecting Reading and Writing**
Comprehension—Distinguish Between Fact and Nonfact; Interpret

35

---

# UNIVERSAL ACCESS
## Meeting Individual Needs

### Visual Learners

Show students photographs of people at work in various careers. Encourage students to look for details in the photographs. Have them ask, *What are employees wearing; What does the workplace look like; Are people working alone or with others?* Have students refer to these details as they fill out a story-structure chart.

### Logical Learners

Tell students that when they interpret information they compare it with facts they already know. Ask students to list facts about a career they think they would enjoy. Have students read about the career and then list new information. Ask them to think about whether the new information changes their opinions about the career.

### Learners with Special Needs

Additional strategies for supporting learners with special needs can be found on page 29L.

Ashley dreams of becoming a country-music star. Do you have a dream like hers? How could you make your dream come true?

★ **Think about a career that you would like to have someday. Write a story about how you might reach your goal. Be creative. Remember that in stories good things can happen! Use at least two of these words in your writing.**

| | | | | | | | |
|---|---|---|---|---|---|---|---|
| inspire | dream | follow | goal | believe | speech | achieve | draw |
| career | tried | seize | details | disappointed | road | boast | bloom |

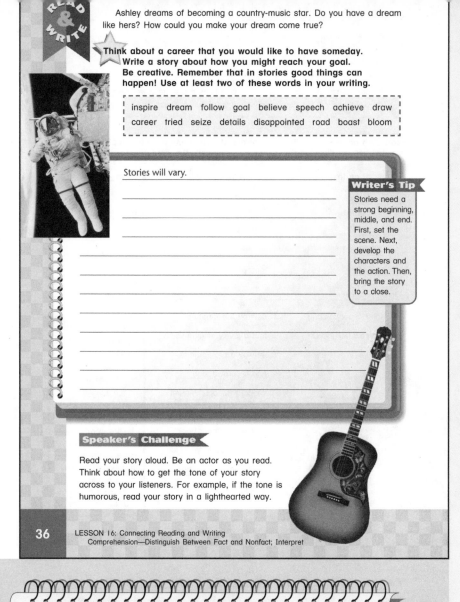

Stories will vary.

### Writer's Tip

Stories need a strong beginning, middle, and end. First, set the scene. Next, develop the characters and the action. Then, bring the story to a close.

### Speaker's Challenge

Read your story aloud. Be an actor as you read. Think about how to get the tone of your story across to your listeners. For example, if the tone is humorous, read your story in a lighthearted way.

**36**    LESSON 16: Connecting Reading and Writing
Comprehension—Distinguish Between Fact and Nonfact; Interpret

### English-Language Learners/ESL

Have English-language learners discuss their career goals with a more fluent student who can supply specific words for the story events or the chosen career. Allow students to write their sentences as a list if necessary, rather than in paragraph form.

### Gifted Learners

Challenge students to rewrite their stories as plays. Remind them to include a cast of characters, stage directions, and to indicate dialogue by showing each character's name followed by a colon. Students might enjoy staging their productions with the help of their classmates.

## The Writing Process

Discuss the purpose of a story—to relate events that inform or entertain. Tell students that their story will be about how their career goal could become a reality.

**Prewrite** Have students think about a personal career goal. Have them create a story-structure chart in which they list characters, setting, story events, and resolution.

**Write** Encourage students to write a beginning sentence that captures their readers' attention. Then have students refer to their story-structure charts as they write.

**Revise** Have students trade stories with a partner. Tell them to keep these questions in mind as they read: *Do I understand the career goal? Is there a clearly defined beginning, middle, and end?* Partners should give each other constructive feedback.

**Proofread** Have students proofread their work for errors in punctuation, grammar, and spelling.

**Publish** Have students copy their final drafts onto page 36 or a separate sheet of paper.

**Computer Connection**

Share the following tip with students who use a word processor to do their writing.

● To save an earlier draft, first open the draft document. Then go to the File menu and highlight "Save As."

● A window called Save As will appear on the screen, and it will show the name of the current document. Keep the original name and add a number after it. For example, label documents Draft1, Draft2, Draft3, and so on.

**Portfolio** Have students add their completed stories to their portfolios.

# Diphthongs
## oi, oy, ou, ow, ew

### Objectives

- To recognize the sounds of the diphthongs **oi, oy, ou, ow,** and **ew**
- To use words that include the diphthongs **oi, oy, ou, ow,** and **ew**
- To distinguish between the sounds of the diphthong **ow** and the vowel pair **ow**

## Warming Up

- Write this rhyme on the board and read it aloud to students:

  You've seen that every English word includes a **vowel** or two;

  You've seen vowels short and long and paired,

  But here is something **new**:

  You put two vowels together and slide them both **around**.

  Listen to the way they **join** to make a different **sound**.

- Underline the words **vowel**, **new**, **around**, **join**, and **sound**. Call on volunteers to pronounce each word slowly, drawing out the vowel sounds.

## Teaching the Lesson

- Explain that sometimes when two vowels blend together they make a new sound called a diphthong.
- Read aloud the Helpful Hints on pages 37–38. Create column headings for the dipthongs **oi, oy, ou, ew, ow** on the board. Pronounce them with students. Point out that **ou** and **ow** form two sounds: **ow** as in **now** and long **o** as in **show**.
- Have students suggest and write words for each column.

---

Name _____

**Helpful Hint**

A **diphthong** is two vowels that blend together to form one vowel sound. If you say a diphthong *very* slowly, you can hear both vowel sounds.

The diphthongs oi in sp**oi**l and oy in b**oy** have the same vowel sound. The diphthong ew has the vowel sound you hear in ch**ew**.

Read each phrase below the three boxes. Underline the word in the phrase that has the diphthong oi, oy, or ew. Then write the word in the box below.

| oi as in | oy as in | ew as in |
|---|---|---|
| **point** | **toy** | **screw** |
| voice | joyous | outgrew |
| appointment | destroy | shrewd |
| join | employ | renew |
| foil | oysters | cashew |

1. sang a joyous song
2. outgrew her jacket
3. destroy the furniture
4. had a lovely singing voice
5. employ a programmer
6. had a shrewd idea
7. cancel your appointment
8. ate some oysters
9. renew the library books
10. join the photography club
11. ate some salty cashew nuts
12. wrapped in aluminum foil

**CHALLENGE**

Circle the diphthongs in these words:

news
trapezoid
turquoise

Which is a math word? A social studies word? An art word? List other words with diphthongs that you might use in math, science, gym, social studies, art, or music.

LESSON 17: Diphthongs **oi, oy, ou, ow, ew**          37

---

# UNIVERSAL ACCESS
## Meeting Individual Needs

### Tactile Learners

Have students play a game of "Diphthong Crosswords." Prepare two sets of letter cards, including all the letters of the alphabet with extra vowels. Have partners place cards crossword-style to make as many words as they can using words with diphthongs from this lesson.

### Visual Learners

Supply students with a variety of print ads from magazines or newspapers and have them search for words with the diphthongs **oi, oy, ou, ow,** and **ew.** Before students begin, create a color key—a different color for each diphthong. When they locate a diphthong have them mark it with the appropriate color.

The **diphthongs** ou and ow can stand for the vowel sound in **cloud** and **clown**.

The **vowel pair** ow usually has the **long** o sound.

| bowl | show | throw |

The silversmith's shop in Colonial Williamsburg, Virginia

Read each sentence. Underline the word that has the sound of ow. Then circle the *flower* 🌸 or the *bowl* 🥣 to show the ow sound in the underlined word.

1. Williamsburg is a <u>town</u> with hundreds of tourists.
2. Let's <u>browse</u> through the silversmith's shop.
3. Look at that <u>yellow</u> hammer.
4. <u>How</u> far is Virginia Beach from here?
5. I can't sit near that <u>rowdy</u> group.
6. Has Williamsburg <u>grown</u> much in recent years?
7. <u>Tomorrow</u> we will tour the rest of the village.
8. Mom is <u>allowing</u> my brother to take us.

Complete each sentence with a word from the box below.

| proud | houses | snow | brown | sounds | flows |

9. She was ___proud___ to be from Virginia.
10. Which body of water ___flows___ through the state?
11. What charming ___sounds___ those birds make!
12. Does it ever ___snow___ in Virginia?
13. The ___houses___ look as they did long ago.
14. Many women's dresses are white and ___brown___.

**38** LESSON 17: Diphthongs
oi, oy, ou, ow, ew

**Home Involvement Activity** Brainstorm ideas to create a list of words that have the diphthongs ou and ow, as in m**ou**nd and d**ow**n.

---

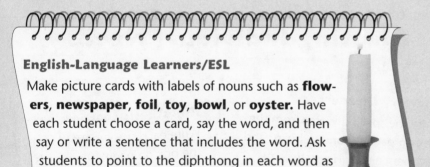

**English-Language Learners/ESL**

Make picture cards with labels of nouns such as **flowers**, **newspaper**, **foil**, **toy**, **bowl**, or **oyster**. Have each student choose a card, say the word, and then say or write a sentence that includes the word. Ask students to point to the diphthong in each word as they say the word.

**Gifted Learners**

Have students write sentences about a vacation they have taken or would like to take. Ask them to include words with diphthongs in each sentence. Encourage students to make their sentences creative and humorous.

**Learners with Special Needs**

Additional strategies for supporting learners with special needs can be found on page 29L.

---

## Practicing the Skill

Read aloud the directions on pages 37–38. Explain that the words for the exercise on page 37 come from the phrases 1–12 at the bottom of the page.

**Intervention Strategy**

Turn to page 29K for an Intervention Strategy designed to help students who need extra support with this lesson.

## Curriculum Connections

### Spelling Link

● Read these sentences aloud and have students write the words in bold type. Tell students that each word contains a diphthong or vowel pair.

> The village of Colonial Williamsburg **employs** many people.
>
> Our guide has a pleasant **voice**.
>
> Williamsburg's popularity has **grown** over the years.
>
> In the bakery, we tried **cashew** pie.
>
> This trip has **renewed** my interest in American history.
>
> **Tomorrow**, we will go home.

● Have students circle the diphthong or vowel pair in each word.

### Writing Link

● Have students research Colonial Williamsburg and then write an essay about what it would have been like to live there.

● Encourage students to use words that have diphthongs from the lesson and the vowel pair **ow** in their essays.

● Have students exchange their work with a partner and circle the words with a diphthong or the vowel pair **ow**.

## Observational Assessment

*Check to see that students are able to distinguish between the diphthong* **ow** *and the vowel pair* **ow**.

# Connecting Spelling and Writing

## Objectives

- To say, spell, sort, and write words with vowel pairs, vowel digraphs, and diphthongs
- To write a biographical sketch

## Warming Up

- Write the following paragraph on the board and underline the words in bold type. Have a volunteer read it aloud.

  In 1775, Patrick Henry made a famous **speech** in Virginia. He challenged his **neighbors** to **proclaim** themselves independent and fight for a **new**, democratic republic. The **rows** of listeners caught their **breath** as he **exclaimed**, "Give me liberty, or give me **death**."

- Ask students what they notice about the underlined words. (There is a vowel pair, a vowel digraph, or a diphthong in each.)

## Teaching the Lesson

- Create a chart on the board with three headings: **Vowel Pairs, Vowel Digraphs,** and **Diphthongs.**
- Ask volunteers to list the vowel pairs, digraphs, or diphthongs they have learned in previous lessons. Have students write them in the correct place on the chart. (Vowel pairs: **ai, ay, ee, ei, ie, oa, oe, ow;** Vowel digraphs: **ea, ei, ey, ie, au, aw, oo;** Diphthongs: **oi, oy, ou, ow, ew**)

## Practicing the Skill

Read aloud the directions on page 39. Ask a student to read each phrase aloud. Then have students complete the page independently.

---

Name _____

 Read each group of words. Say and spell each word in bold type. Repeat the word. Then sort the words according to their vowel sound. Write the words in the correct column below.

- **oath** of office
- **receives** a medal
- **overthrew** the dictator
- gave a rousing **speech**
- soothing **ointment**
- a happy **childhood**
- a heart filled with **woe**
- her first **choice**
- **praise** their efforts
- **loyalty** to the cause
- taking a **survey**
- may never **believe** me
- move with **caution**
- **grown** to respect them

- a helpful **neighbor**
- a **rowdy** group
- **threaten** to rain
- an imaginary **boundary**

Monticello, Thomas Jefferson's house in Virginia

| Words with Vowel Pairs | Words with Vowel Digraphs | Words with Diphthongs |
|---|---|---|
| oath | childhood | overthrew |
| receives | survey | ointment |
| speech | believe | choice |
| woe | caution | loyalty |
| praise | neighbor | rowdy |
| grown | threaten | boundary |

---

# UNIVERSAL ACCESS
## Meeting Individual Needs

### Auditory Learners

Write the spelling words from the box on page 40 on the board and say them aloud. Have students respond with another word that has that vowel sound and uses the same vowel pair, vowel digraph, or diphthong. For example, they could respond to the word **grown** with the word **flow,** but not the word **sew.**

### Learners with Special Needs

Additional strategies for supporting learners with special needs can be found on page 29L.

### Kinesthetic Learners

Write each spelling word from the box on page 40 on cards and place them around the room. Write the vowel pair, vowel digraph, or diphthong in each word on cards and place them in a hat. Have a student draw a card and say the vowel sound. He or she then searches for a matching word card that has that vowel sound. Continue until all cards have been found.

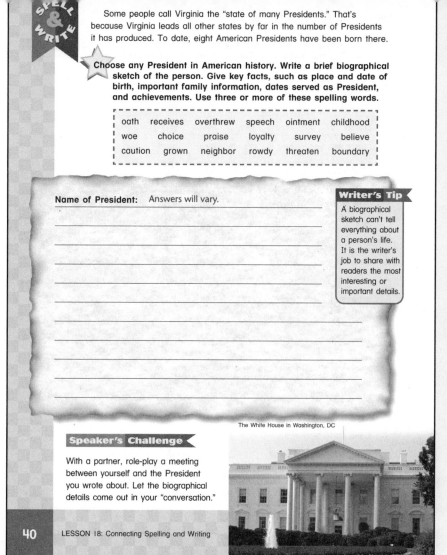

## SPELL & WRITE

Some people call Virginia the "state of many Presidents." That's because Virginia leads all other states by far in the number of Presidents it has produced. To date, eight American Presidents have been born there.

**Choose any President in American history. Write a brief biographical sketch of the person. Give key facts, such as place and date of birth, important family information, dates served as President, and achievements. Use three or more of these spelling words.**

| | | | | | |
|---|---|---|---|---|---|
| oath | receives | overthrew | speech | ointment | childhood |
| woe | choice | praise | loyalty | survey | believe |
| caution | grown | neighbor | rowdy | threaten | boundary |

**Name of President:** Answers will vary.

### Writer's Tip
A biographical sketch can't tell everything about a person's life. It is the writer's job to share with readers the most interesting or important details.

The White House in Washington, DC

### Speaker's Challenge

With a partner, role-play a meeting between yourself and the President you wrote about. Let the biographical details come out in your "conversation."

40    LESSON 18: Connecting Spelling and Writing

---

### English-Language Learners/ESL

Have English-language learners work with a more fluent partner to complete the chart on page 39. Have students pronounce each word, one column at a time, and make up a sentence that uses the word correctly. Allow students to refer to a dictionary to check word meaning.

### Gifted Learners

Give students a copy of Patrick Henry's famous speech. Tell them to underline any vowel pairs, vowel digraphs, or diphthongs that they have studied in this lesson. Ask a volunteer to give a dramatic reading of the speech for their class.

---

## The Writing Process

Tell students that on page 40 they will write a brief biographical sketch of an American president. Read the directions and the spelling words. Make sure students know the meaning of each spelling word.

**Prewrite** Discuss the sources students might use for research. Encourage them to use their library's reference section. Remind students to include the key facts that were asked for in the directions and also to take additional notes about details that interest them.

**Write** Direct students' attention to the Writers' Tip on page 40. Tell them to present the interesting details they find within the context of other facts about this president's life.

**Revise** Have students trade papers with a partner and give constructive feedback. Students should check to see that their partner's biography includes all the information asked for.

**Proofread** Have students read their work slowly and carefully to check for errors in grammar, punctuation, and spelling.

**Publish** Have students copy their final drafts onto page 40 or a sheet of paper.

### Computer Connection

Share the following tip with students who use a word processor to do their writing.

- With a click of the mouse, you can highlight a word, sentence, or paragraph to make editing go more quickly.

- Your program should do the following: Two clicks highlight a word; three clicks highlight a paragraph, even if it is only one sentence long.

- The highlighted section may then be deleted or moved. You may also change font size, color, and so on.

### Portfolio

Have students add their biographical sketches to their portfolios.

**40**

# Reviewing and Assessing
## Vowel Sounds

## Objective

To review and assess vowel pairs, vowel digraphs, and diphthongs

## Warming Up

● Write these words on the board in rows.

| thief | sea | stain | cheese |
| zoo | cook | soon | clue |
| stood | could | shout | wood |
| town | tough | round | south |

● Have students read the words and circle three words in each row that have the same vowel sound. (Row 1: **thief, sea, cheese**; Row 2: **zoo, soon, clue**; Row 3: **stood, could, wood**; Row 4: **town, round, south**)

● Ask students to name two additional words that have the vowel sound in each row.

## ★ Teaching the Lesson

● Point out that the first exercise on page 41 is similar to the activity in *Warming-Up*.

● For the second exercise, make sure that students can distinguish between long and short vowel sounds.

● When doing the exercises on page 42, encourage students to use context clues to help them find the correct answer. Point out to students that in items 5–14 the same letter pair must be used in both spaces.

41

---

Name _____

 Read each group of words. Say the word in bold type and listen for its vowel sound. Cross out three words in the row that have a *different* vowel sound.

| | | | | | | | |
|---|---|---|---|---|---|---|---|
| 1 | **receive** a gift | try | mean | play | believe | eye | deed |
| 2 | deep **voice** | vowel | joy | choice | vine | point | slice |
| 3 | **cloudy** day | brown | tough | cough | young | sound | round |
| 4 | **ready**, set, go | bed | steady | meal | head | vein | feed |
| 5 | **seize** the moment | praise | bread | yeast | key | blew | tease |
| 6 | **clown** around | crow | show | proud | doubt | rough | plow |
| 7 | birds of **prey** | vein | quaint | press | boat | grand | late |
| 8 | feelings of **grief** | siege | gripe | death | doe | team | leaf |
| 9 | **should** call | scout | stood | could | sauce | cool | wood |
| 10 | sore **throat** | flower | hoe | power | foot | grown | mow |
| 11 | **sprain** my wrist | arrow | friend | chase | spray | break | review |
| 12 | **browse** for food | grow | crown | four | though | loud | ground |
| 13 | great **wealth** | squeak | step | worth | spend | peach | feather |
| 14 | **zoom** lens | moon | comb | spoon | look | foot | smooth |

 Underline the word in each pair that has the *same* vowel sound as the sound given at the start of the row.

| 15. **Long** a | grain or grand? | tall or weigh? | toy or tray? |
|---|---|---|---|
| 16. **Long** e | choice or cheese? | size or seize? | team or dread? |
| 17. **Long** i | lie or leaf? | piece or pie? | receive or fly? |
| 18. **Long** o | float or flute? | choose or coat? | woe or wool? |
| 19. **Short** e | health or squeak? | deal or dead? | new or nest? |
| 20. **Short** u | double or doubt? | would or young? | enough or shoulder? |

LESSON 19: Review and Assess    **41**

---

# UNIVERSAL ACCESS
## Meeting Individual Needs

### Auditory Learners

Play a game of "Word Train" with a group of students. Have a student say a word with a vowel digraph, a vowel pair, or a diphthong. The next student in the group says a word that begins with the same last letter as the word just before it. The word should have a different vowel digraph, vowel pair, or diphthong. (For example: **claw**, **way**, **yellow**...)

### Visual Learners

Have students look through Lessons 13–19 for words with vowel pairs, vowel digraphs, or diphthongs. Ask students to mix up the letters of each word, and give the words to another student to unscramble. Once players have unscrambled the words, have them circle the letters that make up vowel pairs, vowel digraphs, or diphthongs.

### Learners with Special Needs

Additional strategies for supporting learners with special needs can be found on page 29L.

**Fill in the circle of the word that completes each sentence. Then write the word on the line.**

1. Rich deposits of ___coal___ lie beneath West Virginia.
   ● coal  ○ breeze  ○ chain

2. Networks of ___train___ lines carry the ore from the mine areas.
   ○ praise  ● train  ○ health

3. Mining does have its risks, but it can ___employ___ many people.
   ○ review  ○ overlook  ● employ

4. Miners ___obey___ strict rules in order to be safe underground.
   ○ play  ○ show  ● obey

**Read each sentence. Choose the letter pair from the three in the row that completes *both* unfinished words. Write that same letter pair in both spaces.**

| | | |
|---|---|---|
| aw | ew | (ow) |
| oi | oe | (oa) |
| (ea) | ei | ie |
| ow | (ou) | aw |
| (oo) | ou | ow |
| aw | (ew) | ow |
| (ay) | ai | ea |
| ea | ie | (ew) |
| (aw) | au | ee |
| oi | ou | (oy) |

5. Let's **foll**___ow___ that **fell**___ow___ to see which restaurant he picks.

6. Button your **c**___oa___**t** all the way to your **thr**___oa___**t**.

7. Emily has thoughts of garlic **br**___ea___**d** in her **h**___ea___**d**.

8. It took us **ab**___ou___**t** four days to paint the **h**___ou___**se**.

9. The **c**___oo___**k sh**___oo___**k** the wooden spoon.

10. Patricia **kn**___ew___ the people in the **n**___ew___**s**.

11. If you **del**___ay___ **spr**___ay___**ing** the rose bush, bugs may infest it.

12. The artist **redr**___ew___ the flowers that **gr**___ew___.

13. Ben will **dr**___aw___ a crab **cl**___aw___ to illustrate his sea garden.

14. The ___oy___**ster** beds will be **destr**___oy___**ed** if we don't save the ocean.

**Extend & Apply**

Write five sentences with two unfinished words that share the same vowel pairs, vowel digraphs, or diphthongs. Have a partner complete your words.

# Reteaching Activities

### Fill It Up

Supply the first and last letters of a word, and have students fill in a vowel pair, vowel digraph, or diphthong to make as many words as they can. Students may add additional letters as needed.
For example:

c_____t (**coat, caught**)

l_____f (**loaf, leaf**)

w____d (**wood, weed, would**)

m____n (**mean, moan**)

r_____d (**read, round**)

### Word Play

Have students use the second exercise on page 42 as a guide to write five or six sentences about a particular subject. Ask students to include two words in each sentence that contain a vowel pair, a vowel digraph, or a diphthong. Students should leave blanks in the words where each vowel pair, vowel dipgrah, or diphthong would go. Have students trade exercises with a partner and work to fill in the blanks correctly.

## Assessing the Skill

**Check Up** Make sure that students understand how to complete the exercises on pages 41–42. Remind students that on page 42 they should use the context of the sentence to help them find the right answer.

**Observational Assessment** Observe students as they complete the exercises in this lesson. Identify specific areas in which students may benefit from additional instruction. Remind students to say words softly to themselves and listen carefully for the vowel sounds.

**Student Skills Assessment** Use the checklist found on page 29H to keep track of each student's progress in understanding vowels, vowel pairs, vowel digraphs, and diphthongs.

**Writing Conference** Meet informally with each student to discuss his or her written work. Note areas of improvement and make constructive suggestions for other areas in which the student can improve. Encourage the student to do self-evaluation, naming areas in which he or she thinks there has been improvement, and areas that could use additional work. Set informal goals for the next meeting.

Group together students who need further instruction in vowel pairs, vowel digraphs, and diphthongs and have them complete the *Reteaching Activities*. Turn to page 29C for alternate assessment methods.

# Combining Consonants with Phonograms

## Objectives

- **To understand how phonograms combine with consonants to make words**

- **To read, form, and write words made by combining phonograms with consonants**

## Warming Up

- Write the following rhyme on the board and have a student read it aloud.

  When the blazing sun is gone,

  When it nothing shines upon,

  Then you show your little **light,**

  Twinkle, twinkle all the **night.**

- Ask a volunteer to underline the words **light** and **night.** Tell students that the letters **ight** form a phonogram.

## Teaching the Lesson

- Have students read the definition of phonogram in the Helpful Hint on page 43. Emphasize that a phonogram is one syllable. Ask for examples of other phonograms.

- Explain that words with more than one syllable may have more than one phonogram.

- Have students read the rest of the Helpful Hint to discover how phonograms and consonants combine.

- Ask students to give other examples of words made by combining consonants with the phonograms in the Helpful Hint box.

---

Name _____

> **Helpful Hint**

You know that a **phonogram** is a syllable that has a vowel or vowels plus one or more consonants. Phonograms have only one vowel sound. Here are some phonograms:

all     ame     en     ight     ing     uck     ump

Notice how **phonograms** and **consonants** are combined in each of these words:

luck = l + uck          tightening = t + ight + en + ing

ballgame = b + all + g + ame

 **Three words in each set have the same phonogram. Underline those words. On the line, write the phonogram they share.**

1. bump  lamp  lumpy  Durham  umpire     The phonogram is ___ump___.
2. wick  line  link  refine  Pinehurst      The phonogram is ___ine___.
3. stall  bawl  mayor  today  Fayetteville    The phonogram is ___ay___.
4. rocket  Roanoke  pickle  mock  locker    The phonogram is ___ock___.
5. stung  linger  Wilmington  single  winter  The phonogram is ___ing___.
6. valley  awning  paws  alley  fawn        The phonogram is ___aw___.

**On the lines, write the six phonograms that you wrote above. For each, write two words that share that phonogram.**

Possible answers:

7. Phonogram ___ump___ : ___dump___ and ___jump___
8. Phonogram ___ine___ : ___fine___ and ___mine___
9. Phonogram ___ay___ : ___way___ and ___day___
10. Phonogram ___ock___ : ___sock___ and ___rock___
11. Phonogram ___ing___ : ___sing___ and ___wing___
12. Phonogram ___aw___ : ___saw___ and ___law___

> **CHALLENGE**
>
> Nashville, Tennessee, and Asheville, North Carolina, are cities that have the phonogram ash in their names. Write the names of two Southern cities or towns that share a different phonogram.

---

# UNIVERSAL ACCESS
## Meeting Individual Needs

### Tactile Learners

Prepare consonant cards and phonogram cards. Have students work with a partner to make words combining the consonant and phonogram cards. One partner may arrange the cards, while the other partner keeps a record of the words they make. Students may use a dictionary to check their words.

### Logical Learners

Have students prepare a "Guide to Phonograms," in which they show how phonograms can be combined with consonants to form words. They may display the information as a chart or a graphic organizer. Have students present the chart to their classmates and invite them to use it to form new words.

| ale | all | ame | est | ide | ight | in | ink | ore |
|-----|-----|-----|-----|-----|------|----|----|-----|

1. We begin our trip from home in the Florida city of Fort Lauderd**ale**.

2. We dec**ide** to leave early in the morning, just after dawn.

3. This early start was at my fathers requ**est**.

4. The long, scenic route took us far **in** to the Florida Keys.

5. My best friend Juanita c**ame** along.

6. She said that we m**ight** see dolphins along the way.

7. Our d**est**ination was the popular resort town of Key West.

8. Juanita had been there bef**ore**. She spoke of its fabulous sunsets.

9. We arrived at our hotel at nightf**all**, just in time for dinner.

10. "We serve any fish you can n**ame**," the waiter told us.

11. Juanita and I ordered the yellowf**in** tuna.

12. My parents were del**ight**ed with the menu. They ordered pasta with fresh clams.

13. After dinner, we all walked barefoot along the beach in the moonl**ight**.

14. On the following day, we explored the t**ide**pools near our hotel.

15. I th**ink** our wake-up call will be at 6:00 A.M. tomorrow. That's my dad for you!

**44**

LESSON 20: Combining Consonants with Phonograms

 **Home Involvement Activity** Together, look at a map of Florida, the Sunshine State. Follow the route from Fort Lauderdale to Key West. Make a list of the places you spot along the way that contain the phonograms listed above.

● Read aloud the direction lines on pages 43–44. Have students be creative in items 7–12, but remind them to write actual words.

● Encourage students to consider sentence context in choosing the appropriate phonogram for exercises 1–15 on page 44.

● Make sure students understand the meaning of the words **destination**, **yellowfin**, and **tidepools**. Then have students complete the exercises independently.

## Curriculum Connections

### Spelling Link

Read aloud the words and sentences below. Then have a volunteer spell each word in bold type orally and write it on the board.

| | |
|---|---|
| **decided** | I **decided** to take a vacation. |
| **moonlight** | I wanted to see the Smoky Mountains by **moonlight**. |
| **destination** | Tennessee was my final **destination**. |
| **nightfall** | At **nightfall** the mountain casts long shadows. |
| **delighted** | We were **delighted** by the views. |
| **request** | I may **request** time off for another vacation soon. |

### Social Studies Link

Display a map of the United States and the Caribbean. Have students locate the Florida Keys. Tell students to use the distance scale to answer these questions: *How many miles do the Florida Keys cover from their northernmost to their southernmost point? How many miles is the southernmost Key from Cuba?*

### Observational Assessment

*Check to see that students can add consonants to phonograms to make new words.*

### English-Language Learners/ESL

Give students phonogram cards **ish, ice,** and **int** and consonant cards. Then give students picture cards for **dish, rice,** and **mint.** Have students make words to match the pictures by placing the correct consonant card in front of the phonogram card.

### Gifted Learners

Challenge students to make a crossword puzzle using words with the phonograms from this lesson. Show students an example of a crossword puzzle for reference. Encourage students to complete one another's puzzles.

### Learners with Special Needs

Additional strategies for supporting learners with special needs can be found on page 29L.

# Combining Consonant Blends with Phonograms

## Objectives

- **To combine consonant blends with phonograms to make words**
- **To use words made by combining consonant blends and phonograms**

## Warming Up

- Write these one-liners on the board:

  Did you hear the one about:

  the new vegetable that can **brush** your teeth? Bristle **sprouts**!

  the banana that saw the monkeys and **split**?

  the **grape** that called for help because it was in a jam?

- Underline the words containing consonant blends and then circle the blends.

- Have students pronounce the underlined words, listening for the sounds the consonant blends make.

## Teaching the Lesson

- Explain that many words begin with letter combinations called consonant blends.

- Write consonant blends such as **fl**, **bl**, and **scr** on the board. Ask students how they are the same and how they are different. (same: all consonants; different: different letters, the first two have two letters and the last one has three)

- Remind students that you can hear individual letter sounds in a consonant blend.

- Read aloud the Helpful Hint on page 45. Have students add different consonant blends to the phonograms in the box. Challenge them to list as many words as they can and then sort the words by phonogram.

---

Name _____

### ► Helpful Hint

A **consonant blend** is two or three consonants sounded together so that each letter is heard. Notice how the **phonograms** and the **consonant blends** are combined in each of these words:

block = bl + ock        flight = fl + ight        scrap = scr + ap

**Complete the name of each picture. Combine the consonant blend in the box with one of the phonograms in the yellow box next to it.**

| 1 | 2 |
|---|---|
| sn _ore_ | fl _ock_ |

| 3 | 4 |
|---|---|
| cl _ap_ | cr _ane_ |

ane
ap
ock
ore

### ► WORK TOGETHER

Get together with a partner to list as many words as you can that combine a consonant blend with the phonogram ap or ight. Then choose three words and write a sentence for each.

**Read about the writer Zora Neale Hurston. Fill in the circle of the word that completes each sentence. Then write the word on the line. Hint: Each answer combines a consonant blend with a phonogram.**

5. Zora was a ___bright___ girl who grew up in the South.
   ● bright     ○ thin     ○ tired

6. She loved to listen to stories told in the general ___store___.
   ● store     ○ ship     ○ pharmacy

7. Later, she studied anthropology and took ___trips___ through the South.
   ○ caps     ● trips     ○ chores

8. She used her experiences to write about ___small___-town life.
   ○ poor     ● small     ○ shop

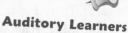

Zora Neale Hurston
(1903–1960)

LESSON 21: Combining Consonant Blends with Phonograms     **45**

---

# UNIVERSAL ACCESS
## Meeting Individual Needs

### Logical Learners

Have students make a chart with several columns, and label each column head with a consonant blend: **sp, pr, st, pl, cl.** Give students a list of words. Tell students to write the words on the chart under the heading that matches the consonant blend. Then have students sort the words by phonogram.

### Auditory Learners

Make cards for the consonant blends **cl, st, pr, gr, sp, spr, pr, fl,** and **pl.** Then read these words aloud: **flat, places, prices, sports, springs, great, pride, climb,** and **state.** Emphasize the sound of each consonant blend. Have students hold up the card for the consonant blend they hear at the beginning of each word.

**Each box gives three consonant blends and three phonograms. Match the blends and the phonograms in each box to build three words. Then write the words on the lines.**

| 1 | | | 2 | | | 3 | | |
|---|---|---|---|---|---|---|---|---|
| cl | — | ide | gr | — | orts | pr | — | aces |
| st | — | imb | sp | — | eat | fl | — | ices |
| pr | — | ate | spr | — | ings | pl | — | at |

1.
climb

state

pride

2.
great

sports

springs

3.
prices

flat

places

**Use a word from the boxes above to complete each sentence about West Virginia, the Mountain State.**

4. With a population of about 2 million, West Virginia is the 35th largest _____state_____.

5. About two-thirds of the state is _____flat_____.

6. Yet there are also hills and mountains to _____climb_____.

7. West Virginia boasts _____prices_____ that tourists can afford.

8. It also offers interesting _____places_____ to see.

9. For example, you might take a dip in one of the state's mineral water _____springs_____.

10. Harpers Ferry is another _____great_____ place to visit.

11. Skiers can enjoy winter _____sports_____ at the Snowshoe Ski Resort.

12. The state parks are another source of state _____pride_____.

*Harpers Ferry, West Virginia*

LESSON 21: Combining Consonant Blends with Phonograms

**Home Involvement Activity** Imagine that relatives or family friends are visiting your state for the first time. List some top tourist attractions in your area. Which do you like best? Which might they like? Talk about why.

---

## English-Language Learners/ESL

List these verbs on the board: **flight, snore, clap, climb, snap, scratch,** and **trot.** Demonstrate the action and have students pronounce each word. Then have students point to the consonant blend at the beginning of the word. Extend the activity by asking students to use the words in sentences.

## Gifted Learners

Have students list words that contain a consonant blend and the phonogram **ing.** (**spring, string, swing, sling, fling, bring, cling**) Then have them write song lyrics about spring. If possible, have them use a melody they already know and teach the song to the class.

## Learners with Special Needs

Additional strategies for supporting learners with special needs can be found on page 29L.

---

• Read aloud the directions on pages 45–46. Tell students they will need to use context clues to make the correct choice for items 5–8 on page 45.

• For items 1–3 on page 46, tell students to draw a line to connect the consonant blend with the correct phonogram before they write the word on the line. Remind students that they will be using the words from the first exercise on page 46 to answer items 4–12.

**Intervention Strategy**

Turn to page 29K for an Intervention Strategy designed to help students who need extra support with this lesson.

## Curriculum Connections

### Spelling Link

Hold an informal spelling bee. Ask students to take turns spelling these words aloud: **bright, great, climb, spring, flock, snore, scrap,** and **block.** After they spell the word correctly, ask students to write the word on the board and identify the consonant blend and the phonogram.

### Multicultural Connection

Zora Neale Hurston spent much of her life in Eatonville, Florida, which is famous as "the first incorporated African American municipality in the United States." Eatonville hosts an annual Zora Neale Hurston festival, which showcases cultural workshops and artistic performances. Have students research Zora Neale Hurston and her writings and read selected items to their classmates.

### Observational Assessment

*Note whether students can read, form, and write words made by combining consonant blends with phonograms.*

# Combining More Consonant Blends with Phonograms

## Objectives

- **To combine consonant blends with phonograms to make words**
- **To identify consonant blends and phonograms in longer words**
- **To read, form, and write words containing consonant blends and phonograms**

## Warming Up

- Write this advertisement on the board and have a student read it aloud.

  Are you a hungry bookworm? Take a **break** at the **Springtime** Bookshop. We sell books about **greenhouses**, **blacksmiths**, **brownstones**, **blueberries**, and much more.

- Have students list all the words that have consonant blends before a phonogram. Ask a volunteer to identify the words that have more than one blend. (**blacksmiths**, **brownstones**)

## Teaching the Lesson

- Remind students that they have learned how to combine consonant blends with phonograms to make words. Explain that some words contain more than one consonant blend and combination of a phonogram.

- Return to the words identified during the *Warming-Up* exercise. Have students circle the consonant blends and underline the phonogram.

- Write the blends **pl, str, gr, br** and the phonogram **ay** on the board. Have volunteers combine and say the words: **play**, **stray**, **gray**, and **bray.** Ask students to suggest other blends to combine with the phonogram. (**spray, clay, sway, stay**)

- Read aloud the Helpful Hints on page 47.

47

---

Name _____

### Helpful Hints

Many words combine **consonant blends** and **phonograms**. Look at these examples:

flake = fl + ake          prank = pr + ank

Some words can have more than one **consonant blend** and one **phonogram**.

screenplay = scr + een + pl + ay

Sprockets

**Each pair of words has the same phonogram. Find the phonogram and underline it in both words.**

| | | | | | | |
|---|---|---|---|---|---|
| 1. sprocket | smock | 2. spice | splice | 3. blink | crinkle |
| 4. bright | frightful | 5. plump | trumpet | 6. request | presto |
| 7. strainer | drainage | 8. crankshaft | blanket | 9. explore | restore |
| 10. strip | clipper | 11. hideaway | bride | 12. squall | mall |

**Write a word from above to complete each statement.**

13. To travel in an unknown place is to ___explore___.
14. Something that causes fear is ___frightful___.
15. An Italian word meaning "fast" is ___presto___.
16. To separate liquids from solids, you could use a ___strainer___.
17. To cause to wrinkle is to ___crinkle___.
18. A covering for a bed is a ___blanket___.
19. An apronlike garment worn over clothing is a ___smock___.
20. A musical instrument is a ___trumpet___.

### WORD STRATEGY

Words with two or more syllables can have more than one consonant blend and one phonogram. To unlock a long word, look for blends and phonograms. Try it:

blacksnake
bridegroom

Write a sentence for each word.

---

# UNIVERSAL ACCESS
## Meeting Individual Needs

### Auditory Learners

Have students work with a partner. Give pairs the following set of word cards: **blink, spice, strainer, bright, flake, slate,** and **smock.** One student turns over a card and reads it aloud. The partner must say a word that begins with a different consonant blend but contains the same phonogram. Give one point for every correct word.

### Visual Learners

On the board, write the words from the box on page 48. Give a different color chalk to each of four students. Assign one of these phonograms to each student: **ip, ay, ink,** and **oke.** When you say, "Go!" have students find their phonograms in three words and underline them. Then have students add to the list one more word with the same phonogram.

⭐ **Read the twelve words in the box. Four phonograms appear three times each. Write these four phonograms on the lines below.**

| | | | | | |
|---|---|---|---|---|---|
| clay | smoke | sprinkler | clipping | drink | crayfish |
| brink | slipshod | broke | stray | spoke | trip |

1. ___ay___    2. ___oke___    3. ___ink___    4. ___ip___

⭐ **Use the words from the box above to complete the sentences.**

5. It's a good idea to ___drink___ plenty of water in the hot sun.

6. Another word for *voyage* is ___trip___.

7. I cut out the newspaper ___clipping___ that had a photograph of my dog.

8. Mom let me keep the ___stray___ cat I found.

9. Roberto made puppets out of modeling ___clay___.

10. I was on the ___brink___ of tears when I didn't make the team.

11. The plumbers did a ___slipshod___ job, and the pipe burst.

12. Three synonyms of ___broke___ are *cracked, fractured,* and *split.*

13. ___Crayfish___ look like little lobsters.

14. The past tense of *speak* is ___spoke___.

15. Dad installed a new ___sprinkler___ system for watering our lawn.

16. Thick black ___smoke___ covered the Everglades as the fire raged.

48    LESSON 22: Combining More
Consonant Blends with Phonograms

**Home Involvement Activity** Look over the words from this lesson. Try to make up a funny story that uses several of the words. Take turns telling your stories. Tape-record the best ones to play back and assess at a later time.

---

**English-Language Learners/ESL**

Have students work with partners to look through magazines for pictures of items whose names contain consonant blends combined with phonograms. Have students cut out the pictures and write the names of the items pictured on cards. Then have students match the cards with the pictures.

**Gifted Learners**

Have students invent compound words following this rule: The word must make sense and must use the same phonogram twice. Some examples might be: **smartcart** (a self-propelled shopping cart), **knockrock** (a door knocker made of stone). Students may illustrate their favorites.

**Learners with Special Needs**

Additional strategies for supporting learners with special needs can be found on page 29L.

---

## Practicing the Skill

- Read aloud the direction lines on pages 47–48. Do the first item in each exercise together.

- Point out that the second exercise on page 47 uses some of the words from the first exercise.

- Tell students they will need to use context clues to make the correct choice for items 5–16 on page 48.

## Curriculum Connections

### Spelling Link

Read each sentence and emphasize the spelling words the students are to write. Remind students that these words contain consonant blends.

> The **sprinklers** came on by themselves one night at school.
>
> We think it might have been a **prank**.
>
> Luckily, there was good **drainage**.
>
> It took weeks to **restore** the school back to normal.
>
> Mrs. Fuller wore a **smock** to clean up the mess.
>
> She is never one to do a **slipshod** job.

### Writing Link

- Write the term **compound words** on the board and then write these words below the heading: **crayfish, flagpole, placecard, daybreak,** and **slipshod.**

- Review the definition of compound words. Then have students add more compound words to the list on the board.

- Finally, ask students to choose three words from the list. Challenge them to write a story incorporating the three words.

### Observational Assessment

*Note whether students can identify consonant blends and phonograms in words of more than one syllable.*

# Connecting Reading and Writing

## Objectives

- **To read a nonfiction piece and respond to it in writing**
- **To practice comparing, contrasting, and synthesizing information**
- **To write a paragraph that compares and contrasts**

## Warming Up

### Comprehension Skills

- Display two pictures of things that are similar, such as an apartment house and a private house. Ask students how they are alike and different. List responses on the board. Explain that when you **compare and contrast**, you analyze how things are alike and how they are different.
- Remind students that **synthesizing** is putting together the ideas within a piece of writing and making sense of them.

## Teaching the Lesson

- Suggest that students review the selection to answer the first question.
- For the second question, students should synthesize the ideas presented in the article.
- To answer the third question, students can use reference sources to find information about pollution areas. Have them list similarities and differences between the Everglades and another polluted area.

## Practicing the Skill

Read the directions on page 50. Discuss reference sources that students can use to find the information they need. Remind students to first list the similarities and differences. Ask students to use some words and phrases found in the box on page 50.

---

Name _____

⭐ Read about how people are rescuing the Everglades from pollution. Then answer the questions that follow.

# Saving the Everglades

from a nonfiction article in **Time for Kids** magazine

Everglades National Park in Florida doesn't look like much from an airplane. But a closer look shows a busy natural world. Hundreds of kinds of animals live in the Everglades.

FLORIDA

But the Everglades is in serious trouble. After years of bad planning, the Everglades is dying. Dozens of its many animals are threatened. Some of its plants and flowers are disappearing. But help for the Everglades is under way. Humans are rescuing the Everglades and its wildlife from death by pollution.

When large numbers of people first moved to Florida more than a century ago, the Everglades was thought to be nothing but swampland. Builders tried to drain the swamp. Farms and cities sprang up where alligators used to run freely. In the 1920s, engineers straightened rivers. They hoped to stop flooding and keep water supplies stable for farms and cities. The plan worked.

But the changes also harmed the Everglades. The area shrank in size by half. Much of the fresh water disappeared. And the numbers of birds, alligators, and other animals shrank, too.

Now everyone is aware of the importance of the Everglades. Farmers are aware of the dangers of the chemicals they are using. And engineers are putting rivers back on their old winding courses. In all, billions of dollars will be spent to help the Everglades. For most people, that is money well spent.

1. People tried to drain the swamp and straighten rivers, which harmed plants and animals.
2. People are learning about the dangers of farm chemicals, and engineers are putting the rivers back on old courses.
3. Answers will vary.

###  Reader's Response

1. What happened to Florida's Everglades?
2. How are people trying to save the Everglades today?
3. Compare the Everglades with another place that has been hurt by pollution. How are the two places alike? What are the differences?

---

# UNIVERSAL ACCESS
# Meeting Individual Needs

### Visual Learners

Remind students that a Venn diagram can represent similarities and differences. Draw a Venn diagram on the board. Explain that the overlapping area is where students should list similarities, and the areas to the right and the left are for differences. Have students use a Venn diagram to display the information they gathered to answer the third Reader's Response question.

### Kinesthetic Learners

Make a sentence strip for each similarity and difference that students named in the *Warming-Up* exercise. Make a Venn diagram on the floor with tape. Have students place sentence strips in the appropriate sections of the Venn diagram.

### Learners with Special Needs

Additional strategies for supporting learners with special needs can be found on page 29L.

You probably know that alligators and crocodiles are cousins. But did you know that the Everglades is the only place in the United States where American alligators and crocodiles live together? Look at the pictures below. Can you tell the difference between an alligator and a crocodile? How?

⭐ Write one or more paragraphs that compare the American alligator with the American crocodile. Do some research. Describe at least two ways that these animals are alike. Then write about their differences. Include a drawing. Use at least two of these words.

American alligator

| Words to Show Similarities: | both | similarly | in the same way |
| | like | alike | by comparison |
| Words to Show Differences: | but | yet | however | unlike |
| | by contrast | | differs from |

Answers will vary.

_____

_____

_____

_____

_____

_____

_____

_____

**Writer's Tip**

Make a comparison chart before writing. In one column, list how the animals are alike. In the other column, list how they are different. Use your chart to write your essay.

**Writer's Challenge**

Choose two animals that are similar, such as a panda and a raccoon or a panda and a bear. In a paragraph, explain how these two animals are alike. Then describe their differences. Compare the two animals' size and shape as well as their diet and habits. Summarize your "findings" at the end.

American crocodile

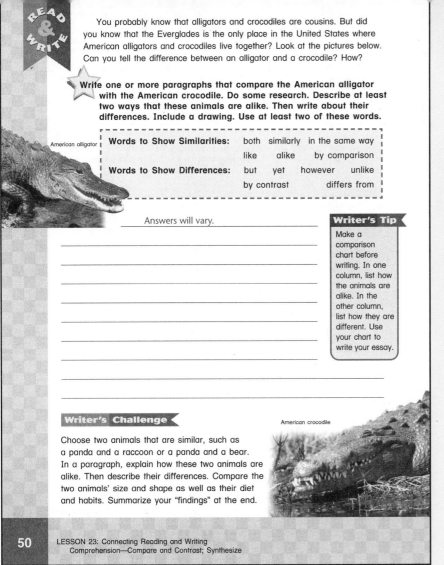

LESSON 23: Connecting Reading and Writing
Comprehension—Compare and Contrast; Synthesize

# The Writing Process

Discuss the purpose of comparing and contrasting. (to explain how things are alike and different) Explain that students will synthesize the information they gather and present it clearly to readers.

**Prewrite** Have students use two columns or a Venn diagram to organize information about the American alligator and the American crocodile. Suggest that they use encyclopedias and nature magazines, or call a local zoo for information. Remind them to take clear notes.

**Write** Ask students to use words and phrases that signal whether they are comparing or contrasting information as they write. Make sure they use some of the words and phrases found in the box on page 50.

**Revise** Have students trade their work with a partner. Ask them to check that the questions have been answered. Suggest that students include a drawing that relates to the written text.

**Proofread** Have students proofread their work to check for errors in grammar, punctuation, and spelling.

**Publish** Have students copy their final drafts onto page 50 or a separate sheet of paper. They may attach the picture to the final draft.

 **Computer Connection** Share the following tip with students who use a word processor to do their writing.

● You can choose fonts (typefaces), type sizes, and styles such as bold or italic for your documents.

● Most programs show the font name and size in a toolbar on the screen. Highlight and click on the font or type size you want.

● Remember to first highlight the text you want to change.

**Portfolio** Have students add their completed comparisons to their portfolios.

## English-Language Learners/ESL

Show photographs of the American alligator and the American crocodile. Ask students to discuss the similarities and differences with fluent speakers. Encourage students to use the phrases of comparison and contrast from the box on page 50 as they conduct their discussions.

## Gifted Learners

After students have written their comparisons, invite those who are interested to continue researching an aspect of the topic for a more in-depth report. Have students reread their comparisons, underlining the most interesting ideas or points. Students can choose one of these ideas for the focus of their new research. Encourage volunteers to use class time to work on their reports. Invite students to present their findings to the class.

# Combining Consonant Digraphs with Phonograms

## Objectives

- **To combine consonant digraphs with phonograms to create words**
- **To use words that contain consonant digraphs and phonograms in writing**

## Warming Up

- Write this sentence on the board and have a student read it aloud.

   The fire **chief shook** his head when he saw the **wheat** field had burned.

- Write the words **chief, shook,** and **wheat** on the board and ask students to find the phonograms and underline them. **(ief, ook, eat)**

- Have students pronounce the first two letters of each word. Remind students that pairs of consonants that represent one sound are called consonant diagraphs.

## ⭐ Teaching the Lesson

- Remind students that consonant diagraphs are different from consonant blends. To review the differences between them, give students the following example.

- Write the words **stock** and **shock** on the board. Pronounce the first two letters of each word with students. Point out that when you say the word **stock,** you can hear both the **s** and the **t** sounds that make up the **st** blend.

- In contrast, when you say the **sh** that begins the word **shock,** you do not hear two letter sounds. You hear one sound— the **sh** sound. The **sh** sound is unlike the **s** sound of the **h** sound.

- Read aloud the Helpful Hint on page 51 as students follow along silently.

**51**

---

Name _____

### Helpful Hint

Remember that a **consonant digraph** is two consonants that together stand for one sound. Notice how the **phonograms** and **consonant digraphs** combine to form these words:

chip = ch + ip          shop = sh + op          thick = th + ick

⭐ **Complete the name of each picture by combining the consonant digraph in the box with one of the phonograms in the yellow box below.**

| ack | alk | orn | ip |
|-----|-----|-----|-----|

| 1 | 2 | 3 | 4 |
|---|---|---|---|
| th_orn_ | wh_ip_ | ch_alk_ | sh_ack_ |

⭐ **Read about South Carolina's Spoleto Festival. Write the word from the yellow box below that completes each sentence. Note that each word combines a consonant digraph with a phonogram.**

| things | chance | where | shares |
|--------|--------|-------|--------|

5. South Carolina is ___where___ the Spoleto Festival takes place every year.

6. The state's largest port, Charleston, ___shares___ this arts festival with the world.

7. Visitors can watch dancers dance, hear singers sing, and do many other interesting ___things___.

8. Although the festival attracts famous artists, it also gives local performers the ___chance___ to perform.

**WORK TOGETHER**

Work with a group. List music-related words, such as song titles or instruments, that combine a consonant digraph with a phonogram.

LESSON 24: Combining Consonant Digraphs with Phonograms   **51**

---

# UNIVERSAL ACCESS
## Meeting Individual Needs

### Visual Learners

On the board, write the consonant digraphs **sh, wh, ch,** and **th.** Have students list several words for each. Tell students to make a word-search puzzle in which the words appear horizontally, vertically, and diagonally. When students have finished, ask them to trade puzzles with a partner.

### Logical Learners

Ask students to make a Venn diagram showing similarities and differences between consonant blends and consonant digraphs. (Possible similarity: Both are made up of consonants. Possible difference: Consonant blends stand for more than one sound, whereas consonant digraphs represent only one sound.)

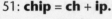

⭐ **Add** the correct phonogram from the box to complete the word in each sentence. Use a phonogram only once.

| ame | are | at | est | ill | ine | ing | ink | ock | uck |

1. Is there another town with the same name as your town? Which one took the name first is probably the furth___est___ thing from your mind.

2. You might th___ink___ that people don't care about such things.

3. However, the people of Wash___ing___ton, Georgia, care very much. This town claims to be the first town named for our very first President.

4. This claim might get a ch___ill___y reception in other towns with that name.

5. The people of Washington, North Carolina, for one, would be sh___ock___ed to hear of Georgia's claim.

6. In Washington, North Carolina, people say th___at___ the honor of being the first town named for George Washington belongs to them.

7. These people would ch___uck___le at Georgia's claim. They would politely explain that Washington actually visited their town in 1791.

8. One town that used to sh___are___ in this "competition" was Washington, Kentucky, but this is no longer the case.

9. In 1990, this town left the battle with barely a wh___ine___ or a whimper. In that year, the town joined with a neighboring town and took the name "Old Washington."

10. Yet the battle still rages in other towns, and the claim for Washington's n___ame___ lives on.

A statue of George Washington

⭐ **Choose** two of the words you wrote above. On the lines below, write a sentence for each of the words.

11. ___Answers will vary._____

12. _____

LESSON 24: Combining Consonant Digraphs with Phonograms

 **Home Involvement Activity** Many towns and cities share the same name, like Springfield or Portland. With your family, brainstorm a list of places with identical names. How many can you list?

---

## Practicing the Skill

● Read aloud the direction lines on pages 51–52. Do the first item in each exercise with students.

● For exercises 1–10 on page 52, explain that the phonogram may be "buried" within the word if it has more than one syllable.

● For exercises 11–12 on page 52, encourage students to include context in their sentences to help show the meaning of the words they chose.

## Curriculum Connections

### Spelling Link

● On a separate sheet of paper, have students write these spelling words as you read them aloud: **chilly, chuckle, furthest, share, shocked, think,** and **whine**.

● Ask students to circle consonant digraphs and underline phonograms. Then have students write a sentence using each word.

### Social Studies Link

● The Charleston Museum of the Karpeles Manuscript Library in South Carolina houses many national treasures. Among them is the original draft for the *Bill of Rights,* as well as the *Thanksgiving Proclamation* signed by George Washington.

● Have students do research to find the address of the museum. Then ask them to write to the museum's education department requesting information about its collection.

### Observational Assessment

*Check to see that students can correctly identify and pronounce consonant digraphs in words.*

---

### English-Language Learners/ESL

Tell students to read the words for items 1–4 on page 51. Have students work with a fluent partner to combine the same consonant digraphs **(ch, sh, th,** and **wh)** with different phonograms. Suggest that students write their answers in the format used at the top of page 51: **chip = ch + ip.**

### Gifted Learners

Ask students to find out about the "Charleston," a lively dance that originated in South Carolina in the early 1900s. Have students research how to do the dance. Help students locate the music and have volunteers demonstrate the dance for the class.

### Learners with Special Needs

Additional strategies for supporting learners with special needs can be found on page 29L.

# Combining Consonants, Consonant Blends, and Consonant Digraphs with Phonograms

## Objectives

- **To combine consonants, consonant blends, and consonant digraphs with phonograms to create new words**
- **To write words with consonants, consonant blends, or consonant digraphs combined with phonograms**

## Warming Up

- Write this rhyme on the board and read it aloud to students:

  Words of every **shape** and **stripe**,

  Words like "**grape**" and words like "**ripe**,"

  share one feature but not two.

  Phonograms alike, it's true,

  What's the difference? Now you know!

  The word beginnings change the show.

- Ask students what the words **shape/grape** and **stripe/ripe** have in common. (the same phonogram) Ask how they are different. (the beginnings are different)

## Teaching the Lesson

- Direct students' attention to the chart on page 53. Have volunteers identify the phonograms, the consonant blends, and the consonant digraphs.

- Read aloud the Helpful Hints on pages 53–54. Discuss the descriptions of hink-pinks, hinky-pinkys, and hinkity-pinkities.

53

---

Name _____

> **Helpful Hint**
>
> You know that you can build many words by combining **consonants**, **consonant blends**, and **consonant digraphs** with **phonograms**.

 Combine the phonogram in each box and the consonants, consonant blends, and consonant digraphs to form words below.

| 1 **ain** | 2 **ake** | 3 **op** |
|---|---|---|
| r___ain___y | f_ake_ | sl_op_py |
| gr_ain_ | br_ake_ | st_op_ped |
| ch_ain_ | clamb_ake_ | dr_op_ping |
| dr_ain_pipe | milksh_ake_ | l_op_sided |
| eyestr_ain_ | sn_ake_root | sharecr_op_per |

⭐ Use each phonogram below and the consonants, consonant blends, and consonant digraphs in the yellow boxes to form words. Then use the words to complete the sentences.

___aw   | s   cl   th   str |

4. Drink your milkshake with a _straw_.

5. Some animals can grow a new _claw_.

6. The past tense of *see* is _saw_.

7. You'll need to _thaw_ the steak before eating it.

___oke   | y   str   br |

8. The team of oxen are in a _yoke_.

9. The rope _broke_ under the weight.

10. The golfer led by one _stroke_ after the first round.

> **CHALLENGE**
>
> Use the phonogram ip and one initial consonant, one consonant blend, and one consonant digraph to write a sentence that makes sense. Here are some sample words you could use to write your sentence:
>
> dip
>
> drip
>
> ship

---

# UNIVERSAL ACCESS
## Meeting Individual Needs

### Auditory Learners

Have students use the words on pages 53–54 in a poetry-writing workshop. Tell students to be creative but to make sure that their writing makes sense. After they have finished, have students read their work aloud to their classmates.

### Kinesthetic Learners

Prepare cards with words from this unit, such as **grain, shake, stopped, stroke, claw, rain, chain, thick, sloppy.** Place the cards around the room where students can easily see them. Call out a description, such as *starts with a consonant digraph, rhymes with* **cake.** Have students walk to the correct word card.

A **hink-pink** is a pair of 1-syllable words that rhyme.    **square chair**
A **hinky-pinky** is a pair of 2-syllable words that rhyme.    **quicker ticker**
A **hinkity-pinkity** is a pair of 3-syllable words that rhyme.    **persistent assistant**
These word pairs combine consonants with phonograms.
All three of these rhyming word pairs also have meaning.
Note that **reachable teachable** is not a hinkity-pinkity.
It rhymes, but it has no real meaning on its own.

 Complete each sentence by writing the other half of the hink-pink, hinky-pinky, or hinkity-pinkity. Choose words from the box below. Be careful! Just because the words rhyme doesn't mean that they are spelled alike.

| | | | | | |
|---|---|---|---|---|---|
| latitude | woolly | drab | French | frock | hefty |
| election | shocking | standing | couch | fleeting | construction |

1. When we saw the strange clothing in the fashion show, we went into ___frock___ **shock.**

2. A person who sits on the sofa and complains is a ___couch___ **grouch.**

3. The gymnast made a ___standing___ **landing** after her vault.

4. In a Paris park, we sat down on a ___French___ **bench.**

5. The overweight left-handed pitcher is quite a ___hefty___ **lefty.**

6. Our quick get-together was a ___fleeting___ **meeting.**

7. My friend in the candidate's office is my ___election___ **connection.**

8. A boring conversation is filled with ___drab___ **blab.**

9. If you insist that your town is located in the very best position, you have a ___latitude___ **attitude.**

10. Anything that slows down building is a ___construction___ **obstruction.**

11. An unexpected loud banging on your door is a ___shocking___ **knocking.**

12. That big, mean, nasty sheep is a ___woolly___ **bully.**

LESSON 25: Combining Consonants, Consonant Blends, and Consonant Digraphs with Phonograms

 **Home Involvement Activity** Make up your own hink-pinks, hinky-pinkies, and hinkity-pinkities. Say them aloud to each other for some **winning grinning**!

---

### English-Language Learners/ESL

Encourage students to share rhymes from their language of origin. Have students write them on the board and read them aloud to their classmates.

Ask students to translate the rhymes into English and teach them to the class. Point out that the English translations will probably not rhyme.

### Gifted Learners

Have students prepare hink-pinks, hinky-pinkies, and hinkity-pinkities. Challenge students to customize them by creating "consonant blend hink-pinks," "consonant digraph hink-pinks," and so on. For example a "consonant digraph hink-pink":
**What is a skinny facial feature?** (a thin chin)

### Learners with Special Needs

Additional strategies for supporting learners with special needs can be found on page 29L.

---

## Practicing the Skill

● Read aloud the direction lines on pages 53–54. For items 4–10 on page 53, point out the two phonograms that students will use to build their answers. **(aw, oke)**

● On page 54, work through the first item with students. If they need additional help, allow them to complete exercises 2–12 with a partner.

## Curriculum Connections

### Spelling Link

Have students write these spelling words on the board: **fake, chain, chair, square, grain,** and **brake.** Tell students they can create three hink-pinks with these words. Have them write the hink-pink that fits each description.

1. What is a phony floor pedal in a car? **(fake brake)**

2. What is a seat with four equal sides? **(square chair)**

3. What is a head full of wheat? **(grain brain)**

### Math Link

Supply students with an Amtrak train schedule for the *Auto Train*, which begins in Silver Springs, Maryland, travels through the Southeast and terminates in Sanford, Florida. Have students study the train schedule and then write one- or two-word problems about train travel, based on the information it contains. Ask them to trade their word problems with a partner and solve each other's problems.

### Observational Assessment

*Check to see whether students can easily identify and pronounce words containing consonants, consonant blends, and/or consonant digraphs.*

# Connecting Reading and Writing

## Objectives

- **To read a nonfiction article and respond to it in writing**
- **To practice summarizing and identifying the main idea and details**
- **To write a paragraph**

## Warming Up

### Comprehension Skills

- Display a magazine article and read the title and subheadings. Ask students what they think the article is about.

- Write the title and subheads in outline form. Have students list details from the article and add them to the outline.

- Remind students that finding the **main idea** and **details** and then **summarizing** the ideas are reading skills. Point out that not every statement in an article supports the main idea.

## Teaching the Lesson

- To answer the first Reader's Response question, have students reread the article carefully.

- Suggest that students look for clues in the title and in the introduction to answer the second question.

- For the third question, remind students to include details to support their main idea.

## Practicing the Skill

- Read the directions on page 56. Discuss how finding 400-year-old artifacts is like opening a time capsule. Have students list items they would put in a time capsule and ask them to explain the importance of the items.

- Refer students to the Writer's Tip for transition words they may use to connect ideas.

**55**

---

Name _____

Read about how a new discovery in Virginia is showing people what life was like in Jamestown, the first permanent English settlement in North America. Then answer the questions that follow.

## Digging Up the Past

from a nonfiction article in Time for Kids magazine

**B**rent Smith of Houston, Texas, cannot take his eyes off the skeleton. Lying in a glass case at the National Geographic Society in Washington, D.C., the skeleton is a mystery. "I just need to know what happened to this guy," says Brent. "What was his name? How did he die?"

That's what historians are wondering, too. The skeleton is nearly 400 years old. It was found in Jamestown, Virginia, site of the first permanent English settlement in America. For years, people thought that the old fort there had been washed away by the James River. But new discoveries, including this skeleton, prove that the fort and its clues to colonial life are buried under the soil.

On May 13, 1607, a ship carrying 104 men and boys from England arrived in Virginia. They named their settlement Jamestown, after Britain's King James. The colonists built a triangle-shaped fort along the river to protect themselves.

Eventually, Jamestown, Virginia's capital, was moved to nearby Williamsburg. Jamestown began to disappear—at least above ground. But what about underground? In April 1994, archaeologist Bill Kelso and others found bits of pottery that could only have been from the 1607 fort. "That first day, we knew we had found it!"

The discoveries are giving scientists and historians the best picture ever of how early colonists lived. They hope to come up with more answers for kids like Brent Smith.

1. Archaeologists have discovered the fort at Jamestown and are digging for clues that will show how colonists lived.
2. A new discovery in Virginia is showing people what life was like in Jamestown.
3. Answers will vary.

*James Fort Construction, May–June 1607*

**Reader's Response**

1. What is happening today in Jamestown, Virginia? Why is it important?

2. What is the main idea of this article?

3. If you could speak to one of the Jamestown settlers, what would you say? Why?

LESSON 26: Connecting Reading and Writing
Comprehension—Main Idea and Details; Summarize

**55**

---

# UNIVERSAL ACCESS
# Meeting Individual Needs

### Tactile Learners

Have students reread the article and then write the main idea and details on separate cards or sentence strips. Mix up the cards or strips and then have students arrange them in outline form. When they have finished, have them discuss how they organized the outline.

### Visual Learners

Students may use an encyclopedia yearbook as a resource for this activity. As they look through the book, have them make notes about issues and events that were significant during a specific time period. Have students list objects to include in a time capsule that would best represent the key issues and events.

### Learners with Special Needs

Additional strategies for supporting learners with special needs can be found on page 29L.

Scientists have uncovered skeletons, armor, beads, keys, pottery, and toys from the original Jamestown settlement. So far, more than 180,000 items have been uncovered, and the digging is still going on! All these discoveries are showing people how the original colonists lived 400 years ago.

**Make a list of items that you and your classmates could put in a time capsule for scientists to find 400 years from now. Your list might include maps, sports equipment, and computers. Then write a paragraph explaining what these items would tell about you and the twenty-first century. State a clear main idea and give your details in logical order. Summarize your ideas at the end. Use at least two of these words.**

| explain | demonstrate | discover | scientists | historians |
|---|---|---|---|---|
| to begin with | besides | also | however | now |
| then | on the other hand | as a result | finally | |

Answers will vary.

_____

_____

_____

_____

_____

_____

_____

### Writer's Tip

Use **transition words**, such as *to begin with*, *however*, and *finally*, to show how your ideas are related. Some transition words can also help you combine shorter sentences.

### Speaker's Challenge

Use the paragraph you wrote to give a speech about what people might find if they "uncovered" your time capsule in the future. Make an outline of your main idea and details. Include a good topic sentence at the beginning and a strong summary at the end.

LESSON 26: Connecting Reading and Writing
Comprehension—Main Ideas and Details; Summarize

### English-Language Learners/ESL

Have students cut out pictures from magazines or make sketches of items they would like to include in a time capsule. Have them work with fluent partners to identify and write the English words for the items.

### Gifted Learners

Encourage students to write a another paragraph about a time capsule from the point of view of someone who lived 400 years ago. This imaginary historical figure should write what he or she would want future generations to learn about and why. Before they begin, have students research the kinds of equipment that were used in the Jamestown settlement or other locations that date back to colonial times.

# The Writing Process

Discuss reasons why informational writing is organized around a main idea and supporting details. (to present information clearly so that it is more useful to the reader) Explain that a summary helps the reader understand the main idea better.

**Prewrite** Have students organize their ideas in an outline with the main ideas as outline headings and details as lettered items under the headings. Remind them to include details that support each main idea. Ask students to check their outlines to see where they use transition words.

**Write** Have students develop a paragraph with an introductory statement, a body, and a conclusion that summarizes their ideas. Remind them that the first sentence in the paragraph should catch the reader's attention.

**Revise** Have students exchange papers to make sure that the main ideas and details are presented in an organized way, that transition words are used properly, and the paper ends with a summary.

**Proofread** Remind students to proofread their work carefully to check for errors in grammar, punctuation, and spelling.

**Publish** Have students copy their final draft onto page 56 or on a separate sheet of paper.

**Computer Connection** Share the following tip with students who use a word processor to do their writing.

● Some word processors contain an outlining feature, which adds bullets to main headings (main ideas) and indents supporting details to show that they are part of the main idea.

● Practice using this feature as you organize your ideas.

**Portfolio** Have students add their finished paragraphs to their portfolios.

# LESSON 27 • UNIT 2
## Student Pages 57–58

# Reviewing and Assessing
## Combining Consonants with Phonograms

## Objective

To review and assess combining consonants, consonant blends and consonant digraphs with phonograms

## Warming Up

Write these two columns of words on the board and then read them aloud.

| | |
|---|---|
| rain | seat |
| law | twice |
| sight | tape |
| greed | sauce |

Ask a volunteer to say the phonograms in each word and then draw lines to match the words that have the same vowel sound. **(rain/tape; law/sauce; sight/twice; greed/seat)**

## Teaching the Lesson

- Read aloud the direction lines for the exercises on page 57. Tell students that in the first exercise they will be looking for words with the same vowel sound. They may find it helpful to say the words softly to themselves.

- Do the first item of the second exercise with students. Suggest that they use the process of elimination if they are having difficulty choosing the correct phonogram.

- Remind students to use context clues in the first exercise on page 58. They may also try the process of elimination to help them find the correct word.

- In the second exercise, suggest that students reread the passage before answering the questions.

57

---

Name _____

⭐ Circle the letter of the word in each row that has the same vowel sound as the phonogram in red.

1. grain   a. grind   b. grin   c.（crane）
2. broke   a.（croak）   b. streak   c. break
3. pale   a. reality   b.（sail）   c. steeple
4. paw   a.（claw）   b. cow   c. blow
5. cake   a. eke   b. weak   c.（steak）
6. play   a. rely   b.（maintain）   c. ready
7. blink   a. blank   b. arch   c.（crinkle）
8. shame   a.（claim）   b. steam   c. sham
9. flight   a. caught   b.（kite）   c. ought
10. slide   a.（rawhide）   b. lid   c. bleed

⭐ Read each sentence. Choose the phonogram from the three in the row that completes *both* unfinished words. Write that phonogram in both spaces.

11. They ch_op_ped off the last act of the very long _op_era.
12. I th_ink_ I know why the stars tw_ink_le in the sky.
13. To my del_ight_, we danced until midn_ight_.
14. Our teacher overs_aw_ the care of a rare tropical mac_aw_.
15. The bl_eat_ing sheep totally def_eat_ed my chance to sleep.
16. It was sh_ock_ing when the manager padl_ock_ed the door.
17. If you want my adv_ice_, it's not worth the sacrif_ice_.
18. Dad bought an _ug_ly new pl_ug_ for the toaster.
19. Firefighters spr_ay_ed water on the runw_ay_.
20. How well can you rec_all_ the plays in baseb_all_?

| | | |
|---|---|---|
|（op）| ip | up |
|（nk）| ing | ick |
| oke | ash |（ight）|
|（aw）| an | at |
| unk |（eat）| ill |
|（ock）| oke | ick |
| ale | ance |（ce）|
| on |（ug）| in |
| ash | or |（ay）|
|（all）| ine | ump |

---

# UNIVERSAL ACCESS
# Meeting Individual Needs

### Kinesthetic Learners

Write a series of phonograms on the chalkboard, such as **ash, ug, ice, eat, unk, an, oke, ought.** Have students pronounce them aloud. Then say a sentence that contains a word with one of the phonograms. Tell students they should stand up when they hear a word with one of the phonograms on the board. Ask the first student who stands up to name the word and the phonogram.

### Visual Learners

Write several phonograms on the board, such as those in the grid on page 57. Have students search through advertising flyers, magazines, or newspapers for words with those phonograms. Have students cut out the words, and any images they wish to include, and arrange them in a phonogram collage. Display students' completed collages.

### Learners with Special Needs

Additional strategies for supporting learners with special needs can be found on page 29L.

Read this passage about Florida's Everglades. For each numbered blank, there is a choice of words below. Circle the letter of the word that best completes the sentence.

The Florida Everglades is a large region of flat, low land. Much of the year, slowly **1** water covers it. In places, the Everglades has **2** of tall, sharp saw grass. There are also small tree islands called hammocks. Deer, panthers, and **3** live on the hammocks.

You have read that in the past, people **4** parts of the Everglades. They dug canals and built roads there for Florida's growing population. Yet development had a high cost. It caused fires and threatened to endanger the land's natural water cycles and animals. People soon saw that if the **5** disappeared, so would the fresh water supply for Florida's cities.

Florida needs the Everglades. It must save its plants and animals. It must protect its water supply. These are great challenges. Luckily, Florida has been taking steps in the **6** direction. The Everglades is now a national park, protected by government laws.

1. a. flowing  b. floating  c. flapping     2. a. foods  b. choices  c. fields

3. a. beaks  b. bears  c. breaks     4. a. drained  b. chained  c. grained

5. a. highlands  b. headlands  c. wetlands     6. a. mighty  b. nightly  c. right

Read the passage again to answer these questions. Circle the letter of the correct answer.

7. The author feels that the Everglades should be
a. drained and covered.
b. painted and photographed.
c. protected and preserved.
d. developed and burned.

8. The word saw grass probably got its name from its
a. short, thick, grasses.
b. sea islands.
c. wispy stems.
d. tall, sharp, teethlike leaves.

Airboat exploring the Everglades

**Extend & Apply**

In a sentence, state the problem faced by Florida's Everglades. In a second sentence, suggest a way to solve it.

58    LESSON 27: Review and Assess

# Reteaching Activities

## Word Chain

Make a 4 x 6 gameboard with these phonograms:

| ance | ick | ame | aw |
|------|-----|-----|-----|
| ight | ock | eak | in |
| unk | aim | ale | op |
| ump | ank | oke | ug |
| ash | all | ide | ow |
| eed | ink | ite | ein |

With a partner, students take turns writing a word using one of the phonograms. The first student to get four words horizontally, diagonally, or vertically, wins the round.

## Poetic License

Have students work together to compile a list of words that rhyme with **Everglades** (words with the **-ade** or **-aid** phonogram). Then ask students to write a short poem about the Everglades. They should base it on what they already know about the Everglades and what they learn from the passage on page 58.

## Assessing the Skill

**Check Up** The exercises on page 57–58 are discussed in *Teaching the Lesson*. Before students complete items 1–6 on page 58 remind them that they are being asked to choose the best answer from three words that combine consonants, consonant blends, and consonant digraphs with phonograms. Point out that using sentence context will help them with this exercise.

Make sure that students understand the directions on pages 57–58 before beginning.

**Observational Assessment** Observe students as they complete the two exercises on page 57. Observe whether they can identify two spellings for the same vowel sound in the first exercise. Also observe whether they can find the phonogram that completes both words in the second exercise.

**Student Skills Assessment** Use the checklist on page 29H to keep a record of each student's progress in combining consonants, consonant blends, and consonant digraphs with phonograms.

**Writing Conference** Meet informally with students to discuss the writing they have done in this unit. Point out areas where improvement has occurred, and make constructive suggestions for other areas in which students need to improve. Encourage students to evaluate their own writing.

Group together students who need further instruction in combining consonants, consonant blends and consonant digraphs with phonograms, and have them complete the *Reteaching Activities*. Turn to page 29C for alternative assessment methods.

# Word Endings, Contractions, and Compound Words

## Theme: Middle West

<table>
<tr><td>

### STANDARDS

- ✪ Read expository text with grade-appropriate fluency and understand its content
- ✪ Develop and strengthen vocabulary by reading and studying words in context
- ✪ Use regular and irregular plurals, contractions, and possessives correctly
- ✪ Identify the number of syllables in compound words

</td><td>

### OBJECTIVES

- ▶ To appreciate nonfiction works about the Middle West
- ▶ To identify inflectional endings and plurals, contractions and the words that form them, and compound words
- ▶ To identify and distinguish between singular and plural possessives
- ▶ To write plurals, possessives, contractions, and compound words

</td></tr>
</table>

### LESSONS

## Assessment Strategies

An overview of assessment strategies appears on page **59C.** It offers multiple suggestions for ways in which teachers can use a variety of unit-specific assessment tools, including **Pretests** and **Post Tests** (pages **59D–59G**), the **Activity Master** (page **59M**), and the **Assessment Checklist** (page **59H**).

## Thematic Teaching

In Unit 3 students learn about inflectional endings, plural nouns, singular and plural possessives, contractions, and compound words. Students encounter these words and word parts in the context of nonfiction selections and exercises related to the theme the *Middle West.*

Students begin their investigation of the Middle West by creating an ad campaign for products from this region, also known as "The Heartland." The resource list below provides titles of books, videos, and other materials that can help students focus their study of the region. Many of the Teacher's Edition lessons in this unit open with theme-related poems, riddles, or tongue twisters. These "hooks" can spark students' interest in the theme and in the play of words.

## Curriculum Integration

### Social Studies
Students research automobile production on page **60,** design a license plate on page **64,** and learn about the word **Hoosier** on page **78.**

### Art
Students list art supplies on page **62** and research different art media on page **70.**

### Math
Students create a bar or line graph on page **68** and write "equations" with compound words on page **86.**

### Science
Students study lakes and waterways on page **66** and research water pollution on page **84.**

## Optional Learning Activities

### Meeting Individual Needs
Most of the Teacher's Edition lessons offer activities for students with distinct learning styles or particular intellectual or sensory strengths. The activities are labeled for learners with the following "styles": **Visual, Kinesthetic, Auditory,** and **Logical.**

### Multicultural Connections
Students research Native American cultures on page **60** and study the Oglala Sioux on page **80.**

### Word Study Strategies
Pages **59I–59J** offer activities that give students practice with word study strategies. Students sort words, build words, and define words in context.

### Universal Access
Exercises tailored to meet the needs of **English-Language Learners** and **Gifted Learners** can be found in almost every Teacher's Edition lesson. Strategies designed to help **Learners with Special Needs,** such as students with Attention Deficit Disorder, can be found on page **59L.**

### Intervention
Page **59K** offers **Intervention Strategies** designed to help students performing below grade level understand the concepts taught in **Lessons 32, 37,** and **40.**

### Reteaching
On page **76** students sort and spell words, and on page **90** students play a game and classify words.

### Technology
Page **59N** offers activities for students who enjoy working with computers or audio/video equipment. In addition, **Computer Connections**—tips for students who use a word processor—can be found on pages **72, 74, 82,** and **88.**

### RESOURCES

**Books**
Harness, Cheryl. *Mark Twain and the Queens of the Mississippi,* NY: Simon & Schuster, 1998.
Warren, Andrea. *Pioneer Girl: Growing Up on the Prairie,* NY: Morrow Junior, 1998.

**Videos**
*Chicago's Riverfront: Where the Present Meets the Past,* Perspective Films, 1992.
*Crazy Horse,* Turner Home Entertainment, 1996.

**CDs**
*Big River,* MCA, 1990.

In Unit 3 students study word endings, contractions, and compound words. To evaluate students' mastery of these skills, use any or all of the assessment methods suggested below.

## Pretests and Post Tests

The tests on pages **59D–59G** assess how well students understand word endings, contractions, and compound words. These tests may be used at the beginning of the unit as a diagnostic tool or at the end of the unit as a formal measure of progress.

## Observational Assessment

Most lessons include a boxed feature prompting teachers to observe students as they work. Each reminder offers specific suggestions for errors, patterns, or signs that indicate whether or not students have grasped key concepts taught in the lesson.

## Using Technology

The activities on page **59N** may be used to evaluate students whose language skills are best shown when using computers or audio/video equipment.

## Performance Assessment

Have students copy the chart below. Then have them complete the chart by adding **s** or **es**, **ed**, and **ing** to each base word. Finally, ask students to write two new base words and add the endings.

| Base Word | s or es | ing | ed |
|-----------|---------|-----|-----|
| mix | _____ | _____ | _____ |
| carry | _____ | _____ | _____ |
| select | _____ | _____ | _____ |
| brag | _____ | _____ | _____ |

## Portfolio Assessment

The portfolio icon in the lesson plans indicates an opportunity for students to add to the body of work in their portfolios. Each student's portfolio will be unique and should contain pieces that the student feels represents his or her best work. You may wish to give students additional opportunities to add to their portfolios.

## Rubric for Writing

| | Always | Sometimes | Never |
|---|---|---|---|
| Uses capitalization, punctuation, spelling, and grammar appropriately | | | |
| Creates a variety of sentences containing words with inflectional endings, contractions, plurals, possessives, and compound words | | | |
| Uses time-order words appropriately to explain a process | | | |
| Uses vivid words to convey meaning through writing | | | |

## Answer Key

**Page 59D**
1. sketches
2. occurring
3. bullied
4. applying
5. they're
6. you'll
7. won't
8. could've
9. valleys
10. lives
11. zeroes
12. women
13. brothers'
14. friend's
15. heroes'
16. cliff's
17. double-park
18. shoelace
19. poison ivy
20. loudspeaker

**Page 59E**
1. hurries, hurried, hurrying
2. splashes, splashed, splashing
3. skips, skipped, skipping
4. wouldn't
5. I've
6. didn't
7. we're
8. batches

9. stories
10. fields
11. wolves
12. echoes
13. feet
14. farmer's
15. parks'
16. wives'
17. moose's
18. class's
19. children's
20. airport
21. flashlight
22. lifeguard
23. teammate
24. turtleneck
25. weekend

**Page 59F**
1. rallied
2. permitting
3. matches
4. marrying
5. who's
6. you're
7. shouldn't
8. we'll
9. batches
10. pantries
11. reefs
12. solos
13. ladies'
14. visitor's
15. men's
16. farmers'
17. trade-off
18. time clock

19. barnyard
20. polar bear

**Page 59G**
1. erases, erased, erasing
2. admits, admitted, admitting
3. applies, applied, applying
4. can't
5. I'm
6. it's
7. they're
8. taxes
9. cavities
10. shelves
11. cuffs
12. cellos
13. trout
14. captain's
15. steamboats'
16. mice's
17. men's
18. visitors'
19. trail's
20. rattlesnake
21. sunrise
22. barefoot
23. waterfall
24. applesauce
25. windmill

Name _____

**Fill in the circle next to the correct form of the word.**

| | | | |
|---|---|---|---|
| **1. sketch** (add **s** or **es**) | ○ sketchs | ○ sketches | ○ sketchies |
| **2. occur** (add **ing**) | ○ occuring | ○ occurying | ○ occurring |
| **3. bully** (add **ed**) | ○ bullied | ○ bullyed | ○ bulled |
| **4. apply** (add **ing**) | ○ appliing | ○ appling | ○ applying |

**Fill in the circle next to the correct contraction form of the words.**

| | | | |
|---|---|---|---|
| **5. they are** | ○ they'er | ○ they're | ○ the'yre |
| **6. you will** | ○ you'll | ○ you'ill | ○ youw'll |
| **7. will not** | ○ will'nt | ○ willn't | ○ won't |
| **8. could have** | ○ could've | ○ couldh've | ○ could'hve |

**Fill in the circle next to the correct plural form of the word.**

| | | | |
|---|---|---|---|
| **9. valley** | ○ valleies | ○ valleyies | ○ valleys |
| **10. life** | ○ lifes | ○ lives | ○ lifies |
| **11. zero** | ○ zeroes | ○ zeros | ○ zeroies |
| **12. woman** | ○ womans | ○ womanes | ○ women |

**Fill in the circle next to the correct possessive form of the word.**

| | | | |
|---|---|---|---|
| **13. brothers** | ○ brother's | ○ brothers' | ○ brothers |
| **14. friend** | ○ friend's | ○ friends' | ○ friends |
| **15. heroes** | ○ heroes's | ○ heroes' | ○ heroes |
| **16. cliff** | ○ cliff's | ○ cliffs' | ○ cliffs |

**Fill in the circle next to the correct compound form of the words.**

| | | | |
|---|---|---|---|
| **17. double + park** | ○ doublepark | ○ double park | ○ double-park |
| **18. shoe + lace** | ○ shoelace | ○ shoe lace | ○ shoe-lace |
| **19. poison + ivy** | ○ poisonivy | ○ poison ivy | ○ poison-ivy |
| **20. loud + speaker** | ○ loudspeaker | ○ loud speaker | ○ loud-speaker |

Possible score on Unit 3 Pretest 1 is 20. Score _____

# Pretest 2

Name _____

**Complete the chart by adding *s* or *es, ed,* and *ing* to each base word.**

| Base Word | add *s* or *es* | add *ed* | add *ing* |
|-----------|-----------------|----------|-----------|
| 1. hurry | | | |
| 2. splash | | | |
| 3. skip | | | |

**Write the contraction for each pair of words.**

4. would not _____    5. I have _____

6. did not _____    7. we are _____

**Write the plural form of each word.**

8. batch _____    9. story _____

10. field _____    11. wolf _____

12. echo _____    13. foot _____

**Write the possessive form of each word.**

14. farmer _____    15. parks _____

16. wives _____    17. moose _____

18. class _____    19. children _____

**Combine the two words to make a compound word.**

20. air + port = _____    21. flash + light = _____

22. life + guard = _____    23. team + mate = _____

24. turtle + neck = _____    25. week + end = _____

Possible score on Unit 3 Pretest 2 is 25. Score _____

**Fill in the circle next to the correct form of the word.**

| | | | |
|---|---|---|---|
| **1. rally** (add **ed**) | ○ rallyed | ○ rallied | ○ ralled |
| **2. permit** (add **ing**) | ○ permiting | ○ permitying | ○ permitting |
| **3. match** (add **s** or **es**) | ○ matchs | ○ matches | ○ matchies |
| **4. marry** (add **ing**) | ○ marrying | ○ marreing | ○ marring |

**Fill in the circle next to the correct contraction form of the words.**

| | | | |
|---|---|---|---|
| **5. who is** | ○ who'is | ○ who's | ○ whoi's |
| **6. you are** | ○ your'e | ○ youar'e | ○ you're |
| **7. should not** | ○ shouldn't | ○ should'nt | ○ shoul'dnt |
| **8. we will** | ○ we'wll | ○ we'll | ○ wel'l |

**Fill in the circle next to the correct plural form of the word.**

| | | | |
|---|---|---|---|
| **9. batch** | ○ batchs | ○ batches | ○ batchies |
| **10. pantry** | ○ pantrys | ○ pantryes | ○ pantries |
| **11. reef** | ○ reefs | ○ reeves | ○ reef |
| **12. solo** | ○ solos | ○ soloes | ○ solo |

**Fill in the circle next to the correct possessive form of the word.**

| | | | |
|---|---|---|---|
| **13. ladies** | ○ ladies's | ○ ladies' | ○ ladies |
| **14. visitor** | ○ visitor's | ○ visitors' | ○ visitors |
| **15. men** | ○ men's | ○ mens' | ○ men |
| **16. farmers** | ○ farmer's | ○ farmers' | ○ farmers |

**Fill in the circle next to the correct compound form of the words.**

| | | | |
|---|---|---|---|
| **17. trade + off** | ○ tradeoff | ○ trade off | ○ trade-off |
| **18. time + clock** | ○ timeclock | ○ time clock | ○ time-clock |
| **19. barn + yard** | ○ barnyard | ○ barn yard | ○ barn-yard |
| **20. polar + bear** | ○ polarbear | ○ polar bear | ○ polar-bear |

Possible score on Unit 3 Post Test 1 is 20. Score _____

Name _____

Complete the chart by adding *s* or *es, ed,* and *ing* to each base word.

| Base Word | add *s* or *es* | add *ed* | add *ing* |
|-----------|-----------------|----------|-----------|
| 1. erase  |                 |          |           |
| 2. admit  |                 |          |           |
| 3. apply  |                 |          |           |

Write the contraction for each pair of words.

4. can not _____     5. I am _____

6. it is _____      7. they are _____

Write the plural form of each word.

8. tax _____      9. cavity _____

10. shelf _____     11. cuff _____

12. cello _____     13. trout _____

Write the possessive form of each word.

14. captain _____     15. steamboats _____

16. mice _____      17. men _____

18. visitors _____     19. trail _____

Combine the two words to make a compound word.

20. rattle + snake = _____     21. sun + rise = _____

22. bare + foot = _____      23. water + fall = _____

24. apple + sauce = _____     25. wind + mill = _____

Possible score on Unit 3 Post Test 2 is 25. Score _____

# UNIT 3 STUDENT PROGRESS CHECKLIST

Student Name ______________________________

## UNIT THREE STUDENT SKILLS ASSESSMENT CHECKLIST

☑ Assessed ☒ Retaught ■ Mastered

- ☐ Inflectional Endings
- ☐ Contractions
- ☐ Plurals
- ☐ More Plurals
- ☐ Irregular Plurals
- ☐ Singular Possessives
- ☐ Plural Possessives
- ☐ Compound Words
- ☐ Compound Words and Syllables

## TEACHER COMMENTS

In Unit 3 students study word endings, contractions, and compound words. To give students practice with word study strategies, use any of the activities suggested below.

## Word Endings

Add the word endings **s** or **es, ed,** and **ing** to each base word and write the new words on the lines. Then choose one of the numbered sets of words and use them in a paragraph.

1. talk     select     wait
   _____   _____   _____
   _____   _____   _____
   _____   _____   _____

2. guess     brush     mix
   _____   _____   _____
   _____   _____   _____
   _____   _____   _____

3. admit     ship     brag
   _____   _____   _____
   _____   _____   _____
   _____   _____   _____

4. give     leave     shape
   _____   _____   _____
   _____   _____   _____
   _____   _____   _____

5. fizz     crash     bleach
   _____   _____   _____
   _____   _____   _____
   _____   _____   _____

6. scurry     sketch     delay
   _____   _____   _____
   _____   _____   _____
   _____   _____   _____

7. wave     echo     sleep
   _____   _____   _____
   _____   _____   _____
   _____   _____   _____

## Word Sort

Write the plural form of each word below. Then sort the plural forms of the words using the headings provided.

**glass** _____   **acre** _____   **county** _____
**knife** _____   **chimney** _____   **hero** _____
**studio** _____   **wolf** _____   **strap** _____
**family** _____   **branch** _____   **dish** _____
**wish** _____   **gulf** _____   **pitch** _____

| Add **s** | Add **es** | Change **y** to **i**, add **es** |
|---|---|---|
| _____ | _____ | _____ |
| _____ | _____ | _____ |
| _____ | _____ | **Change f to v, add es** |
| _____ | _____ | _____ |
| _____ | _____ | _____ |

## Singular or Plural?

Write the singular or plural form of each word in parentheses. Then select one word and write a sentence using its singular or plural form.

1. four (**woman**) _____

2. one (**mice**) _____

3. several (**crisis**) _____

4. many (**sheep**) _____

5. one (**children**) _____

6. some (**ox**) _____

7. this (**oases**) _____

8. two (**moose**) _____

sentence: _____

_____

## Possessive Forms

Write the possessive form of the word in parentheses to complete each sentence. Write the new words on the lines.

1. Some _____ ties have blue stripes.
   (**men**)

2. This _____ flag is red, white, and blue.
   (**country**)

3. That _____ tail is brown.
   (**fox**)

4. One _____ eyes are green.
   (**child**)

5. These _____ eyes are black.
   (**trout**)

6. Many _____ feathers are yellow.
   (**parakeet**)

## Building Words

Replace the underlined word in each compound with a word from the box to make a new word. Write the new word on the line.

| | | |
|---|---|---|
| ball | bath | mark |
| sister | spring | any |
| where | proof | head |

1. summer<u>time</u> _____

2. <u>every</u>body _____

3. <u>bed</u>room _____

4. <u>spot</u>light _____

5. <u>son</u>-in-law _____

6. some<u>thing</u> _____

7. snow<u>flake</u> _____

8. book<u>shelf</u> _____

9. water<u>fall</u> _____

## Word-Part Match-Up

Choose a contraction from the box that stands for the underlined words in each sentence. Write the contraction on the line.

| | | |
|---|---|---|
| won't | couldn't | I've |
| you're | we'll | isn't |

1. <u>We will</u> visit my aunt in Chicago. _____

2. <u>I have</u> visited her before. _____

3. Her house <u>is not</u> far from town. _____

4. The ride <u>will not</u> take long. _____

5. If <u>you are</u> going, leave earlier. _____

6. I <u>could not</u> find the train schedule. _____

| **LESSONS** | **32** More Plurals | **37** Singular Possessives | **40** Compound Words |
|---|---|---|---|
| **Problem** | Student confuses spelling rules when forming plural nouns. | Student has difficulty forming the possessive of a singular noun that ends in **s**. | Student has trouble defining compound words whose components have obscure or obsolete meanings. |
| **Intervention Strategies** | • Have the student list each Helpful Hint for forming plurals on a separate index card.<br><br>• Then have the student find words in the lesson that exemplify the spelling rule stated on each card. The student should list the singular and plural forms of the words on the back of each card.<br><br>• Have the student and a partner take turns quizzing each other with the cards. Finally, have the students scramble the list of example words and sort them by spelling rule. | • Point out to the student that though a noun such as **bus** ends in **s**, it is still singular. Remind the student that almost all singular nouns form the possessive by adding an apostrophe and an **s**. Write the following sentence: *James's dog can do tricks.* Ask the student to substitute a common noun for **James. (boy)** Point out that both words form the possessive in the same way. **(James's, boy's).**<br><br>• Have the student find other examples of singular nouns that end in **s** and form the singular possessive of each. | • Tell the student to underline the part of the compound word that is easy to understand—for example, **berry** in **strawberry.** Explain that these berries got their name because straw is used to protect these berries as they are growing.<br><br>• Encourage the student to research words with one or two parts whose meanings are not obvious, such as **breakfast, anchorperson,** and **broadcast.** Have the student share his or her findings with the rest of the class. |

The following activities offer strategies for helping students with special needs to participate in selected exercises in Unit 3.

## Memory Deficit

### Irregular Plurals

Students with memory deficits may have difficulty recalling the rules that tell how to form irregular plural nouns.

- Guide students to make three boxes on a sheet of paper. Label the first box: *No Change;* the second box: *Change **is** to **es**;* the third box: *Change **oo** to **ee**.*

- List the following words from **Lesson 33** on the board: **oasis, foot, deer, tooth, bison, crisis, cod, parenthesis, child, man, woman.**

- Guide the students to write each word and its plural form. Then have them copy the singular and plural forms in the box that describes how the plural was formed.

- Ask students which words couldn't be categorized in any of the boxes. **(child/children, man/men, woman/ women)** Point out that there are very few such words, and that they are usually so common that students can remember them without much difficulty.

- Encourage students to add to the boxes any new irregular plural words they learn. They can also use the boxes for review.

- Point out that the singular roots of some words with regular plurals are similar to the roots of words with irregular plurals. For example, **house** is similar to **mouse** but does not change to **hice** in the plural. Tell students to make a separate list of these words and to make up little rhymes contrasting regular and irregular plurals. *My neighborhood has **houses** not **hice**. Cats don't catch **mouses**; they catch **mice**.*

## Attention Deficit Disorder (ADD)

### Singular and Plural Possessives

Students with short attention spans often have difficulty coping with small details, such as the placement of the apostrophe in singular and plural possessives. Turning the process into a game may help students learn the rules for apostrophe placement.

- Write several phrases involving both singular and plural possessives—without apostrophes—on a sheet of poster board: *the two boys dog, the one teachers car*, etc.

- Review with students the rules for forming singular and plural possessives.

- Display the poster and tell students that they are going to play a version of "Pin the Tail on the Donkey." Then give students a large apostrophe cut out of cardboard, with tape on the back for placement.

- Ask them to place the apostrophe in the phrase where it belongs. If they place the apostrophe correctly, they can then add an apostrophe to the phrase with a colored marker.

## Conceptual Deficits

### Sequence and Time Order Words

Students who have difficulty understanding time relationships or sequence may need help doing the exercise on page **88**. These students may benefit from making a graphic aid that shows the proper sequence for creating a piece of artwork.

- Ask students to outline their instructions in a cartoon strip. Help them organize their ideas by having them act out the process of creating the piece of art.

- Have them describe each step involved in the process. For example: *I have gathered my materials. I am drawing the design. I will add color next, and so on.* Each time students make a statement, they should sketch the action in the appropriate panel in their cartoon strip.

- Then have students label each box with an appropriate time-order word from the box on page **88.**

- Students can use the cartoon as a guide for writing their "how-to" paragraphs.

The **Middle West** contains the richest farming land in the United States and is often called the nation's "breadbasket." Write the plural form of each word that names a crop or animal grown or raised in this fertile region.

| | | | |
|---|---|---|---|
| corn | _____ | blueberry | _____ |
| cherry | _____ | grain | _____ |
| soybean | _____ | potato | _____ |
| sunflower | _____ | chicken | _____ |
| hog | _____ | beet | _____ |
| tomato | _____ | oat | _____ |
| wheat | _____ | calf | _____ |
| ox | _____ | sheep | _____ |
| cranberry | _____ | apple | _____ |
| grass | _____ | grape | _____ |
| cattle | _____ | pea | _____ |
| bean | _____ | lamb | _____ |

## Make a Move on the Internet

Display a map and point out the states in the Middle West. Ask students to imagine that they are moving to a city such as Milwaukee, Chicago, Detroit, Kansas City, and so on. Have them use the Internet to research their "new home" to explore what it has to offer.

- First, have the students brainstorm topics for research. These topics should provide information for someone planning to relocate to a new area. Examples include employment opportunities, housing options, schools, public transportation, entertainment and cultural offerings, recreation facilities, and so on.

- Have students form groups and work together to assign topics to be researched. Have the students use search engines on the Internet such as *www.yahoo.com* and/or *www.altavista.com* to find current information on their topics.

- Then have students compile their information and use the computer to write a paragraph explaining their findings. Students may also wish to include graphics, illustrations, or photos in their paragraphs. Encourage students to use words with inflectional endings, contractions, plurals, and compound words in their paragraphs.

## Make a Documentary

Invite students to use a video camera to create a documentary that showcases the states of the Middle West. If a video camera is not available, have students use a camera to create a photo-essay.

- Arrange students in groups and assign each group a state in the Middle West. Then have each group find out the following kinds of information about its state: capital city, nickname, flower, bird, song, year admitted to the Union, population, places of interest, and famous residents.

- Students should prepare their information as a script for the video presentation. Encourage each group to use words with inflectional endings, contractions, plurals, and compound words in the scripts. Also, have students create visual aids, such as reproductions of the state flag, flower, and so on in order to enhance their presentation.

- Invite other classes in the school to view the students' documentaries.

## Life on the Farm

Explain to students that many farms in the Middle West are changing from family businesses to corporate enterprises. Technology has played a part in this phenomenon by enlarging farms and making them too expensive for private farmers to own and operate. Some cattle ranchers in the Middle West and other regions have dealt with similar situations by charging tourists money to visit their ranches and work as cowhands.

- Invite students to use the same tactic and advertise employment on a family farm as a vacation package. Have the students write and audiotape a humorous commercial that persuades tourists to spend their money and vacation time working on an old-fashioned family farm.

- Have students divide the tasks, including writing the copy, preparing the sound effects, performing the script, and recording the performance.

- Encourage students to include in their script things that would "persuade" tourists to visit, such as the "fun" of milking cows at 5:00 am, pitching hay, collecting eggs, and so forth. The sounds of mooing cows and clucking chickens might serve as appropriate background "music." The "farmer" can act as the announcer and make a sales pitch to the tourists. Have students include compound words such as **haystack, pitchfork, barnyard, pickup truck** in their scripts.

- Share the commercial with other classes and invite students to discuss their responses.

# Introduction to
## Word Endings, Contractions, and Compound Words

### Objectives

- **To enjoy a nonfiction piece related to the theme the *Middle West***
- **To identify word endings, contractions, plurals, possessives, and compound words**

## Starting with Literature

Ask a student to read "The Heart of the Country" aloud for the class. On the board, write these words from the selection: **breadbasket, heartland, skyscraper,** and **skyline.** Call on volunteers to read the words and to say what they think they mean.

## Critical Thinking

For the first question, ask students to reread paragraph two. In question two, have students reread paragraphs three and four. Encourage students to share their reasons in question three.

## Introducing the Skill

Write these terms on the board: **word endings, contractions, plurals, possessives, compound words**, and list a few examples of each. Tell students to reread the selection looking for examples of these word forms.

## Practicing the Skill

Have students work in small groups. Ask them to list additional examples of words for each of the word forms.

# The Heart of the Country

The Middle West has been called the breadbasket of the United States. There, in the heart of the country, this land produces wheat and corn for the nation. Yet in 1871, fire raged through the largest city in America's heartland. After two days of fire, Chicago lay in ruins.

The great Chicago fire of 1871 killed 300 people, left 90,000 homeless, and destroyed 18,000 buildings. It ruined businesses, too. Yet it couldn't destroy Chicago's location on Lake Michigan. From its important placement in the Midwest, Chicago linked the industrial cities of the Northeast with the farms and ranches of the West. As soon as the rubble was cleared, Chicago began to build a new city from the ground up.

Luckily, architects and city planners had two important new tools. They could work with a strong new material—steel. They could also use a new invention—the elevator. With these two improvements, architects could build high into the sky. One new skyscraper after another was built. Chicago soon had an impressive skyline.

Today, you can see the results of this remarkable construction. Yet there is more to see in Chicago than just tall buildings. Chicago is as beautiful on the ground as it is high above.

### Critical Thinking

1. What caused the people of Chicago to rebuild the city?
2. What effect did this rebuilding have on Chicago?
3. Do you think you would like to be an architect someday? Give reasons for your answer.

---

1. The Chicago fire of 1871 destroyed 18,000 buildings.
2. Architects built skyscrapers, which created an impressive skyline.
3. Answers will vary.

LESSON 28: Introduction to Word Endings,
Contractions, Plurals, Possessives, and Compound Words
**59**

# Theme Activity

**THE HEARTLAND** Have students create an ad campaign for products from the Middle West. Ask them to look through magazines for pictures related to wheat and corn, the crops grown in the "breadbasket" of the country. Pictures may include pancakes, pizza, hotdog rolls, and muffins for wheat; cornbread, corn on the cob, tacos, and grits for corn.

Have students make a poster for their product, using the pictures they found, and write a slogan, such as "Wheat: Good and Good For You," or "It May be Corny, but I Love It!"

Then have students write radio or television ads for their products. Encourage them to include Unit 3 words: contractions, words with inflectional endings, plurals, possessives, and compound words.

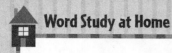

## Word Study at Home

Visit us at
www.sadlier-oxford.com

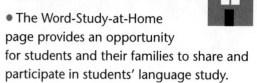

## Dear Family,

In Unit 3, your child will explore and use word endings, contractions, plurals, possessives, and compound words. The theme of this unit is the *Middle West*, including its people and history.

A **contraction** usually combines two words into one by leaving out one or more letters. An **apostrophe (')** shows where the missing letter or letters were. Examples of contractions are **I'm** (*I am*), **doesn't** (*does not*), and **aren't** (*are not*).

A **possessive noun** shows ownership. An **apostrophe** and an **s ('s)** are used to form a singular possessive noun (one **mayor's** plan) or a plural possessive noun not ending in **s** (the **men's** ties). An apostrophe alone is used to form most plural possessives (two **girls'** books).

A **compound** word is made up of two or more smaller words. Your child often uses compound words, such as **backpack** and **homework.**

## Family Focus

- Together, look at a map of the United States. Identify the states of the Middle West: Illinois, Indiana, Iowa, Kansas, Michigan, Minnesota, Missouri, Nebraska, Ohio, North Dakota, South Dakota, and Wisconsin. Talk about the states you would like to visit.

- The Middle West hosts many professional sports teams. Work together to list baseball, basketball, football, soccer, and hockey teams whose fields or stadiums are in this region.

### LINKS TO LEARNING

To extend learning together, you might explore:

**Web Sites**
www.ci.chi.il.us
www.chicagohistory.net/history/fire.html

**Video**
*The Mighty Mississippi,* Discovery Channel Video, 2 videos.

**Literature**
*Chicago* by R. Conrad Stein, ©1997.
*A Place Called Freedom* by Scott Russell Sanders, ©1997.

LESSON 28: Introduction to Word Endings, Contractions, Plurals, Possessives, and Compound Words—Word Study at Home

---

• The Word-Study-at-Home page provides an opportunity for students and their families to share and participate in students' language study.

• On the Word-Study-at-Home page for Unit 3, students and their families will find the Family Focus activities that relate to the theme the *Middle West.* These activities provide opportunities for further study of word endings, contractions, plurals, possessives, and compound words.

• Have students remove page 60 from their books. Tell them to take the page home so that their families may share in the Word-Study-at-Home Family Focus activities.

• Families may want to discuss the essay on page 59, particularly the details about the Chicago fire, or the city's important link to Northeastern industrial cities and farms and ranches in the West.

### Theme-Related Resources

**Books**

*Cut From the Same Cloth: American Women of Myth, Legend, and Tall Tale* edited by Robert D. San Souci, Philomel, 1993

*Death of the Iron Horse* by Paul Goble, Aladdin Books, 1993

*From Sea to Shining Sea: A Treasury of American Folklore and Folk Songs* edited by Amy L. Cohn, Scholastic, 1993

*The Huckabuck Family and How They Raised Popcorn in Nebraska and Quit and Came Back* by Carl Sandburg, Farrar, Strauss & Giroux, 1999

**Audiotapes**

*Sarah, Plain and Tall* written by Patricia MacLachlan, narrated by Glen Close, Caedmon Audio Cassette; 1995

---

## Multicultural Connection

The area now known as the Midwest was home to many Native Americans before the European settlers arrived. Have students research the tribes found in the states of Ohio, Indiana, Illinois, Michigan, Wisconsin, Minnesota, Iowa, Missouri, Kansas, and Nebraska. Ask students to include information about their way of life.

## Social Studies Link

A revolutionary industry was based in Detroit, Michigan. Have students research the history of Henry Ford's assembly-line method of automobile production, including its impact on American life. Then ask students to think about and present their views on some of the effects the automobile has had on transportation, our lives, and the world.

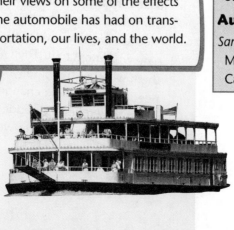

# Inflectional Endings

## Objectives

- **To add endings to base words to make new words**

- **To follow the spelling rules for adding inflectional endings to base words**

## Warming Up

- Write this rhyme on the board and read it aloud to students.

   When a base word needs an ending for its meaning to be clear,

   Please stop and see which letters were originally there.

   Then check the rules for dropping **e**'s, or changing **y**'s to **i**'s,

   Or doubling the last letter—avoid a word surprise.

- Explain that sometimes an ending is added to a word to change its meaning or use in a sentence. Say the following sentences: *I **write** a letter. I am **writing** to my friend.* Ask a student to explain how the word **write** changed in the second sentence. (the **e** was dropped and **ing** was added) Ask if the following sentence makes sense: *I am **write** to my friend.* (no)

## Teaching the Lesson

- Explain that to show the plural form of a noun, or to show a different verb tense, inflectional endings are added to a base word. Some of these endings are **s, ed,** or **ing.**

- Tell students that the word that receives the ending is called the base word. Then explain that depending on how it is spelled, a base word may undergo a spelling change. It may drop a final letter, double a final letter, or change **y** to **i.**

---

Name _____

### Helpful Hints

Add s, ed, or ing to most **base words** to make a new word.

| talks | talked | talking |

Add es to words that end in s, ss, ch, sh, x, z, or zz.

| guesses | teaches | crushes | boxes | fizzes |

When a **base word** ends in a **consonant** followed by y, change the y to i before adding es or ed. Just add ing to words that end in y.

scurry → scurries      scurried      scurrying

 Add s or es, ed, and ing to each base word. Change y to i as needed. Write the new words on the lines.

| Base Word | Add s or es | Add ed | Add ing |
|---|---|---|---|
| 1. marry | marries | married | marrying |
| 2. reach | reaches | reached | reaching |
| 3. relax | relaxes | relaxed | relaxing |
| 4. impress | impresses | impressed | impressing |
| 5. rush | rushes | rushed | rushing |
| 6. bully | bullies | bullied | bullying |
| 7. buzz | buzzes | buzzed | buzzing |
| 8. select | selects | selected | selecting |

Write the base word for each word below.

| 9. mixing | mix | 10. kisses | kiss |
|---|---|---|---|
| 11. geniuses | genius | 12. carrying | carry |
| 13. waltzed | waltz | 14. sketches | sketch |
| 15. rallied | rally | 16. frizzes | frizz |

### CHALLENGE

Use the spelling strategies you have just learned to add s or es, ed, and ing to the words below. Then write a sentence for one form of each word.

   fix
   screech
   crash
   hurry

LESSON 29: Inflectional Endings      **61**

---

# UNIVERSAL ACCESS
# Meeting Individual Needs

## Visual Learners

Write these words on the board: **advised, surprising, plotting, canned, regretted, forgetting, flurries, bodies, losses, fizzing, sweated,** and **folds.** Have volunteers choose a word and write its base word next to it. Then ask them whether the base word needed any spelling changes when the ending was added, and what those changes were.

## Kinesthetic Learners

Write ten base words and the word endings **s, es, ing,** and **ed** on index cards (one per card). Have students work with partners and begin by turning the word cards face down. Then a student turns the first card over, while the partner chooses an ending card and places it next to the base word. Finally, that partner respells the word with the ending in place. Students take turns matching the cards.

When a **base word** ends in silent **e**, drop the **final** e before adding ed or ing. For most words ending in **silent** e, keep the e when adding s.

bake → baked baking bakes    erase → erased erasing erases

When a **base word** with one syllable ends in one **vowel** followed by a **consonant**, usually double the final consonant before adding ed or ing.

pat + ed = patted    brag + ing = bragging    ship + ing = shipping

For most two-syllable words ending in one **vowel** and one **consonant**, double the consonant only if the accent is on the second syllable.

permit + ed = permitted        occur + ing = occurring

The following sentences tell about an unusual project that honors a brave Native American. Add **s** or **es**, **ed**, or **ing** to each base word in parentheses (). Write the new words on the lines.

1. A sculptor ___applies___ many unusual techniques. (apply)

2. One creative man ___committed___ half his life to turning a mountain in South Dakota into a work of art. (commit)

3. Polish-American Korczak Ziolkowski proposed ___creating___ a huge monument to honor Crazy Horse, the great chief of the Oglala Sioux nation. (create)

*Crazy Horse Memorial still under construction*

4. He was just ___guessing___ when he predicted it would take him 30 years. (guess)

5. Korczak knew that such a huge project would require a lot of ___planning___. (plan)

6. ___Beginning___ in 1958, he set off the first blast on Thunderhead Mountain in the Black Hills. (Begin)

7. He worked on that mountain for years, ___shaping___ stone into a magnificent sculpture. (shape)

8. After ___giving___ nearly 36 years to the Crazy Horse project, time ran out for the artist. (give)

9. Korczak died, ___leaving___ an incomplete statue and unfinished dreams. (leave)

**Home Involvement Activity Beat, burst,** and **cut** are verbs that are the same in the present and in the past tense. Work together to make a list of other verbs that do not change from the present to the past.

---

• Read aloud the directions on pages 61–62 and complete the first item in each set of exercises as a group.

• Remind students to refer to the Helpful Hints at the top of each page as they complete the exercises.

## Curriculum Connections

### Spelling Link

Stage a spelling bee in which students take turns spelling these words: **baking, patted, occurring, applies, leaving, planning, guessing, reaches, relaxed, rallied.** After students spell the word, have them say the base word and whether or not the spelling of the base word changed when the ending was added. If the base word changed, students must spell the base word before the change was made.

### Art Link

• Have students think about their favorite art medium: drawing, painting, film, sculpture, and so on.

• Then have them prepare a shopping list of supplies needed to create a piece of art in that medium. Tell students to prepare a list of art supplies as if they were going to an art supply store and to note how many of each item they would buy.

• Make sure students write items in the plural form or the singular form, depending on how much they think they will need.

### Observational Assessment

*Note whether students can differentiate between base words that require a spelling change before adding an inflectional ending and those that do not.*

---

### English-Language Learners/ESL

Ask students to read the Helpful Hints on pages 61–62. For each rule, have students draw a sketch and write a word or sentence that demonstrates the rule. For example, for the first rule on page 61, a student might draw a person holding a telephone. The student could write, *He **talks** on the phone.*

### Gifted Learners

Write these categories on the board: **creating, planning, building.** Have students determine what changes occurred when adding **ing.** Then have students add **ing** to the verbs **read, dig, hire, weld, spin, pull, permit,** and place them in the correct category according to the type of spelling change made, if any.

### Learners with Special Needs

Additional strategies for supporting learners with special needs can be found on page 59L.

# Contractions

## Objectives

- **To identify and write contractions**
- **To use an apostrophe in a contraction**

## Warming Up

● Write this dialogue on the board and have two students read it aloud.

Apostrophe 1: **What's** new?

Apostrophe 2: **I'm** new at this job! **It's** a lot of work holding words together.

Apostrophe 1: **You'll** get used to it. But I wonder what happens to the letters we replace?

Apostrophe 2: I **don't** dare let go to find out.

● Remind students that an apostrophe is a kind of punctuation mark. Have volunteers read and underline every word that has an apostrophe. Explain that these words are called contractions.

## Teaching the Lesson

● Write the words **are not** on the board and demonstrate how to combine the words to form a contraction.

Step 1: are not

Step 2: arenot

Step 3: aren't

● Tell students that the apostrophe takes the place of one letter: the **o** in **not**.

● Explain that apostrophes can take the place of more than one letter. Show this example:

Step 1: they would

Step 2: theywould

Step 3: they'd

● Ask how many letters were replaced by the apostrophe. (4)

---

Name _____

### ▷ Helpful Hint

A **contraction** usually combines two words into one by leaving out one or more letters. An **apostrophe** (') shows where the missing letter or letters were.

it + is = it's     is + not = isn't     do + not = don't     will + not = won't

I + have = I've     you + are = you're     he + would = he'd     we + will = we'll

Write the contraction for each pair of words. Then write the letter or letters that have been left out of the contraction.

|  |  | Contraction | Letter(s) Left Out |
|---|---|---|---|
| 1. | are not | aren't | o |
| 2. | you have | you've | ha |
| 3. | does not | doesn't | o |
| 4. | would not | wouldn't | o |
| 5. | I am | I'm | a |

 The sentences below are about the amazing Corn Palace in Mitchell, South Dakota. Underline the contraction in each sentence. Then write the two words for which each contraction stands.

6. In Mitchell, South Dakota, they're just nuts about corn.

 they        are

7. Mitchell is where you'll see the famous Corn Palace.

 you        will

8. What's most striking about the Corn Palace is that its outside is covered with South Dakota corn and grain!

 What        is

### WORK TOGETHER

With a group, list the features of a special building in your town. Then write two short passages that describe the building. Use contractions in one description but none in the other. Compare the passages. Which do you prefer? Why?

LESSON 30: Contractions    **63**

---

# UNIVERSAL ACCESS
## Meeting Individual Needs

### Kinesthetic Learners

Ask students to make letter cards for these words: **he is, did not, should not, we have, he will,** and **does not.** Also make an apostrophe card. Have students take a letter card and arrange themselves to spell one of the word pairs. Another student, holding the apostrophe card, removes the correct letters (students) and stands in their place so that what is left is a contraction. Have the students who were replaced read the contraction aloud.

### Logical Learners

Have students write a paragraph explaining how to form a contraction. Then, have them share it with another student to see if the explanations work. If so, ask students to create a diagram or flowchart of the process they described, and display the finished diagram or chart to the class.

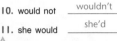 **Read the words. Write their contractions on the lines.**

1. he is — he's
2. did not — didn't
3. should not — shouldn't
4. we have — we've
5. had not — hadn't
6. will not — won't
7. he will — he'll
8. Bob is — Bob's
9. does not — doesn't
10. would not — wouldn't
11. she would — she'd

12. could not — couldn't
13. he has — he's
14. they have — they've
15. she is — she's
16. I will — I'll

Scene from the movie *It's a Wonderful Life*, 1946

 **These movie, book, and song titles should have contractions. Rewrite each title correctly by using a contraction.**

17. *It Is a Wonderful Life* — It's a Wonderful Life
18. "Let Us Fall in Love" — "Let's Fall in Love"
19. "Who Is That Knocking?" — "Who's That Knocking?"
20. *You Have Got Mail* — You've Got Mail
21. "Do Not Be Cruel" — "Don't Be Cruel"
22. *We Are No Angels* — We're No Angels
23. *Look Who Is Talking* — Look Who's Talking
24. *You Cannot Go Home Again* — You Can't Go Home Again
25. "You Are My Everything" — "You're My Everything"
26. *I Have Heard the Mermaids Singing* — I've Heard the Mermaids Singing

LESSON 30: Contractions

**Home Involvement Activity** Brainstorm another list of movie, book, or song titles that have contractions. Work together to replace each contraction with the words for which it stands.

**English-Language Learners/ESL**

Write the following on the board: **I am = I'm.** Then play the "I am" game. Point to yourself and say: *I am a teacher. I'm a teacher.* Choose a student to continue by saying, *I am a ___. I'm a ___.* Students may use their names, or describe themselves in another way. For example: *I am a dancer. I'm a dancer.* The game may be played with other contractions, such as *You are, You're.*

**Gifted Learners**

Inform students that contractions often indicate informal speech or writing. Have students take a passage from a textbook and find the words that can be made into contractions. Then have students rewrite the passage with contractions and read it aloud.

**Learners with Special Needs**

Additional strategies for supporting learners with special needs can be found on page 59L.

## Practicing the Skill

● Read aloud the directions for the exercises on pages 63–64. Make sure students understand what they are to do.

● For the second exercise on page 64, students should be able to check their work if they recognize the title.

## Curriculum Connections

### Spelling Link

Read each sentence aloud, and tell students to listen for and write the words that can be combined to form a contraction.

I heard that **you are** planning a vacation in South Dakota. (you're)

**Do not** miss the spectacular Black Hills. (Don't)

**They are** of great interest to me. (They're)

**You will** see strange rock formations there. (You'll)

**It is** important to hike with a skilled guide. (It's)

When **you have** made your plans, please let me know. (you've)

I **would not** like to miss the opportunity. (wouldn't)

### Social Studies Link

Tell students that South Dakota issued a redesigned license plate that displays Mount Rushmore. Tell them that it is also possible to personalize license plates, for example, I'M COOL. Have students create a license plate of 8–10 letters that includes a contraction. If possible, show photos of license plates as examples.

## Observational Assessment

*Note whether students correctly place the apostrophe in contractions.*

# Plurals **s, es, ies**

## Objectives

- To form plurals by adding **s, es,** or **ies** to base words
- To follow the spelling rules for forming plurals.

## Warming Up

- Write this rhyme on the board, and read it aloud for students.

  What do you do

  When you want to show two?

  The answer's not always the same.

  A few simple rules

  Will give you the tools

  This challenging matter to tame.

- Remind students that inflectional endings change the meaning and use of base words. Ask how the meaning of **tool** is different from the meaning of **tools.**

## Teaching the Lesson

- Write these words on the board: **clocks, shells,** and **faces.** Have students find and circle the letter at the end of each word that makes it plural. (**s**)

- Write these words on the board: **watches, foxes,** and **bosses.** Tell students to find and circle the letters that make each word plural. (**es**)

- Write these words on the board: **families, stories, berries, ponies,** and **cities.** Ask students to write the base words. (**family, story, berry, pony, city**) Have students describe how the base words changed in order to form the plurals. (change **y** to **i** and add **es**)

---

Name _____

> **Helpful Hints**
>
> **Plural** means "more than one." Add **s** to make most **base words** plural.
>
> farm + s = farms     rope + s = ropes     statue + s = statues
>
> Add **es** to words that end in s, ss, ch, sh, x, z, or zz.
>
> genius + es = geniuses     dish + es = dishes     waltz + es = waltzes

Add **s** or **es** to form the plural of each word. Write the plural word on the line.

1. walrus     walruses
2. box     boxes
3. glass     glasses
4. noise     noises
5. batch     batches
6. farmer     farmers

*World's largest ball of twine, in Darwin, Minnesota*

Add **s** or **es** to each word in bold type so that the sentence makes sense. Write the new plural word on the line.

7. One of our **wish** was to see the world's largest ball of twine.     wishes

8. In fact, two Midwestern towns boast very large **ball** of twine. The one in Darwin, Minnesota, measures 12 feet across!     balls

9. A man from Cawker City, Kansas, liked **challenge,** so he made his own ball of twine. But his had a diameter of only 11 feet.     challenges

10. These two creations were made without paint, **brush,** or other art supplies. Both are on display in their Midwestern towns.     brushes

> **CHALLENGE**
>
> Brainstorm ideas to create a list of movies, television programs, songs, books, stories, or poems that have plural words in their titles. Circle each plural word on your list.

LESSON 31: Plurals **s, es, ies**     65

---

# UNIVERSAL ACCESS
## Meeting Individual Needs

### Visual Learners

Write these headings on the board: **base word, plural form.** Under **base words** write: **boy, passport, pocket, bench, box, fox, buddy, monkey, donkey, visitor,** and **story.** Have students write the correct plural form next to each singular noun, and then explain what changes, if any, they made to the base word.

### Kinesthetic Learners

Make a card for each singular noun: **dish, couch, chair, puppy, brush, umbrella, statue, box, clock, scooter, chimney, penny, turkey,** and **pony.** On each card have students paste a photograph or draw an illustration of the object. Play a game in which one student takes a card and the other student flips a coin. If the coin toss is "heads," the student spells the plural form of the noun. If the coin toss is "tails," the student reads the singular form on the card.

## Helpful Hints

When a **base word** ends in a **consonant** followed by y, change the y to i before adding es.

melody + es = melodies          county + es = counties

When a **base word** ends in a **vowel** and y, keep the y and just add s.

key + s = keys          journey + s = journeys          boy + s = boys

 **Use a word from the box below for each clue in the puzzle. Write one letter in each space. Then read down the shaded column to answer the question at the bottom.**

| stories | pantries | poppies | delays | buoys |
|---|---|---|---|---|
| paddies | currencies | injuries | dairies | bodies |

1. money used in different countries — c u r r e n c i e s
2. floating objects used to warn ships — b u o y s
3. our physical shapes — b o d i e s
4. small rooms or closets for storing food — p a n t r i e s
5. series of wrongs done to someone — i n j u r i e s
6. postponements — d e l a y s
7. round, showy red flowers — p o p p i e s
8. farms where milk cows are raised — d a i r i e s
9. fields where rice is grown — p a d d i e s
10. tales of fictional or true events — s t o r i e s

**Question:** Which town in Iowa is building the world's largest ear of corn—a 50-foot giant?

**Answer:** Coon Rapids

**66** LESSON 31: Plurals s, es, ies

 **Home Involvement Activity** The following farm-related words are scrambled. They are also in the plural form. Unscramble the words and write a sentence for each one.
**lossi    lebasst    sdraynrab    seidlf    ratcrost**

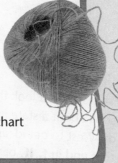

## Practicing the Skill

- Read aloud the directions on page 65. Before students begin the activities, preview some of the words and ask if they will require any spelling change to write the plural form. (no) Then read aloud the directions for the exercise on page 66. Ask the same question, and make sure students understand that most of these words will require a spelling change.

- If students need help, encourage them to reread the Helpful Hints.

## Curriculum Connections

### Spelling Link

Have students make a three-column chart. In the left column, have them write these words: **walrus, noise, batch, waltz, challenge, story,** and **currency.** If the plural form requires a spelling change, have students write what to do in the middle column, for example: "Drop silent **e**, add **es**." If they should not change the word, have them write, "no change." Then, in the last column, have students write the plural form of each word. **(walruses, noises, batches, waltzes, challenges, stories, currencies)**

### Science Link

- Minnesota has more than 15,000 lakes, in addition to the enormous Lake Superior. Geologists say that glaciers carved Minnesota's watery landscape.

- Have students research Minnesota's landscape—its lakes and waterways—and write a paragraph about their findings. Remind students to pay close attention to the spelling of plural forms they use.

### Observational Assessment

*Note whether students can identify the correct ending to form the plural of a base word.*

# Plurals with
# f, lf, fe, ff, and o

## Objectives

- To recognize, form, and use irregular plural nouns

- To follow the spelling rules for forming plurals

## Warming Up

- Write this ad on the board and read it aloud to students:

  Everything for your outdoor summer fun: **Half** price on **radios**, plastic **igloos**, and **stereos**; canned **tomato** paste and **potato** salad; books on **wolves**, build-your-own **patio**, and **auto** repair.

- Have students decide which words are singular and which are plural. (Singular— **half, tomato, potato, patio, auto**; Plural—**radios, igloos, stereos, wolves**)

## Teaching the Lesson

- Tell students that for most words ending in **f, lf,** or **fe,** they form the plural by changing **f** to **v** and adding **es.** For example: **wife/wives, calf/calves, half/halves, life/lives, loaf/loaves.**

- Give students examples of words that end in **o** after a vowel. (**patio, radio, rodeo, stereo**) Tell them to add **s** to form the plural. (**patios, radios, rodeos, stereos**)

- Where an **o** follows a consonant, students will add **es** to make the plural form. For example: **potatoes, tomatoes,** and **heroes.**

- Point out that there are exceptions to all of these rules.

---

Name _____

### Helpful Hints

For most words ending in f, lf, or fe, form the plural by changing the f to v and adding es.

  loaf = loaves          wolf = wolves          knife = knives

There are some exceptions to this rule. You form the plural of some words ending in f, lf, or fe and most words ending in ff by adding s.

  gulf = gulfs          safe = safes          cliff = cliffs

Write the plural form of each word.

1. leaf _leaves_        2. calf _calves_
3. half _halves_        4. life _lives_
5. belief _beliefs_     6. bluff _bluffs_
7. reef _reefs_         8. shelf _shelves_

Complete each sentence with the plural form of a word from the box. Look in a dictionary if you need help.

  sniff    thief    roof    safe    loaf    wharf

9. Violent tornadoes in the Midwest had destroyed the town and both __wharves__, or docks.

10. All the houses in the village once had red __roofs__.

11. We hoped that the new alarm system would prevent __thieves__ from looting the stores.

12. New __safes__ were installed in the bank to protect the money of the merchants and townspeople.

13. After several __sniffs__, the police dog decided that there were no survivors in the rubble.

14. __Loaves__ of bread were given to the victims.

A Midwestern tornado

### CHALLENGE

Each of these words has two plural forms. Write the two plurals. Then write a sentence for one of the plural forms of each word.

  hoof
  scarf
  staff

LESSON 32: Plurals with f, lf, fe, ff, and o          67

---

# UNIVERSAL ACCESS
# Meeting Individual Needs

### Visual Learners

Have students look through a book about a state in the Middle West to get ideas for nouns that end in **f, lf,** or **fe;** that end in an **o** following a vowel; or an **o** following a consonant. Tell students to make a list of these nouns and then write them in their plural form. Finally, have students write a paragraph about the state using the plural nouns on their list.

### Auditory Learners

Have students work with a partner to brainstorm a list of nouns that end in **f, lf,** or **fe;** an **o** following a vowel; and an **o** following a consonant. Partners should then make an answer key of the correct plural spelling for each word. Finally, have partners challenge another pair of students to spell each word on the list.

**67**

For most words ending in **o** after a **vowel**, add **s** to form the plural.

studio + s = studios          igloo + s = igloos

For most words ending in **o** after a **consonant**, add **es** to form the plural.

tomato + es = tomatoes          hero + s = heroes

However, there are many exceptions. For some words that end in **o**, just add **s**.

piano = pianos          auto = autos

 **Write the plural form of each word. If you aren't sure whether to add s or es, look in a dictionary.**

| | | | | |
|---|---|---|---|---|
| 1. video | videos | 2. torpedo | torpedoes | |
| 3. radio | radios | 4. photo | photos | |
| 5. potato | potatoes | 6. oboe | oboes | |
| 7. duo | duos | 8. rodeo | rodeos | |
| 9. banjo | banjos | 10. lasso | lassos | |

 **Write the plural form of the eight words below. Then circle those eight plural words in the puzzle. The words can appear across, on a slant, or up and down.**

| | |
|---|---|
| 11. echo | echoes |
| 12. cello | cellos |
| 13. half | halves |
| 14. solo | solos |
| 15. poncho | ponchos |
| 16. soprano | sopranos |
| 17. oaf | oafs |
| 18. self | selves |

s e o r a i d s s
o c a u f f s o e
p h f c h o l l l
r o s c e o t o v
a e s r c l a s e
n s e g e l l o s
o t i p r u x o e
s p h a l v e s s
d p o n c h o s e

Workers assembling **autos** at a Michigan auto plant

 **Home Involvement Activity** Work together to look through some newspapers or magazines. Circle the plural form of words ending in f, lf, fe, ff, and o.

68          LESSON 32: Plurals with **f, lf, fe, ff,** and **o**

---

Read aloud the directions on pages 67–68. Explain to students that the word-search puzzle on page 68 has two parts. The first part is writing the plural form of the word on the line. The second part is searching for the plural form of the word—across, on a diagonal, or up and down—in the puzzle.

 **Intervention Strategy** Turn to page 59K for an Intervention Strategy designed to help students who need extra support with this lesson.

## Curriculum Connections

### Spelling Link

Have students make a three-column chart. In the left column, have them write these words: **potato, photo, half, self, knife, wolf, cliff,** and **safe.** Have students write the rule for the spelling change in the middle column. For example: "for words ending in **o** after a consonant, add **es**." If the base word does not change, have them write, "no change." In the last column have students write the plural form of each word. (**potatoes, photos, halves, selves, knives, wolves, cliffs, safes**)

### Math Link

● The Midwest and the central United States are known as "Tornado Alley". It includes the area from Austin, Texas to central South Dakota. The reason for so many tornadoes in this region is a combination of climate and geographical features.

● Have students research the number of tornadoes in the United States since 1974, and prepare a bar graph or a line graph that shows the information. Title the graph, "Tornadoes in the United States."

## Observational Assessment

*Note whether students can form irregular plurals.*

---

### English-Language Learners/ESL

Encourage students to find pictures or to illustrate these objects: **loaves, igloos, wolves, videos, roofs, patios, potatoes, echoes, pianos.** Then have students create a story based on some or all of the images. They can work with a more fluent student who can help them.

### Gifted Learners

Have students work in a group to create a "Dictionary of Plurals." Students should brainstorm a list of words. Then, they should alphabetize the words, write the singular form, and write a brief definition. Finally, students should write guide words at the top of each page for reference.

### Learners with Special Needs

Additional strategies for supporting learners with special needs can be found on page 59L.

# Irregular Plurals

## Objectives

- To recognize that some nouns have an irregular plural form
- To recognize that some nouns have the same form in the singular and the plural

## Warming Up

- Write this rhyme on the board and read it aloud to students.

   A **mouse** needed a **blouse** and went shopping for one in the town.

   But when she passed by,

   two ____ caught her eye,

   and also an evening gown.

- Help students fill in the blank in the rhyme. **(blouses)** Explain that the plural form of **blouse (blouses)** is a regular plural form. The letter **s** is added to the word to make it plural.

- Then tell students that the plural form of **mouse** is **mice**, which is an irregular plural form.

## Teaching the Lesson

- Tell students that some nouns, like **mouse,** have irregular plural forms. These words do not follow usual spelling rules.

- Explain that other nouns stay the same in both the singular and plural forms.

- Have a student read the Helpful Hints aloud. Then ask: *What do some of the nouns with irregular plural forms have in common?* (The double **o** in **tooth, goose,** and **foot** all change to double **e—teeth, geese,** and **feet.)**

- Encourage students to think of other nouns with irregular plurals. (Examples include **man, woman, child,** and **deer.)** Have them check the plural forms in a dictionary.

---

Name _____

### Helpful Hints

The **plurals** of some words do not have s or es at the end. These words become plural in irregular ways.

man → men    foot → feet    tooth → teeth    goose → geese

Some words stay the same whether singular or plural.

gross    series    species    trout    deer    sheep    moose

Read the irregular plural forms in the box below. Write each plural on the line next to the singular form of the word.

| children | lice | crises | oases | mice | oxen |
| teeth | feet | media | parentheses | men | women |

1. mouse _mice_    2. child _children_    3. woman _women_

4. ox _oxen_    5. louse _lice_    6. crisis _crises_

7. foot _feet_    8. tooth _teeth_    9. man _men_

10. oasis _oases_    11. medium _media_    12. parenthesis _parentheses_

 All the words below have the same singular and plural form. Write each word under the correct category. The first answer is given.

| alfalfa | bacon | asparagus | wheat | cattle |
| cod | deer | bison | spinach | popcorn |

| Plant Kingdom | Animal Kingdom |
| --- | --- |
| alfalfa | bacon |
| asparagus | cattle |
| wheat | cod |
| spinach | deer |
| popcorn | bison |

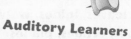

### WORD STRATEGY

The saying "Rules are made to be broken" is true for some plurals. Check a dictionary to write the *two* plural forms for these words:

fungus    index
radius    appendix

LESSON 33: Irregular Plurals    69

---

# UNIVERSAL ACCESS
## Meeting Individual Needs

### Logical Learners

Have students make word cards of the nouns with irregular plural forms on pages 69 and 70. Have them add other nouns with irregular plural forms, such as **crisis, oasis, fungus** and **radius**. Then have them exchange papers with a classmate and sort the words into the categories that apply. Have them explain the logic behind their sorting methods.

### Auditory Learners

Display a list of nouns with irregular plurals from pages 69–70. Tell students they are going to make up a "chain" story, using sentences that follow a narrative. Have the first student choose one of the nouns and make up a sentence using the singular form. Have the next student add a sentence using the plural form. Have students continue using the nouns to make up sentences, until they reach a natural end to the story.

| Across | Down | | |
|--------|------|------|------|
| 1. safe | 2. fungus | 10. louse | 17. gross |
| 3. rope | 3. radius | 11. pony | 19. reef |
| 5. man | 4. parenthesis | 12. self | 21. patio |
| 7. index | 5. medium | 14. sheep | 22. key |
| 9. alfalfa | 6. child | 16. echo | 23. cod |
| 12. shelf | 8. wax | | |
| 13. noise | | | |
| 15. series | | | |
| 18. deer | | | |
| 20. eight | | | |
| 24. species | | | |
| 25. moose | | | |
| 26. oasis | | | |

*(Crossword puzzle grid with answers: safes, ropes, men, indices, alfalfa, shelves, noises, series, deer, eights, species, moose, oases, and down answers including fungi, radii, parentheses, media, children, wax, lice, ponies, selves, sheep, echoes, gross, reefs, patios, keys, cod.)*

**Home Involvement Activity** Make up small word-search puzzles that include irregular plurals, such as **geese** and **crises**. Write your words across, on a slant, or up and down. Then exchange and solve each other's puzzles.

## English-Language Learners/ESL

Make picture cards and word cards for nouns with irregular plural forms, and for nouns that are the same in the singular and plural form. (Examples: Irregular—**teeth, feet, men, children, oxen, mice, radii**; Same—**deer, sheep, moose, fish, bison**) Display the word and picture cards, and have students match them. Then have them say or write a sentence that correctly uses the word.

## Gifted Learners

Invite students to use a dictionary to research the background of the nouns below, and to answer these questions: *What is the plural of this noun, and why?* Suggest the following words, and encourage students to add to the list: **criterion, nucleus, curriculum,** and **cactus.**

## Learners with Special Needs

Additional strategies for supporting learners with special needs can be found on page 59L.

## Practicing the Skill

● Read aloud the directions on pages 69–70. Complete the first item in each exercise with students.

● Before students begin the crossword puzzle, point out the format, including the clues that go across and down.

● Encourage students to write the plural forms on a separate sheet of paper and check their answers in a dictionary before they begin.

## Curriculum Connections

### Spelling Link

● Write the following nouns and their irregular plurals on the board.

| | |
|---|---|
| **child/children** | **tooth/teeth** |
| **woman/women** | **medium/media** |
| **ox/oxen** | **louse/lice** |
| **man/men** | **foot/feet** |

● Then ask students to write sayings to help them remember the spellings of the irregular plurals, for example: It's not n<u>ice</u> when one louse becomes many l<u>ice</u>.

### Art Link

● In art, the term **medium** means the art material that is used to communicate an idea. Examples of media are watercolor, oils, pen and ink, photography, and so on.

● Have students research some of the media that interest them and find out the equipment involved, how the equipment is used, and the visual effects those media produce.

● Students may present their findings in a table or in a written paragraph titled "Art Media."

## Observational Assessment

*Check to see that students understand which nouns have a regular plural form and which have an irregular plural form.*

**70**

# Connecting Spelling and Writing

## Objectives

- To say, spell, sort, and write contractions and the plural forms of nouns
- To write a personal narrative that includes contractions and plurals

## Warming Up

- Write this journal entry on the board and read it aloud to students.

  **Today's** the day **we've** prepared for all our **lives**. This evening, when our team boards the **buses** for the trip back home, **it'll** be a bus full of **winners**, or so we hope.

- Circle the words in bold type, and ask students to categorize them as contractions or as plurals.

- Have students name the two words that each contraction stands for (**Today's—today is; we've—we have; it'll—it will**), and to name the singular noun for each plural form. (**lives—life; buses—bus; winners—winner**)

## Teaching the Lesson

- List the following phrases on the board: **I will, she is, you are.** Call on volunteers to write the contraction next to each phrase. Review contractions with students.
- List the following words on the board: **wish, fence, border, sheaf, roof, sheep,** and **body.** Call on volunteers to write the plural form of each word, and to use the plurals in sentences.

## Practicing the Skill

Read aloud the directions for page 71. Ask students to read each phrase aloud. Then have students write each word in the correct column in the chart.

---

Name _____

Read each group of words. Say and spell each word in bold type. Repeat the word. Then sort the words. Write each word in the correct box below.

- varieties of **wheat**
- danced the lively **waltzes**
- **wouldn't** want to stay
- cuts that need **stitches**
- a pair of **oxen**
- a **series** of steps
- sang sweet **melodies**
- **haven't** had lunch yet
- captured the **thieves**
- repairing the **chimneys**
- too many **crises**

- as her **injuries** heal
- **calves** in the meadow
- so **they'll** agree
- grazing **cattle**
- as **I've** always said
- **echoes** down the canyon
- if **we're** on time

| Contractions | Plurals That Follow Rules | Irregular Plurals |
|---|---|---|
| wouldn't | waltzes | wheat |
| haven't | stitches | oxen |
| they'll | melodies | series |
| I've | thieves | crises |
| we're | chimneys | cattle |
| | injuries | |
| | calves | |
| | echoes | |

LESSON 34: Connecting Spelling and Writing

71

---

# U N I V E R S A L   A C C E S S
# Meeting Individual Needs

### Auditory Learners

Play the "Match Game" with students. Write the plural nouns from page 72 on the board. Write the singular form of these nouns on word cards, and place them in a pile. Have students take turns choosing a word card and saying the word aloud. The first person to find the correct plural on the board gets to choose the next word card, and so on.

### Learners with Special Needs

Additional strategies for supporting learners with special needs can be found on page 59L.

### Logical Learners

Have partners play "Twenty Questions." Tell one partner to choose a contraction from page 71 or 72. Tell the other partner to ask "Yes" or "No" questions to guess what the word is. For example: *Does it have more than five letters? Does it begin with a vowel?* Players keep a list of the contractions as they are guessed. After each contraction, partners switch roles and play again.

The Middle West has produced many great American writers. These writers were either born there or made the Midwest their home. Carl Sandburg, Willa Cather, Mark Twain, Ernest Hemingway, Laura Ingalls Wilder, and Mari Sandoz are six great writers whose names and works you may know. Like most good authors, these writers began writing about what they knew. In fact, many of them set their stories or poetry in the Midwest.

Now it's your turn to write about something you know. Write a personal narrative about an exciting adventure you have had. Use the people from the real-life experience and the actual setting. Include a logical sequence of events, and use the "I" point of view. Include at least two of these spelling words in your true story.

| | | | | | |
|---|---|---|---|---|---|
| wheat | waltzes | wouldn't | stitches | oxen | series |
| melodies | haven't | thieves | chimneys | crises | injuries |
| calves | they'll | cattle | I've | echoes | we're |

Willa Cather
(1873–1947)

Answers will vary.

_____
_____
_____
_____
_____
_____
_____
_____

**Writer's Tips**

As you revise, combine sentences to give more complete ideas. Then proofread your story for correct capitalization, punctuation, and spelling.

**Speaker's Challenge**

Use storytelling techniques to tell your story to your group or the class. Vary your tone of voice to emphasize a change of action in the plot. Speak loudly and clearly, and use appropriate gestures and body movement.

72    LESSON 34: Connecting Spelling and Writing

Carl Sandburg
(1878–1967)

### English-Language Learners/ESL

Have students create a drawing to illustrate a personal experience. Then have students use self-stick notes to label parts of the drawing that show plural objects. Also have them label characters with appropriate contractions (such as **they've**, **we're**, **I'll**, and so on).

### Gifted Learners

Invite students to play "Blank Out." Have them delete the nouns in their narratives, substituting blanks. Then have them exchange papers and replace the blanks with silly nouns. Invite students to share their finished products.

## The Writing Process

Tell students that on page 72 they will write a personal narrative about an exciting adventure they have had. Read the introductory paragraph, directions, and spelling words at the top of the page.

**Prewrite** Discuss with students the idea of brainstorming in order to find a topic. They should create a list of ideas, and then review the list to narrow the possibilities. When students have selected a topic, tell them to outline the main idea and supporting details.

**Write** Have students use their outline as the framework for their narrative. Remind them to use at least two of the spelling words in their writing.

**Revise** Call students' attention to the Writer's Tip on page 72. Have them share their narratives with a partner and exchange constructive feedback. Tell them to ask, *Are the details about setting realistic?*

**Proofread** Have students check their work to make sure there are no run-on sentences or sentence fragments in their writing.

**Publish** Have students copy their final draft onto page 72 or onto a separate sheet of paper. If possible, have them illustrate their writing with a drawing of the event.

**Computer Connection**

Share the following tip with students who use a word processor to do their writing.

● Headers in your document will help you identify the name of the document, the date you created it, the page number, and any other information you want to include.

● To create a header, click "Header and Footer" on the View menu.

● Write the name of your document. Then click the icons for page numbers, date, time, etc. When you finish, click "Close."

**Portfolio** Suggest that students add their personal narratives to their portfolios.

# Connecting Reading and Writing

## Objectives

- **To read a nonfiction piece and respond to it in writing**
- **To make inferences and interpret information**
- **To write a descriptive paragraph**

## Warming Up

### Comprehension Skills

- Tell students that **making inferences** is a reading skill. Explain that when you infer, you combine clues in the passage with your own knowledge to determine what the writer meant but has not stated directly. For example, if you read that a mountain was ice-covered most of the year, you could infer that only well-trained people with appropriate equipment would attempt to climb it.

- Remind students that when you **interpret** a piece of writing, you construct meaning from what you have read.

## Teaching the Lesson

- Have students focus on the first and last paragraphs in the passage to help them answer the first Reader's Response question.

- Have students reread the fourth paragraph to help them infer the answer to the second Reader's Response question.

## Practicing the Skill

Read aloud the directions on page 74. Point out that natural settings often inspire writers or artists. Discuss sources that students can use for inspiration, such as photographs.

---

Name _____

Read about our nation's greatest river.
Then answer the questions that follow.

READ & WRITE

# Life Along the Mississippi River

**M**ark Twain, whose real name was Samuel Langhorne Clemens, often wrote about the Mississippi River. He once described it is a "wonderful book [with] a new story to tell every day."

The Native Americans who lived by the shores of the Mississippi were the first to tell the river's story. They used the river for traveling, hunting, and fishing. The river was the center of their lives.

When Thomas Jefferson made the Louisiana Purchase in 1803, the United States took ownership of the Mississippi River. Soon, new settlements followed. Later, riverboats came.

Steamboats brought another wave of change. These steam-powered giants could carry tons of goods to market. Steamboat traffic led to the rapid growth of cities along the river.

Early European explorers who mapped the river called it a "gathering of waters." Yet they could have called it a gathering of animals and people. Nearly half of North America's ducks, geese, and swans use the river as a migration path. More than 200 kinds of fish swim in its waters. Beaver, muskrats, otters, and turtles also make the river their home.

Millions of people also flock to the Mississippi River each year. These people are inspired by the new stories the river has to tell.

Mark Twain (1835–1910)

### Reader's Response

1. **What do you think Mark Twain meant by his description of the river?**

2. **How do you think steamboat traffic led to the growth of cities along the river?**

3. **Would you like to take a riverboat ride down the Mississippi River? Why? What do you think the trip would be like?**

1. There is always something new to see on the river.
2. People were able to trade and buy goods that were delivered by steamboat so it was profitable for towns to grow along the river.
3. Answers will vary.

---

# UNIVERSAL ACCESS
# Meeting Individual Needs

## Auditory Learners

Play musical pieces that evoke a mood, such as Prokofiev's "Peter and the Wolf," Copland's "Appalachian Spring," or Gershwin's "Rhapsody in Blue." Encourage students to make notes as they listen to and reflect on the music. Have them write an essay to interpret the music they have heard.

## Kinesthetic Learners

Place in a paper bag several unrelated items, such as a feather, a stone, a button, a crayon, and a postage stamp. Have students empty the bag and examine its contents, imagining something these objects might relate to, such as a person, a place, or a particular event. Have students write a paragraph explaining what they have inferred from the objects.

## Learners with Special Needs

Additional strategies for supporting learners with special needs can be found on page 59L.

Writers and artists who travel on the Mississippi are inspired by the beauty of the river. In fact, these people are often inspired by their natural surroundings. They may even form special attachments to mountains, oceans, forests, deserts, or plains. Indeed, they may create poems and paintings that show the beauty of something special in nature.

**Describe something in nature that is special to you. Examples may include a canyon, a field, a mountain, or even a river. Write a vivid description of this natural feature and tell why you feel it is special. Use at least two of these words to describe.**

| | | | | | |
|---|---|---|---|---|---|
| majestic | wildlife | dramatic | silence | peaceful | magnificent |
| scenery | inspiring | breathtaking | beautiful | awesome | private |

 Answers will vary.

**Writer's Tip**

Use vivid verbs and adjectives to give your readers a mental picture of your description. Keep your audience in mind as you write.

**Writer's Challenge**

Imagine the perfect photograph of the natural feature you have described. Now create the perfect caption for that photo. Use exact words and vivid language. Answers will vary.

Scotts Bluff towers above the flat plains in Nebraska.

LESSON 35: Connecting Reading and Writing
Comprehension—Make Inferences; Interpret

## The Writing Process

Tell students that on page 74 they will write a description of something in nature. Remind students to use clues to help readers infer information about their subject. Read the directions, introductory paragraph, and list of words at the top of the page.

**Prewrite** Have students create a Main Idea Web. Tell them to write the name of their subject in the central circle. Then have them write five "sensory" words or phrases in circles connected to the central circle.

**Write** Have students use their webs to help them organize their descriptions. Then call their attention to the Writer's Tip on page 74. Suggest that students provide clues for readers to infer information about the subject.

**Revise** Have students share their descriptions with a partner. Have them check to see whether they have provided clues for readers to make inferences.

**Proofread** Have students check their work for errors in grammar, punctuation, and spelling.

**Publish** Have students copy their final drafts onto page 74 or onto a separate sheet of paper. Ask them to think of an interesting title for their description.

**Computer Connection** Share the following tip with students who use a word processor to do their writing.

● You can save time when you are working on a document by using special keys.

● Press the CTRL key at the same time as the Home key to go to the beginning of a document. Press the CTRL key at the same time as the End key to go to the end of a document.

**Portfolio** Have students add their descriptive paragraphs to their portfolios.

### English-Language Learners/ESL

Have students work with a fluent speaker. Ask students to draw the subject they want to describe and have their partners write descriptions based on the illustrations. Encourage English-language learners to make a list of phrases or key points they want to include. Invite partners to share their illustrations and descriptions with the class.

### Gifted Learners

Have students refer to the Main Idea Webs they used in the Prewriting stage of their descriptions. Have them write a poem about the subject, either in rhyme or in free verse. Have students compare the finished works to see which one more clearly describes the subject. Ask students to share their poems with the class.

# Reviewing and Assessing

## Word Endings, Contractions, and Plurals

### Objective

To review and assess word endings, contractions, and plurals

## Warming Up

- Write the following paragraph on the board.

  <u>Haven't</u> you <u>noticed</u> the high <u>winds</u> that blow here? <u>You'll</u> see that <u>sometimes</u>, weather <u>permitting</u>, the laundry <u>dries</u> very quickly. Other <u>times</u>, it <u>flies</u> away and <u>lands</u> on <u>roofs</u>, television <u>antennae</u>, and even in <u>gardens</u>.

- Write these headings on the board. Have students categorize the underlined words:

| Word Endings | Plurals | Contractions |
|---|---|---|
| (noticed) | (winds) | (Haven't) |
| (permitting) | (sometimes) | (You'll) |
| (dries) | (times) | |
| (flies) | (roofs) | |
| (lands) | (antennae) | |
| | (gardens) | |

## Teaching the Lesson

- Lessons 28–35 introduce students to the rules for inflectional endings, plural forms, and contractions. Have students work in pairs to find the lesson in which the item in each exercise is taught.

- Point out that the last exercise on pages 75–76 requires students to use context clues to choose the correct form to complete the sentence.

---

Name _____

 Add s or es, ed, and ing to each base word. Write the new words on the lines. Make spelling changes as needed.

| Base Word | Add s or es | Add ed | Add ing |
|---|---|---|---|
| 1. arch | arches | arched | arching |
| 2. talk | talks | talked | talking |
| 3. fizz | fizzes | fizzed | fizzing |
| 4. mix | mixes | mixed | mixing |
| 5. crash | crashes | crashed | crashing |
| 6. occur | occurs | occurred | occurring |
| 7. apply | applies | applied | applying |
| 8. erase | erases | erased | erasing |

Write the base word for each word below.

9. brushed _____ brush
10. admitting _____ admit
11. scurrying _____ scurry
12. rallies _____ rally

Add ed or ing to the base word in bold type to complete each sentence.

give 13. Mom has been _____giving_____ arts-and-crafts classes to senior citizens.

cut 14. She is _____cutting_____ up small fabric squares for a quilting project.

hurry 15. Last night, she _____hurried_____ to class with a large box of stuffing.

stitch 16. The class watched as she _____stitched_____ and filled part of a quilt.

display 17. All the students will be _____displaying_____ their crafts at the fair.

Gateway Memorial Arch in St. Louis, Missouri

---

# UNIVERSAL ACCESS
## Meeting Individual Needs

### Auditory Learners

Supply a set of letter cards, including several apostrophe cards, and read aloud word pairs such as: **he is, we are, you are, they would, could not, will not, does not,** and so on. Have students work with a partner to make the correct contraction that goes with each word pair. Allow students time to arrange the cards correctly before they go to the next contraction.

### Learners with Special Needs

Additional strategies for supporting learners with special needs can be found on page 59L.

### Kinesthetic Learners

Supply magazines and have students cut out objects and paste them on cards. Then have them write the singular form on the front of the card and the plural form on the back. Arrange cards along the chalk ledge. Have students read the singular form and spell the plural without looking at the back of the card. When a student spells a word correctly, he or she picks up the card.

**Write the plural form of each word.**

1. tax _____taxes_____
2. roof _____roofs_____
3. calf _____calves_____
4. deer _____deer_____
5. child _____children_____
6. series _____series_____
7. crisis _____crises_____
8. knife _____knives_____
9. ox _____oxen_____
10. bush _____bushes_____
11. man _____men_____
12. wolf _____wolves_____
13. potato _____potatoes_____
14. piano _____pianos_____

**Fill in the circle of the words that make up the contraction in bold type.**

15. I **shouldn't** complain.   ○ would not   ● should not   ○ will not
16. **She'll** be surprised.   ○ She all   ● She will   ○ She would
17. **Who's** at the door?   ● Who is   ○ Who has   ○ Who was
18. **Let's** go swimming.   ○ Let is   ● Let us   ○ Let as
19. I **won't** argue.   ○ could not   ● will not   ○ would not

**Underline the word that correctly completes each sentence. Then write the word on the line.**

20. Many ____cities____ serve good pizza, but Chicago's pizza stands alone.
    city          citys          <u>cities</u>

21. Chicago-style pizza is thick—two ____inches____ thick in some cases!
    inchs          inch          <u>inches</u>

22. Deep-dish pizza is so gooey that people eat it with ____knives____ and forks.
    knifes          <u>knives</u>          knifves

**Extend & Apply**

How do you like your pizza? Give your answer in a short paragraph. Use at least one plural word and one contraction.

# Reteaching Activities

## Categories

Write these column headings on a sheet of paper or on the board: **fox/foxes, shelf/shelves, tooth/teeth, moose/moose.** Point out that the first column is for nouns with regular plural forms; the second is for nouns that end in **f, lf,** or **fe;** the third is for nouns with irregular plural forms; and the last is for nouns that are the same in the singular and plural forms. Have students work in groups to add as many words to each category as they can. Vary the activity for inflected endings and contractions.

## Together We Stand

Have students work in a small group to choose and write ten plural nouns, ten inflected verbs, and five contractions from pages 61–76. Have them use a separate sheet for each category: **nouns, verbs,** and **contractions.** One group reads a word for the other team to categorize and spell. After one team misses, play passes to the other team.

**Check Up** The exercises on page 75 are discussed in *Teaching the Lesson.* Assign them now if you have not already done so. Page 76 will help you assess students' ability to choose the correct plural form, and to use contractions and apostrophes correctly. Read aloud the sets of directions. Make sure students understand that they must fill in the circle of the correct words in the contractions exercise on page 76 (15–19). Then have them complete the page.

**Observational Assessment** As students complete the exercises, check to make sure they understand how to add inflectional endings to verbs, how to form contractions, and how to construct the plural forms of nouns. Observe which exercises appear to pose the greatest difficulty for students. You may wish to refer back to observations you made during lessons 29–35.

**Student Skills Assessment** Use the checklist on page 59H to keep a record of students' mastery of inflectional endings, contractions, and plural forms.

**Writing Conference** As you complete the unit, meet with students individually. Review portfolio samples and other written work from earlier in the unit. Help students identify contractions, plurals, and words with inflectional endings, and make sure those words are spelled correctly. Ask students to recall a favorite piece of writing in their Home Portfolios and invite them to share it with the class.

Group together students who need further instruction on inflectional endings, contractions, and regular and irregular plural forms, and have them complete the *Reteaching Activities.* Turn to page 59C for other assessment methods.

# Singular Possessives

## Objectives

- To recognize the singular possessive form of a common or proper noun
- To write the singular possessive form of a common or proper noun

## Warming Up

- Write this poem on the board and read it aloud.

  You've seen the apostrophe spring into action;

  it's often used to form a contraction.

  It plays many roles, I think you'll agree;

  the apostrophe's uses are great, as you'll see.

- Call on volunteers to summarize the poem. (Apostrophes are used in contractions, but they serve other functions, too.) Tell students that there is a clue to the role an apostrophe plays in the next-to-last line of the poem.

## Teaching the Lesson

- Tell students that an apostrophe is used to show ownership or possession:

  **singular noun + apostrophe + s = possessive form of the noun**

- Point out to students that the possessive form of a noun is easier and less awkward to use. Read aloud the first example in the Helpful Hint box on page 77. Point out that not all the words in the phrase were used in the possessive form, **Beth's basketball.** Ask students what words were dropped. **(the, belonging to)**
- Ask a volunteer to read the Helpful Hint on page 77.

---

Name _____

**Helpful Hint**

Add an **apostrophe** and an s ('s) to the end of a singular noun to show who or what has or owns something.

the basketball belonging to Beth = Beth's basketball

the challenges facing one champion = one champion's challenges

the cell phone that James has = James's cell phone

Each of the following phrases is about one of Indiana's state record holders. Rewrite each phrase. Add 's to the word in bold type to show who or what has or owns something.

| | |
|---|---|
| 1. the speed record set by a **turkey** | a turkey's speed record |
| 2. the best archer in **Muncie** | Muncie's best archer |
| 3. the first lighthouse in **Indiana** | Indiana's first lighthouse |
| 4. the fastest elevator in the **state** | the state's fastest elevator |
| 5. the gold medals won by that **swimmer** | that swimmer's gold medals |
| 6. the largest barn in this **county** | this county's largest barn |
| 7. the biggest salad ever made in **Greenwood** | Greenwood's biggest salad |
| 8. the 57-pound catfish caught by a **Hoosier** | a Hoosier's 57-pound catfish |

Write the possessive form of each word.

| | | | |
|---|---|---|---|
| 9. student | student's | 10. staff | staff's |
| 11. cyclist | cyclist's | 12. editor | editor's |
| 13. fox | fox's | 14. country | country's |
| 15. teacher | teacher's | 16. boy | boy's |
| 17. Ms. Kim | Ms. Kim's | 18. Charles | Charles's |
| 19. Pedro | Pedro's | 20. brother | brother's |

**WORK TOGETHER**

Work with a partner. Write five sentences that use the possessive form of a noun, but leave out the **apostrophe** and the s ('s). Exchange papers. Insert the **apostrophe** and the s ('s) correctly in each sentence.

---

# UNIVERSAL ACCESS
## Meeting Individual Needs

### Logical Learners

Have students create a chart or other graphic organizer to compile what they have learned about apostrophes so far: Apostrophes are used in contractions, and they are used to show the singular possessive form. Have students title their organizers "All About Apostrophes." Encourage them to leave room in their organizers to add information they will learn in the next lesson.

### Visual Learners

Have students reread their answers for the second exercise on page 77, and highlight the **'s** in each word with a colored marker. Then have them look again at items 9–20, and turn those words into plurals by adding an **s**. Have students highlight the **s**-ending with a different colored marker so that they can see the difference between plurals and possessives.

☆ **Read the following phrases. Underline the ten phrases that show who or what has or owns something. Then write a sentence for each phrase you have underlined.**

| | | |
|---|---|---|
| Fort Wayne's courthouse | three nights | the team's mascot |
| the mayor's plan | this city's nickname | a golfer's paradise |
| huge horse farms | creeks and streams | Dave's Dairy Barn |
| the town's location | highway repairs | the governor's idea |
| summer sunsets | Gus's tickets | the speedway's turns |

1. Answers will vary.
_____

2. _____
_____

3. _____
_____

4. _____
_____

5. _____
_____

6. _____
_____

7. _____

The **track**'s hairpin turns at the Indy 500

8. _____
_____

9. _____
_____

10. _____
_____

 **78** LESSON 37: Singular Possessives

 **Home Involvement Activity** Read together an article or a column from the sports pages of a newspaper. Circle each singular possessive noun that you find.

## Practicing the Skill

● Read aloud the directions on pages 77 and 78.

● Refer students to the examples in the Helpful Hint box to show them how to make the possessive form of a phrase.

● On page 78, point out that not all the phrases show ownership. Allow students to work with a partner, if necessary, to complete the page.

 Turn to page 59K for an Intervention Strategy designed to help students who need extra support with this lesson.

## Curriculum Connections

### Spelling Link

● Have students write the possessive form of each underlined phrase to complete each sentence.

Ana was the <u>youngest champion of the state</u>. **the state's youngest champion**

She broke <u>the record of her brother</u>. **her brother's record**

She became the <u>fastest swimmer of the Midwest</u>. **Midwest's fastest swimmer**

### Social Studies Link

● Tell students that the word **Hoosier** is used as a nickname for a native or resident of Indiana. There are several theories as to how the term "Hoosier" came into the English language.

● Have interested students research a few of these theories, using the dictionary, the encyclopedia, or the Internet.

● Then have them summarize their findings in a few sentences. Each sentence should use the possessive form.

### Observational Assessment

*Note whether students can correctly position the apostrophe to make the singular possessive form.*

---

### English-Language Learners/ESL

Supply name tags for students, and ask students to wear them. Then ask each student to hold an object, such as a pencil, pen, or notebook. Have English-language learners write **'s** on self-stick notes and attach them to the right side of the name tag. Have students read the card, which now shows the possessive form, and use it to name the object that the student is holding, for example: "Maria's folder."

### Gifted Learners

As students use the possessive phrases to complete the exercise on page 78, encourage them to organize their sentences so that they tell a story.

### Learners with Special Needs

Additional strategies for supporting learners with special needs can be found on page 59L.

# Plural Possessives

## Objectives

- **To recognize the plural possessive form of common and proper nouns**
- **To write the plural possessive form of common and proper nouns**

## Warming Up

- Write this sentence on the board and read it aloud to students.

  Sid's **horses'** horseshoes were rusted.

- Help students see that only one word with an apostrophe is in the singular possessive form. **(Sid's)**

- Tell students that the apostrophe after **s** is another kind of possessive form. Ask a volunteer to explain the meaning of the *Warming-Up* sentence.

## Teaching the Lesson

- Review with students how to show ownership in the singular form.

- Write the words **men, women,** and **children** on the board. Ask students to name the singular form of each word **(man, woman, child),** and then to write the singular possessive form of each. **(man's, woman's, child's)** Explain that when the plural form of a noun does not end in **s**, the possessive form is an apostrophe followed by **s**.

- Tell students that this rule is also true of words that have the same singular and plural forms (such as **moose**).

- Have students read the Helpful Hints aloud. Call on volunteers to provide additional examples for each rule.

---

Name _____

### Helpful Hints

Add only an **apostrophe** (') to form the **possessive** of a plural noun that ends in s.

  the new ship of the owners = the owners' new ship
  the farm owned by her parents = her parents' farm

Add an **apostrophe** and an s ('s) to form the possessive of a plural noun that does not end in s.

  the bird that belongs to the children = the children's bird
  the vacation of the women = the women's vacation

The Midwestern **states'** busy waterways

 **Rewrite each phrase. Add an apostrophe (') or an apostrophe and an s ('s) to the word in bold type to show who or what has or owns something.**

1. the cargo ships on the **lakes** — the lakes' cargo ships
2. the sailboats of my **friends** — my friends' sailboats
3. the fishing trip of our **teachers** — our teachers' fishing trip
4. the tools of these **engineers** — these engineers' tools
5. the boat race for the **women** — the women's boat race
6. the bicycles that belong to the **children** — the children's bicycles
7. the view from their **cabins** — the cabins' view
8. the cameras of those **tourists** — those tourists' cameras

 **Write the possessive form of each word.**

9. swimmers — swimmers'  10. students — students'
11. drivers — drivers'  12. trout — trout's
13. brothers — brothers'  14. captains — captains'
15. workers — workers'  16. ladies — ladies'
17. men — men's  18. doctors — doctors'

### CHALLENGE

Change these words to the plural form. Then write the possessive form of each plural word.

city  hero
cliff  wolf

LESSON 38: Plural Possessives    **79**

---

# UNIVERSAL ACCESS
## Meeting Individual Needs

### Logical Learners

Refer students to the "All About Apostrophes" graphic organizer that they created in Lesson 37. In addition to contractions and the singular possessive form, they should include how apostrophes are used to create the plural possessive form. Students may need to revise their format to include the new material.

### Kinesthetic Learners

Refer students to the phrases at the top of page 80. Have them write each singular and plural noun on a separate strip of paper. Then have them cut out an **'s** from a piece of paper with texture, such as sandpaper. Have students add the **'s** to make the singular and plural form for each noun, and then trace the written letters and the sandpaper additions with a finger.

**Read each phrase. If the words show that one person or thing has or owns something, write the word *one*. If the words show that more than one has or owns something, write *more than one*.**

1. the forest rangers' lookout — more than one
2. the leader's responsibilities — one
3. the farmers' crops — more than one
4. the sailors' voyage — more than one
5. the city planner's new proposal — one
6. the guide's maps — one
7. the calves' owner — more than one
8. the parks' natural beauty — more than one

South Dakota's Badlands National Park

**Read the sentences about Badlands National Park. Underline the word that completes each sentence correctly. Then write the word on the line. Watch out! Don't confuse plurals and possessives.**

9. This national __park's__ location is in southwestern South Dakota. — parks   <u>park's</u>   parks'
10. It has nearly 244,000 __acres__ of rock formations mixed with grass prairie. — <u>acres</u>   acre's   acres'
11. The park contains the __world's__ richest fossil beds from 23–35 million years ago. — worlds   <u>world's</u>   worlds'
12. Badlands National Park averages about 1.1 million __visitors__ each year. — <u>visitors</u>   visitor's   visitors'
13. The summers are hot and dry, and the __Badlands'__ winters are usually cold. — <u>Badlands'</u>   Badland's   Badland
14. One __camp's__ facilities are primitive; there is no running water. — <u>camp's</u>   camps   camps'
15. Some of the __trails__ take hikers past huge prairie dog towns. — <u>trails</u>   trail's   trails'

**Home Involvement Activity** Write one sentence each for the following pairs:
**trails** and **trail's**   **visitor's** and **visitors'**   **rangers** and **rangers'**

- Review the directions for the exercises on pages 79–80.

- In the second exercise on page 80, tell students to use clues in the sentences to make the correct answer choice.

## Curriculum Connections

### Spelling Link

Have students write the plural possessive form of the underlined nouns to complete each sentence.

The <u>cabins</u> windows faced an impressive scene. **cabins'**

The <u>rangers</u> tours leave at different times of day. **rangers'**

Sean's <u>friends</u> photos are on display at the library. **friends'**

The <u>lakes</u> bottoms have become fossil beds. **lakes'**

Our <u>students</u> science projects include fossil studies. **students'**

There are many <u>children</u> books about our national parks. **children's**

### Multicultural Connection

- Sections of Badlands National Park are watched over by the Oglala Sioux and the National Parks Service.

- Ask students to research the role of the Oglala Sioux at Badlands National Park. The Oglala Sioux stage a reenactment of a ritual known as the Ghost Dance, and they co-manage the Stronghold Region, which was a training ground during World War II.

### Observational Assessment

*Note whether students can correctly position the apostrophe to make the plural possessive form.*

### English-Language Learners/ESL

Write the following word pairs on the board: **doctors/patients; parents/sons; swimmers/pools; drivers/cars.**

Have students add an apostrophe to form the plural possessive form of the words in bold type. Help them write a sentence using each word pair. For example, *The doctor's patients were very pleased.*

### Gifted Learners

Introduce students to the concept of **collective nouns**—nouns that name a group but follow the rules for forming singular possessives. Write these words on the board:

**class   family   crowd**

Have students write the possessive form of each word.

### Learners with Special Needs

Additional strategies for supporting learners with special needs can be found on page 59L.

# Connecting Spelling and Writing

## Objectives

- **To say, spell, sort, and write words with plurals, contractions, singular possessives, and plural possessives**
- **To write a persuasive speech**

## Warming Up

- Write this passage on the board, and have a volunteer read it aloud.

    **We've** heard the **men's** and **women's cheers.** They filled the **musician's ears**.

- Write these column headings on the board: **plural, singular possessive, plural possessive,** and **contraction.** Then, underline the words in bold type and work with students to categorize each underlined word. (Plural—**cheers, ears;** Singular possessive—**musician's;** Plural possessive—**men's, women's;** Contraction—**We've**)

## Teaching the Lesson

- List these categories on the board: **singular possessive, plural possessive, plural.** Then write these words on the board: **parents', brother's, sisters.**
- Ask students to correctly categorize the words. (Singular possessive—**brother's;** Plural possessive—**parents', women's** Plural—**sisters**)
- Ask students to suggest other words that fit these categories.

## Practicing the Skill

Review the directions for page 81. Point out that each word belongs in one box or category only. Have students complete the page independently, but check their answers before going on to page 82.

---

⭐ Read each group of words. Say and spell each word in bold type. Repeat the word. Then sort the words. Write each word in the correct box below.

- strong **arguments**
- **aren't** going to win
- the **reporters'** coverage
- in the **editor's** column
- for the **country's** own good
- agree with their **viewpoints**
- if **you're** interested
- **won't** get their attention
- at a **women's** club
- to hold the **debates**
- closing **statements**
- what they **might've** said
- explain our **positions**
- get **supporters'** comments
- if **you'll** listen
- obeying the **official's** rules
- the **opponent's** remarks
- in the **speakers'** own words

Lincoln-Douglas debate, 1858

| Singular Possessives |
| --- |
| editor's |
| country's |
| official's |
| oponent's |

| Plural Possessives |
| --- |
| reporters' |
| women's |
| supporters' |
| speakers' |

| Plurals |
| --- |
| arguments |
| viewpoints |
| debates |
| statements |
| positions |

| Contractions |
| --- |
| aren't |
| you're |
| won't |
| might've |
| you'll |

---

# UNIVERSAL ACCESS
# Meeting Individual Needs

## Auditory Learners

Have students read aloud the spelling words from the box on page 82, and respond to each word they hear with another form of that word. For example, if the word is a plural, students should respond with the singular form. Encourage students to explain how they can hear the difference between using the plural possessive and the singular possessive forms of a noun. (Possible answer: listen for context clues)

## Kinesthetic Learners

Have a group of students sit in a circle. Give each student two strips of paper and a pencil. Tell students to observe the others in the circle. Then, have them write on one strip of paper a sentence about something that belongs to one of the people in the group. On the second strip, have them write about something that belongs to several people in the group. Have students share their sentences.

## Learners with Special Needs

Additional strategies for supporting learners with special needs can be found on page 59L.

In the 1800s, Americans flocked to hear public speeches. Large crowds listened to readings, lectures, and debates. The audience would stay for hours to hear good speakers make sound arguments.

Abraham Lincoln held several famous debates with Stephen A. Douglas in 1858. Lincoln was running against Douglas in an Illinois state election. Both men were fine speakers. Both had strong ideas. Lincoln lost that election. Yet his great speeches against slavery won him national attention.

★ **Choose a topic that you feel strongly about. Write a persuasive speech. Present your main idea or argument in a strong topic sentence. Give convincing supporting details. Use at least two of these spelling words.**

| | | | | | |
|---|---|---|---|---|---|
| arguments | aren't | reporters' | editor's | country's | viewpoints |
| you're | won't | women's | debates | statements | might've |
| positions | supporters' | you'll | official's | opponent's | speakers' |

Answers will vary.

**Writer's Tip**

Arguments are most convincing if you support them with facts. Don't rely on opinions alone to try to persuade your audience.

**Speaker's Challenge**

In formal debates, teams argue both sides of an issue. Yet team members cannot always represent the side in which they believe. Choose an issue. Plan arguments for the side you do *not* support. All the same, make your arguments strong and persuasive. Save your strongest argument for last.

## The Writing Process

Tell students that on page 82 they will write a speech to persuade others to agree with something they feel strongly about.

**Prewrite** Discuss with students that a persuasive speech should begin with a strong statement of the speaker's opinion, followed by reasons to support this opinion. Tell students to begin with a strong opening sentence, and to end with their most powerful argument.

**Write** Direct students' attention to the Writer's Tip on page 82. Allow students time to gather facts that will support their arguments.

**Revise** Have students trade papers with a partner and exchange constructive feedback. Then have students revise their own work.

**Proofread** Have students check their work for errors in spelling, grammar, and punctuation.

**Publish** Have students copy their final drafts onto page 82 or onto a separate sheet of paper. Then call on volunteers to give their speeches to the class.

*Computer Connection* Share the following tip with students who use a word processor to do their writing.

● An outline can help organize your notes when you deliver a speech orally. You can format an outline automatically, inserting numbers or bullets.

● Go to the "View" menu and click "Outline View." Start to type your headings. The word processor automatically applies the built-in heading styles. When you finish, you can number the headings.

*Portfolio* Suggest that students add their persuasive speeches to their portfolios.

### English-Language Learners/ESL

Have students work in pairs with fluent speakers. Each student should have a few objects in a bag, such as pencils and pens. A student selects an item and says a complete sentence, including the possessive form. For example, *"This red pen belongs to Jason. It is Jason's red pen."* Have students continue the activity. If possible, have them include the plural possessive form.

### Gifted Learners

Have students transfer their notes to cards and plan to deliver their speeches accompanied by visual aids such as posters or photographs. Have students practice giving their speeches from their note cards. Tell students to plan each point in the speech where they will show an illustration or visual image.

# Compound Words

## Objectives

- **To identify and form compound words**
- **To recognize the words within a compound word**

## Warming Up

- Tell students to imagine they are ordering their breakfast, and they have to choose from this menu:

  Grapefruit

  Pancakes

  Cornflakes

  Blueberries

- Encourage students to name the different foods they would order. Then ask them to find smaller words hidden in these words.

- Discuss with students what some of the hidden words are, and how they relate to the larger word.

## Teaching the Lesson

- Explain to students that a **compound word** is made up of two or more smaller words. Point out that the meaning of the smaller words is related to the meaning of the compound word. (For example, **weekday** means a day of the week besides Saturday or Sunday.)

- Have students keep this important rule in mind as they continue through the lesson. When forming compound words, keep the original spelling of both words.

- Have a student read aloud the Helpful Hints. Discuss and compare the three different kinds of compound words.

---

Name _____

### Helpful Hints

A **compound word** is made up of two or more smaller words.

back + pack = backpack      farm + land = farmland

Some compound words use hyphens.

drive-in          mother-in-law

Other compound words are two separate words.

control tower          poison ivy

Cleveland's busy **waterfront**

Write the compound word described in each clue. Check a dictionary if you are not sure whether to write the compound as one word, as a word with a hyphen, or as two words.

1. This ship travels in space. _____ spaceship
2. You can dive off this board. _____ diving board
3. This shoe is used to walk on snow. _____ snowshoe
4. This building rises high into the sky. _____ highrise
5. This "dog" is served hot on a bun. _____ hotdog
6. Here's a place to rest your foot. _____ footrest
7. He's the husband of your sister. _____ brother-in-law
8. This bear lives in polar regions. _____ polar bear
9. You might play on this ground. _____ playground

Underline the compound word in each phrase. Draw a line up and down to separate the two smaller words that make up the compound word.

10. saw birds on a rooftop
11. waited for the countdown
12. slept in the bed|room
13. carrying a suit|case
14. mails a post|card
15. decided not to double|park

### WORD STRATEGY

Divide an unfamiliar **compound word** into two smaller words when you read. This strategy will help you figure out the meaning and pronunciation of the word. Use this strategy to write definitions for these compound words:

footbridge
pathfinder

LESSON 40: Compound Words          **83**

---

# UNIVERSAL ACCESS
## Meeting Individual Needs

### Visual Learners

Give the word list below to a group of students, but don't let other classmates see the list. Ask students to illustrate the words' literal meanings, not their definitions as compound words: **football, string bean, buttermilk, mother-of-pearl, airplane, lighthouse, shoehorn, highway.** Have students display their drawings and ask other classmates if they can guess which compound word each illustration represents.

### Kinesthetic Learners

Assign students to two teams, and give each team a set of word cards. Team members take turns pantomiming interesting compound words, such as **airplane, honeycomb, lunar module, bulldog, leapfrog,** and so on. Invite students to come up with their own compound words to pantomime.

★ Match a word from Column A with a word from Column B to build seven compound words. Write the compound words on the lines. Check a dictionary if you are not sure whether to write the compound as one word or two.

| A | | B |
|---|---|---|
| roller | 1. roller coaster | light |
| rain | 2. rainbow | coaster |
| spot | 3. spotlight | drill |
| fire | 4. fire drill | comb |
| honey | 5. honeycomb | hive |
| book | 6. bookshelf | bow |
| bee | 7. beehive | shelf |

★ Read the seven compound words that you wrote. Write a sentence for each word.

8. Answers will vary. _____

9. _____

10. _____

11. _____

12. _____

13. _____

14. _____

**Home Involvement Activity** Work together to make a list of compound words that begin or end with fire and light. Your list may include fire **engine, bon**fire, **light**house, and **candle**light.

---

**English-Language Learners/ESL**

Prepare word and picture cards for the following compound words: **shoelace, gas station, toenail, pillbox, matchstick, blueberry,** and **necklace.** Do not label the picture cards. Have students match the word card with the picture card, and then make up a sentence that includes the compound word correctly.

**Gifted Learners**

Have students create a crossword puzzle using the compound words they listed on page 84. Show students how to number the items in the puzzle. You may want to show them an example of a simple crossword puzzle to follow. Then have them write clues for the "Across" words and the "Down" words.

**Learners with Special Needs**

Additional strategies for supporting learners with special needs can be found on page 59L.

---

## Practicing the Skill

• Read aloud the directions for the exercises on pages 83–84.

• Have dictionaries available so that students can check whether the compounds are one word, two words, or hyphenated.

Turn to page 59K for an Intervention Strategy designed to help students who need extra support with this lesson.

## Curriculum Connections

### Spelling Link

Have students match the words on the left with the words on the right, and then use them to complete each sentence.

| count | park |
|---|---|
| double- | tower |
| control | down |

The pilot radioed the (**control tower**) for permission to take off.

The astronauts excitedly watched the (**countdown**) before the launch.

Do not (**double-park**) your car here or you will get a traffic ticket.

### Science Link

• Read the following aloud to students:

By 1969, Cleveland's Cuyahoga River was so polluted that it caught fire. This resulted in the passage of several important laws, including the Clean Water Act. Industrial companies can no longer run roughshod over the environment.

• Have students work in groups to prepare a presentation about the clean-up of the Cuyahoga River. As they do their research, have students take note of any compound words they encounter, and include as many as they can in their final presentations.

## Observational Assessment

*Note whether students can separate a compound word into smaller words.*

# Compound Words and Syllables

## Objectives

- To identify and form compound words of more than two syllables
- To recognize the words within a compound word
- To identify the number of syllables in a compound word

## Warming Up

Read this description of an imaginary baseball game aloud to students.

Ladies and **gentlemen**, as a seasoned **sportscaster**, I have never seen a **play-off** game as heart stopping as this one. The batting is **red-hot**, the **bull pen** is alive, and the **outfield** is unbeatable. What a day for **baseball**!

- Have students identify the compound words and write them on the board. Help students define any unfamiliar words, such as **bull pen**, and invite them to brainstorm about out how these terms came into being.

## Teaching the Lesson

- Review with students why these words are called compound words.
- Point out that words are made up of parts called syllables. Have students read aloud the compound words from the *Warming-Up* activity. Point to and count the syllables as you say the words.
- Read aloud the Helpful Hints. Tell students that identifying the syllables can help them read and understand compound words.
- Return to the list of compound words and ask volunteers to draw a line between the two parts. Then have students say each part as you count the syllables.

---

Name _____

### Helpful Hints

Many **compound words** have more than two syllables. Look at the compound word **doubleheader**. How many syllables does the word have? Here's a way to figure it out.

First, separate the compound word into two smaller words.

doubleheader = double + header

Then count the number of syllables in each smaller word.

**Dou/ble** has 2 syllables.
**Head/er** has 2 syllables.
2 + 2 = 4

The compound word **doubleheader** has 4 syllables.

Divide each compound word into two smaller words. Write the two words. Count the number of syllables in each smaller word. Then add the number of syllables. The first one has been done for you.

| Compound Word | Smaller Words | | Syllables | | |
|---|---|---|---|---|---|
| 1. turtleneck | turtle | + neck | 2 | + 1 | = 3 |
| 2. double-jointed | double | + jointed | 2 | + 2 | = 4 |
| 3. motor scooter | motor | + scooter | 2 | + 2 | = 4 |
| 4. grasshopper | grass | + hopper | 1 | + 2 | = 3 |
| 5. summertime | summer | + time | 2 | + 1 | = 3 |

Underline the compound word in each phrase. Draw a line up and down to separate the compound word into syllables.

6. runs to home|plate

7. watched the towns|people

8. drenched in the down|pour

9. listens to the loud|speaker

10. took her rain|coat

11. avoids the rattle|snakes

12. sees every|body at the game

13. plays in the after|noon

### CHALLENGE

Write a sports paragraph that includes these four compound words:

baseball
doubleheader
left-handed
home run

LESSON 41: Compound Words and Syllables   **85**

---

# UNIVERSAL ACCESS
## Meeting Individual Needs

### Auditory Learners

Have students work with a partner to complete items 1–5 on page 85. Have teams read each word aloud, clapping their hands to mark the syllables. After they have clapped the total number of syllables, have students clap the number of syllables in each part, pausing before they move on to the next syllable. Finally, students should say how many syllables there are in each compound word.

### Logical Learners

Have students choose a word and combine it with other words to make as many compound words as possible. For example:

**water + fall = waterfall**

**water + fountain = water fountain**

**water + cooler = watercooler**

**water + lily = water lily**

Students can work in teams to see who can make the longest list.

Match a word from Column *A* with a word from Column *B* to form six compound words that name different kinds of food. Write the words on the lines. Then draw a line up and down to separate each compound "food" word into syllables.

| A | | B |
|---|---|---|
| lamb | 1. lamb|chop | corn |
| water | 2. water|melon | meal |
| grape | 3. grape|fruit | berry |
| pop | 4. pop|corn | fruit |
| blue | 5. blue|berry | chop |
| corn | 6. corn|meal | melon |

Play a food-naming game. Brainstorm with a group for five minutes to list ten compound food names. Then separate each compound word into two smaller words. Count the number of syllables in each word. Finally, add the total number of syllables of all the words.

| | Compound Words | Smaller Words | Syllables |
|---|---|---|---|
| 7. | Answers will vary. | _____ + _____ | ___ + ___ = ___ |
| 8. | _____ | _____ + _____ | ___ + ___ = ___ |
| 9. | _____ | _____ + _____ | ___ + ___ = ___ |
| 10. | _____ | _____ + _____ | ___ + ___ = ___ |
| 11. | _____ | _____ + _____ | ___ + ___ = ___ |
| 12. | _____ | _____ + _____ | ___ + ___ = ___ |
| 13. | _____ | _____ + _____ | ___ + ___ = ___ |
| 14. | _____ | _____ + _____ | ___ + ___ = ___ |
| 15. | _____ | _____ + _____ | ___ + ___ = ___ |
| 16. | _____ | _____ + _____ | ___ + ___ = ___ |

Total: _____

LESSON 41: Compound Words and Syllables

**Home Involvement Activity** Brainstorm a list of imaginary compound food names. For example, would you like to drink a **meatball shake?** How about some **knuckleberry pie?** Create a menu of your funny foods.

## Practicing the Skill

• Read aloud the directions on pages 85–86. Complete the first item in each exercise with students.

• Suggest that students read the phrases quietly to themselves in the second exercise on page 85.

• Assign students to work in small groups to complete the second half of page 86.

## Curriculum Connections

### Spelling Link

Have students match the words on the left with the words on the right to form compound words. Have them say the total number of syllables in the compound word. Then have them write the compound words.

| | |
|---|---|
| **motor** | **quake** |
| **every** | **cream** |
| **ice** | **pour** |
| **down** | **body** |
| **after** | **cycle** |
| **earth** | **noon** |

### Math Link

• Challenge students to write addition exercises in which they add two compound words to make a third compound word. Ask students to count the syllables.

• Encourage students to use at least one word of three syllables. Some examples are:

**strawberry + shortcake =
strawberry shortcake**

**computer + software =
computer software**

### Observational Assessment

*Check to see that students can identify syllables and count syllables correctly.*

### English-Language Learners/ESL

Have students use a variation of a potato-head toy to practice using compound words. Begin with a potato or a stuffed paper bag. Draw the mouth, nose, and eyes. Then have students cut out decorations for the potato-head that describe compound words from construction paper, such as eyeglasses, earrings, eyebrows, and so on. Students should name the compound word as they attach the decorations.

### Gifted Learners

Have students prepare a glossary of compound words. Have them list as many compound words as they can. Then have them sort the words alphabetically. Finally, ask them to look up each definition and rewrite it in their own words. Students can publish their glossaries as reference books for the classroom.

### Learners with Special Needs

Additional strategies for supporting learners with special needs can be found on page 59L.

# Connecting Reading and Writing

## Objectives

- To read a nonfiction piece and respond to it in writing
- To sequence and synthesize information
- To write a how-to paragraph

## Warming Up

### Comprehension Skills

- Ask students to discuss the importance of following directions in order. Explain that order is the sequence in which steps are carried out. Using sequence is both a reading and writing skill. Readers can better understand how something is done if the directions are written in sequence.

- Remind students that to synthesize is to put together ideas within a piece of writing and make sense of them.

## Teaching the Lesson

- Tell students to look at the photograph, read the title, and read the second paragraph to answer the first Reader's Response question.

- Have students skim the passage to find the time-order words to answer the second Reader's Response question.

- Have students evaluate the information they read to help them answer the third Reader's Response question. Remind them to list specific points to support their reasons.

## Practicing the Skill

Read the directions for page 88. Then discuss different kinds of artistic expression. Encourage students to look through books on art to give them ideas for their topic.

---

Name _____

 Read about an amazing artist who uses Midwestern farmland as his canvas. Then answer the questions that follow.

**READ & WRITE**

# How to Grow a Painting
### by Gail Skroback Hennessey

*The Statue of Liberty in a wheat field in Kansas*

Stan Herd isn't your everyday artist. His brush is a tractor, his canvas is the Earth and his paints are sunflowers and other plants!

Herd is a "crop artist." None of his "paintings" would fit on the wall of a museum. Take, for example, his picture of a sunflower in a vase. The sunflower is 150 feet long and the vase is 300 feet high. The painting sits in a field of Lawrence, KS. The sunflower is made of, well, sunflowers. The vase is green clover.

Herd got the idea to do crop art when he was flying over Kansas. Herd said, "I saw beautiful designs of the farmlands below. I thought, 'This is a wonderful art form for people who fly.'"

Herd can't just paint on the spur of the moment. He first spends a lot of time checking out the land he's going to use. Herd looks for running water that can destroy the work. He checks for chemicals in the ground that can change the colors of the field. He then flies above the field to get a better view of his "canvas." Next, Herd sits down and draws his picture on grid paper.

Once that's finished, Herd sticks bright orange flags in the ground. Each flag corresponds to a dot on his grid. Then he digs lines into the ground, connecting the flags. It's like a connect-the-dot drawing!

Herd digs with tractors, plows, rakes, hoes—even his feet. Then he checks his work. Says Herd, "Unlike most artists, who take a step back to inspect their paintings, I have to drive to the airport, get in a plane and fly above my painting!"

1. "Crop art" uses earth and plants as artistic materials.
2. First, he checks out the land. Then flies above it to get a better view. Next, he draws his design on grid paper. Then, he sticks flags in the ground to match the grid. Next, he uses a tractor to connect the flags. Finally, he views his work from an airplane.
3. Answers will vary.

 **Reader's Response**

1. Describe "crop art." Why is it unusual?
2. What does Stan Herd do to create a work of crop art? Give the steps in order, from first to last.
3. Would you like to be a "crop artist"? Explain your reasons.

LESSON 42: Connecting Reading and Writing
Comprehension—Sequence; Synthesize
**87**

---

# UNIVERSAL ACCESS
## Meeting Individual Needs

### Visual Learners

Encourage students to look into the artwork of realistic illustrators such as Norman Rockwell. Tell students to study some of his magazine covers and then list details of what they see. Tell students to organize their details so that they indicate a possible sequence of events leading up to the scene in the illustration.

### Kinesthetic Learners

Have students plant fast-growing grass seeds in a small jar or coffee can, if a garden is not available. Students can complete this activity over a matter of days. Show students how to water their plants and wait for the fast-growing seeds to bloom. (a few days) When the experiment is completed, have students work with a partner to explain and list the steps of the experiment.

### Learners with Special Needs

Additional strategies for supporting learners with special needs can be found on page 59L.

Stan Herd follows a sequence of steps before he begins to create a piece of crop art. First, he tries to find a piece of land to use. Next, he checks for running water and for chemicals in the ground that can hurt his work. After that, he flies over the field to get a better view of his "canvas." Then, he draws his picture on grid paper.

⭐ **Imagine you are going to create an interesting work of art. Your artwork might be a sculpture of "found" objects or a collage. Write a "how-to" paragraph of the steps you would take to create your artwork. Explain what you would do first, next, and finally. Use some of these time-order words.**

| first | next | then | finally | when | still | meanwhile | while |
|-------|------|------|---------|------|-------|-----------|-------|
| now | then | last | soon | later | before | during | after |

Answers will vary.

_____

_____

_____

_____

_____

_____

_____

**Writer's Tips**
- Arrange your steps in the best order.
- Combine shorter steps.
- Summarize your information at the end.

**Speaker's Challenge**

Present your writing as a "how-to" speech. Vary the tone of your voice to stress the important steps in the process. Use visual aids to help you explain.

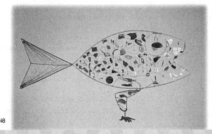

*Finny Fish* sculpture by Alexander Calder, 1948

88   LESSON 42: Connecting Reading and Writing
Comprehension—Sequence; Synthesize

## English-Language Learners/ESL

Provide students with magazines to use for picture cards. Have students select a picture of a painting, a sculpture, or any other work of art. Invite students to work with fluent speakers to describe the art process in the picture they have chosen. Then have the teams create a "how-to" poster about the work of art, using pictures and labels.

## Gifted Learners

Invite students to conduct a demonstration of the art techniques they have researched. Students may also wish to lead classmates through the steps in the process. In this case, the whole class will make the art project the student researched. You may wish to do this with a few students' "how-to" paragraphs.

## The Writing Process

Tell students that on page 88 they will write a "how-to" paragraph about the steps they would take to create a work of art. Read aloud the introduction, directions, and time-order words at the top of the page.

**Prewrite** Tell students to choose an art process and to research it. Students should then prepare an outline of their main topic and supporting details. The outline should show the structure of the paragraph—with a beginning, middle, and end. Remind students to use time-order words from the box.

**Write** Suggest that students write an interesting opening sentence. Remind them to present the instructions clearly and sequentially. Tell students to make sure that they have explained or defined any unfamiliar terms.

**Revise** Direct students to read their paragraphs with a partner and exchange feedback. Then have students revise accordingly.

**Proofread** Have students check that they have used at least three time-order words. Have them review their work for errors in punctuation, spelling, and grammar.

**Publish** Students can copy their final drafts onto page 88 or onto a separate sheet of paper.

**Computer Connection** Share the following tip with students who use a word processor to do their writing.

- You may want to "code" your writing as you revise. For example, you may want to use different colors to separate the beginning, middle, and end.

- Select the text you want to make a different color. Click on "Font" in the Format menu. Click the arrow on the right of the Color box, select the color you want, and then click the button.

**Portfolio** Have students add their how-to paragraphs to their portfolios.

# Reviewing and Assessing

## Word Endings, Contractions, Plurals, Possessives, and Compound Words

### Objective

To review and assess word endings, contractions, plurals, possessives, and compound words

## Warming Up

- Write the following words on the board. Have students circle the word that gives the correct plural or possessive form. Encourage students to use the dictionary to check spellings.

| | | |
|---|---|---|
| **pulley** | **pullies** | **pulleys** |
| **city** | **city's** | **cityes** |
| **box** | **boxs** | **boxes** |
| **mayor** | **mayors'** | **mayores** |

- Explain to students that in each group, only one choice is possible. After students make their selection, have them explain what it is. (**pulleys**—plural; **city's**—singular possessive; **boxes**—plural; **mayors'**—plural possessive)

## Teaching the Lesson

- Direct students' attention to the first exercise, about plural forms, on page 89. Explain that students may have to change the spelling of the base word.

- Explain that the second exercise on the page will ask students to form the singular possessive or the plural possessive form. Explain that students can use context clues in the second and third exercises to help them determine the answer.

---

Name _____

 Write the plural form of each base word. Then write the possesive form of each plural word.

1. radish ____radishes____  ____radishes'____
2. statue ____statues____  ____statues'____
3. monkey ____monkeys____  ____monkeys'____
4. wife ____wives____  ____wives'____
5. mouse ____mice____  ____mice's____

 Rewrite each phrase. Use an apostrophe and an s ('s) or an apostrophe (') to show who or what has or owns something.

6. the roar of that engine _____that engine's roar_____
7. the rattles that belongs to those babies _____those babies' rattles_____
8. the mayor of this city _____the city's mayor_____
9. the badges that belong to the captains _____the captains' badges_____
10. the locker room meant for the women _____the women's locker room_____
11. the medals of those heroes _____those heroes' medals_____
12. the feed for the animals _____the animals' feed_____
13. the books of these students _____these students' books_____

 Fill in the circle of the word that correctly completes each sentence. Then write the word on the line.

14. The Middle West is known as our ___nation's___ breadbasket.
    ● nation's ○ nation ○ nations'

15. ___Farmers'___ lives in the Corn Belt depend on their ability to grow corn.
    ○ Farmers ● Farmers' ○ Farmer's

16. Here, on the flat land of the Great Plains, growing wheat and corn
    is a way of life for men, women, and ___children___.
    ● children ○ child's ○ children's

LESSON 43: Review and Assess **89**

---

# UNIVERSAL ACCESS
## Meeting Individual Needs

### Kinesthetic Learners

Prepare a beanbag and a six-square hopscotch board. Instead of labeling the boxes with numbers, label them as follows: action word, drop the **e**, change **y** to **i**, plural, compound word, contraction. Students toss the beanbag into a square, as in hopscotch. Then they say a word that fits the rule before they jump on the board.

### Learners with Special Needs

Additional strategies for supporting learners with special needs can be found on page 59L.

### Auditory Learners

Have groups of students generate a list of onomatopoeia, such as animal noises (**hiss, bark, squeak**), or environmental sounds (**honk, crash, hum**). Give each group a five-part spinner, labeled as follows: **present, past, contraction, plural,** and **possession.** Students spin the spinner and say a sentence using one of the verbs on the list. They must also use the word form set up by the spinner.

**Complete each sentence with a compound word. Write the word on the line.**

1. A chair mounted on wheels is a ___wheelchair___.

2. Boats that you row are ___rowboats___.

3. The way you send someone off on a trip is a ___send-off___.

Wheelchair race at Goodwill Games

★ **Read the passage. For each numbered blank, there is a choice of words below. Fill in the circle of the word that completes the sentence correctly.**

The National Road was built in **4**, starting in 1811. It was our **5** response to change. People were moving to the West in great numbers, and they needed a way to get there. By 1850, the National Road had reached Illinois. However, by then, the coming of the railroad had stopped **6** to extend the National Road. Much later, the old National Road became part of U.S. Highway 40.

4. ○ stage's   ● stages   ○ stage

5. ● country's   ○ countries   ○ countries'

6. ○ plan's   ○ plans'   ● plans

★ **Reread the passage. Circle the letter of each answer below.**

7. Why was the National Road started?
   a. There were too many cars.
   (b.) People were moving to the West.
   c. Workers needed jobs.
   d. The railroad was coming.

8. How long did it take for the road to reach Illinois?
   a. more than a century
   b. nearly 11 years
   (c.) about 40 years
   d. less than 10 years

**Extend & Apply**

Suppose that you and your family wanted to drive from Maryland, where the National Road began, west to the Pacific Ocean. Use a road atlas to plan the route. Answers will vary.

90   LESSON 43: Review and Assess

# Reteaching Activities

## Number Your Words

Prepare a table with the column heads below.

Singular (1)

Plural (2)

Singular possessive (3)

Plural possessive (4)

Compound word (5)

Free toss (6)

Ask students to take turns rolling a number cube. Have them say and spell a word for the category of the number on the cube. For example, if a student rolls a two, he or she could say and spell **monkeys.** If a six is rolled, student gets a free toss.

## Change, or Not?

Have students make a list of all the objects they see in the classroom. When they have compiled their lists, have them begin to classify the words. The first classification should be whether the word is singular or plural. The second should be, "If it's plural, was there a spelling change?" If there was a change, have students write the singular noun in parentheses next to the plural noun.

## Assessing the Skill

**Check Up** The exercises on page 89 are discussed in *Teaching the Lesson*. Assign them now if you have not already done so.

Page 90 will help you assess students' understanding of word endings, plurals, possessives, and compound words.

Read aloud the directions for the exercises. Point out that for items 4–6, students will read a passage from which certain words are missing. They will choose the correct answer and fill in the circle. Then have students complete the page.

**Observational Assessment** As students complete the exercises, observe which areas appear to pose the greatest difficulty. For items 1–3, check whether they can use the photograph and clues in the sentence to infer the compound words. For items 4–6, make sure students understand the variety of forms that are presented. You may wish to refer back to your observational notes from lessons 29–35 as you evaluate overall progress of the students.

**Student Skills Assessment** Keep a record of students' mastery of inflectional endings, contractions, plurals, possessives, and compound words, using the checklist on page 59H.

**Writing Conference** Meet with each student individually to discuss recent writing efforts: the descriptive essay on page 74, the persuasive speech on page 82, and the how-to paragraph on page 88. Have students recall a favorite piece of writing in their Home Portfolios. Discuss areas in which the student has shown improvement, and set goals for the next writing opportunity.

Group together students who need further instruction in inflectional endings, contractions, plurals, possessives, and compound words, and have them complete the *Reteaching Activities.* Turn to page 59C for alternative assessment methods.

# UNIT 4 PLANNING RESOURCE

# Prefixes, Roots, Base Words, and Suffixes

## Theme: Southwest

### STANDARDS

✪ Read expository text with grade-appropriate fluency

✪ Develop and strengthen vocabulary by reading and studying words in context

✪ Use knowledge of prefixes, suffixes, roots, and base words to determine the meanings of new words

✪ Divide words with prefixes and suffixes into syllables

### OBJECTIVES

▶ To appreciate nonfiction works about the Southwest

▶ To determine the meanings of words with roots, base words, prefixes, and suffixes

▶ To identify and write words with roots, base words, prefixes, and suffixes

▶ To separate words with prefixes and suffixes into syllables

### LESSONS

## Assessment Strategies

An overview of assessment strategies appears on page **91C**. It offers suggestions for using a variety of assessment tools, including **Pretests** and **Post Tests** (pages **91D–91G**), the **Activity Master** (page **91M**), and the **Assessment Checklist** (page **91H**).

# Thematic Teaching

In Unit 4 students learn about prefixes, roots, base words, and suffixes. Students encounter words with one or more of these word parts in the context of authentic nonfiction selections and exercises related to the theme the *Southwest*.

Students begin their investigation of the theme by creating an Almanac of the Southwest. The resource list below offers titles of books, videos, and other materials that can help students focus their study of the region. Many of the Teacher's Edition lessons in this unit open with poems, riddles, or tongue twisters related to the Southwest. These "hooks" can spark students' interest in the theme and in the play of words.

# Curriculum Integration

### Writing
Students outline spelling rules on page **128** and create a simple thesaurus on page **132**.

### Science
Students research the planet Pluto on page **96**, study the uses of wire on page **112**, list inventions on page **116**, prepare a glossary on page **118**, and research hurricane damage on page **126**.

### Art
Students study Georgia O'Keeffe on page **102**.

### Social Studies
Students prepare a time line on page **92**, map the transcontinental railroad on page **100**, research the history of television on page **114**, and study the Declaration of Independence on page **130**.

### Math
Students make bar graphs on page **122** and count suffixes on page **124**.

# Optional Learning Activities

### Meeting Individual Needs
Most of the Teacher's Edition lessons offer activities for students with distinct learning styles or particular intellectual or sensory strengths. The activities are labeled for learners with the following "styles": **Visual, Kinesthetic, Auditory, Logical,** and **Tactile.**

### Multicultural Connections
Students research cultural influences on page **92,** look up word histories on page **94,** study pueblos on page **98,** collect recipes on page **104,** and research Latin roots on page **110.**

### Word Study Strategies
Pages **91I–91J** offer activities that give students practice with word study strategies. Students sort words, build words, and define words in context.

### Universal Access
Exercises tailored to meet the needs of **English-Language Learners** and **Gifted Learners** can be found in almost every Teacher's Edition lesson. Strategies designed to help **Learners with Special Needs,** such as students with Conceptual Deficits, can be found on page **91L.**

### Intervention
Page **91K** offers **Intervention Strategies** designed to help students performing below grade level understand the concepts taught in **Lessons 45, 49,** and **63.**

### Reteaching
On page **108** students search for words, and on page **138** students build words from word parts.

### Technology
Page **91N** offers activities for students who enjoy working with computers or audio/video equipment. In addition, **Computer Connections**—tips for students who use a word processor—can be found on pages **106, 120, 134,** and **136.**

## R E S O U R C E S

### Books
Green, Carl R. and Sanford, William Reynolds. *Zebulon Pike: Explorer of the Southwest,* NJ: Enslow Publishers, 1996.
Meltzer, Milton. *Driven from the Land: The Story of the Dust Bowl (Great Journeys),* NY: Benchmark Books, 2000.

### Videos
*The American Experience: Lost in the Grand Canyon,* PBS Home Video, 1999.
*The American Experience: The Iron Road,* PBS Home Video, 1990.

### CDs
*Pecos Bill,* Rabbit Ears Series, Madacy Records, 1999.

In Unit 4 students study base words, roots, prefixes, and suffixes. To evaluate students' mastery of these skills, use any or all of the assessment methods suggested below.

## Pretests and Post Tests

The tests on pages **91D–91G** objectively assess how well students understand base words, roots, prefixes, and suffixes. These tests may be used at the beginning of the unit as an informal diagnostic tool or at the end of the unit as a more formal measure of students' progress.

## Observational Assessment

Opportunities for observing students as they work are suggested throughout the unit. Lesson-specific recommendations are included for assessing students' work. Check students' work on a regular basis to see whether they are applying what they are learning to their own writing.

## Using Technology

The Technology activities on page **91N** may also help evaluate students whose language skills are best shown when using computers or audio/video equipment.

## Performance Assessment

Select ten words from the lessons in this unit. Have students print the words on a sheet of paper. Then ask students to underline the base word or root, and circle the prefix and/or suffix in each word.

## Portfolio Assessment

The portfolio icon in the lesson plans indicates an opportunity for students to add to the growing body of work in their portfolios. Each student's portfolio will be unique and should contain pieces that the student feels represent his or her best work. You may wish to give students additional opportunities to add to their portfolios.

## Rubric for Writing

| | Always | Sometimes | Never |
|---|---|---|---|
| Uses capitalization, punctuation, spelling, and grammar appropriately | | | |
| Creates a variety of sentences containing words with roots, prefixes, suffixes, and multisyllabic words with prefixes and suffixes | | | |
| Uses rhyming pairs appropriately for intended purpose | | | |
| Conveys meaning through writing | | | |

## Answer Key

**Page 91D**
1. dis
2. in
3. de
4. en
5. pre
6. un
7. trans
8. semi
9. port
10. graph
11. pod
12. vis
13. duct
14. scope
15. audi
16. gram
17. less
18. some
19. y
20. ity
21. ment
22. ance

**Page 91E**
1. de 2
2. out 2
3. ir 4
4. com 2
5. semi 4
6. re 2
7. con 2
8. sub 2
9. em 2
10. pre 2
11. pos 3
12. ject 2

13. script 3
14. vis 3
15. aster 3
16. ped 2
17. spect 2
18. gram 3
19. phone 3
20. spect 3
21. ful 2
22. ness 2
23. ive 2
24. ance 3
25. hood 3
26. some 2
27. y 2
28. age 2
29. less 2
30. ence 3

**Page 91F**
1. un
2. mid
3. co
4. post
5. en
6. in
7. ex
8. il
9. vid
10. log
11. duct
12. scope
13. tract
14. audi
15. graph
16. port
17. ful

18. ance
19. ity
20. ness
21. ion
22. able

**Page 91G**
1. un 3
2. mid 2
3. dis 3
4. post 2
5. ex 2
6. il 4
7. trans 2
8. in 3
9. en 3
10. co 4
11. port 2
12. pel 2
13. vid 3
14. graph 3
15. log 3
16. scope 3
17. duct 3
18. tract 2
19. script 3
20. audi 5
21. less 2
22. est 2
23. able 4
24. ible 4
25. hood 3
26. ity 4
27. like 2
28. ly 3
29. ship 2
30. sion 3

Name _____

**Fill in the circle next to the prefix that can be added to each base word.**

1. _____qualify
○ un      ○ de      ○ dis

2. _____accurate
○ un      ○ in      ○ re

3. _____fault
○ mis     ○ de      ○ re

4. _____circle
○ en      ○ un      ○ pre

5. _____caution
○ mis     ○ pre     ○ post

6. _____familiar
○ co      ○ ex      ○ un

7. _____form
○ trans   ○ il      ○ mid

8. _____private
○ out     ○ semi    ○ trans

**Fill in the circle next to the root that is found in each word.**

9. transport
○ trans   ○ pos     ○ port

10. autograph
○ auto    ○ togr    ○ graph

11. podium
○ um      ○ diu     ○ pod

12. television
○ tele    ○ ion     ○ vis

13. conductor
○ duct    ○ tor     ○ cond

14. microscope
○ scope   ○ crosc   ○ micro

15. audience
○ ence    ○ dien    ○ audi

16. diagram
○ dia     ○ agra    ○ gram

**Fill in the circle next to the suffix that can be added to each base word.**

17. care_____
○ y       ○ less    ○ ness

18. quarrel_____
○ ity     ○ some    ○ ance

19. cloud_____
○ ity     ○ y       ○ ly

20. possible_____
○ ful     ○ ity     ○ ment

21. measure_____
○ ion     ○ ly      ○ ment

22. avoid_____
○ ence    ○ ment    ○ ance

Possible score on Unit 4 Pretest 1 is 22. Score _____

**Underline the prefix in each word. On the line, write the number of syllables the word has.**

1. defrost ____
2. outweigh ____
3. irregular ____
4. combine ____
5. semicircle ____
6. rewrite ____
7. confirm ____
8. submerge ____
9. embrace ____
10. preschool ____

**Underline the root in each word. On the line, write the number of syllables the word has.**

11. deposit ____
12. reject ____
13. prescription ____
14. visible ____
15. asterisk ____
16. pedal ____
17. inspect ____
18. diagram ____
19. microphone ____
20. spectacle ____

**Underline the suffix in each word. On the line, write the number of syllables the word has.**

21. wishful ____
22. kindness ____
23. active ____
24. avoidance ____
25. adulthood ____
26. tiresome ____
27. juicy ____
28. package ____
29. painless ____
30. persistence ____

Possible score on Unit 4 Pretest 2 is 30. Score _____

Name _____

**Fill in the circle next to the prefix that can be added to each base word.**

I. _____equal
○ un    ○ de    ○ dis

2. _____week
○ un    ○ semi    ○ mid

3. _____operate
○ co    ○ de    ○ re

4. _____script
○ en    ○ un    ○ post

5. _____able
○ mis    ○ pre    ○ en

6. _____correct
○ co    ○ in    ○ un

7. _____claim
○ en    ○ il    ○ ex

8. _____logical
○ il    ○ semi    ○ trans

**Fill in the circle next to the root that is found in each word.**

9. video
○ id    ○ deo    ○ vid

10. dialogue
○ dia    ○ log    ○ alo

II. aqueduct
○ aqu    ○ duct    ○ que

12. telescope
○ tele    ○ lesc    ○ scope

13. attract
○ ttract    ○ att    ○ tract

14. auditorium
○ ium    ○ tori    ○ audi

15. autograph
○ graph    ○ togr    ○ auto

16. import
○ port    ○ po    ○ imp

**Fill in the circle next to the suffix that can be added to each base word.**

17. pain_____
○ ly    ○ ness    ○ ful

18. annoy_____
○ ity    ○ some    ○ ance

19. sincere_____
○ ity    ○ ness    ○ y

20. dark_____
○ ful    ○ ness    ○ ment

21. digest_____
○ ion    ○ ly    ○ ment

22. manage_____
○ ion    ○ ity    ○ able

Possible score on Unit 4 Post Test 1 is 22. Score _____

**Underline the prefix in each word. On the line, write the number of syllables the word has.**

1. unequal ____        2. midweek ____

3. disagree ____       4. postscript ____

5. exclaim ____        6. illogical ____

7. transform ____      8. incorrect ____

9. enable ____        10. cooperate ____

**Underline the root in each word. On the line, write the number of syllables the word has.**

11. import ____        12. expel ____

13. video ____         14. telegraph ____

15. dialogue ____      16. telescope ____

17. production ____    18. retract ____

19. description ____   20. auditorium ____

**Underline the suffix in each word. On the line, write the number of syllables the word has.**

21. painless ____      22. darkest ____

23. manageable ____    24. digestible ____

25. adulthood ____     26. sincerity ____

27. dreamlike ____     28. rapidly ____

29. hardship ____      30. division ____

Possible score on Unit 4 Post Test 2 is 30. Score _____

**Student Name** _____

## UNIT FOUR
## STUDENT SKILLS ASSESSMENT CHECKLIST

☑ Assessed     ☒ Retaught     ■ Mastered

- ❏ Base Words, Roots, Prefixes, and Suffixes
- ❏ Prefixes **un-, re-, dis-, de-**
- ❏ Prefixes **pre-, post-, ex-, out-**
- ❏ Prefixes **sub-, trans-, mid-, semi-**
- ❏ Prefixes **in-/il-/im-/ir-**
- ❏ Prefixes **co-, com-/con-, en-/em-, in-/im-**
- ❏ Roots **-pos-, -pel-, -tract-, -ject-, -port-**
- ❏ Roots **-ped-/-pod-, -ven-/-vent-, -duc-/-duct-**
- ❏ Roots **-spect-, -vid-/-vis-, -audi-, -phon-, -scope-**
- ❏ Roots **-scrib-/-script-, -graph-/-gram-, -log-**
- ❏ Roots **-fac-** and **-astro-/-aster-**
- ❏ Suffixes **-er** and **-est**
- ❏ Suffixes **-y, -ly, -ish, -like, -ful, -less**
- ❏ Suffixes **-ship, -ness, -hood, -ment, -some**
- ❏ Suffixes **-ity, -ive, -age, -ion/-sion/-tion**
- ❏ Suffixes **-able/-ible** and **-ance/-ence**
- ❏ More Than One Prefix or Suffix

## TEACHER COMMENTS

# WORD STUDY STRATEGIES

In Unit 4 students study prefixes, roots, and suffixes. To give students opportunities to master word study strategies, use any or all of the activities suggested below.

## Word-Part Match-Up

Combine the prefix with each of the three base words that follow it. Write the new words on the lines. Then write an additional word that includes the prefix.

1. **un-**

   **lock**         **known**         **familiar**

   _____  _____  _____

   additional word: _____

2. **re-**

   **apply**         **paid**         **occur**

   _____  _____  _____

   additional word: _____

3. **dis-**

   **cover**         **agree**         **honest**

   _____  _____  _____

   additional word: _____

4. **de-**

   **code**         **frost**         **fault**

   _____  _____  _____

   additional word: _____

5. **pre-**

   **school**         **view**         **historic**

   _____  _____  _____

   additional word: _____

## Word-Part Search

Circle the prefix in each word. Determine whether each word contains a base word or a root and underline that word part. If you underlined a base word, write **BW** on the line. If you underlined a root, write **R** on the line.

**conform**      _____

**midterm**      _____

**postscript**   _____

**expel**        _____

**outweigh**     _____

**distract**     _____

**subtopic**     _____

**enforce**      _____

**inject**       _____

**semicolon**    _____

**transport**    _____

**describe**     _____

## Build on Word Roots

Answer each clue by matching a prefix in the box to a root in the box to form a new word. Write the new words on the lines.

| Prefixes: | Roots: |
|---|---|
| trans | duct |
| ex | port |
| re | spect |
| con | pel |
| in | ject |

1. To force to leave is to _____

2. To carry across is to _____

3. To direct or lead is to _____

4. To look at closely is to _____

5. To throw back is to _____

## Build with Suffixes

Circle the suffix in each word. Then write two new words that include the same suffix.

1. careless _____ _____

2. friendly _____ _____

3. finest _____ _____

4. yellowish _____ _____

5. sadness _____ _____

6. improvement _____ _____

7. childhood _____ _____

8. troublesome _____ _____

9. partnership _____ _____

10. active _____ _____

## Consider the Context

For each word pair, choose the word that best fits the context of the sentence. Write the word. Then write a sentence using the word you did not choose.

1. The **(management/manageable)** did not offer pay raises this year. _____
   _____
   _____

2. He gave his apology with complete **(sincerely/sincerity)**. _____
   _____
   _____

3. Writers and artists are **(creativity/creative)** people. _____
   _____
   _____

4. Most fairy tales and fables are not based on **(really/reality)**. _____
   _____
   _____

## Word Deconstruction

Circle the prefix or suffix in each word. (Some words may have more than one prefix or suffix.) Write the base words on the lines.

1. rediscover _____

2. creativity _____

3. helplessness _____

4. disagreement _____

5. impolitely _____

6. wholesomeness _____

7. redirection _____

8. unhappiness _____

| LESSONS | **45** Base Words, Roots, Prefixes, and Suffixes | **49** Prefixes **in-, il-, im-, ir-** | **63** Suffixes **-able/-ible** and **-ance/-ence** |
|---|---|---|---|
| **Problem** | Student has difficulty distinguishing roots from base words. | Student can't remember which base words are used with the prefixes **il-, im-, in-,** and **ir-**. | Student has difficulty spelling words that end with the suffixes **-able/-ible** and/or **-ance/-ence**. |
| **Intervention Strategies** | • Student may have difficulty distinguishing between roots and base words because some roots, such as **-port-, -pod-,** and **-log-,** can stand alone as base words. Although these roots and words look and sound alike, they have different meanings. For example, the word **port** means "harbor town" while the root **-port-** means "to carry."<br><br>• Ask the student to look up the meanings of **pod** and **log** as base words and as roots. | • Tell the student that these prefixes can mean **not** and can be regarded as one prefix that changes according to the first letter of the word to which it is added.<br><br>• Point out that using different versions of the prefix makes words easier to pronounce. Demonstrate that it is easier to say *"imp"* than *"inp"* and *"ill"* than *"irl"*.<br><br>• Ask the student to add the prefixes **il-, im-, in-,** and **ir-** to each of the following base words and say them aloud: **correct, mature, regular,** and **legal.** Then ask the student to note which prefix is easiest to pronounce with the base word. | • Suggest to the student that he or she use pronunciation as a strategy to help remember the spellings of words that end in these suffixes. For example, when the student learns that the base word **break** takes the suffix **-able** and that the base word **flex** takes the suffix **-ible,** have the student then pronounce each suffix with an exaggerated long vowel sound.<br><br>• Stress to the student that this strategy is not to be used for learning to pronounce the words, but rather to help identify and remember the appropriate suffix to use. |

OKLAHOMA CITY

The following activities offer strategies for helping students with special needs to participate in selected exercises in Unit 4.

## Conceptual Deficits

**Base Words, Roots, Prefixes, and Suffixes**
Students who have difficulty with classification activities may become confused when asked to analyze words according to their prefixes, base words, roots, and suffixes. These students may find using a graphic organizer to classify word parts will help them identify the prefix, base word, root, or suffix in a word.

- Read the definitions for prefix, base word, root, and suffix on page **93.** Have students make a four-column chart and head each column with the name of these word parts. Suggest that they put **prefix** in the first column to remind them that a prefix is added to the beginning of a word and **suffix** in the last column to remind them that it is added to the end of a word.

- Ask students to write the definition of each word part in each column under its name. Guide students to use the charts to divide the words on page **94** into word parts.

## Memory Deficits

**Prefixes un-, re-, dis-, de-**
Students who have trouble remembering details may find the lessons on word parts frustrating. Engaging these students' prior knowledge may give them a field of reference in which to integrate the new material.

- Use **Lesson 46** as a model. Tell students to look at the Helpful Hints and to think of other examples of words with the prefixes **un-, re-, dis-, de-**. (Point out that the slang word **dis** comes from the word **disrespect.**)

- Encourage students to find ways to familiarize themselves with words that consist of prefixes, roots, and suffixes. For example, suggest that students keep a list of such words as they encounter them in their reading. Make time available for students to share these words with a partner and to use them in sentences.

## Conceptual Deficits

**Story Map**
Students who have difficulty with inferential thinking may need help filling in the story map on page **120.** Before they map their own story, help them map a story or a movie that they have read or seen and enjoyed.

- Make and photocopy a new story map substituting questions for the labels given in the map on page **120.** For example, instead of using the label **Setting,** use the question **Where did the story take place?** Instead of the label **Hero,** use the question **Who was the story about?**

- Continue to ask specific questions that focus on the kind of information the students are being asked to give. After students have mapped a story they already know, encourage them to map the story they have created.

## Visual/Perception Deficits

**Coding Activity**
Students who have difficulty keeping their place while reading may need help with activities such as the one on page **137.**

- Have students write each letter/number combination on index cards. For example **A1** written on one side and **un** written on the other.

- Then have them use the labeled cards to complete the exercises by choosing the appropriate cards and writing the corresponding prefix, base word, and suffix on the line.

- Students may find the task easier to manage if they keep the index cards in piles according to the letters **A, B, C,** and so on.

Name _____

**Sort the words in the box and write the words on the lines.**

| poisonous | discover | beautiful | attract | enclose |
|---|---|---|---|---|
| opposite | return | midweek | boldest | pedal |
| insight | educate | manuscript | cloudless | freedom |

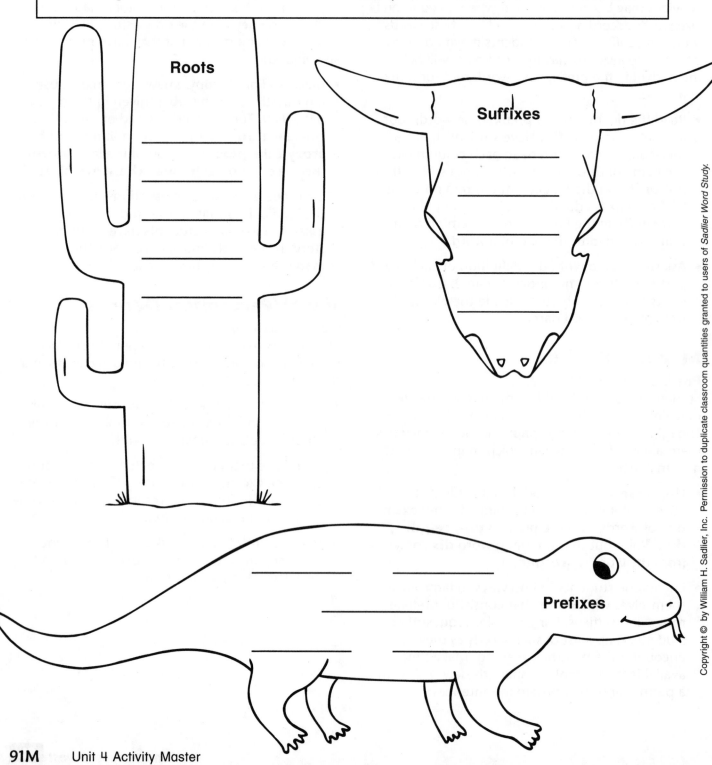

**Roots**

_____
_____
_____
_____
_____

**Suffixes**

_____
_____
_____
_____
_____

**Prefixes**

_____
_____
_____

## Create a Sonoran Desert Guidebook

 Invite students to use the Internet to create a guidebook about Arizona's Sonoran Desert.

- Ask the class to discuss topics to research related to the desert environment. They may want to include the following: climate, temperature, geographic features or land forms, and indigenous plants and animals.

- Encourage (and assist if needed) the students to use search engines to obtain and compile information about the Sonoran Desert. If a scanner is available, have students scan photographs, maps, charts, and graphs to include in the guidebook.

- Tell students to use words that contain prefixes, roots, and suffixes in the text of the guidebook, for example: **aridity, humidity, adaptation, development, survival, midsummer, midday, edible, successful, sandy,** and so on.

- Help the students create a display for the guidebook that showcases the beauty of the Sonoran Desert. The display and guidebook can be presented as a learning center in the classroom or shared with others in the school library.

## Videotape a Regional Art Exhibition

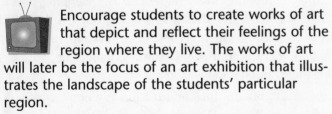 Encourage students to create works of art that depict and reflect their feelings of the region where they live. The works of art will later be the focus of an art exhibition that illustrates the landscape of the students' particular region.

- Show students examples from artists with Southwestern influences, such as Georgia O'Keeffe, Frederic Remington, and Edward Sheriff Curtis. Encourage the students to note how each artist captures the essence of the Southwestern environment in his or her specific type of art.

- Have a discussion about the characteristics of the students' particular region that can be the focal points of their art. For example, students may want to include the plains and farm lands of the Middle States, the coastal and industrial areas in the Northeast states, etc.

- After students have completed their works of art have them write a brief commentary about their work. The class will then work together to produce a video presentation of the art exhibit. The narrative should introduce each piece of art and read the commentaries. Encourage students to include words with prefixes, roots, and suffixes both in their commentary and narrative.

- Have the class select a student to act as the narrator for the exhibition. Encourage volunteers to take turns operating the video camera.

## Record Myths and Legends of Carlsbad Caverns

Encourage students to write and record myths or legends that give an imaginative explanation of how the caverns of New Mexico's Carlsbad Caverns were formed.

- Introduce students to examples of myths and legends of the Southwest, such as the legend of Pecos Bill. Have students note the use of humor that is an important feature in these tales.

- Provide students with photographs of New Mexico's Carlsbad Caverns. Encourage them to write a myth or legend that recounts an event that occurred there, real or imaginary.

- Tell students to use as many descriptive words as possible in their stories with the suffixes **-er, -est, -ful, -like, -y, -ly, -ness, -ment, -ive,** and **-tion.**

- When all the stories are written, read them aloud to the class. Then tell the students that they may record the stories on an audiocassette. Students may read their own stories or ask a classmate to read and record the story for them.

- The finished audiocassette can be used in a listening center or shared with another class.

## Introduction to
### Prefixes, Roots, Base Words, and Suffixes

### Objectives

- **To enjoy a nonfiction passage related to the theme the *Southwest***
- **To identify prefixes, roots, base words, and suffixes**

## Starting with Literature

Have volunteers read aloud "Mountain Lying Down." On the board, write the word **enchantment.** Draw lines separating the word parts as follows: **en/chant/ment.** Tell students that they will learn about these word parts in this unit.

## Critical Thinking

- For the first question, review the meaning of the word **awesome.**

- Have students reread paragraph three to find the answer to the second question.

- Encourage students to think about what they know from experience or reading to answer the third question.

## Introducing the Skill

- Write the following terms on the board: **base word, root, prefix,** and **suffix.** Ask students to use what they already know as well as clues within the words to determine the meaning of each term.

- Help students label the word parts in the word **enchantment.**

## Practicing the Skill

Make a chart with the column heads: **en-, -ish, -ion, -ist, -ment,** and **-some.** Call on volunteers to find words in the passage that contain the word part in each heading. **(enchantment, Spanish, elevation, tourists, awesome)**

91

# "Mountain Lying Down"

**T**he Southwest is indeed a "land of enchantment." The Grand Canyon is just one of the wonders of the Southwest.

The Grand Canyon is 277 miles across. In some spots it is 10 miles wide. The Paiute call it *Kaibab,* or "Mountain Lying Down." To the Spanish explorers, it was *Gran Cañón.*

Native Americans knew about the Grand Canyon long before the first Europeans arrived in the 1500s. In about the year A.D. 500, the Anasazi came. They farmed the dry land and made baskets, pottery, and sandals. They lived in small villages in houses they built with stone. A thousand years later, these people were gone.

On the rim of the Grand Canyon are thick forests of aspen and fir. The temperatures there are cool. Much snow falls in the winter. Yet the floor of the canyon is a desert. It is hot and dry—and home to many different kinds of cacti. Because of the huge differences in elevation and moisture in the Grand Canyon, a wide variety of plants and animals can live there.

Today, more than 4 million people visit the Grand Canyon each year. You can be sure that most of these tourists leave with a new understanding of the word—*awesome!*

### Critical Thinking

1. **What is "awesome" about the Grand Canyon?**
2. **What was life like for the Anasazi who lived in the Grand Canyon area?**
3. **Have you ever been to the Grand Canyon? If so, what was it like? If not, would you like to go? Explain why.**

1. The Grand Canyon is huge, contains both forest and desert, and has a wide variety of plants and animals.
2. The Anasazi farmed, made baskets, pottery, and sandals, and lived in stone houses.
3. Answers will vary.

LESSON 44: Introduction to Prefixes, Roots, Base Words, and Suffixes    **91**

# Theme Activity

**ALMANAC OF THE SOUTHWEST** Display the area known as the Southwest on a map of the United States (Texas, Oklahoma, New Mexico, and Arizona). Have students work in groups to research the region. Assign a separate topic to each group: historical information, tourist information, plant and animal life, weather and climate, and natural resources.

Encourage students to present their information as a book, which they can publish with the title "Almanac of the Southwest." Maps, charts, and graphs should have explanations about the information included.

As you continue to work on the lessons in Unit 4, have students add words that contain prefixes, roots, and/or suffixes to the glossary of their "Almanac of the Southwest."

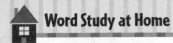

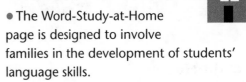

Visit us at
www.sadlier-oxford.com

## Dear Family,

Your child has begun Unit 4 of Sadlier's *Word Study* program. Lessons in this unit focus on prefixes and suffixes and on how they change the meaning of the base words and roots that include them. The theme of this unit is the *Southwest*.

A **prefix** is a word part added to the beginning of a base word or root. Some common prefixes are **un-, re-, dis-, de-,** and **ex-**.

A **suffix** is a word part added to the end of a base word or root. Some common suffixes are **-ful, -less, -ness,** and **-ion**.

A **root** is the main part of a word. Roots become words when a prefix or a suffix is added to them. Add the prefix **ex-** ("out of") and the suffix **-ion** ("act or result of") to the root **-tract-** ("pull"): **ex- + -tract- + -ion = extraction.** This word means "the act of pulling out, as a tooth."

### Family Focus

- Create a Word Wall of prefixes and suffixes that your child will study in this unit. Add new words as they arise—in conversation or on the radio or television.

- Read together the nonfiction selection on page 91. Discuss it with your child. Has your family been to the Grand Canyon? Would your family like to visit this natural wonder? How would you get there from where you live?

### LINKS TO LEARNING

To extend learning together, you might explore:

**Web Sites**
www.nps.gov/grca
www.johngregg.com

**Video**
*The American Experience: Lost in the Grand Canyon,* PBS Home Video.

**Literature**
*Desert Dwellers: Native People of the American Southwest* by Scott S. Warren ©1997.

*Race to the Moonrise: An Ancient Journey* by Sally Crum ©1998.

## Multicultural Connection

The Spanish influence and the influence of Native Americans are felt strongly in the present-day culture of the Southwest. Have students choose a group and research the influences of the group on this region. Have students pay particular attention to place names, and words that have been incorporated into the English language. Students may wish to find out about food, music, dance, and styles of architecture contributed by the Spanish or Native American peoples.

## Social Studies Link

The region called the Southwest includes the state of Texas, the only state ever to have been a separate country. Have students prepare a time line of Texas history from the time it became a republic until the present. Students may wish to incorporate this research into the theme project.

## Word Study at Home

- The Word-Study-at-Home page is designed to involve families in the development of students' language skills.

- On the Word-Study-at-Home page for Unit 4, students and their families will find activities that relate to the theme, the *Southwest,* and focus on prefixes, suffixes, base words, and roots.

- Invite students to remove page 92 from their books carefully and take it home to share with their families.

- Families may want to discuss some of the information about the Grand Canyon included in the passage on page 91. If any family members have visited the Grand Canyon, students may want to interview them and share their findings with the class.

### Theme-Related Resources

**Books**

*The Best Town in the World* by Byrd Baylor, Macmillan, 1983

*Grand Canyon: Exploring a Natural Wonder* by Wendell Minor, Scholastic, Inc., 1998

*Walks Alone* by Brian Burks, Harcourt Brace, 1998

**Web Sites**

Cinco de Mayo:
**www.worldbook.com/fun/cinco/ html/cinco.htm**

The U.S.-Mexican War (1846–1848):
**www.pbs.org/kera/usmexicanwar**

# Base Words, Roots, Prefixes, and Suffixes

## Objectives

- **To identify base words, roots, prefixes, and suffixes**
- **To read and write words containing base words, roots, prefixes, and suffixes**

## Warming Up

- Call on two students to act out this dialogue for the class.

   **Student 1:** Pete and Re-Pete took the bus home. The bus stopped, and Pete got off. Who was left?

   **Student 2:** Re-Pete.

   **Student 1:** Pete and Re-Pete took the bus home. The bus stopped...

- Encourage students to "ham it up" as they read the dialogue several times.

- Have a student explain the joke. ("Re-Pete" is heard as "repeat," so the first student repeats from the beginning again.)

- Explain that some word parts added before or after a word can change the meaning of the word.

## Teaching the Lesson

- Tell students that each numbered item on page 93 has its own Helpful Hint. Call on a student to read the hint for the first item and then complete item one as a group. Ask students to name other prefix/base word combinations they know.

- Call on a student to read the hint that explains roots. Read the instructions and have students complete item two. Review the difference between a base word and a root.

- Have students read the hints and instructions for items three and four and complete the sentences.

93

---

Name _____

> ▶ **Helpful Hint**
>
> Prefixes, suffixes and roots are word parts. You can discover the meaning of a word through its word parts.

**HINT:** You can add a prefix *or* a suffix *or* both to a **base word** to form a new word or change a word's meaning. For example, **read** is the base word in **unread**able.

⭐ **Write the base word that completes the sentence correctly.**

1. The base word in **refillable** is ___fill___.     refill    fillable    fill

**HINT:** A **root** is the main part of a word. A root usually cannot stand alone. Add a prefix *or* a suffix *or* both to a root to form a word. The root **pel** means "drive." The prefix **ex** means "out." To **expel** is "to drive out."

⭐ **Write the root that completes the sentence correctly.**

2. The root in **injection** is ___ject___.     in    ject    inject

**HINT:** A **prefix** is a word part added to the beginning of a base word or root. The prefix in **disagree** is **dis**. **Dis** means "not." To **disagree** is "not to agree."

⭐ **Write the prefix that completes the sentence correctly.**

3. The prefix in **return** is ___re___.     re    turn    return

**HINT:** A **suffix** is a word part added to the end of a base word or root. The suffix in **friendship** is **ship**. **Ship** means "state." **Friendship** is "the state of being friends."

⭐ **Write the suffix that completes the sentence correctly.**

4. The suffix in **unhappiness** is ___ness___.
   ness    happy    un

> **WORK TOGETHER** ▶
>
> Work with a partner. Brainstorm a list of prefixes and suffixes that you can add to the following roots to build words:
>
> **ject**   **port**   **tract**

---

# UNIVERSAL ACCESS
## Meeting Individual Needs

### Tactile Learners

Make a card for each prefix, suffix, base word, and root used on page 94. (There will be more than one of some cards.) Assign students to teams of three and have them work cooperatively to form each word on page 94. Then have them rearrange the cards to make new words.

### Logical Learners

Make word cards for some easily recognizable pairs of antonyms that contain base words, roots, prefixes, and/or suffixes. Have students work with a partner to match the antonyms. Remind students to use a dictionary for words they don't know. Possible pairs include the following:

**enjoyable/unpleasant**
**reusable/disposable**
**exact/inexact**
**logical/unreasonable**

Use what you know about word parts. Write the prefix, the base word, and the suffix in each word.

| | Prefix | Base Word | Suffix |
|---|---|---|---|
| 1. unsuccessful | un | success | ful |
| 2. cooperative | co | operate | ive |
| 3. reusable | re | use | able |
| 4. semimonthly | semi | month | ly |
| 5. encouragement | en | courage | ment |
| 6. nonpoisonous | non | poison | ous |
| 7. unreasonable | un | reason | able |
| 8. disappearance | dis | appear | ance |
| 9. incompletion | in | complete | ion |
| 10. disgraceful | dis | grace | ful |

Write the prefix, the root, and the suffix in each word.

| | Prefix | Root | Suffix |
|---|---|---|---|
| 11. contraction | con | tract | ion |
| 12. respectful | re | spect | ful |
| 13. invisible | in | vis | ible |
| 14. description | de | script | ion |
| 15. protractor | pro | tract | or |
| 16. producer | pro | duc | er |
| 17. subtraction | sub | tract | ion |
| 18. importance | im | port | ance |
| 19. rejection | re | ject | ion |
| 20. inventive | in | vent | ive |

LESSON 45: Base Words, Roots, Prefixes, and Suffixes

**Home Involvement Activity** Look for words in advertisements that have prefixes *or* suffixes *or* both. Make a list. Then circle the base word or root in the words that you find. Make a Word Wall of these words.

- Point out that the words in the first half of page 94 contain base words and the words in the second half contain roots.

- Listing the prefixes, suffixes, and roots will help students complete the exercises on page 94.

Turn to page 91K for an Intervention Strategy designed to help students who need extra support with this lesson.

## Curriculum Connections

### Spelling Link

Have a three-way spelling bee with these words: **unsuccessful, encouragement, rejection, cooperative, nonpoisonous,** and **contraction.** Arrange students in groups of three. Give a word to one group and allow them time to divide it into its parts. Then have group members answer as follows: one student says and spells the prefix, one student says and spells the base word or root, and one student says and spells the suffix. Continue with the next word and the next group.

### Multicultural Connection

Tell students that most dictionary entries tell the etymology of a word, or its origin and development. The word **etymology** is from the Greek word *etymon*, which means "true sense." The Greeks, like other ancient peoples, believed that the name of an object described its essence. In a dictionary, have students look up the etymology of words from the lesson, such as **return, encouragement,** and **subtraction.**

### Observational Assessment

*Check whether students are able to identify which part of a word is a prefix or a suffix.*

### English-Language Learners/ESL

The English language includes elements of so many other languages that nonnative speakers may see words in English that are similar to words in their home language. Have students review the list of words on page 94 and ask them to point to or name words or word parts that look familiar. Ask students to discuss the similarities with their classmates.

### Gifted Learners

Ask students to think of a specialized field in which they have an interest, such as a sport or computers. Have them list words that are related to that activity. Then have them add prefixes or suffixes to their words. Examples might be **reboot, kicker, artist.**

### Learners with Special Needs

Additional strategies for supporting learners with special needs can be found on page 91L.

# Prefixes
## un-, re-, dis-, de-

### Objectives

- To identify and use the prefixes **un-, re-, dis-, and de-**

- To understand how a prefix combines with a base word to form a new word

## Warming Up

- Write the following rhyme on the board and read it aloud to students.

    Do you think it usual

    Or do you think it **un**,

    That adding a prefix to a base word

    Gives it uses more than one?

- Ask students to find a prefix in the rhyme. **(un-)** Explain that the word **unusual** is formed by adding the prefix **un-** to the base word **usual.**

- Have a student separate **unusual** into two parts. **(un** and **usual)**

- Ask what the word **usual** means. (ordinary or commonplace) Then ask what **unusual** means. (out of the ordinary or uncommon)

## Teaching the Lesson

- Have students read the Helpful Hints and discuss how each prefix changes the meaning of the base word as it makes a new word.

- Discuss with students any patterns of meaning they see in the prefixes. (Some prefixes, such as **un-** and **dis-**, add a negative meaning to base words.)

- Point out that some prefixes have more than one meaning. For example, **re-** can mean "again," as in **rewrite,** or "back," as in **repay.**

---

Name _____

### ▶ Helpful Hints

A **prefix** is a word part added to the **beginning** of a **base word.** Adding a prefix to a word can change the meaning of the word. It can also make a new word.

The **prefix** un means "not," as in un**equal.**

The **prefix** re means "again," as in re**make,** or "back," as in re**pay.**

The **prefix** dis means "not or opposite of," as in dis**agree.**

The **prefix** de means "from," as in de**scribe,** "off," as in de**rail,** "reverse," as in de**frost,** or "bring down," as in de**value.**

Some words seem to have prefixes but do not. For example, when you remove the un from **under,** no base word remains.

The sentences below are about Arizona's Kitt Peak National Observatory. Complete each sentence by adding the prefix un, re, dis, or de to the base word in parentheses. Be sure the new word is spelled correctly.

1. Astronomers took three years to ___disqualify___ 149 other Southwestern peaks before they chose Kitt Peak as the place for an observatory. **(qualify)**

2. The observatory's 21 telescopes help scientists to ___unlock___ some of the mysteries of our vast universe. **(lock)**

3. The telescopes are aimed at distant stars and galaxies and can predict when certain events will happen again, or ___reoccur___. **(occur)**

4. The scientists use computers that can ___decode___ complex information. **(code)**

### CHALLENGE

Each of the following words has two prefixes. Underline both prefixes. Then tell a partner what each word means.

rediscovered

unrestrained

Kitt Peak Observatory

---

# UNIVERSAL ACCESS
## Meeting Individual Needs

### Visual Learners

Have students look through store flyers for words or phrases that contain the prefixes **un-, re-, dis-,** or **de-,** such as **decaffeinated soda, instant rebate, unbeatable prices,** or **discount.** Ask students to cut out these examples and use them in a collage. As part of the collage, students may write their own phrases, using the prefixes **un-, re-, dis-,** and **de.**

### Auditory Learners

Write words that contain the prefixes **un-, re-, dis-,** and **de-** on cards. Examples include **unaware, delight, review, displease, replace, unlikely, disappear,** and **unwilling.** Have students each take a card and sit in a circle. The first student holds up his or her card and says a sentence using the word correctly. The next student does the same with his or her word, building on the previous student's sentence in order to tell a story.

⭐ **Add un, re, dis, or de to each of the following base words. Write the new word on the line.**

1. think ___rethink___
2. live ___relive___
3. happy ___unhappy___
4. honest ___dishonest___
5. fault ___default___
6. please ___displease___
7. frost ___defrost___
8. apply ___reapply___
9. loyal ___disloyal___
10. familiar ___unfamiliar___
11. regard ___disregard___
12. elect ___reelect___

⭐ **Complete each sentence with a word from the box.**

> unpolluted    repaid    discover    unknown    disagree

13. The achievements of the astronomer Percival Lowell may be ___unknown___ to many people.

14. In 1894, Dr. Lowell built an observatory in Flagstaff, Arizona. He knew that Flagstaff's cloudless skies and ___unpolluted___ air would be ideal for studying the Solar System.

15. Lowell hoped that his many hours of looking through his telescope would be ___repaid___ one day.

16. In 1930, a worker at the observatory was the first to ___discover___ the planet Pluto. Lowell had predicted that there was another planet out there past Uranus and Neptune.

17. The work at Lowell Observatory has been recognized and appreciated by astronomers. Yet some astronomers have begun to ___disagree___ with the idea that Pluto is in fact a planet.

Telescope at Lowell Observatory

LESSON 46: Prefixes un-, re-, dis-, de-    **Home Involvement Activity** *The Return of the Pink Panther* is a movie that has a prefix in its title. What other movies have the prefix un, re, dis, or de in their names? Make a list together.

---

**English-Language Learners/ESL**

Write these pairs of words on the board: **happy/unhappy, frost/defrost, write/rewrite,** and **agree/disagree.** Have partners create picture cards for each word. Invite them to quiz each other with the picture cards and label each with the correct word.

**Gifted Learners**

Have students create original words that include the prefixes **un-, re-, dis-,** and **de-,** for example: **reagree, desubtract, disfrown,** and **unlaugh.** Ask students to use each word in a sentence that will suggest its meaning to the reader.

**Learners with Special Needs**

Additional strategies for supporting learners with special needs can be found on page 91L.

---

## Practicing the Skill

Read aloud the directions on pages 95 and 96. Point out that on page 95 and in the first exercise on page 96, students must use what they know about the meaning of the prefix and the base word to decide which prefix to use.

## Curriculum Connections

**Spelling Link**

Write these scrambled words on the board: **ckolnu, dedeoc, lyappre, nohsidste, tecerle, seeasidlp.** Have students write the correct unscrambled word to complete each clue.

> Something you do not like will ___ you. **(displease)**
>
> Do not trust someone who is ___ . **(dishonest)**
>
> Use a key to ___ the door. **(unlock)**
>
> How would you ___ a secret message? **(decode)**
>
> If sun block washes off, ___ it quickly. **(reapply)**
>
> Voters may ___ a candidate they like. **(reelect)**

**Science Link**

● Pluto, the ninth and outermost planet in our solar system, remains mysterious. Recently, Pluto's moon, Charon, was discovered. Within the next twenty years, an unmanned space mission is planned to learn what lies beyond Pluto.

● Have students choose a topic and research it: 1) Discoveries made about Pluto by the Hubble Telescope, 2) Pluto's unusual orbit, 3) Pluto's unclear origins. Tell students to look for words with prefixes as they conduct their research.

## Observational Assessment

*Note whether students can form words by adding the prefixes **un-, re-, dis-,** and **de-** to base words.*

## Student Pages 97–98

# Prefixes
## pre-, post-, ex-, out-

### Objectives

- **To identify and use the prefixes pre-, post-, ex-, and out-**
- **To understand how a prefix combines with a base word to form a new word**

## Warming Up

- Write these sentences on the board and have students read them aloud.

   During the **postwar** period, the nation became **preoccupied** with fitness. Was it reasonable to expect American youth to **extend** themselves to the utmost degree in order to **outperform** and **outdistance** young people from other countries?

- Write the prefixes **pre-**, **post-**, **ex-**, and **out-** as column headings on the board. Tell students to find words in the sentences that contain these prefixes and then write the words under the correct column heading.

## Teaching the Lesson

- Ask a student to read the Helpful Hint for the prefix **pre-** on page 97. Have students name words that begin with the prefix **pre-**. Ask them to explain what each word means and use it in a sentence.

- Do the same for the prefixes **post-**, **ex-**, and **out-**.

- Have students read the words in the box on page 97 and the words in items 4–7 on the same page. Ask them to identify the prefixes and determine their meanings. Students may use a dictionary to verify their answers.

---

Name _____

> **Helpful Hints**

The **prefix** **pre** means "before."

Children attend **pre**school before kindergarten.

The **prefix** **post** means "after."

A **post**script is an extra note placed after the end of a signed letter. Its abbreviation is P.S.

The **prefix** **ex** means "out of or from."

To **ex**claim is "to cry out."

The **prefix** **out** means "outside" or "greater than."

To **out**number is to have a greater number.

*Archaeologists at an Anasazi ruin*

 **Complete each sentence with a word from the box.**

| precautions | outweigh | prehistoric |
|---|---|---|

1. Throughout the Southwest, _____prehistoric_____ peoples, like the Anasazi, left evidence of the lives they had led long ago.

2. Archaeologists take great _____precautions_____ so as not to disturb the remains of past cultures.

3. Usually, their findings _____outweigh_____ their efforts.

**Underline the prefix in each word. Then use what you know about prefixes to write the meaning of the word on the line. Use a dictionary, if needed.**

4. postdate    to date later _____

5. exchange    to give up for something else _____

6. preplan    to plan before _____

7. outlast    to last longer than _____

> ### CHALLENGE
>
> Pre and post are prefixes used to describe periods in time. For example, **pre-Columbian** means "before the arrival of Columbus in the Americas." Write the meaning of these words:
>
> prewar
> postwar

---

# UNIVERSAL ACCESS
# Meeting Individual Needs

### Visual Learners

Have students list all the words on pages 97 and 98 that start with the prefixes **pre-**, **post-**, **ex-**, and **out-**. Ask students to create a word-search puzzle using the words. Tell them they may arrange the words horizontally, vertically, or diagonally. Then have them share their completed puzzles with a partner.

### Auditory Learners

Have students listen as you call out several phrases containing words with the prefixes **pre-**, **post-**, **out-**, and **ex-**. Ask them to write down each word they hear and then compare their lists with a partner's. Possible phrases include **a postponed game, to prepare the recipe, add a postscript, a gift exchange, a movie preview.**

**Choose a word from the box to answer each question correctly. Write the word on the line.**

| | | | | |
|---|---|---|---|---|
| postpone | prejudge | exclaim | preface | exhale |
| outburst | preview | outskirts | exclude | exchange |

1. Which word means "a showing of something ahead of time"? _____preview_____

2. Which word means "to cry out, as in surprise"? _____exclaim_____

3. Which word means "introduction to a book, often written by the author"? _____preface_____

4. Which word means "the area at the edge of a town or city"? _____outskirts_____

5. Which word means "to give or take one thing in return for another"? _____exchange_____

6. Which word means "to pass judgment before knowing all the facts"? _____prejudge_____

7. Which word means "to keep out"? _____exclude_____

8. Which word means "a bursting forth"? _____outburst_____

9. Which word means "to breathe out"? _____exhale_____

10. Which word means "to put off until later"? _____postpone_____

**Write a sentence for six of the words you wrote above.**

11. _____Answers will vary._____

12. _____

13. _____

14. _____

15. _____

16. _____

LESSON 47: Prefixes **pre-, post-, ex-, out-**

**Home Involvement Activity** Write the four prefixes from this lesson, each on an index card. Shuffle the cards and place them face-down. Take turns picking cards. Build two words from the prefix on each card.

**English-Language Learners/ESL**

Write these words on the board: **preview, exchange, outburst, postscript.** Make sure students understand the meanings of each word and how the prefixes change the meanings. Ask students to work with a partner and use pantomime and gestures to show the meaning of each word before the prefix was added and after.

**Gifted Learners**

Have students add one of the four prefixes taught in this lesson to each word and then write a definition and an example sentence for it: **produce, determine, hypnotic, press, port, test, race.** (**overproduce, predetermine, posthypnotic, express, export, pretest, outrace**)

**Learners with Special Needs**

Additional strategies for supporting learners with special needs can be found on page 91L.

● Read aloud the directions on pages 97 and 98. Point out that on page 97 and in the first exercise on page 98, students will use context as well as their knowledge of the prefix and base word in order to choose the correct word.

● Tell students to refer to the Helpful Hints box as they complete the exercises on pages 97–98.

## Curriculum Connections

### Spelling Link

Tell students to write a column heading for each prefix: **pre-, post-, ex-,** and **out-.** Then read each sentence, have students listen for the word that has one of these prefixes, and write it in the correct column.

**Exchange** these gloves for some that fit.

Jason's **outburst** surprised us.

We plan to attend a **preview** of the new show.

I had to **postpone** my trip.

"Bravo!" **exclaimed** the members of the audience.

Your last reason **outweighs** all the others.

### Multicultural Connection

● In the Southwest, the pueblo, a Native American dwelling, bears a noticeable resemblance to modern-day apartment houses. Some of these structures were built more than a thousand years ago.

● Students may wish to research some of the southwestern Native American groups, with emphasis on pre-Columbian history (history before the arrival of Columbus). Encourage students to display their findings in a poster or a labeled illustration.

## Observational Assessment

*Check whether students can identify when to use the prefixes **pre-** and **post-**.*

# Prefixes sub-, trans-, mid-, semi-

## Objectives

- To identify and use the prefixes **sub-**, **trans-**, **mid-** and **semi-**

- To understand how a prefix combines with a base word to form a new word

## Warming Up

- Write the following passage on the board and read it aloud to students.

  On Monday, Mason takes a **subway** to school. But **midweek**, he takes a bus to the science lab. He is learning how to conduct successful **transplants** in vegetable gardens. The plants are grown in a **semicircle** around a light source.

- Write these prefixes on the board: **mid-**, **sub-**, **trans-**, and **semi-**. Ask students to find and underline the words in the passage that have one of these prefixes.

- Call on volunteers to circle the prefixes and, using sentence context, tell what they think each word means.

## Teaching the Lesson

- Have students read the Helpful Hints on pages 99 and 100.

- Ask students if the prefixes on page 99 have anything in common. (They both have to do with position or motion.)

- Ask students how the prefixes on page 100 are similar. (They both have to do with halves: **semi-** refers to one half of something, and **mid-** refers to the middle point of something.)

---

Name _____

### Helpful Hints

Sub is a **prefix** that means "under" or "less than."

A sub**marine** is a ship that can go underwater.
The sub**plot** of a play or novel is less important than the main plot.

Trans is a **prefix** that means "across," "beyond," or "through."

The first trans**continental** railroad sped across the country in 1869.
Trans**lucent** material, like frosted glass, lets light pass through.

 Underline the prefix in each word.

1. transport
2. subcommittee
3. transatlantic
4. subtitle
5. transform
6. subfreezing
7. submerge
8. subtopic
9. transplant
10. transmit
11. transform
12. subway

*The Last Spike* by Thomas Hill

 Read each clue. Then unscramble the letters to form the word that fits the clue. Write the word on the line. All the words appear in the list above.

13. a title that usually explains the main title — ubslitte — subtitle
14. across the Atlantic Ocean — citlantarants — transatlantic
15. a committee acting under the main committee — mostbeeticum — subcommittee
16. move a plant from one pot to another — sanntpralt — transplant
17. topic under the main topic — busoptic — subtopic
18. underground train — swabyu — subway

### CHALLENGE

Use what you know about American history and the prefix trans to write the meaning of this statement:
*The* **transcontinental** *railroad linked the East and the West.*

LESSON 48: Prefixes **sub-**, **trans-**, **mid-**, **semi-**    99

---

# UNIVERSAL ACCESS
## Meeting Individual Needs

### Visual Learners

Have students design a jigsaw puzzle. In each space, they will write a word that starts with a prefix from this lesson. The puzzle should have a color key, so that words that include the same prefix are the same color. When the pieces are put together they should create a simple design. Distribute copies of students' puzzles for their classmates to solve.

### Auditory Learners

Arrange students in groups of four. Make a spinner whose arrow points to spaces marked **trans-**, **sub-**, **mid-**, and **semi-**. Students spin the spinner and call out the prefix on which the pointer lands. Then they say a word that starts with that prefix and write it down. Students may refer to a dictionary for help in finding words with these prefixes.

Underline the prefix in each word in the box below. Then complete each sentence with a word from the box. Use a word only once.

midweek  semicircle  midterm  midyear  semicolon  semiprivate

semiprecious  midway  semifinal  midtown  semiformal

1. Chicago is _____midway_____ between New York and Los Angeles.

2. Our team lost in the _____semifinal_____ round of the play-off.

3. We always schedule our _____midyear_____ checkup in June.

4. At a _____semiformal_____ dinner, a man would wear a suit, not a tuxedo.

5. We sat in a _____semicircle_____ around the fireplace.

6. We call the _____midweek_____ special in our cafeteria the "Wednesday Surprise."

7. The central part of a city between its uptown and downtown areas is known as _____midtown_____.

8. We are having a _____midterm_____ exam on everything we have studied since the beginning of the fall term.

9. Turquoise is a _____semiprecious_____ gem. It is not as valuable as a diamond or a ruby, but it is more valuable than a plain rock.

10. A _____semicolon_____ is a punctuation mark that is less final than a period, but greater than the pause for a comma.

11. A _____semiprivate_____ hospital room is shared by two patients.

Turquoise—a semi**precious** stone

 **Home Involvement Activity** Find out the names and features of some semi**precious** gems. Does anyone in your family have jewelry made from these stones? If so, create a display and exhibit cards to share.

**100** LESSON 48: Prefixes sub-, trans-, mid-, semi-

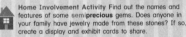

# Prefixes
# in-/il-/im-/ir-

## Objectives

- **To identify and use the prefixes in-, il-, im-, and ir-**

- **To understand the rules for using these prefixes**

## Warming Up

- Write the following rhyme on the board and read it aloud to students.

  There once were four prefixes,

  **in-, il-, im-,** and **ir-**

  They did the same jobs,

  So decided to share.

- Write these words on the board:

  **perfect, correct, responsible, legal**

- Have students use the prefixes in the poem to make new words that have the opposite meaning. **(imperfect, incorrect, irresponsible, illegal)**

- Have volunteers use the words in sentences.

## Teaching the Lesson

- Explain that the prefixes **im-, in-, ir-,** and **il-** all mean "not." Explain that when they are added to a base word, they change its meaning to the opposite meaning.

- Tell students that studying prefixes will help them understand unfamiliar words. Demonstrate by using the word **inability.** Explain that if they understand the meaning of **ability,** then they can determine the meaning of **inability** by thinking about how the prefix changes it. The prefix **in-** means "not," so the word **inability** means "no ability."

---

Name _____

> ### Helpful Hints
>
> The **prefixes** in, il, im, and ir mean "not."
>
> **in**complete = not complete       **im**possible = not possible
> **il**logical = not logical            **ir**regular = not regular
>
> The **prefixes** in and im appear before many different base words and roots.
> The **prefix** il goes before words that begin with l.
> The **prefix** ir goes before words that begin with r.

 Underline the prefix in each word. Then on the line, use what you know about prefixes and base words to write the meaning of the word.

1. illegal — not legal
2. impolite — not polite
3. irresponsible — not responsible
4. impatient — not patient
5. illiterate — not literate
6. inaccurate — not accurate
7. impractical — not practical
8. insensitive — not sensitive
9. illegible — not legible
10. insincere — not sincere
11. immortal — not mortal
12. incorrect — not correct
13. impure — not pure
14. immature — not mature
15. irrelevant — not relevant
16. inactive — not active

> ### WORD STRATEGY
>
> To figure out the meaning of an unfamiliar word with a prefix, cover the prefix and read the rest of the word. Try that strategy with these words:
>
> impartial
> inability
>
> Discuss how using the strategy helped you figure out the meaning of the words.

---

# U N I V E R S A L   A C C E S S
# Meeting Individual Needs

### Kinesthetic Learners

Have students make a set of cards for the prefixes **in-, il-, im-, ir-.** Then write on the board these words and point to each one in turn: **responsible, measurable, audible, decisive, legal, logical, mature, mobile, capable, movable, reparable, legible, direct,** and **regular.** Have students hold up the correct prefix card that could be used with each base word.

### Auditory Learners

Explain to students that to figure out which word and prefix go together, it's helpful to listen for the combinations that are easiest to pronounce. Have students test this by making prefix cards for **in-, il-, im-,** and **ir-,** and base word cards for the words on page 101. Tell students to mismatch prefixes and base words and try to pronounce them, such as **irlogical.** Then have them read the correct word and notice that the word flows more smoothly.

**Read each passage. Then on the lines, write the answer to each question.**

1. Georgia O'Keeffe (1887–1986) was a great American artist. As a young child, she showed a strong talent for art. She felt **impatient** to grow up. She couldn't wait to become an artist.

New Mexican painting by Georgia O'Keeffe, 1941

   Why was the young Georgia O'Keeffe **impatient**? _She couldn't wait to become an artist._

2. Georgia O'Keeffe was born in Wisconsin and grew up on a farm. After she finished high school, she went to art school. She lived in New York City and in Chicago. Yet deep in her heart, she felt **incapable** of adjusting to city life. She longed for open space and clear light.

   Why did Georgia O'Keeffe feel **incapable** of living in a city? _She longed for open space and clear light._

3. Later on, New Mexico became O'Keeffe's home. She loved the clear light, fresh air, and freedom. She was a fiercely **independent** woman. She did not rely on others. She loved to hike, to spend time alone, and to paint.

   In what ways was O'Keeffe **independent**? _She did not rely on others. She loved to spend time alone._

4. The images in O'Keeffe's artwork are bold and clear. O'Keeffe felt that bright light was **indispensable** to the creation of her lifelike art. She could not paint without it.

   What does **indispensable** mean? _absolutely necessary; essential_

5. When she was in her late seventies, O'Keeffe's eyesight began to fail. This change had an **irreversible** effect on her life as a painter. With great sadness, she had to give up painting.

   What had an **irreversible** effect on Georgia O'Keeffe? _her failing eyesight_

LESSON 49: Prefixes **in-/il-/im-/ir-**

 **Home Involvement Activity** Talk with family members about the meaning of the words **mature** and **immature**. Discuss the opportunities available to students when they show they are mature.

---

### English-Language Learners/ESL

Write these word pairs on the board and have students say each word. Ask them to work with a partner to act out the words for the rest of the class. Have the class guess which word pair the students are acting out.

| | |
|---|---|
| polite—impolite | patient—impatient |
| mature—immature | legible—illegible |
| active—inactive | responsible—irresponsible |

### Gifted Learners

Provide students with several slang expressions, such as **couch potato, spacey, full of hot air, off base, no way,** and **free as a bird.** Tell them to look for words with the same meaning on pages 101–102. **(inactive, impractical** or **irresponsible, insincere, impossible, incorrect, independent)**

### Learners with Special Needs

Additional strategies for supporting learners with special needs can be found on page 91L.

---

- Read aloud the directions on pages 101 and 102.

- Ask students if they are familiar with the art on page 102. Explain to students that the artist Georgia O'Keeffe was a real person and that they will learn more about her life as they complete the exercises.

 Turn to page 91K for an Intervention Strategy designed to help students who need extra support with this lesson.

## Curriculum Connections

### Spelling Link

Write the following phrases on the board. Tell students that the phrases are clues. Have volunteers read each clue aloud and answer it with a word from the lesson.

   doesn't relate to anything
   can't read or write
   doesn't depend on anyone
   hasn't grown up
   can't be reversed
   isn't able to do something
   isn't lawful

(Answers: **irrelevant, illiterate, independent, immature, irreversible, incapable, illegal**)

### Art Link

- The Georgia O'Keeffe Museum opened in Santa Fe in 1997. Many, but not all, of her works are there.

- Have students study the art of Georgia O'Keeffe and write their reactions using as many words as they can that start with **in-, il-, im-,** and **ir-.** Students' responses may be in essay form or as verse.

### Observational Assessment

*Check whether students know which prefix to use with a particular base word.*

# Prefixes
## co-, com-/con-, en-/em-, in-/im-

## Objectives

- **To identify and use the prefixes co-, com-/con-, en-/em-, in-/im-**
- **To understand that more than one prefix can have the same meaning**
- **To understand that a prefix can have different meanings**

## Warming Up

- Write the following on the board, underline the words in bold type, and read it aloud to students.

  Dear Diary,

  Mom's new **coworker** invited her to lunch. After they **enjoyed** their meal, they asked the chef for the recipe. By **coincidence**, he had **compiled** his recipes in a book, which **included** some great desserts.

- Have students write the underlined words on a separate sheet of paper. Encourage students to look for similarities in the meaning of the words that start with **co-** or **com-**; the words that start with **in-** or **en-**.

## ★ Teaching the Lesson

- Ask students to read the Helpful Hint on page 103. Encourage them to use a dictionary to find other words that begin with the prefixes **co-, com-,** or **con-**.

- Read with students each section of the Helpful Hints box on page 104. Point out that the prefixes **in-** and **im-** can mean "not," or they may mean "in," "into," "within," or "on." When a prefix has more than one meaning, the context of the sentence may help students determine the meaning of the word.

---

Name _____

> **Helpful Hint**
>
> The **prefixes co** and **com** or **con** mean "with or together."
>
> coexist = exist with          compile = gather and put together
> conjoin = join together

★ **Read each phrase below. Underline the word that has the prefix co, com, or con. Then circle the prefix in the word.**

1. a crowded airport (con)course
2. (com)piles a list of names
3. (com)poses a song about Texas
4. performs at a rock (con)cert
5. one of the two (co)signers
6. (con)firms the answer
7. (con)cedes victory to the other team
8. will (con)front the issue

An airport con**course**

★ **Answer each question. Use a word from the box below. Write the word on the line.**

> | concurrent | compare | cooperate | combine |

9. Which word means "happening at the same time"? ____ **concurrent**

10. Which word means "to join or mix together"? ____ **combine**

11. Which word means "to work together for a common purpose"? ____ **cooperate**

12. Which word means "to examine together"? ____ **compare**

**WORK TOGETHER**

Work with a group to brainstorm words that begin with the prefixes co, com, or con. Then scramble the letters of each word. Write each scrambled word on an index card. Take turns unscrambling the words.

LESSON 50: Prefixes **co-, com-/con-, en-/em-, /in-/im-**    **103**

---

# UNIVERSAL ACCESS
# Meeting Individual Needs

### Visual Learners

Write the following on the board.

| co- | joy |
| com- | cert |
| con- | ploy |
| en- | bine |
| em- | vite |
| in- | operate |
| im- | merse |

Have students copy the lists and then draw lines to match a prefix with a base word or a root, to form a new word. Encourage students to use a dictionary when necessary.

### Logical Learners

Write these words on the board in random order: **insight, incisor, invitation, impossible, inability, import, impress, impartial, immeasurable.** Have students decide in which words the prefix **in-** or **im-** means "in" and in which words the prefix means "not." Ask students to give reasons to support their conclusions.

The **prefixes** en and em have the same meaning.
En and em mean "to put into or on."

> encode    enforce    enjoy    embalm

The **prefixes** en and em may also mean "to cause to be or make."

> enable    enrich    enslave    embitter

En and em also mean "to cover or surround."

> encircle    enclose    entangle    embrace

You know that the **prefixes** in and im mean "not."
They also mean "in, into, within, or on."

> insight = can see into        import = bring in

Carlsbad Caverns

 **New Mexico is called the "Land of Enchantment."
Some of the enchantment happens underground.
Underline the word that best completes each
sentence about Carlsbad Caverns National Park.
Then write the word on the line.**

| | | |
|---|---|---|
| 1 | Every year, about 750,000 people travel to southeastern New Mexico to ___enjoy___ a fantastic experience. | inhale<br>enlarge<br>enjoy |
| 2 | Visitors to Carlsbad Caverns can ___inspect___ an underground world of rarely seen treasures within 75 caves. | engulf<br>include<br>inspect |
| 3 | Cave visitors will not ___endanger___ themselves if they stay on the trails and listen to the park rangers who guide them. | employ<br>endanger<br>enrage |
| 4 | Daring cave explorers can ___immerse___ themselves in a more adventurous cave experience. | immerse<br>encounter<br>embody |
| 5 | Adventurers actually ___embrace___ the opportunity to crawl through an underground wilderness of newly found caves. | encircle<br>embrace<br>inscribe |

104    LESSON 50: Prefixes co-, com-/con-,
en-/em-, in-/im-

 **Home Involvement Activity** Discuss the features of
a place that might earn the description "enchanted."
Talk about enchanting places that you have visited
together. What made them charming or enchanting?

## Practicing the Skill

● Read aloud the directions to each exercise on pages 103 and 104. Point out to the students that on page 104, they will choose one of three words.

● Encourage students to refer to the Helpful Hints boxes on page 103 and 104 whenever necessary. Students may wish to work with a partner to complete items 1–5 on page 104.

## Curriculum Connections

### Spelling Link

Have students write the word that correctly completes each definition.

> To breathe in is to ___. **(inhale)**
>
> To risk one's safety is to ___ oneself. **(endanger)**
>
> To work together is to ___. **(cooperate)**
>
> To admit defeat is to ___. **(concede)**
>
> To write music is to ___. **(compose)**
>
> To wrap one's arms around someone is to ___ him or her. **(embrace)**

### Multicultural Connection

● The cuisine of the Southwest is a blend of Native American and Mexican foods. Some dishes and ingredients students may be familiar with are chile peppers, corn flour, tortillas, chorizo burritos, huevos rancheros, fajitas, tamales, and enchiladas.

● Have students work in a group to collect recipes for dishes native to the Southwest. They may wish to prepare some of the dishes, photograph them, and include the recipes in a class cookbook.

### English-Language Learners/ESL

Write the prefixes **co-, con-,** and **com-** on slips of paper. Then write **worker, cert,** and **pass** on other slips of paper. Finally, have a picture of a coworker, an orchestra, and a compass. Have students match the correct prefix and root or base word that corresponds to the picture. Have students say each completed word and use it in a sentence.

### Observational Assessment

*Check whether students can distinguish between words in which the prefix **in-** or **im-** means "not" and words in which it means "in."*

### Gifted Learners

Have students research the etymology of these words: **company, combine,** and **encyclopedia.** Ask students to write or diagram their findings and share them with the class.

 **Learners with Special Needs**

Additional strategies for supporting learners with special needs can be found on page 91L.

# Connecting Spelling and Writing

## Objectives

- To say, spell, sort, and write words with prefixes before a base word or a root
- To write a persuasive speech

## Warming Up

- Write the following speech on the board and have a student read it aloud:

  I believe it is time to <u>embrace</u> the idea of a TV-free week. Why should we <u>unquestioningly</u> watch the <u>irresponsible</u> <u>nonstop</u> programming? Although it would be <u>impossible</u> to <u>enforce,</u> those who did <u>cooperate</u> would see how a TV-free week can change one's life.

- Ask students to read and underline the words with the prefixes **em-**, **un-**, **im-**, **ir-**, **non-**, and **co-**. Have a volunteer draw a line between the prefixes and base words. (em|brace, un|questioningly, ir|responsible, non|stop, im|possible, en|force, co|operate)

## Teaching the Lesson

Discuss the meaning of each word above. Show how the meaning of the prefix combines with the meaning of the base word in each case. Have students read the words in bold type on page 105 and analyze the relationship between the prefix and base word in each.

## Practicing the Skill

Read aloud the directions on page 105. Ask students to read each group of words aloud. As they say each word in bold type, have them listen for the number of syllables in each word. Have students sort the words by number of syllables and write them in the correct column.

---

Name _____

 Read each group of words. Say and spell each word in bold type. Repeat the word. Then sort the words. Write each word in the correct box below.

- **combine** business with pleasure
- **cooperate** with the police
- **displease** his family
- that we should **embrace**
- **enforce** the law
- an **illegal** contract
- an **impolite** remark
- an **irresponsible** act
- **inhale** pollution
- a **midseason** sale
- **outlasted** its usefulness
- **postdated** the check
- the **preface** to her book

- **reelect** her to another term
- in a **semiprivate** room
- added a funny **subtitle**
- in **unfamiliar** territory
- **transform** our government

Senate Room of Texas State Capitol

| Words with Two Syllables | Words with Three Syllables | Words with Four or More Syllables |
|---|---|---|
| combine | illegal | irresponsible |
| displease | impolite | semiprivate |
| embrace | midseason | unfamiliar |
| enforce | outlasted | |
| inhale | postdated | |
| preface | reelect | |
| transform | subtitle | |

# UNIVERSAL ACCESS
## Meeting Individual Needs

### Visual Learners

Have students work with a partner to identify and list all the prefixes that appear on page 105. Then have them use as many words with these prefixes as they can in one sentence. Give students five minutes to compose and write their sentence. The students who correctly use the most words in a single sentence win the game.

### Learners with Special Needs

Additional strategies for supporting learners with special needs can be found on page 91L.

### Kinesthetic Learners

Make a set of cards with the base words from page 105, and another set with the prefixes: **com-**, **co-**, **dis-**, **em-**, **en-**, **il-**, **im-**, **ir-**, **in-**, **mid-**, **out-**, **post-**, **pre-**, **re-**, **semi-**, **sub-**, **trans-**, and **un-**. Arrange students into two teams. Have students draw a card from each stack and write the word they make, whether correct or not. If the word is correct, the team gets another turn. If not, play passes to the other team. When all cards are used, each team totals the number of correct words they made.

Barbara Jordan (1936–1996) was one of our nation's greatest speakers and defenders of the Constitution. She represented the people of Texas with "a will of iron and a voice of gold." Barbara was determined to get a good education. She worked to be strong and independent. With her eloquent voice, she spoke out for causes in which she believed.

★ **Choose an issue that you feel strongly about, such as saving the environment. Write a short persuasive speech to your classmates. Try to get your audience to agree with your opinions and point of view. Use at least two of these spelling words in your speech.**

| | | | | | |
|---|---|---|---|---|---|
| combine | cooperate | displease | embrace | enforce | illegal |
| impolite | irresponsible | inhale | midseason | outlasted | postdated |
| preface | reelect | semiprivate | subtitle | unfamiliar | transform |

Answers will vary.

_____

_____

_____

_____

_____

_____

**Writer's Tip**

Use the 5 steps of the writing process: prewrite, write, revise, proofread, and publish.

Barbara Jordan speaking in 1992

_____

_____

**Speaker's Challenge**

Learn more about the life of Barbara Jordan. Then give an oral report about this great American. Write your main ideas and important facts on note cards. Practice using your note cards before giving your report. Also practice pacing your speech.

106    LESSON 51: Connecting Spelling and Writing

---

## The Writing Process

Tell students that on page 106 they will write a persuasive speech. Have them read the instructions and the spelling words.

**Prewrite** Tell students that a persuasive speech should begin with a statement of their opinion. The middle should contain reasons to support this opinion. The speech usually concludes with the speaker restating his or her opinion.

**Write** Have students write their opinion and their reasons on a separate sheet of paper before they begin. Then have them review their reasons and number them in order of importance. Remind students to use at least two spelling words.

**Revise** As students read over their speech to revise it, tell them to keep these questions in mind: *Did I present my reasons in a way that encourages others to agree with me?*

**Proofread** Have students check their speeches for errors in grammar, punctuation, and spelling.

**Publish** Have students recopy their final draft onto page 106 or onto a separate sheet of paper. Students should include any diagram, photo, or illustration that supports their opinion.

 **Computer Connection**

Share the following tip with students who use a word processor to do their writing.

• Many word-processing programs have the capability of creating graphs or charts. These documents can be printed directly onto transparent acetate for use as graphic aids during a speech.

• Encourage students to familiarize themselves with the computer's graphics capability. Remind them to print out drafts of their chart or graph on paper before transferring the image onto acetate.

**Portfolio** Suggest that students add their persuasive speeches to their portfolios.

---

### English-Language Learners/ESL

Create base-word cards, such as **cover, play, known, able.** Make prefix cards for the prefixes students have learned. Have students experiment to find out how many prefix cards make words when combined with a base word. Show students how to make a graphic organizer with the base word at the center and the words with prefixes radiating outward.

### Gifted Learners

Write several prefixes, such as **un-, dis-, re-,** and **pre-** on the board, and base words, such as **do, cut, fold, order, light, send, view.** In small groups, have one student select a base word and use it in a sentence. Another student must respond using the same base word with a prefix. For example, a student might say, "Please fold this shirt," to which another student might say, "I will unfold this shirt first." Have students continue to add prefixes as long as they can make new words.

# Reviewing and Assessing
### Prefixes

## Objective

To review and assess adding prefixes to base words

## Warming Up

● Write these words on the board:

| | | |
|---|---|---|
| **disband** | **renew** | **outboard** |
| **precook** | **submarine** | **transatlantic** |
| **illogical** | **irreparable** | **semisweet** |
| **derail** | **enact** | **coworker** |

● Ask students to identify the prefix in each word, define the word, and then give a definition for the prefix. In each case, ask students how the prefix affects the base word's meaning.

## Teaching the Lesson

● Lessons 44–50 introduced students to several prefixes (**un-, re-, dis-, de-, pre-, post-, ex-, out-, sub-, trans-, mid-, semi-, il-, im-, in-, ir-, co-, com-, con-, em-,** and **en-**). They also introduced the rules for adding them to a base word to form a new word.

● Remind students that a base word and a prefix combine to form a word that is more than the meaning of its parts, in the same way that a compound word is a synthesis of its parts. Some prefixes, like **pre-** or **re-**, have a simple, obvious meaning. Other prefixes, like **dis-** or **en-**, have more subtle meanings. Refer to the words in the *Warming-Up* exercise as examples of this point.

---

Name _____

☆ Add the prefix **dis** to two of the following base words. Add the prefix **re** to the two other words. Write the meaning of each new word.

| Base Word | Word with Prefix | Meaning of New Word |
|---|---|---|
| 1. cover | discover | to find out; gain knowledge |
| 2. appear | reappear | appear again |
| 3. apply | reapply | apply again |
| 4. please | displease | to cause displeasure |

☆ Add the prefix **out** to two of the following base words. Add the prefix **pre** to the two other words. Write the meaning of each new word.

| Base Word | Word with Prefix | Meaning of New Word |
|---|---|---|
| 5. caution | precaution | to be careful beforehand |
| 6. last | outlast | to last longer than |
| 7. historic | prehistoric | before history |
| 8. burst | outburst | a sudden release or bursting forth |

 Add the prefix **sub** to one of the following base words. Add the prefix **trans** to the other word. Write the meaning of each new word.

| Base Word | Word with Prefix | Meaning of New Word |
|---|---|---|
| 9. plant | transplant | to move from one place to another |
| 10. merge | submerge | to sink below the surface |

 Add the prefix **il** to one of the following base words. Add the prefix **ir** to the other base word. Write the meaning of each new word.

| Base Word | Word with Prefix | Meaning of New Word |
|---|---|---|
| 11. responsible | irresponsible | not responsible |
| 12. legal | illegal | not legal |

# UNIVERSAL ACCESS
## Meeting Individual Needs

### Auditory Learners

List these prefixes on the board: **un-, re-, dis-, de-, pre-, post-, ex-, out-, sub-, trans-, mid-, semi-, il-, im-, in-, ir-, co-, com-, con-, em-, en-.** Have students work with a partner. One student chooses a prefix and says it. The partner says a word with that prefix and tells what the word means. Students can check off each prefix when it is used correctly.

### Learners with Special Needs

Additional strategies for supporting learners with special needs can be found on page 91L.

### Visual Learners

On the board, write the prefixes taught so far in this unit. In teams, have one player write a prefix and blank spaces for the rest of the letters that would form a word. An opposing team member guesses which letters make up the word. If a guess is correct, a student writes that letter in its correct place. When the opposing team has enough letter clues, they may guess the word. If they guess correctly, they get a point. If they guess incorrectly they lose a turn.

**REVIEW & ASSESS**

**Fill in the circle of the word that best completes each sentence. Then write the word on the line.**

1. Do you picture Arizona as a desert? Well, the Grand Canyon State also has ___unspoiled___ mountain ski areas and snow-shoeing trails.
   ○ defrosted   ● unspoiled   ○ impossible

2. Our family is taking a(n) ___midwinter___ ski trip to Arizona.
   ● midwinter   ○ postwar   ○ exchange

3. Maybe our trip will ___coincide___ with a lunar eclipse. If it does, we will watch it at the Lowell Observatory in Flagstaff.
   ○ discover   ○ engulf   ● coincide

4. We'll also pan for ___semiprecious___ stones in one of Arizona's streams.
   ○ outnumbered   ○ semiformal   ● semiprecious

**Complete each sentence by combining a prefix with a base word in the box to form a new word. Write the new word on the line.**

| Prefixes |
| --- |
| de |
| dis |
| en |
| out |
| **Base Words** |
| large |
| lasted |
| parted |
| satisfied |

The southeastern corner of Arizona was once a busy mining region. The land held silver and copper. Miners found great veins of these valuable metals. Once word got out, miners and fortune hunters hurried there. Eager bosses hired cheap workers to help them strike it rich. Miners quickly built "boom towns." They dreamed of how they would (5) ___enlarge___ their cash boxes. Indeed, a few bosses got very rich. Yet most failed and left (6) ___dissatisfied___.

When the boom ended, the miners (7) ___departed___. They left behind houses, shops, schools, and even jails. Some abandoned houses have (8) ___outlasted___ the miners who once lived in them. Today, in towns such as Gleeson, Pearce, and Cochise, visitors can see the "ghost towns" that remain.

**Extend & Apply**

Find out more about the old mining towns of the Southwest. Write a paragraph about one of these towns. Use at least two words that have prefixes.

Abandoned mining town in Arizona

LESSON 52: Review and Assess

---

## Assessing the Skill

**Check Up** The exercises on page 107 are discussed in *Teaching the Lesson*. Assign them now if you have not already done so. Page 108 asks students to demonstrate their ability to choose the correct word to complete each sentence, a process that requires them to understand both the meaning of the prefixes and the base words.

**Observational Assessment** As students complete each set of exercises, watch to evaluate how well they understand the meaning of each prefix, each base word, and the two word parts combined to form a word with its own meaning.

**Student Skills Assessment** Use the checklist on page 91H to keep track of students' mastery of each family of prefixes, how they are added to base words, and how adding a prefix changes the meaning of the base word.

**Writing Conference** Hold informal meetings at which you and the student can look over the writing he or she has done so far in this unit. Together, look for places where the student has improved, and look for places where the student could improve further. Encourage students to continue adding to their portfolios.

Group together students who need further instruction in adding prefixes to base words and have them complete the *Reteaching Activities*. Turn to page 91C for alternative assessment methods.

---

# Reteaching Activities

## What's the Word?

Write the following sentences on the board:

The Sonoran Desert is an [not a good host] environment for plants that need a lot of water. **(inhospitable)**

Some of the [put into danger] plants and animals are protected by law. **(endangered)**

In the desert, the [middle of the night] sky is full of stars. **(midnight)**

Have students replace the clues in brackets with words that start with one of the prefixes they have learned.

## Scavenger Hunt

Have students work in small groups. Assign each group four or five prefixes. Tell students they are on a scavenger hunt for words with these prefixes. Encourage students to look through books in their class or their school library. Have one student in each group keep a list of all the words that group members find. Set a 30-minute limit, after which time the recorder can present the group's list.

# Student Pages 109–110

## Roots -pos-, -pel-, -tract-, -ject-, -port-

### Objectives

- To identify and use the roots -pos-, -pel-, -tract-, -ject-, and -port-
- To use roots of words as clues to the words' meaning

## Warming Up

- Write this rhyme on the board and read it aloud to students.

  Our language has not always been
  the one that we all know.
  Many voices, many words
  combined to make it grow.

- Explain that the English we use derived many of its words from the ancient Greek and Latin languages.

- Point out that the prefixes students have just learned are examples of Latin and Greek word parts, and that their meanings affect the meanings of the word to which they are attached.

## Teaching the Lesson

- Focus student's attention on the Helpful Hints. Have students read a root and its explanation one at a time. When they have finished, ask them to suggest other words that contain the root. When they name a word, have them also point out prefixes. Students should give the meaning of the word they name.

- Point out to students that they can sometimes infer the meaning of an unknown word from the context in which it appears, as with the exercise on page 110.

- Ask students to suggest why these roots were grouped together in one lesson. (Possible answer: They all have to do with moving objects from place to place.)

---

Name _____

### Helpful Hints

A **root** is the main part of a word. Roots have meaning, but few can stand alone. Roots become words when **prefixes** or **suffixes** are added to them. If you know the meaning of a root, you can often figure out the meaning of a word.

The **root** pos means "put or place."  →  To **deposit** is "to put money in a bank."

The **root** pel means "push" or "drive."  →  To **repel** is "to drive back."

The **root** tract means "pull, draw back, or drag."  →  A **tractor** is a farm vehicle that pulls heavy loads.

The **root** ject means "throw" or "force."  →  To **reject** is "to throw back."

The **root** port means "carry."  →  To **export** is "to carry goods out of one country to sell in another."

---

Underline the root in each numbered word below. Then match each word with its meaning. Write the letter of the correct definition on the line.

| | | |
|---|---|---|
| e | 1. opposite | a. to draw to or pull toward |
| c | 2. expel | b. the way a person or thing is placed |
| g | 3. portfolio | c. to drive out by force |
| b | 4. position | d. to draw away attention |
| a | 5. attract | e. placed at the other end or side |
| f | 6. projector | f. a machine that throws an image onto a screen |
| h | 7. import | g. a case for carrying loose papers or drawings |
| d | 8. distract | h. to bring in or carry goods from another country |

### WORK TOGETHER

Work with a partner to look through a newspaper or a book to find words formed from the roots given in this lesson. Make a list of the words that you find. Then exchange your list with the list prepared by another partner team.

---

# UNIVERSAL ACCESS
## Meeting Individual Needs

### Auditory Learners

Give students a set of root cards for each root in the lesson: **-pos-, -pel-, -tract-, -ject-, -port-.** Then read aloud in random order the words from the lesson. Students should hold up the card with the root that is found in that word.

### Logical Learners

Have students make concept webs for these roots: **-pos-, -pel-, -tract-, -ject-,** and **-port-.** They should organize each web with the root in the middle and all the words that contain that root around it. First students should categorize all the words on pages 109–110, but they may wish to extend the activity with additional words.

⭐ **Choose the best word from the box to complete each sentence. Write the word on the line.**

| compel | dispel | expose | portable | positive |
|--------|--------|--------|----------|----------|
| propel | reject | retract | traction | transport |

1. Mules have dependable __traction__. This makes them well suited for the rugged canyons of the Southwest, like those in the Grand Canyon.

2. These pack animals can safely __transport__ people and equipment up and down steep and winding trails.

3. People experienced in the outdoors hope to __dispel__ the idea that it is too dangerous to hike in the desert. They know the importance of bringing a good supply of water, high-energy food, and sunscreen.

4. The intense desert heat should __compel__ any hiker to bring along a full canteen.

5. With their __portable__ tent and lightweight gear, some hikers make their way down to the canyon floor for an overnight stay.

6. Because of a late start, some hikers have to __reject__ their original plan.

7. Some adventurers __expose__ themselves to the dangers (and excitement!) of white-water rafting.

8. The knowing guides __retract__, or draw back, the oars when the boats reach the rapids.

9. The rushing water will __propel__ the boats forward.

10. Plan your trip carefully. Know what to expect and what to take with you. If you respect the desert environment, you are more likely to have a __positive__ outdoor experience.

Mule riders above the Grand Canyon

110  LESSON 53: Roots
-pos-, -pel-, -tract-, -ject-, -port-

🏠 **Home Involvement Activity** Brainstorm a list of words that have the roots in this lesson. Then take turns telling a cumulative story, one sentence at a time, about a family adventure. Use words from your list.

---

## Practicing the Skill

● Read aloud the directions to each exercise on pages 109–110. On page 109, call students' attention to the Work-Together activity.

● For the exercise on page 110, suggest that students first analyze the words in the boxes to understand their meaning.

## Curriculum Connections

### Spelling Link

Have students write a word from this lesson that correctly completes each sentence.

> When you breathe out, you ___ air. **(expel)**
>
> You can ____ goods by ship or by plane. **(import)**
>
> Too much noise in the car will ____ the driver. **(distract)**
>
> A ____ television is small and lightweight. **(portable)**
>
> The mayor did not ____ her decision to run again. **(retract)**
>
> An optimist has a ____ attitude. **(positive)**

### Multicultural Connection

● About half of our English words derive from Latin and often reflect the Roman way of life. For example, the word **mile** comes from the Latin word *mille,* meaning "one thousand." As Roman cartographers began to make maps, they needed a unit of measurement to show the distance between settlements. They used the term *mille* to refer to the distance that could be covered by a thousand steps.

● Challenge students to become word detectives and find the origins of other English words that are derived from Latin.

### Observational Assessment

*Check whether students can combine a prefix and a root to make a new word.*

---

### English-Language Learners/ESL

Have students act out these tasks: making a **deposit,** driving a **tractor,** giving an **injection,** moving a **portable** object, **extracting** liquid from something. Before students begin, have them write the above phrases on the board. As students begin their pantomime, classmates should point to or say the phrase that names the action.

### Gifted Learners

Have students research the development of the English language. Tell them to pay particular attention to the Viking invasions and the conquest of England by the French-speaking Normans. Encourage them to find out how the language we speak today was influenced by these events.

### Learners with Special Needs

Additional strategies for supporting learners with special needs can be found on page 91L.

# Roots -ped-/-pod-, -ven-/-vent-, -duc-/-duct-

## Objectives

- To identify and use the roots -ped-/-pod-, -ven-/-vent-, and -duc-/-duct-

- To use roots of words as clues to the words' meaning

## Warming Up

- Write the following sentences on the board and read them aloud to students.

  **Ven** to a party and **duc** a friend.

  Watch your **peds** so they don't get stepped on.

- Underline the words in bold type. Have students substitute words that might make more sense, based on the context of the sentences. **(come, bring, feet)**

- Explain that **ven, duc,** and **peds** are roots, and as students will learn, **ven** means "come," **duc** means "bring," and **ped** means "foot."

## Teaching the Lesson

- Have students read the Helpful Hints on page 111. Ask them to name other words that contain the roots listed.

- Discuss with students why these roots were grouped together in this lesson. (Possible answer: They all have to do with moving from place to place.)

- Discuss the pictures on page 111. Make sure students understand what is being shown. Ask which words have prefixes. (items 3, 4, and 6)

- Call students' attention to the Challenge activity on page 111 and explain that it is an extension of the picture activity.

111

---

Name _____

### Helpful Hints

Ped or Pod, ven or vent, and duc or duct are **roots**.

Ped or pod means "foot."

A **bi**ped is a two-footed animal.

Ven or vent means "come."

A **convention** is a meeting where people come together.

Duc or duct means "lead" or "bring."

An **aqua**duct is a pipe that brings water over a long distance.

★ **Write the root that will complete the name of each picture.**

| 1 | 2 | 3 |
|---|---|---|
| p e d estrian | p o d ium | re d u c t ion |

| 4 | 5 | 6 |
|---|---|---|
| con d u c t or | p e d al | in v e n t ion |

★ **Write a word from the box below to complete each sentence.**

| adventure | conductors | introduced |
|---|---|---|

7. Oklahoma _introduced_ people to oil wells. Many people in the state became rich from the oil found on their land.

8. _Conductors_ on transcontinental railroads collected tickets.

9. Later, the automobile made driving a family _adventure_.

### CHALLENGE

Write one sentence for each of the six words shown in the pictures at the top of the page. Share your sentences with classmates.

LESSON 54: Roots -ped-/-pod-, -ven-/-vent-, -duc-/-duct-    111

---

# UNIVERSAL ACCESS
## Meeting Individual Needs

### Auditory Learners

Prepare word cards for the words on this page. Have students work in small groups. Suggest a theme, such as **travel.** One student turns over a card and says a sentence about a trip or a journey, using that word correctly. The next student turns over another card and says a sentence about the same trip or journey containing the word. Students continue until all the cards are used.

### Logical Learners

Make a deck of cards that contains two each of the words in the boxes on pages 111–112, and eight "wild" cards. Two students are dealt five cards each and place the remaining cards facedown. One student places a card faceup on the table. If the other student has a card with the same root, he or she can place it on the first card. If not, he or she has to draw cards until one appears. A "wild" card can change the root.

The small Panhandle town of McLean, Texas, is home to the Devil's Rope Museum. On display there are Mack's twist, Billings' simple 4-point, Corsican clip, and many other varieties. What do you think is in this museum?

 Use a word from the box for each clue. Write one letter in each space. To find out what this little museum has to offer, read down the shaded column. Write those letters in order in the spaces to answer the question at the bottom.

| biped | bipod | educate | inductee | invent |
| pedestal | producer | reduce | ventured | |

1. like a tripod, but a two-legged stand        b i p o d
2. a base on which a statue stands        p e d e s t a l
3. a person who brings people and money together to make a movie, TV series, or play        p r o d u c e r
4. an animal that has two feet        b i p e d
5. to bring knowledge to people        e d u c a t e
6. someone who is brought into military service        i n d u c t e e
7. to come up with something new        i n v e n t
8. to bring down in size or value        r e d u c e
9. "Nothing ____, nothing gained."        v e n t u r e d

**Question:** What does the Devil's Rope Museum collect and exhibit?

**Answer:** b a r b e d   w i r e

LESSON 54: Roots
-ped-/-pod-, -ven-/-vent-, -duc-/-duct-

**Home Involvement Activity** What is the most unusual museum, exhibit, or collection you have ever seen or heard about? What idea do you have for a museum? Discuss your ideas.

- Read aloud the directions for the exercises on page 111. For items 1–6, have students refer to the roots in the Helpful Hints to decide which root completes each word.
- On page 112, show students how to position the answers so that one letter in each item falls within the shaded bar.

# Curriculum Connections

## Spelling Link

Write these scrambled words on the board: **earduvetn, ndorcctuo, ucedtea, anepestrid, urodcerp,** and **nteeuvr.** Have students unscramble the words and then use them to complete the sentences.

Something new can be an exciting ____. (**adventure**)

Someone who walks is a ____. (**pedestrian**)

Metal is a good ____ of electricity. (**conductor**)

It rained so hard we did not ____ out for three days. (**venture**)

To ____ a puppy, you need a lot of patience. (**educate**)

The play has a director but it needs a ____. (**producer**)

## Science Link

Metal wire is used to make barbed wire. It is also one of the best conductors of electricity. Have students research the process of making metal wire, and describe some of its uses. Students may present their findings as a poster, diagram, or a written report.

### Observational Assessment

*Check whether students can explain the meaning of the root **-duc-** in the word **education.***

## English-Language Learners/ESL

Play a game of "Tic-tac-toe." Set up the grid with nine roots. Have students name a word that contains the root in that square in order to mark it off. As with conventional tic-tac-toe, the first one to get three in a row is the winner. If students have difficulty, allow them to work with a more fluent partner.

## Gifted Learners

Have students write an advertisement for a convention to be held on a specific topic, for example, bird watching or baseball-card collecting. In the advertisement, have students use these words: **convention, podium, reduction, invention, introduce, educate,** and **producer.**

## Learners with Special Needs

Additional strategies for supporting learners with special needs can be found on page 91L.

# Roots -spect-, -vid-/-vis-, -audi-, -phon-, -scope-

## Objectives

- **To identify and use the roots -spect-, -vid-/-vis-, -audi-, -phon-, and -scope-**
- **To use roots of words as clues to the words' meaning**

## Warming Up

- Write the following sentences on the board and ask a student to read them aloud.

  Do you **audi** the sweet **phon** of birds?

  **Scope** carefully and you might **spect** a rare **vid.**

- Ask students to identify words in the sentences that are unusual. Have students write them on the board. **(audi, phon, scope, spect, vid)**

- Tell students to use context to guess at each word's meaning. **(audi/hear; phon/sound; scope/look; spect/see; vid/sight)**

## Teaching the Lesson

- Have students read aloud the Helpful Hints on pages 113 and 114. After the description of each root, have students suggest other words with that root. Allow them to use a dictionary, if necessary.

- Discuss with students why these roots were grouped together in this lesson. (Possible answer: These roots all have to do with listening or seeing.)

- The roots in this lesson turn up in many words that students encounter every day. Allow them to explore the variety of terms that come to mind. (For example: **television, videotape, telephone**)

113

---

### Helpful Hints

Spect, vid or vis, audi, and phon are **roots.**

Spect and vid or vis all mean "see."

To in**spect** is to look at closely.
A **vid**eo is a recording you can see.
**Vis**ion is your sense of sight.

**Audi** or audio means "hear."

An **audi**ence is a group of listeners.

Phon, phone, or phono means "sound."

**Phon**ics uses the sounds of letters to help you read.

An audio**logy** test to check hearing

Read each definition. Then find the word in the box that matches it. Write that word on the line. Circle its root.

| audiometer | auditorium | evident | respect | spectacular |
| suspect | symphony | telephone | television | visit |

1. to regard highly — re**spect**
2. a machine that measures your hearing — **audi**ometer
3. a hand-held device that carries sound — tele**phone**
4. to look at with doubt or distrust — su**spect**
5. relating to a remarkable sight — **spect**acular
6. to go to see someone or something — **vis**it
7. an orchestra or a harmony of sounds — sym**phon**y
8. a box for receiving pictures — tele**vis**ion
9. easy to see or understand — e**vid**ent
10. a room or hall for an audience — audi**tor**ium

### CHALLENGE

Use what you know about roots, music, and art to write the meaning of these words:

phonograph
spectrum

---

# UNIVERSAL ACCESS
## Meeting Individual Needs

### Visual Learners

Have students play this game as a small group or as a whole class. Write these words on cards: **microscope, periscope, telescope, telephone, symphony, television, auditorium,** and **videotape.** One student chooses a card and has 30 seconds to draw a picture representing the word on the board. Classmates guess the word the picture shows. Have a student write the word under the illustration.

### Auditory Learners

Write the roots **-spect-, -vid-, -vis-, -audi-, -phon-,** and **-scope-** on the board. Call out the roots in random order and ask students to combine the root with another word in a creative way to make a new word. (For example: **elephone**—made by combining **elephant** with **phone.**) Ask students to define the new words they make and use them in sentences to show what they mean.

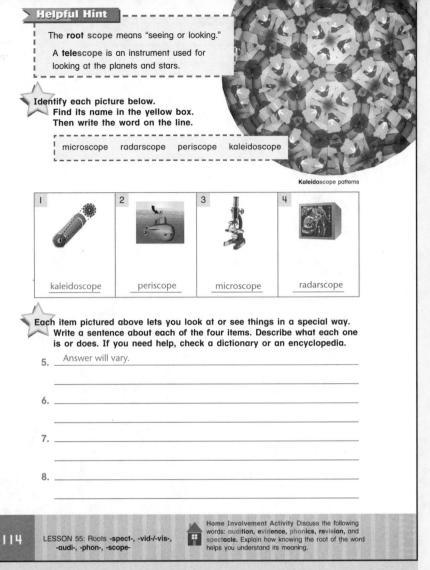

**Helpful Hint** - - - - -

The **root** scope means "seeing or looking."

A **tele**scope is an instrument used for looking at the planets and stars.

**Identify each picture below. Find its name in the yellow box. Then write the word on the line.**

microscope    radarscope    periscope    kaleidoscope

*Kaleidoscope patterns*

| 1 | 2 | 3 | 4 |
|---|---|---|---|
| kaleidoscope | periscope | microscope | radarscope |

**Each item pictured above lets you look at or see things in a special way. Write a sentence about each of the four items. Describe what each one is or does. If you need help, check a dictionary or an encyclopedia.**

5. Answer will vary.

   _____

6. _____

   _____

7. _____

   _____

8. _____

   _____

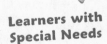

**114**    LESSON 55: Roots -spect-, -vid-/-vis-, -audi-, -phon-, -scope-

**Home Involvement Activity** Discuss the following words: **audi**tion, e**vid**ence, **phon**ics, re**vis**ion, and **spect**acle. Explain how knowing the root of the word helps you understand its meaning.

---

**English-Language Learners/ESL**

Have students find pictures or draw sketches to illustrate the words **telephone, television, videotape, telescope, microscope.** Ask students to label each picture with the correct word. Using a colored marker, have students underline the roots in each word. Point out the connection between the meaning of the root and the meaning of the word.

**Gifted Learners**

Have students play a game of "Twenty Questions" with a partner. One student thinks of a word that includes the root **-spect-, -vid-, -vis-, -audi-, -phon-,** or **-scope-.** The other student can ask twenty "yes" or "no" questions in order to guess the correct word.

**Learners with Special Needs**

Additional strategies for supporting learners with special needs can be found on page 91L.

---

● Read aloud the directions to the exercises on page 113. For items 1–10, have students choose from the words in the box and write the correct word on the line.

● For items 1–4 on page 114, make sure students can correctly identify the pictures. For items 5–8, encourage students to plan their sentences so that they can better explain what each piece of equipment does.

## Curriculum Connections

### Spelling Link

Write the following sentences on the board and have students unscramble the words and spell them correctly.

The fireworks display was awesome and **taspecrcual. (spectacular)**

Every rainbow contains all the colors of the **ecstmrup. (spectrum)**

The city orchestra played Beethoven's Fifth **yhpoynsm. (symphony)**

Before CDs and audiocassettes, there was the **ohnahogprp. (phonograph)**

The spring concert is performed in the school **iaitomurdu. (auditorium)**

A scientist can see tiny organisms under a **icreomscpo. (microscope)**

### Social Studies Link

Have students research the history of television. Their research should include the meaning of the word. They should also mention the introduction of videotape. Challenge them to find information on how new technology is changing television and what new products we may see in the future. Have students present their research visually or in a report.

### Observational Assessment

*Check whether students can differentiate between the meanings of the roots* **-audi-** *and* **-phon-.**

# Roots
## -scrib-/-script-, -graph-/-gram-, -log-

### Objectives

- To identify and use the roots -scrib-/-script-, -graph-/-gram-, and -log-

- To use roots of words as clues to the words' meaning

## Warming Up

- Write this imaginary letter on the board and read it aloud to students.

  Dear Ms. Bunting,

  It's hard to put <u>logs</u> together to <u>scrib</u> you a <u>gram</u> with my <u>graph</u>, but you are my favorite author. Can I please have your autograph?

  Sincerely,

  A friend

- Ask students what they think the underlined words may be. (roots) Call on volunteers to write them on the board. Encourage students to use sentence context to guess the words these roots suggest. **(logs/words; scrib/write; gram/letter; graph/pencil)**

- Tell students to find the word in this fan letter that contains one of the roots. **(autograph)**

## Teaching the Lesson

- Call on volunteers to read aloud the Helpful Hints on page 115. As students finish reading about each root, have them suggest other words with that root.

- Discuss with students why these roots were grouped together in this lesson. (Possible answer: All these roots have to do with communicating through writing and words.)

- Have a student read aloud the Challenge box on page 115 and discuss the questions as a group.

115

---

Name _____

### Helpful Hints

Scrib or Script, graph or gram, and log are **roots**.

Both **scrib** and **script** mean "write."

A **pre**scrip**tion** is a doctor's written directions for using medicine. To **scrib**ble is to write carelessly or quickly.

The root **graph** means "something that writes or records." The root **gram** means "something written or recorded."

A **tele**graph is a system for sending messages by wire. A **tele**gram is a message sent by **tele**graph.

The root **log** means "word or speech." Sometimes, this root is spelled as **logue**.

A **dia**logue is a conversation.

 **Read the sentences. Underline the words that have the roots** scrib/script, graph/gram, **or** log.

1. The photograph of the Alamo on the cover of the book showed how the fort used to look.

2. In the prologue, the author told what had inspired her to write the book.

3. The monologue on the tape is clear and interesting.

4. I found the diagram of the fort very helpful.

5. The author's description of the battle is exciting.

6. My copy of the book has the writer's autograph in it.

7. However, she scribbled her signature.

8. The author's apology included all the people she had forgotten to thank.

 **CHALLENGE**

The roots graph/gram and log are words by themselves. What does each word mean? Write a sentence for each word. Do any of the words match the meaning of the root?

The Alamo in San Antonio, Texas

LESSON 56: Roots **-scrib-/-script-, -graph-/-gram-, -log-** | 115

---

# UNIVERSAL ACCESS
## Meeting Individual Needs

### Visual Learners

Students may be familiar with the profession of scribe, an individual who copied manuscripts before the invention of the printing press. Have students look up the word **manuscript** (handwritten) and write a brief explanation of the history of the word. Ask students to find some examples of the manuscripts that scribes prepared, or prepare a calligraphy demonstration for the class.

### Auditory Learners

Tell students that an early communications device, the telegraph, operated with a code made up of dots and dashes. Have students find out about Morse code, prepare a code key, and do a demonstration as if they were telegraphers in the 1800s.

**Read each phrase. Underline the root in each word in bold type.**

1. **prescribed** rest and relaxation
2. the **dialogue** in the novel
3. a 1-year **subscription** to that magazine
4. **graphite** in the pencil
5. read the **inscription** on the rock
6. uses perfect **grammar**
7. used **logic** to solve the problem
8. was very **apologetic**

**Write an original sentence for each of the eight words in bold type above. Use a dictionary, if needed.**

9. _Answers will vary._ _____
_____
10. _____
_____
11. _____
_____
12. _____
_____
13. _____
_____

Car "sculptures" in Texas

14. _____
_____
15. _____
_____
16. _____
_____

**116**    LESSON 56: Roots
-scrib-/-script-, -graph-/-gram-, -log-

 **Home Involvement Activity** Suppose you could put a large original sculpture in front of your home. What would it be? Brainstorm to create a list of ideas. What did you decide? Write a **description**.

---

# Roots
# -fac- and -astro-/ -aster-

## Objectives

- To identify and use the roots -fac- and -astro-/-aster-

- To use roots of words as clues to the words' meaning

## Warming Up

- Write the sentence below on the board. Call on a student to read it aloud.

   My **astros**! Did you really **fac** that model ship by yourself?

- Challenge students to guess the meaning suggested by the roots in bold type. Supply the following clues: -**astro**- is found in the word **astronomy**; -**fac**- is part of the words **factory** and **manufacture** (-**astro**- means "star" and -**fac**- means "to make something").

- Ask students to think of other words that contain the roots -**astro**- and -**fac**-.

## Teaching the Lesson

- Call on volunteers to read the Helpful Hints on pages 117 and 118. Point out the many variations of the root -**fac**-. On page 117, show that the root -**fic**- can occur at the beginning, middle, or end of a word. (Possible examples: **scientific, difficult, fictitious, sacrifice**)

- Discuss the ideas presented in the Challenge box on page 117. Have students read aloud the sentences they write.

- Ask students to think about the word **disasters** in the box on page 118. Ask students to define the word. (a terrible occurrence) Then ask why the root that means "star" is associated with this word. (Ancient people believed in astrology—the idea that good and bad things are governed by the position of the stars.)

**117**

---

Name _____

### Helpful Hints

The **root** fac means "to make or do." It comes from the Latin word *facere*.

In English, this root is spelled in many ways, including fac, fact, fec, fect, fic, fit, and fy. This root can appear at the beginning, in the middle, or at the end of a word.

fact    effect    fiction    benefit    ratify

 Underline a form of the root fac in each numbered word below. Then match the word to its meaning. Write the letter of the definition on the line.

| | | | |
|---|---|---|---|
| f | 1. scientific | a. | to make larger |
| l | 2. difficult | b. | to make sick |
| b | 3. infect | c. | to make products, usually with machines |
| e | 4. factory | d. | to give up for the sake of another |
| i | 5. perfect | e. | building where things are made in great number |
| h | 6. affect | f. | done according to science |
| k | 7. profits | g. | to inform or make known |
| g | 8. notify | h. | to make a change in or influence |
| d | 9. sacrifice | i. | done without mistakes |
| c | 10. manufacture | j. | to please or make happy |
| j | 11. satisfy | k. | money made after expenses |
| m | 12. efficient | l. | hard to do or make |
| o | 13. artificial | m. | done with little waste |
| a | 14. magnify | n. | lack of something necessary |
| n | 15. deficiency | o. | not made by nature |

### CHALLENGE

Language constantly changes. Roots may take on new spellings. Circle the root related to fac in these two words. Then write a sentence for each word.

counterfeit
fashion

---

# UNIVERSAL ACCESS
# Meeting Individual Needs

### Visual Learners

Write on the board the word "fax" and have students explain what it is. (a machine that uses the phone lines to send an image to another fax machine) Have students look up the derivation of the word. (It is a clipped form of the word **fac-simile**, meaning "make something similar.") Tell students to prepare an advertisement for a fax machine that includes the above information.

### Logical Learners

Have students look at the words **effect, fiction, benefit**, and **ratify** in the Helpful Hints box on page 117. Tell students to use a dictionary to discover the meanings of the prefixes and suffixes that shade the meaning of the root -**fac**-. Have students write a paragraph or prepare a chart explaining their findings.

**Helpful Hint**

The root **astro** or **aster** comes from the Greek word for "star." Notice the root in these words.

astronaut          astronomy          asteroid

★ Use the best word from the box below to complete each sentence. Write the word on the line.

> asterisk     astronomers     disasters     astronauts

You have seen movies about space flight. You have probably heard space travelers talking to "Mission Control" on Earth. The Mission Control Center is a real place. It is located at the Johnson Space Center. This NASA facility is about 25 miles outside of Houston, Texas. Many engineers, mathematicians, computer

scientists, and (1) ___astronomers___ work there. They work in teams to

head off (2) ___disasters___ before they happen.

All American (3) ___astronauts___ are trained here. They must learn to use high-tech tools and space-age instruments before they get the "okay"

to go into space. You may see an (4) ___asterisk___ next to the name of some Americans who have flown in space. This star-shaped mark shows that the person was not a NASA astronaut, but a guest aboard a flight.

Astronaut at Johnson Space Center

★ Match each word to its meaning. Write the letter of the definition on the line.

__b__  5. asteroid      a. causing great loss, damage, or suffering

__c__  6. astral        b. any of the minor planets with orbits
                            between those of Mars and Jupiter

__f__  7. astrology     c. relating to the stars; starry

__a__  8. disastrous    d. an instrument once used to measure stars

__d__  9. astrolabe     e. the science of the planets and stars

__e__  10. astronomy    f. the belief that stars and planets influence people's lives

 **Home Involvement Activity** The Latin root stella means "star," as in **constellation**. Work together to figure out the meaning of **stellar** and **stelliform**. Then write a sentence for each word.

## English-Language Learners/ESL

Draw on the board a building and label it "Word Factory." Have students suggest words that can come out of the factory—only words that have **-fac-** as the root. Students may write the words "inside the building" and underline the root. Repeat the activity with a star labeled, "Astro Words."

## Gifted Learners

Have students find out the word for "to make" or "to do" in other Latin-based languages: Spanish, French, Italian, Portuguese, and Romanian. Students may extend the activity to find the word for "star" in these languages. Have students compare the words and display their findings in a chart.

## Learners with Special Needs

Additional strategies for supporting learners with special needs can be found on page 91L.

---

● Read aloud the directions to the exercises on pages 117 and 118.

● On page 118, suggest that students check the meanings of the words in the dictionary for items 5–10.

● Encourage students to refer to the Helpful Hints boxes on page 117 and 118 whenever necessary.

## Curriculum Connections

### Spelling Link

● Write these words on cards: **asteroid, disastrous, magnify, manufacture, notify, astronomy, satisfy, scientific,** and **sacrifice.**

● Have one student choose a card and say the word aloud. Have another student spell the word and go to the board and write it. If the student spells the word correctly, he or she should use it in a sentence.

● The first student to spell the word correctly chooses the next card and calls out the word. Continue until all cards have been chosen.

### Science Link

Encourage students to prepare a space glossary including terms such as these: **AU** (astronomical unit), **asteroid, astrophysics, astrolabe,** and other terms with the root **-aster-** or **-astro-.** Have students include sketches or other illustrations in the glossary. Tell them to make sure they put the words in alphabetical order to make it easier for the user of the glossary to find the words.

### Observational Assessment

*Check whether students can identify the many variations of the root **-fac-.***

# Connecting Reading and Writing

## Objectives

- **To read and respond to a piece of fiction**
- **To identify problem and solution, and distinguish between fact and fiction as aids to reading comprehension**
- **To write a tall tale**

## Warming Up

### Comprehension Skills

- Explain to students that identifying the **problem and solution** in a story helps the reader to understand the story better.
- Tell students that many folk heroes actually lived, but the details of their adventures were often exaggerated. Point out that being able to **distinguish between fact and fiction** is one way of understanding a tall tale.

## Teaching the Lesson

- Tell students to skim the passage to find the answer to the first question.
- Encourage students to evaluate the actions of Pecos Bill to answer question two.
- Discuss how a person's deeds can "grow in the telling" to answer question three.

## Practicing the Skill

- Read the introduction and the directions on page 120. Discuss with students the folk heroes named in the introduction.
- Guide students to use the story map for preparing their own tall tale.

---

Name _____

Read about the Southwest's roughest, toughest folk hero—Pecos Bill—and think about why this larger-than-life character is the hero of so many tall tales. Then answer the questions that follow.

# Rough, Tough Pecos Bill

### by Lester David

When cowboys of the late 1800's gathered in bunkhouses at the end of the day, the talk naturally turned to Pecos Bill. This mythical cowpoke was the roughest, toughest and best range rider in the Southwest.

The smartest, too. He invented roping and Western movies. He even taught broncos how to buck. He taught his own horse so well that no man—except Bill—could ride him. That's why Bill named him Widow Maker.

During a long dry spell, Bill trekked to the Gulf of Mexico to carry water to his parched home state of Texas. Tiring of the long journey, he decided instead to dig a little trench for the water. The result? The Rio Grande, the river that forms Texas' southern border.

But that dig was nothing compared with the Grand Canyon. Yep, Pecos Bill dug that, too. When a terrific urge to mine for gold struck him one day, he started digging. Before he could yell "Eureka!" he had created the canyon.

Wild stories abound about how his days ended. The best yarn: Bill took one look at a city slicker from the East and just laughed himself to death!

1. He tried to bring water to Texas. He formed the Rio Grande.
2. Answers will vary.
3. Answers will vary.

 **Reader's Response**

1. Name one problem that Pecos Bill tried to solve. What happened as a result?

2. Do you think that Pecos Bill was a real person? Could he have done the things that the stories say he did? Explain.

3. Some heroes of tall tales were real people. Yet the stories about them grew taller each time they were told. Why do you think this happened?

LESSON 58: Connecting Reading and Writing
Comprehension—Problem and Solution; Distinguish Between Fact and Fiction

119

---

# UNIVERSAL ACCESS
# Meeting Individual Needs

### Logical Learners

Have students read a short, objective news story and locate the 5W's (who, what, why, when, where). Let students use the facts as the starting place for an exaggeration. Have them experiment with stretching the facts, finding out which parts of the story lend themselves to exaggeration better than others. Have volunteers share their stories with the class.

### Visual Learners

Show photographs of natural places such as Mt. Everest, the Grand Canyon, the Pacific Ocean. Tell students to think about legends that could develop to explain the natural features. For example: footprints forming the Great Salt Lake, or leaving an oven open and accidentally forming Death Valley. Have students write about these unreal "cause and effect" situations and share them with classmates.

### Learners with Special Needs

Additional strategies for supporting learners with special needs can be found on page 91L.

Folk heroes like Paul Bunyan, John Henry, Davy Crockett, Annie Oakley, and Pecos Bill all had one thing in common. They had what it took to solve problems. Tall tales are full of problems and contests. The hero may be trying to tame the fiercest bear, stop a cyclone from coming, outthink the quickest thinker, or beat the latest machine. Whatever the problem, the hero solves it because of his or her daring, skill, or strength.

Fill in the story map below for a tall tale you will write. First, list a problem that your folk hero will face. Then exaggerate the steps he or she will take to solve the problem. Also, list the setting (where and when the story takes place) and the characters. Remember: Your hero will have traits that are larger than life. Later, use at least two of these words to write your tall tale.

| description | enjoy | exaggeration | fact | fiction |
|---|---|---|---|---|
| greatest | hero | imagination | independent | invent |
| irregular | spectacular | successful | transform | |

**Story Map**

Setting: _____ Answers will vary. _____

Hero: _____

Traits: _____ _____ _____

Other Characters: _____ _____ _____

Problem: _____

    Step 1: _____

    Step 2: _____

    Step 3: _____

Solution: _____

**Writer's Tip**

Mix fact with imagination and exaggeration to write your tall tale.

**Writer's Challenge**

Now use your story map to write your tall tale. Use vivid words to describe your hero, and "speak" in a humorous voice. State your problem and solution clearly, but exaggerate the details. Use two or more of the words from the box above.

Statue of Paul Bunyan and Babe the Blue Ox

120   LESSON 58: Connecting Reading and Writing
Comprehension—Problem and Solution; Distinguish Between Fact and Fiction

---

### English-Language Learners/ESL

Many cultures contain tall tales about folk heroes. Ask students to research tall tales in the literature of their first language, and work with another student to relate the story to classmates. If possible, have the story in print so that you can copy it and distribute it. Read it through first, to see whether it translates well.

### Gifted Learners

Songs were often written about characters from tall tales. Suggest that students use their story maps and completed tall tales to write a song that captures the character's traits, his or her adventures, and the story's problem and solution.

---

## The Writing Process

Discuss with students the features of a good tall tale. Then read aloud page 120.

**Prewrite** Before students begin their tall tale, help them think about the characters, problem, and solution. To help students think about story problems, suggest they start by thinking about common problems such as missing the school bus or not being prepared for a test.

**Write** As students write, encourage them to exaggerate the events in their stories.

**Revise** Have them review their story maps to check if the story's problem and solution are clear.

**Proofread** Encourage students to carefully check their work for errors in grammar, punctuation, and spelling.

**Publish** Ask students to copy their final drafts onto page 120 or a separate sheet of paper.

**Computer Connection** Share the following tip with students who use a word processor to do their writing:

• Students can create a blank template of the story map. The template can be saved and used when they need to write a new story.

• Have them type the blank story map as found on page 120. Save it as "Story Map Template." When students need to create a story map, they can open the template and then go to File and then Save As. At the prompt, they may save the story map by giving it the name of the story. (For example: Story Map Riding the Wind.) They can complete the story map form, while still retaining the original template to be used for other stories.

**Portfolio** Have students add their story maps and their tall tales to their portfolios.

## Suffixes -er and -est

### Objectives

● **To identify and use the suffixes -er and -est**

● **To read and write words containing the suffixes -er and -est**

---

## Warming Up

● Write this sentence on the board and have a student read it aloud.

    Texas is **larger** than Arizona.

● Ask students how the word **larger** was formed. (Start with **large** and then add the ending **-er** to show comparison.)

● Ask what form of **large** would be used to complete this sentence: Of all the southwestern states, Texas is the _____. **(largest)**

● Have a volunteer explain why the suffix **-er** was used in the first sentence and the suffix **-est** was used in the second. (**larger** compares two things; **largest** compares more than two things)

---

## Teaching the Lesson

● Read aloud the Helpful Hints on page 121 and discuss the use of the suffixes.

● Tell students that they have already seen the suffixes **-er** and **-est** when they learned about comparing two or more things.

● To help students remember when to use which suffix, tell them that a two-letter suffix (**-er**) is used to compare two things, and a three-letter suffix (**-est**) is used to compare three or more things.

● Read aloud the Helpful Hints on page 122. Remind students they may need to double final consonants or change **y** to **i** when adding **-er** or **-est** to a base word.

---

Name _____

### Helpful Hints

A **suffix** is a word part added to the end of a **base word** or **root**. Suffixes change the meaning of words or make new words.

    wish + ful = wishful    pain + less = painless    bold + ness = boldness

    Add the **suffix** er to compare *two* things.                    bright + er = brighter

    Add the **suffix** est to compare *more than two* things    dark + est = darkest

Wheeler Peak

 Read each sentence. Draw one line under the word that compares two things. Draw two lines under the word that compares more than two things.

1. The highest peak in New Mexico is Wheeler Peak.

2. At 13,361 feet, Wheeler Peak is 718 feet higher than Arizona's Humphreys Peak.

3. The tallest building in Oklahoma City, the Liberty Tower, has 36 stories.

4. The Liberty Tower is shorter than a bank in Tulsa.

5. The population of Arizona is greater than that of New Mexico.

6. Oklahoma has the smallest area of the four Southwestern states.

7. Texas is the largest Southwestern state of all.

8. Arizona is the newest state in the Southwest; it joined the Union in 1912, about a month after New Mexico did.

9. Texas is the oldest Southwestern state. It joined the Union late in 1845.

10. Texas is an older state than Oklahoma is.

11. The fastest way to get from Albuquerque to Phoenix is to go south through national forest land.

**WORK TOGETHER**

Form a small group. Use an atlas, an almanac, an encyclopedia, or the Internet to find out about these Southwestern states: Arizona, New Mexico, Oklahoma, and Texas. Compare facts by using the suffixes **er** and **est**.

LESSON 59: Suffixes **-er** and **-est**          121

---

# UNIVERSAL ACCESS
## Meeting Individual Needs

### Tactile Learners

Make word cards for these words: **long, mad, sunny, fair, safe, broad, funny, grim.** Have students work in pairs. One student chooses a card and adds **-er** and **-est** to the base word. Have students work together to use the words in phrases about their daily lives. For example, they might discuss **fair, fairer,** and **fairest** exams. Partners should take turns choosing cards.

### Logical Learners

On the board, write the words below in a three-column chart:

| small | (big) | (bigger) | (biggest) |
|-------|-------|----------|-----------|
| light | (heavy) | (heavier) | (heaviest) |
| smooth | (rough) | (rougher) | (roughest) |
| happy | (sad) | (sadder) | (saddest) |

Have students write the opposite of each word and then add the suffix **-er** and **-est.**

## Helpful Hints

Sometimes, you need to make spelling changes before adding **er** or **est**.

Double the final consonant of a one-syllable, short-vowel word before adding **er** or **est**.

red + er = redder          hot + est = hottest

Change **y** to **i** before adding **er** or **est**.

tiny + er = tinier          sturdy + est = sturdiest

Drop **silent e** before adding **er** or **est**.

wide + er = wider          fine + est = finest

Acoma Pueblo in New Mexico

**Add er and est to each base word. Write the new words in the chart.**

| Base Word | Base Word + er | Base Word + *est* |
|-----------|----------------|-------------------|
| 1. nice | nicer | nicest |
| 2. sad | sadder | saddest |
| 3. friendly | friendlier | friendliest |

**Add er or est to the base word in the box below to complete each sentence correctly.**

| grand | keen | old | safe |

4. The Acoma Pueblo in New Mexico is the ___oldest___ continuously lived-in city in the United States.

5. In 1540, Francisco Coronado wrote that the pueblo's location on a huge mesa made it one of the ___safest___ cities he had ever seen.

6. John Wesley Powell wrote that the Grand Canyon was indeed the ___grandest___ place of all.

7. Powell had a ___keener___ knowledge of geology than the explorer, Zebulon Pike.

**122**  LESSON 59: Suffixes **-er** and **-est**

*Home Involvement Activity* What is the **highest** peak, **tall**est building, **old**est town, **deep**est lake, **large**est city, and so on, in your state? Find out together. Record the information on a fact sheet or chart.

---

### English-Language Learners/ESL

Have students work in groups of three for this activity. Students will use items 1–11 on page 121. First, make sure they have underlined the correct word. Then have them act out the word—with two students if the suffix is **-er** and three students if the suffix is **-est**. After they have acted out the word, have students pronounce it as a group.

### Gifted Learners

Invite students to write a character sketch about someone whom they admire. Tell them to begin by compiling a list of adjectives that describe the person. As students write the actual sketch, tell them to use the suffixes **-er** and **-est**.

### Learners with Special Needs

Additional strategies for supporting learners with special needs can be found on page 91L.

---

## Practicing the Skill

● Read aloud the directions for the exercises on pages 121 and 122. Make sure students understand that they have to draw one line under words that compare two things and two lines under words that compare more than two things.

● Call on a volunteer to read the Work Together feature on page 121. Make sure that students have access to reference materials to help them complete the activity.

## Curriculum Connections

### Spelling Link

Write these words on the board: **small, old, fast, sad, friendly, nice.** Have students add the appropriate suffix to each word in parenthesis to complete the sentence.

Pablo is nice but Petra is (nice). **(nicer)**

Our new car is the (small) we have ever had. **(smallest)**

Which student is the (old)? **(oldest)**

Today the students were (friendly) than yesterday. **(friendlier)**

Jeannie wanted the puppy with the (sad) face. **(saddest)**

Which is (fast), the tortoise or the hare? **(faster)**

### Math Link

● In the exercise on page 121, students read that New Mexico's highest point is Wheeler Peak. Have students research the highest points and lowest points in the other western states.

● Have students make a bar graph showing the highest and lowest point in the state. Check to see that they have labeled the graph correctly.

### Observational Assessment

*Note whether students can spell words when they must change **y** to **i** or double the final consonant.*

# Suffixes -y, -ly, -ish, -like, -ful, -less

## Objectives

- To identify and use the suffixes -y, -ly, -ish, -like, -ful, and -less
- To read and write words containing the suffixes -y, -ly, -ish, -like, -ful, and -less

## Warming Up

- Write the following haiku on the board and read it aloud to students.

  A **stately** cactus,

  **leafless**, **spiny**, yet **hopeful**

  **Greenish**, **treelike** pole.

- Underline the words **stately, leafless, spiny, hopeful, greenish,** and **treelike.**

- Ask students to discuss their meaning. Point out that these words are used to describe the cactus.

- Tell students to use what they know about suffixes to identify and circle the suffixes in these words.

## Teaching the Lesson

- Read the Helpful Hints on page 123 and 124. To help students understand the definition of each suffix show them how to substitute the definition for the word with the suffix. For example, in the first line on page 124, there are a number of definitions. Model the substitution: **salty** = "full of salt."

- Call on a volunteer to read the Challenge feature and have students discuss how the words **careful** and **careless** are constructed. (**care** + suffix) Then work as a group to make a list of words with opposite meanings that use the suffixes -**ful** and -**less**. (Possible words: **powerful/powerless, painful/painless**)

123

---

Name _____

> **Helpful Hints**
>
> The **suffix** ful means "full of."    The **suffix** less means "without."
>
> powerful = full of power      painless = without pain
>
> The **suffix** ish means "like," "somewhat," or "belonging to a nation or people."
>
> childish behavior    yellowish light    Spanish dances
>
> If a word ends in **silent** e, drop the e before adding ish.
>
> a whitish color    a bluish sky
>
> The **suffix** like means "resembling."
>
> a lifelike statue    a dreamlike experience

 Combine a base word with a suffix in the box to form a new word. Then use the new word in a phrase or sentence that shows its meaning. Write the words and the sentences on the lines.

| Base Words | | | |
|---|---|---|---|
| baby | beauty | business | desert |
| thought | skill | Swede | worth |
| **Suffixes** | | | |
| ful | ish | like | less |

1. babyish    Answers will vary.
2. beautiful _____
3. businesslike _____
4. desertlike _____
5. thoughtful (or thoughtless) _____
6. skillful _____
7. Swedish _____
8. worthless _____

Cinco de Mayo dancers

> ### CHALLENGE
>
> The suffixes ful and less are opposite in meaning.
>
> careful/careless
>
> Make a list of opposite words that use the suffixes ful and less.

---

# UNIVERSAL ACCESS
# Meeting Individual Needs

## Visual Learners

Have students work with a partner to list words that end in the suffixes -**y, -ly, -ish, -like, -ful,** and -**less.** Students should check the spelling after they make their lists. Then have students prepare a word search puzzle for other students to solve. Have students use the words from page 124: such as, **cloudy, terribly, clingy, wavy, happily, icy, dirty, carelessly, humbly,** and **stormy.**

## Kinesthetic Learners

Tell students to stand if they hear you say a word with the suffix -**y, -ly, -ish, -like, -ful, -less,** and to remain seated if the word does not have one of the suffixes. Use words such as: **weightless, greatest, safely, hopeful, closeness, rocky, thoughtful, brightly, bravely, fearless, darkness, colorful, healthy, painful, helpless, neatness, rainy,** and **brighter.**

The **suffix** y means "full of," "tending to," or "like."

salty          sticky          watery

When a word ends in **silent** e, usually drop the e before adding y.

juice + y = juicy          noise + y = noisy

When a word ends in a single consonant after a short vowel, double the consonant before adding y.

fun + y = funny          drip + y = drippy

The **suffix** ly means "in a certain way."

Quickly means "in a quick way."

When you add ly to a word that ends in le, drop the le.

bubble + ly = bubbly          crumble + ly = crumbly

When a word ends in y, change the y to an i before adding ly.

easy + ly = easily          merry + ly = merrily

 On the line, add y or ly to the word in bold type.

1. full of **storms** _____ stormy
2. in a **humble** way _____ humbly
3. in a **careless** way _____ carelessly
4. full of **dirt** _____ dirty
5. full of or like **ice** _____ icy
6. in a **happy** way _____ happily
7. like a **wave** _____ wavy
8. tending to **cling** _____ clingy
9. in a **terrible** way _____ terribly
10. full of **clouds** _____ cloudy
11. in a **warm** way _____ warmly

**Storm**y sky over Saguaro National Monument

**124** | LESSON 60: Suffixes
-y, -ly, -ish, -like, -ful, -less

 **Home Involvement Activity** Write each suffix from this lesson on an index card. Shuffle the cards. For each card you pick, build a word. Then use the word in a sentence about the weather.

## English-Language Learners/ESL

Display photographs that evoke description, such as cooking food, a volcano, or an exciting sporting event. Have students work with a partner and write a list of descriptive words that include the suffixes **-y, -ly, -ish, -like, -ful,** and **-less.** You may wish to allow students to describe the scene in their language of origin first, and then translate their descriptive words into English.

## Gifted Learners

Have students list the base words and suffixes in the box on page 123. Then have students use those words to write a poem, a descriptive essay, or a short story about the dancing couple in the photograph on that page.

## Learners with Special Needs

Additional strategies for supporting learners with special needs can be found on page 91L.

## Practicing the Skill

● Read aloud the directions to each exercise on pages 123 and 124. On page 123 encourage students to try out the new words first on a piece of paper.

● If students have difficulty completing items 1–11 on page 124, allow them to work with a partner.

## Curriculum Connections

### Spelling Link

Read aloud the following spelling words. Have students write the words and underline the suffixes.

| | |
|---|---|
| beauti<u>ful</u> | thought<u>less</u> |
| life<u>like</u> | drip<u>py</u> |
| bubb<u>ly</u> | worth<u>less</u> |
| skill<u>ful</u> | happi<u>ly</u> |

### Math Link

Have students assign points to each suffix based on the number of letters in the suffix. For example: **-y** = 1; **-ly** = 2; **-ish** and **-ful** = 3; **-like** and **-less** = 4. Ask students to write sentences using words with these suffixes. Have them total the number of points for each suffix used in a sentence and write their highest scoring sentence on the board. Write the following on the board as an example of a "high scoring" sentence: *The **clownlike**, **shabbily** dressed performer was **hopeful** that he would not go away **jobless**.* (4+2+3+4=13)

### Observational Assessment

*Note whether students can correctly use words with the suffixes **-y, -ly, -ish, -like, -ful,** and **-less** in context.*

# Suffixes -ship, -ness, -hood, -ment, -some

## Objectives

● **To identify and use the suffixes -ship, -ness, -hood, -ment, and -some**

● **To use and write words ending in the suffixes -ship, -ness, -hood, -ment, and -some**

## Warming Up

● Write the following passage on the board and have a student read it aloud.

> Mr. Lubbock's class began the "School **Neighborhood**" project. They made posters about good school **citizenship**. They voted to promote **friendliness**, self-**improvement**, and **helpfulness**. The posters were **awesome**. Soon, the entire school was involved in the project.

● Underline the words in bold type and ask a student to identify and circle the base word in each one.

● Ask another student to define the base word and then tell how adding the suffix changes the meaning of each word.

## Teaching the Lesson

● Read aloud the Helpful Hints on page 125. Call on students to supply other examples for each suffix, and have a volunteer write each example on the board.

● Ask a student to read the Challenge feature on page 125. Point out that the suffix **-some,** like other suffixes, has more than one meaning.

---

Name _____

### Helpful Hints

The **suffix** ship means "state or condition of," "office of," or "skill."

**Partnership** is the state of being partners.

The **suffix** ness means "state or quality of."

**Blindness** is the state of being blind.

The **suffix** hood means "state, quality, or condition of."

**Childhood** is the time or state of being a child.

The **suffix** ment means "act or result of" or "state of being."

**Disappointment** is the state of being disappointed.

The **suffix** some means "like or tending to."

**Troublesome** means tending to cause trouble.

**Join each base word and suffix. Write the new word on the line.**

| | | |
|---|---|---|
| 1. | citizen + ship | citizenship |
| 2. | adult + hood | adulthood |
| 3. | nervous + ness | nervousness |
| 4. | measure + ment | measurement |
| 5. | burden + some | burdensome |
| 6. | penman + ship | penmanship |
| 7. | improve + ment | improvement |
| 8. | neighbor + hood | neighborhood |
| 9. | awe + some | awesome |
| 10. | bright + ness | brightness |
| 11. | friend + ship | friendship |

**Citizen**ship ceremony

### CHALLENGE

The suffix some can also describe a grouping, such as a **three**some. Write a sentence about sports using **two**some and **four**some.

---

# UNIVERSAL ACCESS
## Meeting Individual Needs

### Visual Learners

Have students make word cards for each of the base words on pages 125–126. Also have them make multiple sets of cards for the suffixes **-ship, -ness, -hood, -ment,** and **-some.** Each partner takes 6 cards. The other cards are stacked face-down. Have players take turns asking his or her partner for a suffix in order to match it with a base word they are holding in their hand. If there is a match, that player places the two cards on the table. If there is no match, that player chooses another card from the stack.

### Logical Learners

Have each student choose a word from the lesson that ends with the suffix **-ship, -ness, -hood, -ment,** or **-some.** Tell them to write a riddle for their word. For example: "This word has the suffix **-some.** It names the trait of causing difficulty for another. What is it?" **(troublesome)**

★ **Read each phrase. Underline the suffix** ship, ness, hood, ment, or some **in each word in bold type.**

1. his **boyhood** in Arizona
2. won the **championship**
3. new to **parenthood**
4. a worn **pavement**
5. has **leadership** qualities
6. a new **development**
7. takes **ownership**
8. a **quarrelsome** couple
9. graceful **movement**
10. pleasure and **happiness**
11. heated **arguments**

12. the **seriousness** of the problem
13. **tiresome** chores
14. felt deep **sadness**
15. a **fearsome** storm

Galveston Harbor after hurricane

★ **Complete each sentence below. Choose from the words in bold type above.**

16. A _____fearsome_____ hurricane battered the Gulf Coast of Texas.
17. Almost at once, the _____pavement_____ began to buckle under our feet.
18. _____Quarrelsome_____ neighbors argued over how to protect boats and homes.
19. The mayor and the police chief showed strong _____leadership_____ qualities during the crisis.
20. Quick action or _____movement_____ was needed to rescue the victims.
21. The community felt great _____sadness_____ for the town's loss.
22. Everyone was aware of the _____seriousness_____ of the damage.
23. Cleaning up would be a long and _____tiresome_____ process.
24. _____Arguments_____ arose over how to begin the cleanup.
25. We all felt _____happiness_____ when the town was restored.

**126**   LESSON 61: Suffixes
-ship, -ness, -hood, -ment, -some

 **Home Involvement Activity** Discuss the feelings of **enjoyment**, **amazement**, and **resentment**. Talk with family members about situations and events that evoke these feelings.

## English-Language Learners/ESL

Have students work in groups. Give each group word cards for a base word and suffix from items 1–15 on page 126. Tell the groups to match the word parts, write the word with the suffix, and then say, write, or act out a sentence that includes each word. Students may consult with their group to develop a sentence.

## Gifted Learners

Ask students to write each word from this lesson on a sheet of paper. Next to each word, have them list other words that can be described by the word. For example, next to **fearsome**, students might write **lion, storm,** and **monster.**

## Learners with Special Needs

Additional strategies for supporting learners with special needs can be found on page 91L.

## Practicing the Skill

● Read aloud the directions for items 1–11 on page 125. Have students refer to the Helpful Hints and substitute the definition for the suffix when possible to help them figure out the meaning of a word.

● Read aloud the directions for the two exercises on page 126. Point out that items 16–25 use words from the first exercise, but that some words will not be used.

## Curriculum Connections

### Spelling Link

After reading aloud each of the sentences below, repeat the word in bold type. For each word, have a student spell it orally, write it on the board, and circle its suffix.

The **movement** of the waves is rhythmic.

Sailing is rewarding but **tiresome.**

I like my **neighborhood.**

The mayor's **leadership** is strong.

The noisy bluejays seem **quarrelsome.**

Seeing his family again brought him **happiness.**

### Science Link

● On September 8–9, 1900, a hurricane killed about 6,000 people in the city of Galveston, Texas. After that disaster, Galvestonians built a seawall and brought in sand to raise the level of the city to prevent future flooding.

● Have students research the storm and report their findings, using as many of these words as they can: **pavement, development, ownership, movement, happiness, seriousness, tiresome, sadness, fearsome, awesome, neighborhood,** and **improvement.**

## Observational Assessment

*Check whether students know when to change the spelling of a base word before adding a suffix.*

**126**

# Suffixes -ity, -ive, -age, -ion/-sion/-tion

## Objectives

- **To identify and use the suffixes -ity, -ive, -age, -ion/-sion/-tion**

- **To use and write words with the suffixes -ity, -ive, -age, -ion/-sion/-tion**

## Warming Up

- Write the following on the board and read it aloud to students.

  There is some **confusion** as to the right **postage** for this card. It was found in our **luggage** and it included a **creative description** of our trip to the Grand Canyon. It even told our **mileage**. In all **sincerity**, I'd like it to reach you before we arrive back home.

- Rewrite the first sentence this way:

  There is some **state of being confused** as to the right **amount of money paid for mailing** this card.

- Ask students to examine the words **confusion** and **postage** and tell how using these words with suffixes helped make the sentence clearer and more concise.

## Teaching the Lesson

- Have students take turns reading aloud the Helpful Hints on pages 127 and 128. Ask students to give examples of other words that end with these suffixes.

- Point out the spelling changes that occur when suffixes are added to some words.

- On page 128, students are asked to select the correct word and add the correct suffix. Ask them to think about how the suffixes affect the meaning of a root or a base word as they complete these exercises.

---

Name _____

### Helpful Hints

The **suffix** ity means "state or condition."

  real + ity = reality

The **suffix** ive means "relating to" or "tending to."

  protect + ive = protective

When words end in **silent e**, drop the e before adding the suffixes ity or ive.

  sincere + ity = sincerity          create + ive = creative

The **suffix** age means "act, condition, or result of" or "collection of."

  breakage                baggage

The **suffix** age may also mean "cost of," "home of," or "amount of."

  postage              orphanage                shortage

When a word ends in y after a consonant, change the y to i before adding age.

  carry + age = carriage

When a **suffix** that begins with a vowel follows a one-syllable, short-vowel word ending in a consonant, double the consonant before adding the suffix.

  lug + age = luggage

**Underline the suffix in each word in bold type.**

1. picked up the **baggage**
2. put the box in **storage**
3. an **active** volcano
4. the ship's **wreckage**
5. sends a **package**
6. a **destructive** storm
7. **supportive** friends
8. a week of high **humidity**
9. too much **publicity**
10. a happy **marriage**
11. car with low **mileage**
12. **possibility** of rain

### CHALLENGE

Unscramble the word in bold type. Underline its suffix. Then write your own sentence for the unscrambled word.

*Mom is an **xtuevicee** at the bank.*

LESSON 62: Suffixes -ity, -ive, -age, -ion/-sion/-tion   127

---

# UNIVERSAL ACCESS
## Meeting Individual Needs

### Visual Learners

Make word cards using words from the lesson such as **active, orphanage, humidity,** and so on. Cut and laminate the cards in a jigsaw pattern, so that the base word is one jigsaw piece and its suffix is the corresponding jigsaw piece. Place the "pieces" in a bag and have students select one. Then have them find and match the "pieces" to form the original words.

### Logical Learners

Ask students to write the words with suffixes from this lesson. Have students sort the words into two groups—those that are nouns and those that are adjectives. Tell students to keep track of the base word's part of speech. Have students investigate whether each word changes its part of speech when a suffix is added to the base word. Have students collect and analyze the data they find.

The **suffix** ion, sion, or tion means "act or result of."

| reflection | confusion | creation |

Sometimes, when a word ends in **silent** e, drop the e before adding ion.

tense → tension          rotate → rotation

The spelling of a word may change when the suffix ion, sion, or tion is added.

**decide** = decision          **divide** = division
**persuade** = persuasion          **describe** = description

⭐ **Read about the Grand Canyon. Add the suffix ion to the word in the word box that best completes each sentence. Make any needed spelling changes. Write the new word on the line.**

| confuse | create | direct | elevate | protect |

Many people are fascinated by the Grand Canyon. We can all agree that it is

big and beautiful. Yet there is some (1) _____confusion_____ about its age. We do know

that 65 million years ago, the rim was at sea level. Somewhere between 5 million and

20 million years ago, the Colorado River took its present (2) _____direction_____.

Its flow caused the (3) _____creation_____ of the canyon. As the river began to carve

out the canyon, the (4) _____elevation_____ of the land changed. It began to rise.
Today, the South Rim is 7,500 feet above sea level in places. The North Rim is
1,000 feet higher. Nature's masterpiece of the American Southwest deserves our

care and (5) _____protection_____.

A view from the North Rim of the Grand Canyon

**128**

LESSON 62: Suffixes
-ity, -ive, -age, -ion/-sion/-tion

🏠 **Home Involvement Activity** What is the most magnificent natural site you have seen together? Talk about it. Use as many words with the suffix ion, sion, or tion as you can.

● Read aloud the directions to the exercises on pages 127 and 128. Point out that on page 128, they will form new words consisting of a base word and a suffix.

● Encourage students to refer to the Helpful Hints on page 127 and 128 whenever necessary.

## Curriculum Connections

### Spelling Link

Write the following phrases on the board. Ask students to copy each phrase and write a word from the lesson that describes it.

advertising (**publicity**)
items you carry (**baggage**)
something that has been made
    (**creation**)
a chance (**possibility**)
bond between husband and wife
    (**marriage**)
state in which one is not thinking
    clearly (**confusion**)
height above sea level (**elevation**)
in motion (**active**)

### Writing Link

● As students proofread their writing they should pay attention to words in which a spelling change takes place before adding a suffix. Help students understand when they should drop the final **e**, when they should double a consonant, or when they should change the **y** to **i** before adding suffixes.

● Students may make a Helpful Hints sheet outlining these rules and giving examples for each. Have them refer to these hints as they proofread their writing.

### Observational Assessment

*Note whether students can distinguish between meanings of the suffix* **-age.**

**English-Language Learners/ESL**

Prepare cards containing words with suffixes and cards with only suffixes. Post the word cards. Have students find the card whose suffix matches the card exactly, and place it over the suffix on the word card. Then have them pronounce the word. Encourage students to say whether there was a spelling change, and if so, what that change was. Students may refer to the Helpful Hints or discuss their ideas with a partner.

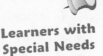

**Gifted Learners**

Supply students with an article from a nature magazine about the Grand Canyon or another feature of the Southwest. Have students read the article to find words with suffixes. Students should keep a list of the words and then write a summary of the article using the words.

**Learners with Special Needs**

Additional strategies for supporting learners with special needs can be found on page 91L.

# Suffixes -able/-ible and -ance/-ence

## Objectives

- **To identify and use the suffixes -able/-ible and -ance/-ence**

- **To make spelling changes in words with suffixes**

## Warming Up

- Write the following statement on the board and read it aloud to students.

    It helps to be **flexible** in figuring out which suffix to use. Your **confidence** will grow and you will soon see a **difference** if you exercise **persistence** and make use of a **manageable** dictionary.

- Underline the words in bold type and ask students to read them to the class. Have students divide each word into a root or base word and a suffix. When students' responses are correct, have them write their answers on the board.

## Teaching the Lesson

- Have volunteers read the Helpful Hints on page 129. Point out that words with the suffixes -**able** or -**ible** are adverbs and that words with the suffixes -**ance** or -**ence** are nouns.

- Ask students to think of other words that end in these suffixes. Write the words on the board and have students use them in sentences.

- Discuss the information in the Word Strategy box on page 129. Point out the exceptions and encourage students to use a dictionary whenever they are in doubt about spelling or choosing a suffix.

---

Name _____

**Helpful Hints**

The **suffix** able or ible means "able to" or "capable of."

An **enjoy**able movie is capable of giving enjoyment.
A **sens**ible person is capable of showing good sense.

The **suffix** ance or ence means "act of" or "state of being."

**Avoid**ance is the act of avoiding.
**Differ**ence is the state of being different.

There is no rule for whether to use able or ible, or ance or ence. It is best to check a dictionary when you are unsure about which spelling is correct.

Read each statement. Add the suffix in parentheses to the word in bold type to form a word that will complete the sentence. Write the word on the line.

**WORD STRATEGY**

If a base word ends in **silent** e, you drop the e before adding able or ible. Add able to these words:

believe  inflate

Notice some exceptions to the rule:

lovable *or* loveable
manageable
knowledgeable

1. (able) If you can **break** this vase, then it must be ___breakable___.

2. (ible) If you can **digest** certain foods, then they must be ___digestible___.

3. (able) If you can **manage** your pets, then they are ___manageable___.

4. (ible) If you can **flex** a drinking straw, then it must be ___flexible___.

5. (ance) If something **annoys** you, then it is an ___annoyance___.

6. (ence) If you **persist** until you finish a task, then you have ___persistence___.

7. (ence) If you are **intelligent,** then you have ___intelligence___.

8. (ence) If you are **confident,** then you have ___confidence___.

---

# UNIVERSAL ACCESS
## Meeting Individual Needs

### Visual Learners

Write the suffixes -**able, -ible, -ance,** and -**ence** at the top of long, thin strips of paper, and post the papers on a wall or bulletin board. Have students work in small groups and, using a dictionary, find as many words as they can for each category. Have students write the words on the list and then use the word lists to write humorous poems.

### Logical Learners

Have students think about and discuss the rules for using the suffixes in this lesson. Tell students to develop "user-friendly" guides for readers to help them understand the meaning of an unfamiliar word that has one of these suffixes. After the guides are ready, have students "field test" them with the class. If the guides aren't clear enough, ask students to revise them and try them out again.

**Use each of the words in the box in a sentence that shows its meaning.**

| independence | predictable | appearance |
|---|---|---|

1. Answers will vary. _____

   _____

2. _____

   _____

3. _____

   _____

**Fill in the circle of the word that completes each sentence correctly. Then write the word on the line.**

4. I can never get __comfortable__ sitting on a wooden bench.
   - ● comfortable  ○ washable  ○ legible

5. Getting to know people of different cultures helps us develop __tolerance__.
   - ○ appearance  ● tolerance  ○ brilliance

6. His __absence__ from school on Tuesday made him miss the test.
   - ○ independence  ● absence  ○ avoidance

7. Bridget was thrilled to get a letter of __acceptance__ to college.
   - ● acceptance  ○ existence  ○ dependence

8. Last year, I won my school's gold medal for __excellence__ in science.
   - ● excellence  ○ difference  ○ confidence

9. Granddad drove a __convertible__ in the 1950s.
   - ○ perishable  ○ deductible  ● convertible

130   LESSON 63: Suffixes
-able/-ible, and -ance/-ence

 **Home Involvement Activity** Ordinary objects are **measurable** in many ways. For example, you can measure a jar by its height, weight, or capacity. Choose objects. List the ways they are **measurable**.

**130**

# More Than One Prefix or Suffix

## Objectives

- **To identify and use words with more than one prefix or suffix**

- **To determine meaning by analyzing word structure**

## Warming Up

- Write the following sentences on the board and read them aloud to students.

  **Unreasonable misunderstandings** led to **unpalatable disagreements**.

  With the **reexcavation** of King Tut's tomb, **researchers** have **reestablished** his claim to **royalty**.

- Point out that even if students don't know the meaning of every word, they are able to identify the words with prefixes, suffixes, or both. Ask volunteers to write these words on the board.

- As a group, identify the prefixes and suffixes. Then discuss how the prefixes and suffixes help in determining word meaning.

## Teaching the Lesson

- Point out that words communicate thoughts and ideas. Adding prefixes and suffixes helps us better communicate the idea we want to get across.

- Read aloud the Helpful Hint on page 131. After students have read the words with more than one prefix, ask them to discuss what the words mean. Do the same for the suffixes.

- Read aloud the Helpful Hint on page 132. Have students analyze the meaning of the words **enjoyable** and **disgraceful.**

- Ask students to suggest other words with more than one prefix or suffix, and words with both a prefix and a suffix.

---

Name _____

### Helpful Hints

Some words have *more than one* **prefix.**

The word redis**cover** adds the **prefixes** re and dis to **cover.**
The word disen**tangle** adds the **prefixes** dis and en to **tangle.**

Some words have *more than one* **suffix.**

Creat**ively** adds the **suffixes** ive and ly to the base word **create.**
Forget**fulness** adds the **suffixes** ful and ness to the word **forget.**

Each of these words has two prefixes or two suffixes. Draw one line under the first prefix or suffix. Draw two lines under the second prefix or suffix.

1. undisclosed
2. endlessly
3. kindliest
4. helpfulness
5. selfishness
6. loneliness
7. reinstate
8. creativity
9. resubmerge
10. carefully
11. carelessness
12. reasonableness

Read these sentences about Oklahoma. Underline the word in each sentence that has *more than one suffix.* Then circle each suffix in the word. Write the base word on the line.

13. In the 1930s, dust storms fearlessly swept through Oklahoma and ruined the land.

    fear

14. Oklahoma-born songwriter Woody Guthrie actively worked to expose the hard lives of farmers during the 1930s.

    act

15. Guthrie told of the powerlessness of poor farmers who had been hurt by the dust storms.

    power

Abandoned farmhouse in the Dust Bowl

### CHALLENGE

List as many words as you can with more than one prefix or suffix that can complete the following sentence:

*Her _____ made her the right choice for mayor.*

LESSON 64: More Than One Prefix or Suffix     **131**

---

# UNIVERSAL ACCESS
## Meeting Individual Needs

### Auditory Learners

Students may know the song, "Supercalifragilisticexpialidocious." Encourage students to find the words and sing it for the class. Write the word on the board, and work together to find any prefixes, suffixes, and even a root. **(fragil)** Remind students that this made-up word contains one or two made-up prefixes and suffixes.

### Tactile Learners

Prepare a five-part spinner with the numbers 2, 3, 4, 5, and 6. Have students play in groups of five. Each student spins the needle and has to write a word on the board with the same number of syllables as the pointer shows. Some of these syllables should be prefixes, suffixes, or both. Then have the student circle the prefixes or suffixes in the word.

Write the prefix, the base word, and the suffix for each word below. Use + signs to separate the three parts. The first one has been done for you. Use a dictionary, if needed, to check the spelling of any base words.

1. enrichment      en + rich + ment
2. disappearance      dis + appear + ance
3. illegally      il + legal + ly
4. coauthorship      co + author + ship
5. replacement      re + place + ment
6. immaturity      im + mature + ity
7. unbelievable      un + believe + able
8. incompletion      in + complete + ion

 Fill in the circle of the word that completes each sentence. Then write the word on the line.

9. ___Disagreements___ arose at the meeting.
   ○ Replacements    ○ Unreasonable    ● Disagreements

10. The arguments were about who would buy the ___refreshments___
    ● refreshments    ○ distrustful    ○ independence

11. We refused to tip the ___unfriendly___ waiter.
    ○ unchangeable    ○ cooperative    ● unfriendly

12. For $1.49, you can get ___refillable___ cups of soda at the all-night market.
    ○ exchangeable    ● refillable    ○ unselfish

LESSON 64: More Than One Prefix or Suffix

**Home Involvement Activity** Choose one of the base words from this page, such as *place.* Have a contest to see who can add the most prefixes and suffixes to this base word to build new words.

---

### English-Language Learners/ESL

Have students compile a list of prefixes and suffixes from the unit. Tell students to write their own definitions of the prefixes and suffixes. Ask students to illustrate the prefix or suffix. For example **not** can be represented by a red circle and a diagonal line going across. Encourage students to make each illustration reflect the meaning of the prefix or suffix.

### Gifted Learners

Have students compile a list of words with prefixes and suffixes. Tell students to create a rhyme or a jingle using words that have the same rhyming suffixes. Point out that they can also rhyme a few short words with one long, multisyllabic word.

### Learners with Special Needs

Additional strategies for supporting learners with special needs can be found on page 91L.

---

## Practicing the Skill

● Read aloud the directions for the exercises on pages 131–132. Remind students to use the + sign as shown in the first item on page 132.

● Explain that in the second exercise on page 132, students should use what they have learned about prefixes and suffixes to help them make the correct word choice.

## Curriculum Connections

### Spelling Link

Write the following sentences on the board. Have students unscramble the word in brackets and write the correct word from the lesson to complete each sentence.

> Woody Guthrie's **[eacrvittiy]** comes through in his folk songs.
>
> I can listen to his songs **[dsllesyen].**
>
> They contain **[liabunelevbe]** tales.
>
> Farmers' **[arseselesncs]** helped pave the way for the Dust Bowl.
>
> People tried to be **[sefiushnl]** and help each other.
>
> Many people in government were **[fryunielnd]** and unsympathetic.

(Answers: **creativity, endlessly, unbelievable, carelessness, unselfish, unfriendly**)

### Writing Link

Have students create a simple thesaurus that they can refer to when writing. They may begin by including words from the lessons in the unit on prefixes and suffixes. Make available several thesauruses for students to examine as they design and write their own.

### Observational Assessment

*Note whether students can distinguish the prefixes and suffixes from the base word or root.*

# Connecting Spelling and Writing

## Objectives

- **To say, spell, sort, and write words containing prefixes and suffixes**
- **To write a sports column including words with prefixes and suffixes**

## Warming Up

- Write this paragraph on the board and have a student read it aloud.

    I can speak with **confidence** about the **importance** of the pioneering spirit in America. Men and women made tough **decisions** as they headed west. They were called on **daily** to make good **judgments.** The **seriousness** of their actions should not be forgotten.

- Ask volunteers to identify the words that contain a suffix. Then have them circle each suffix.

## Teaching the Lesson

- Discuss the meanings of the words in the *Warming-Up* exercise and how each meaning combines the meaning of the root or base word with the suffix.

- Have students read the words in bold type on page 133, and do the same analysis on the words with suffixes.

## Practicing the Skill

- Read the directions on page 133. As students say and spell the words in bold type, have them take note of the first letter.

- Tell students to read the column headings for the table and then write each word in the correct column depending on the first letter of the word.

133

---

Name _____

 Read each group of words. Say and spell each word in bold type. Repeat the word. Then sort the words. Write each word in the correct column below.

- an **active** child
- too much **publicity**
- a **thoughtful** gift
- gave a **sensible** answer
- showed poor **judgment**
- spoke with **confidence**
- **friendliest** student of all
- a **believable** story
- making tough **decisions**
- with all **seriousness**
- a **troublesome** situation
- won the **championship**
- a **subscription** to a magazine
- a **lifelike** statue

- responsibility of **parenthood**
- long and happy **marriage**
- an **unselfish** person
- **importance** to the community

Statue in Oklahoma of a pioneer woman and her son

| Words That Start with A – H | Words That Start with I – P | Words That Start with Q – Z |
| --- | --- | --- |
| active | publicity | thoughtful |
| confidence | judgment | sensible |
| friendliest | lifelike | seriousness |
| believable | parenthood | troublesome |
| decisions | marriage | subscription |
| championship | importance | unselfish |

---

# UNIVERSAL ACCESS
## Meeting Individual Needs

### Visual Learners

Working with a partner, have students identify and list the suffixes found on page 133. Ask them to list words that contain each suffix. Finally, have them write a sentence using as many words as they can with different suffixes. Give students five minutes to compose their sentence. Tell them the sentence may be humorous but it must make sense grammatically.

### Kinesthetic Learners

Make a set of cards with the base words from the lesson such as, **self, life, believe,** and so on. Make a second set with the suffixes: **-able, -age, -ance, -ence, -er, -est, -ful, -hood, -ible, -ion, -ish, -ity, -ive, -less, -like, -ly, -ment, -ness, -ship, -sion, -some, -tion,** and **-y.** Have students draw a card from each and write the word they make. If the word is correct, the student gets another turn. If not, the turn passes to the next player.

### Learners with Special Needs

Additional strategies for supporting learners with special needs can be found on page 91L.

Jim Thorpe was born in 1887. He was one of a pair of twin boys born into the Sac and Fox Indian tribes on land that is now in Oklahoma. His mother gave him a name that means "Bright Path." Thorpe lived up to his name.

At the Olympic Games of 1912, Jim Thorpe won the gold medal in both the pentathlon and decathlon. No athlete has achieved this feat, before or since. The King of Sweden, who presented Thorpe with his medals, called him "the greatest athlete in the world."

☆ **Choose a famous athlete—past or present. Do some research. Write a sports column about the person for your school or local newspaper. Give highlights from your athlete's life and career. Use at least two of these spelling words.**

| | | | |
|---|---|---|---|
| active | publicity | thoughtful | sensible | judgment |
| confidence | friendliest | believable | decisions |
| seriousness | troublesome | championship | subscription |
| lifelike | parenthood | marriage | unselfish | importance |

Answers will vary.

_____

**Writer's Tip**

Answer the 5*Ws* in your column. Your readers need to know *who* your story is about, *what* happened, *when* and *where* it took place, and *why* or *how* it happened.

Jim Thorpe at 1912 Olympics

**Writer's Challenge**

Jim Thorpe had great athletic ability in football, track, baseball, boxing, hockey, lacrosse, archery, tennis, and swimming. In a paragraph, explain why someone might be good at so many sports.

---

## The Writing Process

Tell students that on page 134 they will write a sports article about a famous athlete. Have them read over the introduction, the instructions, and the spelling words.

**Prewrite** Ask students to think of a sport and an athlete they enjoy watching. Using an encyclopedia and other reference works, such as the *Guinness Book of World Records,* have students collect facts about the athlete they chose, and organize the facts into an outline. Refer to the Writer's Tip, and have students include this information in their outline as well. Have students take note of the Writer's Challenge at the bottom of the page, and use the assignment as a writing warm-up.

**Write** Remind students to include main ideas and supporting details. Ask students to clearly state why this athlete was their choice.

**Revise** As students read over their writing, have them use the 5Ws as a checklist.

**Proofread** Have students check their work for errors in spelling, capitalization, and punctuation.

**Publish** Have students copy their final draft onto page 134 or onto a separate sheet of paper. Encourage students to illustrate their articles.

 **Computer Connection**

Share the following tip with students who use a word processor.

• Word-processing programs usually contain a Find feature. Students can use the Find feature as they complete the writing assignment for this lesson. They can check to see whether they have used two spelling words, or if the athlete's name is spelled correctly each time it appears.

• The Find feature is usually in the pull-down menu under Edit. Students may then follow the keyboard commands.

**Portfolio** Have students add their completed sports articles to their portfolios.

---

### English-Language Learners/ESL

Create a number of cards that could be used to describe a sport, for example: **action, active, graceful, popularity, fastest, higher, sportsmanship, entertainment,** and **championship**. Allow students to discuss the meaning of each word with a partner. Then have students find the suffix in each word. Finally, have students create a sentence about a sports figure (real or imaginary) with as many words as possible.

### Gifted Learners

Have students write a descriptive paragraph about someone famous. Have them think about what the person did or does to bring about their fame. Encourage students to use a concept web to help them think of describing words. Then ask students to add suffixes to the descriptive words and use them in their paragraphs.

# Connecting Reading and Writing

## Objectives

- **To read and respond to a non-fiction piece**
- **To make inferences and use interpretation when reading**
- **To write a travel article**

## Warming Up

### Comprehension Skills

- Discuss with students how people make decisions to visit a certain place.

- Ask what kind of information is found in a travel brochure. (facts about a place, interesting features, photographs, maps)

- Explain that a reader may use the information found in a travel brochure or travel article to **make inferences** about what a place is like. The reader can make **interpretations** based on the information presented and then make a decision about whether to visit the place.

## Teaching the Lesson

- Tell students to use the passage to find the answer to the first question.

- Encourage a class discussion about reasons for cliff paintings.

- Have students imagine spending a day at Big Bend. Then have them imagine the same day, but a thousand years ago.

## Practicing the Skill

- Read the introduction and directions on page 136.

- Return to the topic discussed during the *Warming-Up* exercise. Remind students that their articles should give readers a chance to make inferences and interpretations about what a place is like.

---

Name _____

 Take an imaginary hike through Big Bend National Park in America's Southwest and experience the park's unusual plants and animals. Then answer the questions that follow.

# Deep in the Heart of...Big Bend

### by Bud McDonald

To find Big Bend on a map, look at the southwestern portion of Texas, the part of the state that juts out beneath New Mexico. You'll notice that it also lies along the border that divides the United States from Mexico. Big Bend gets its name from the giant U-turn made by the Rio Grande that forms the southern boundary of this national park.

Many prickly desert plants and stinging, biting desert animals make their home at Big Bend. Thirty kinds of snakes live here, including five species of rattlesnakes. Tarantulas and scorpions make their home in this arid land, as well. Herds of deer add their graceful beauty. *Javelina* (a small, native wild pig), roadrunners, and armadillos thrive. Coyotes and mountain lions live here, too.

More than 400 species of birds live at Big Bend or pass through it during the year. That's more birds than are found in any other national park in the United States. There are species of plants at Big Bend that live nowhere else.

One reason for the great variety of life is because Big Bend has many different habitats: deserts, mountains, wooded river bottoms, desert springs, and canyons.

Visitors to Big Bend will see Native American cliff paintings thousands of years old. These ancient pictures help us to imagine the way life was at Big Bend.

Big Bend National Park

1. Big Bend has many different habitats: deserts, mountains, wooded river bottoms, desert springs, and canyons.
2. Answers will vary.
3. Answers will vary.

 **Reader's Response**

1. Why is Big Bend home to so many different kinds of wildlife?

2. Visitors to Big Bend can see ancient cliff paintings. Why do you think people painted these pictures?

3. Imagine that it is thousands of years ago. You are living at Big Bend. What is your life like? Why?

LESSON 66: Connecting Reading and Writing
Comprehension—Make Inferences; Interpret

**135**

---

# UNIVERSAL ACCESS
# Meeting Individual Needs

### Visual Learners

Ask students to skim through a book highlighting a location. Encourage them to look at the photos but to avoid reading the text. Ask students to close the book and write a description of what they think the place is like. Have students compare their descriptions with the book's descriptions. Ask if the inferences and interpretations they made were correct.

### Tactile Learners

Find several detailed photographs of places. Cut them into jigsaw puzzle pieces. As students work to put the puzzles together, tell them to focus on the visual clues in the piece. They can interpret what they see and make inferences about which piece to connect.

### Learners with Special Needs

Additional strategies for supporting learners with special needs can be found on page 91L.

Big Bend's interesting geography—its deserts, mountains, and river canyons—its unusual plants and animals, its ancient cliff paintings, and miles of hiking trails make it an ideal place for people to visit. In fact, its haunting sights and sounds, as well as its lush smells provide the perfect setting for an adventure.

Now choose a place that would make an interesting topic for a travel article. Your place could be a park, a city or village, or your hometown. Include facts about the geography of the area and a brief history. Describe two interesting places to visit. Include a small map, a photograph, or an illustration. Use at least two of these words.

> traveling  protective  features  photograph  description  activity
> recreation  geography  respectful  unfamiliar  transportation  beautiful

Armadillo

Answers will vary.

_____

_____

_____

_____

_____

_____

_____

_____

### Writer's Tip

Choose the most interesting information that will make your audience want to experience the place for themselves.

Javelina, or peccary

### Writer's Challenge ◀

Turn your travel article into a travel brochure. Add a list of interesting places to visit and activities for the whole family to enjoy. You might include information about where to eat, sleep, and shop. Use vivid words that will support your descriptions and details.

136  LESSON 66: Connecting Reading and Writing
Comprehension—Make Inferences; Interpret

## The Writing Process

Read aloud the introduction, instructions, and boxed words on page 136. Discuss the purpose of writing a travel article. Have students explain how making inferences and interpreting information will help the reader better understand the travel article.

**Prewrite** Students should have a clear understanding of what they want to describe. They may organize their information in an outline.

**Write** Remind students to make their descriptions as vivid as possible. Tell students to include the sights and sounds that a visitor would encounter in that particular destination.

**Revise** Ask students to think of these questions as they revise: *Are there sentences that I can combine or reorder? Does every paragraph have a main idea that is supported by the other sentences? Are the descriptions clear? Will the reader want to visit this place?*

**Proofread** Ask students to read their articles slowly to check for errors in grammar, punctuation, and spelling.

**Publish** Have students copy their final paragraphs onto page 136 or a separate sheet of paper.

### Computer Connection

Share the following tip with students who use a word processor.

● Most word-processing programs have a file of images or "clip art." You can insert these images in your document to make it visually interesting.

● From the Insert menu, pull down to Picture and then click on "Clip Art." Scroll through the gallery of images and double-click on the one you want.

● You can position the image in your document by dragging and dropping the image. You can resize the image by clicking on and dragging one of its corners.

### Portfolio

Have students add their completed travel articles to their portfolios.

### English-Language Learners/ESL

Students may be more familiar with places from their country of origin. Suggest that students think of places where they have lived or visited. If students are not yet fluent enough to write a paragraph, allow them to list phrases and descriptions about their place.

### Gifted Learners

Students may wish to work with a group to act out what it would be like to visit the place they have chosen for their article. They should gather props and equipment and decide on the most compelling scene—one that will make others want to visit. Encourage class members to discuss the most important features of this location, based on what they saw.

# Reviewing and Assessing

## Prefixes, Roots, Base Words, and Suffixes

### Objective

**To review and assess adding prefixes and suffixes to roots or base words**

## Warming Up

● Write these words on the board:

**inactive, endless, semisweet, heartiest, react, heavily, readiness, adulthood, merriment, derail, fearsome, supportive, orphanage, portion, cooperate, unable, abrasion,** and **flexible.**

● Ask students to circle each prefix and underline each suffix. Ask volunteers to tell what each root or base word means and explain how the prefix and/or suffix changes the meaning.

## Teaching the Lesson

● Direct students' attention to the first exercise on page 137. Point out that students will decode the words by combining prefixes, roots or base words, and suffixes.

● Explain that for items 11 and 12, they will be doing the opposite—in other words, they will be writing a code for the words.

● Students may extend this activity by writing new codes and trading papers with a partner for decoding.

● For the exercise on page 138, suggest that students try each possible answer in the passage to see which word's meaning best fits the surrounding context.

---

Name _____

 Look at the word-part chart below. You can use it to form many words. For example, you can form the word **contraction** by combining C1 + B2 + H3.

|   | 1 | 2 | 3 |
|---|---|---|---|
| A | un | create | ment |
| B | trans | tract | ible |
| C | con | term | ly |
| D | ex | form | tion |
| E | re | ject | less |
| F | dis | sense | ful |
| G | de | gage | ness |
| H | in | turn | ion |
| I | en | circle | ive |
| J | semi | script | ity |

Century plant at Big Bend National Park

 Use the word-part chart to decode these words. On the lines, write the words that you get from these letters and numbers. Make spelling changes as needed.

1. B1 + D2 _____ transform
2. I1 + I2 _____ encircle
3. J1 + I2 _____ semicircle
4. F2 + B3 _____ sensible
5. B2 + H3 _____ traction
6. D2 + E3 + G3 _____ formlessness
7. F1 + B2 + H3 _____ distraction
8. H1 + E2 + H3 _____ injection
9. D1 + B2 + H3 _____ extraction
10. I1 + G2 + A3 _____ engagement

Use the word-part chart to encode these words. Write the letters and the numbers on the lines.

11. reject _____ E1 + E2
12. creativity _____ A2 + I3 + J3

---

# UNIVERSAL ACCESS
## Meeting Individual Needs

### Visual Learners

Write the suffixes from the unit on the board such as **-er, -est, -y,** and so on. Have students play in teams. One player writes a suffix on the board, but leaves blank spaces for the letters that come before. The other team guesses letters that fill the blanks. If the guess is correct the letter is placed in the blank. Play continues until the team can correctly guess the word.

### Learners with Special Needs

Additional strategies for supporting learners with special needs can be found on page 91L.

### Auditory Learners

Write the following suffixes on the board: **-er, -est, -y, -ly, -ish, -like, -ful, -less, -ship, -ness, -hood, -ment, -some, -tion, -ion, -sion, -ive, -age, -ity, -able, -ible, -ance,** and **-ence.** Have students work with a partner. One student chooses a suffix and says it aloud. The partner says a word that contains the suffix, and uses it in a sentence. Students should try to use all the suffixes and check them off as they are used.

**Read the passage. For each numbered blank, there is a choice of words below. Circle the letter of the word that completes the sentence correctly.**

The Sonoran Desert of Arizona is a land of dry plains and mountains. It hosts a variety of cacti, shrubs, and small trees. It is home to the prickly pear, *cholla*, and barrel cactus. *Palo verde*, ironwood, and mesquite trees grow here. Many desert animals dwell here, too. These hardy creatures know how to live __1__ in this harsh place.

Perhaps the best known __2__ of the Sonoran Desert is a special type of cactus. The stately saguaro [suh-(G)WAHR-oh] cactus grows here and in northern Mexico only. Unlike trees, the saguaro has no leaves. Its shape helps it to hold water and to __3__ water loss. The saguaro loses less than a glass of water a day. (Ordinary trees can lose hundreds of gallons in one day.) Naturally, the saguaro stores water for the desert's long dry spells. It also provides food and shelter for desert animals.

1. (a.) successfully  b. forgetfully  c. helplessly
2. a. infection  b. inspector  (c.) inhabitant
3. a. deduce  b. produce  (c.) reduce

Saguaro Cacti in the Sonoran Desert

**Reread the passage to answer the questions. Circle the letter of the answer.**

4. What is true about the saguaro?
   a. It grows in snowy mountains.
   b. It has bushy leaves.
   (c.) It holds great amounts of water.
   d. It scares away animals.

5. What is a *cholla*?
   a. a kind of home
   b. a kind of fruit
   c. a kind of animal
   (d.) a kind of cactus

**Extend & Apply**

Write a glossary entry for the saguaro. Include its pronunciation, definition, an original sentence, and a picture. Use one word with a prefix and a suffix.

138    LESSON 67: Review and Assess

# Reteaching Activities

## What's the Word?

Write the following sentences. Have students add a suffix to the root or base word in brackets.

In the desert sky, many objects were easily [vis]. **[visible]**

The problem is not the sun's [bril]. **[brilliance]**

Too many streetlights create a phenomenon known as "light [pollute]." **[pollution]**

In even the [small] [neighbor], streetlights interfere with the view. **[smallest, neighborhood]**

## More, More Words

Have students think of roots or base words to which they can add the greatest number of prefixes and/or suffixes in order to change it the greatest number of times. Have students generate lists of words that have the same base word or root but different suffixes. Tell students to extend the activity further by adding prefixes as well as suffixes.

**Check Up** The exercises on page 137 give students practice building words by combining roots, base words, prefixes, and suffixes. Page 138 asks students to choose the correct word to complete each sentence, a process that requires them to understand the meaning of prefixes, suffixes, roots, and base words. Page 138 will help you assess students' mastery of using word parts and context to determine meaning.

**Observational Assessment** As students complete each set of exercises, evaluate their use of word knowledge as they decode the words on page 137 and choose the correct word on page 138. Evaluate specific improvements as well as overall progress by comparing your earlier notes with your current observations.

**Student Skills Assessment** Keep track of students' progress in understanding the use of prefixes and suffixes using the checklist on page 91H.

**Writing Conference** Hold informal meetings at which you and the student can look over the writing he or she has completed in this unit. Discuss how the student's work has improved and what the student can do to make his or her writing even better. Ask students to recall a favorite piece of writing in their Home Portfolios and invite them to share it with the class.

Group together students who need further instruction in prefixes, suffixes, roots and base words and have them complete the *Reteaching Activities*. Turn to page 91C for alternative assessment methods.

# Context Clues

## Theme: West

### STANDARDS

- ✪ Read expository text with grade-appropriate fluency and understand its content
- ✪ Develop and strengthen vocabulary by reading and studying words in context
- ✪ Use context clues to determine word meaning and improve comprehension
- ✪ Use inference to determine word meaning

### OBJECTIVES

- ▶ To appreciate nonfiction works about the West
- ▶ To identify different types of context clues and strategies that involve them
- ▶ To use different types of context clues to determine the meanings of new words
- ▶ To make inferences based on context clues

### LESSONS

## Assessment Strategies

An overview of assessment strategies appears on page **139C**. It offers suggestions for using a variety of unit-specific assessment tools, including **Pretests** and **Post Tests** (pages **139D–139G**), the **Activity Master** (page **139M**), and the **Assessment Checklist** (page **139H**).

## Thematic Teaching

In Unit 5 students will learn about context clues. Students practice different strategies of contextual analysis as they read nonfiction selections and complete exercises related to the theme the *West.*

Students begin their investigation of the West by creating a visual composition (a mural or a collage) depicting famous western people and places. The resource list below provides titles of books, videos, and other materials that can help students focus their study of the region. Many of the Teacher's Edition lessons in this unit open with theme-related poems, riddles, or tongue twisters. These "hooks" can spark students' interest in the theme and in the play of words.

## Curriculum Integration

### Writing

Students write a description of a television program on page **142,** compose a poem on page **156,** and write word analogies on page **164.**

### Science

Students create an "Astronomy Glossary" on page **144,** classify plants and animals on page **148,** and research land formations on page **160.**

### Social Studies

Students create travel brochures on page **140,** map stagecoach routes on page **146,** research Native American cultures on page **162,** and write trivia questions on page **166.**

## Optional Learning Activities

### Meeting Individual Needs

Most of the Teacher's Edition lessons offer activities for students with distinct learning styles or particular intellectual or sensory strengths. The activities are labeled for learners with the following "styles": **Visual, Kinesthetic, Auditory, Logical, Musical,** and **Tactile.**

### Multicultural Connections

Students investigate the history of place names on pages **140** and **158** and research Iceland's hot springs on page **150.**

### Word Study Strategies

Pages **139I–139J** offer an array of activities that give students practice with word study strategies such as using context clues and sorting words.

### Universal Access

Exercises tailored to meet the needs of **English-Language Learners** and **Gifted Learners** can be found in almost every Teacher's Edition lesson. Strategies designed to help **Learners with Special Needs,** such as students with Memory Deficits, can be found on page **139L.**

### Intervention

Page **139K** offers **Intervention Strategies** designed to help students performing below grade level understand the concepts taught in **Lessons 69, 72,** and **80.**

### Reteaching

On page **154** students write context sentences and teach "mini-lessons," and on page **172** students teach their own strategies to the class.

### Technology

Page **139N** offers activities for students who enjoy working with computers or audio/video equipment. In addition, **Computer Connections**—tips for students who use a word processor—can be found on pages **152, 168,** and **170.**

### RESOURCES

**Books**
Roop, Connie and Roop, Peter Geiger. *Girl of the Shining Mountains: Sacagawea's Story,* NY: Hyperion Press, 1999.
Wukovits, John F. *The Black Cowboys (Legends of the West),* NY: Chelsea House Pub., 1997.

**Videos**
*Artists of the West,* PBS Home Video, 2000.
*Lewis & Clark: The Journey of the Corps of Discovery,* PBS Home Video, 1997.

**CDs**
*Prairie Serenade,* Riders In The Sky, Rounder, 1998.

In Unit 5 students study context clues. To evaluate students' mastery of these skills, use any or all of the assessment methods suggested below.

## Pretests and Post Tests

The tests on pages **139D–139G** objectively assess how well students understand a variety of context clues. These tests may be used at the beginning of the unit as an informal diagnostic tool or at the end of the unit as a more formal measure of students' progress.

## Observational Assessment

Most lessons include a boxed feature prompting teachers to observe students as they work. Each reminder offers specific suggestions for errors, patterns, or signs that indicate whether or not students have grasped key concepts taught in the lesson.

## Using Technology

The Technology activities on page **139N** may be used to evaluate students whose language skills are best shown when using computers or audio/video equipment.

## Performance Assessment

Have students sort words or phrases in two columns with the headings: **Words That Signal a Comparison** and **Words That Signal a Contrast.** Ask them to write the following words in the correct columns: **yet, like, instead of, similar to, however, in the same way.** Using the completed chart, have students write a sentence using a pair of signal words to compare and contrast something.

## Portfolio Assessment

The portfolio icon in the lesson plans indicates an opportunity for students to add to the growing body of work in their portfolios. Each student's portfolio will be unique and should contain pieces that the student feels represents his or her best work. You may wish to give students additional opportunities to add to their portfolios.

| Rubric for Writing | Always | Sometimes | Never |
|---|---|---|---|
| Uses capitalization, punctuation, spelling, and grammar appropriately | | | |
| Uses context clues to uncover the meaning of unfamiliar words | | | |
| Uses mixed context clues to better understand the meaning of a sentence or paragraph | | | |
| Uses inference to draw a conclusion | | | |
| Conveys comparison and contrast through writing | | | |

## Answer Key

**Page 139D**
1. conceal
2. tranquil
3. immense
4. debris
5. stroll
6. summit
7. exceed
8. severe
9. precious
10. aquarium
11. exhausted
12. vowels
13. coins
14. oceans
15. mammals

**Page 139E**
1. cellar
2. cushion
3. alphabet
4. tune
5. fierce
6. drought
7. wharf
8. errand
9. humidity
10. barber
11. furious
12. migrate
13. scarce
14. pasture
15. galaxy

**Page 139F**
1. corridor
2. quill
3. late
4. victorious
5. vapor
6. opinion
7. internal
8. fragrance
9. endurance
10. circular
11. neglect
12. instruments
13. directions
14. measurement
15. flowers

**Page 139G**
1. tedious
2. bouquet
3. fabricate
4. equip
5. fragile
6. meddle
7. shrivel
8. grimace
9. adorn
10. digest
11. inspect
12. obvious
13. groove
14. tepid
15. decent

**Fill in the circle of the word that best completes each sentence.**

**1.** The clever spy wore a disguise to _____ his identity.
○ conceal ○ duplicate ○ condition

**2.** After the hurricane, I was glad that the weather was _____.
○ stormy ○ tranquil ○ precious

**3.** He tried and he tried but he could not lift the _____ log.
○ immense ○ tiresome ○ shallow

**4.** The storm left garbage, wood, and other _____ in the streets.
○ debt ○ debris ○ posters

**5.** After dinner I often take a _____ or walk around the garden.
○ run ○ slippery ○ stroll

**6.** The gondola will take the skiers up to the _____ of the mountain.
○ base ○ summit ○ lift

**7.** If you continue to drive fast, you may _____ the speed limit.
○ exceed ○ limit ○ obey

**8.** The _____ lightning from the storm caused the power to be disrupted.
○ calm ○ freezing ○ severe

**9.** Diamonds, opals, and other _____ gems are too expensive for me.
○ adequate ○ small ○ precious

**10.** Our class will see many kinds of fish when we visit the _____.
○ planetarium ○ aquarium ○ stadium

**11.** After a long run, Jay was too _____ to play ball.
○ examine ○ exertion ○ exhausted

**Fill in the circle that best identifies each series.**

**12.** a, e, i, o, u
○ consonants ○ numbers ○ vowels

**13.** penny, nickel, dollar bill
○ coins ○ money ○ circles

**14.** Atlantic, Pacific, Indian
○ oceans ○ rivers ○ continents

**15.** dog, cat, whale
○ pets ○ mammals ○ fish

Possible score on Unit 5 Pretest 1 is 15. Score _____

# Pretest 2

**Choose a word from the box that best completes each sentence.**
**Write the answer on the line.**

| | | | | |
|---|---|---|---|---|
| fierce | cushion | furious | alphabet | pasture |
| humidity | errand | tune | cellar | scarce |
| migrate | barber | drought | galaxy | wharf |

1. The boxes of old clothes were stored in the _____.

2. Place this soft velvet _____ on the seat of the chair.

3. There are twenty-six letters in the English _____.

4. Ken hummed the _____ when he forgot the words to the song.

5. The lion startled the crowd with its _____ roar.

6. We were asked to conserve water during the _____.

7. Many boats are docked at the _____.

8. I went on an _____ for my mother to buy milk.

9. The high _____ made me feel warm and uncomfortable.

10. Our _____ charges twelve dollars for a haircut.

11. Pam was _____ when she missed the last train.

12. Many birds _____, or move from one place to another for the winter.

13. During the famine, food was _____ and difficult to find.

14. The shepherd leads the sheep to graze in the green _____.

15. The Milky Way is the name of a _____, or a large collection of stars.

Possible score on Unit 5 Pretest 2 is 15. Score _____

Name _____

**Fill in the circle of the word that best completes each sentence.**

**I.** The bellhop took our luggage through the long hotel _____.
   ○ roof          ○ corridor          ○ corral

**2.** In the past, a feather, or a _____ was dipped in ink and used to write.
   ○ bone          ○ wing          ○ quill

**3.** If you arrive in class after the bell rings, you are _____.
   ○ absent          ○ late          ○ sick

**4.** After several defeats, the team was eager to be _____.
   ○ victorious          ○ losing          ○ exhausted

**5.** If water is heated to the proper temperature, it becomes _____.
   ○ liquid          ○ solid          ○ vapor

**6** In my _____, I feel that it is too early to leave the party.
   ○ advice          ○ opinion          ○ apology

**7.** The X-ray showed the stomach and other _____ organs.
   ○ external          ○ internal          ○ vertical

**8.** The flowers have a pleasant _____.
   ○ fume          ○ fabric          ○ fragrance

**9.** A marathon runner must have great stamina and _____ to win.
   ○ endurance          ○ sneakers          ○ water

**10.** My father wore a tie that had _____ or round patterns.
   ○ rectangular          ○ circular          ○ bluish

**I I.** Don't be careless and _____ to walk the dog.
   ○ evade          ○ neglect          ○ respond

**Fill in the circle that best identifies each series.**

**12.** viola, cornet, piano
   ○ furniture   ○ colors   ○ instruments

**13.** north, south, east
   ○ directions   ○ topics   ○ numbers

**14.** inch, foot, yard
   ○ money   ○ measurement   ○ books

**15.** daisy, rose, zinnia
   ○ trees   ○ birds   ○ flowers

Possible score on Unit 5 Post Test I is 15. Score _____

## Post Test 2

Name _____

**Choose a word from the box that best completes each sentence.
Write the answer on the line.**

| | | | | |
|---|---|---|---|---|
| digest | obvious | groove | meddle | tedious |
| adorn | equip | fragile | tepid | shrivel |
| fabricate | grimace | bouquet | decent | inspect |

**1.** I was easily bored during the _____ lecture.

**2.** Mom received a _____ of roses, tulips, and other flowers.

**3.** He was very clever to _____ an excuse to miss the lecture.

**4.** It is necessary to _____ the boat with extra life preservers.

**5.** Please be careful with the vase, it is _____ and will break easily.

**6.** Please do not _____, or interfere with my plans for the trip.

**7.** Without water, the plant will _____ and die.

**8.** Her face made a _____ when she tasted the bitter medicine.

**9.** We will _____ the room with balloons for the party.

**10.** It took some time for the winner to _____ the surprising news about the race.

**11.** The mechanic will _____ the tires of the car in order to fix the leak.

**12.** When I saw his smile, it was _____ that he was happy with the results.

**13.** The snowmobile left tracks or a _____ in the snow.

**14.** It will be comfortable in the bath if you use _____ water.

**15.** He is not on the honor roll, but he gets _____ grades in school.

Possible score on Unit 5 Post Test 2 is 15. Score _____

**Student Name** _____

## UNIT FIVE
## STUDENT SKILLS ASSESSMENT
## CHECKLIST

☑ Assessed    ☒ Retaught    ▣ Mastered

- ❑ Context Clues—Experience
- ❑ Context Clues—Definitions 1
- ❑ Context Clues—Definitions 2
- ❑ Context Clues—Words in a Series 1
- ❑ Context Clues—Words in a Series 2
- ❑ Context Clues—Comparison
- ❑ Context Clues—Contrast
- ❑ Context Clues—Compare and Contrast
- ❑ Context Clues—Inference 1
- ❑ Context Clues—Inference 2
- ❑ Context Clues—Mixed Strategies

## TEACHER COMMENTS

# WORD STUDY STRATEGIES

In Unit 5 students study context clues. To give students practice with word study strategies, use any or all of the activities suggested below.

## Sentence Meaning

Circle the word in bold type that best completes each sentence. Write the word on the line.

1. I felt tremors and heard things rattle during the _____ .

   **earthquake**  **heat wave**  **thunderstorm**

2. The clown learned how to _____ a plate on the end of a broomstick.

   **wash**  **break**  **balance**

3. Even though a string on her violin _____, she kept on playing.

   **melted**  **crumbled**  **snapped**

4. The school _____ blew the whistle to signal the start of the basketball game.

   **nurse**  **coach**  **librarian**

5. The campers hiked along a _____ in the woods.

   **trail**  **street**  **jungle**

## Definition Clues

Each sentence contains a definition for the underlined word. Write the word from the box to answer the question that follows each sentence.

| quarrelsome | farmer | museum |
|---|---|---|

1. Dad collects mining <u>relics,</u> displaying these precious old objects in his office. Where else would you find **relics** on display? _____

2. A rude digger at the mining site was a <u>curmudgeon;</u> he was always in a bad mood.

   How is a **curmudgeon** likely to act?

   _____

3. The lack of <u>arable</u> soil made desert living difficult; the soil was not suitable for growing crops.

   Who is concerned about **arable** soil?

   _____

## Words in a Series

Circle the category in the box that describes how the series of words are linked. Then choose two remaining categories and write a series of words.

1. cornea, lash, tear duct, iris

   | eye parts | mouth parts | ear parts |
   |---|---|---|

   _____

2. harp, flute, glockenspiel, ocarina

   | songs | musicians | instruments |
   |---|---|---|

   _____

3. pastels, oils, charcoal, watercolors

   | snack foods | art supplies | fabrics |
   |---|---|---|

   _____

4. _____

   _____

5. _____

   _____

Colorado

## Compare and Contrast

Circle the word(s) in each sentence that signal a comparison or contrast. Then write the two things that are being compared or contrasted.

1. The skirmish on the bridge was equal to an earlier fight.

   _____  _____

2. The sink pipes are made of galvanized steel whereas the toy sink pipes are plastic.

   _____  _____

3. My friend is athletic, as opposed to my brother, who does not play sports.

   _____  _____

4. This jetty is similar to the pier at the other end of the harbor.

   _____  _____

## Make Inferences

Circle the word in bold type that has the same meaning as the underlined word. Then write a sentence using the word in bold type.

1. The hungry child ate every morsel on his plate.

   **vegetable**   **bit of food**   **tasty dish**

   sentence: _____

2. The directions gave precise measurements, so there was no guesswork.

   **exact**   **unclear**   **lengthy**

   sentence: _____

3. An owner's pet is as precious to him as gold is to a miner.

   **worthless**   **valuable**   **costly**

   sentence: _____

## Mixed Strategies

Write the type of context clue from the box that is used in each sentence. Then write the meaning of the underlined word in each sentence.

| experience | definition | inference |
|---|---|---|
| contrast | words in a series | compare |

1. The dog's barking deterred the thief from entering the house.

   context clue type: _____

   **Deterred** means _____.

2. Many European towns have open, public squares, such as plazas, piazzas, and commons.

   context clue type: _____

   **Plaza** means _____.

3. While the water damage to the barn is irreparable, the roof of the house can be fixed.

   context clue type: _____

   **Irreparable** means _____.

4. A truck laden, or loaded, with bags of cement will ride low to the ground.

   context clue type: _____

   **Laden** means _____.

5. A sailor is comfortable on a ship but a person who is a landlubber is not.

   context clue type: _____

   **Landlubber** means _____.

| LESSONS | 69 Context Clues— Experience | 72 Context Clues— Words in a Series | 80 Context Clues— Inference |
|---|---|---|---|
| **Problem** | Student has difficulty finding the precise word that fits the context clue. | Student may be confused by a series of unfamiliar words. | Student has difficulty defining a word by using indirect clues. |
| **Intervention Strategies** | • Write sentences in which more than one answer choice is appropriate. For example: *I took a (**bus, car, bicycle**) to the train station.*<br><br>• Guide the student to edit the sentences to limit the choice to one possible answer. Ask: *Which form of transportation would not give protection against rain or snow?*<br><br>• Encourage the student to edit the sentence by including a limited condition such as: *I got wet because I took a (**bus, car, bicycle**) to the train station.* **(bicycle)** | • Tell the student to identify one familiar word in the series. Then look for other clues in the sentence that may help identify the word.<br><br>• The student may identify **stone** as the only familiar word in the first example on page 147. Point out that the word **other** in the sentence identifies **stone** with the less familiar words. | • Point out that often the context clue is like a riddle but with a more obvious answer.<br><br>• Explain to the student that sometimes they may have to draw a conclusion about something that is not directly stated. Ask: *What stores water and supplies electric power?* **(dam)**.<br><br>• Help the student create riddles from the examples on page 163. Ask: *What left behind burned trees and ash?* (an **inferno**) |

The following activities offer strategies for helping students with special needs to participate in selected exercises in Unit 5.

## Memory Deficits
### Context Clues—Definitions
Students who have difficulty retaining or comprehending information (especially when it has been presented orally or read aloud) may benefit from extra practice in using context clues that define difficult words.

* The exercises on page **143** all contain clues or possible definitions of the words in bold type. The clues are either linked to the word in bold by the verb **is** or they appear near the word in bold and are set off by a comma.

* Encourage students to take a more active role while reading to help them better understand and remember what they read. One way to do this is to ask questions while they read. For example, when they come across a word they are unfamiliar with while reading, have them highlight the word and isolate the sentence.

* Have students ask themselves what the highlighted word might mean by looking at the surrounding text for context clues or possible definitions. Have them circle these words that offer clues about the unfamiliar word's meaning. Then have them check these clues by looking up the highlighted word in a dictionary and compare their findings.

## Conceptual Deficits
### Context Clues—Compare and Contrast
Students with difficulty understanding the concepts of **comparison** and **contrast** may need assistance with **Lessons 76** through **78.** Students may find using a graphic organizer may help them visualize and understand these concepts.

* Display a Venn diagram by drawing two overlapping circles on the board. Explain that the two circles illustrate how two things are alike **(compare)** in some way and how two things are different **(contrast)** in some way. Use a simple example by showing two objects such as a red ball and a red block. Label one circle **ball** and the other **block**. Write the word **red** in the Venn diagram where the two circles overlap.

* Write this sentence on the board: **The ball is like the block, because it is red**. Underline the word **like.** Then ask the students how the two objects are different and write their responses in the appropriate circles of the Venn diagram. Using their responses, write another sentence on the board, for example: **The ball is round, but the block is flat.** Underline the word **but**. Point out that some words or phrases such as **like, but, either, and, too, different, however, also, rather, whereas, yet, opposed to,** and so on act as signals in a sentence for the reader to know when a comparison or contrast is being made.

* Encourage the students to first identify or highlight the "signals" in each sentence and then ask themselves if the two things in each sentence are being compared **(alike)** or contrasted **(different)** when completing the exercises on pages **155–160.**

Name _____

**Match each state in Column A with its capital in Column B.
Then use a reference book to check your work.**

_____ 1. California      a. Cheyenne

_____ 2. Nevada      b. Denver

_____ 3. Montana      c. Sacramento

_____ 4. Utah      d. Salt Lake City

CO

_____ 5. Colorado      e. Helena

_____ 6. Idaho      f. Carson City

_____ 7. Wyoming      g. Boise

ID

**Match each state in Column A with its nickname in
Column B. Then use a reference book to check your work.**

_____ 8. California      a. Beehive State

_____ 9. Nevada      b. Treasure State

_____ 10. Montana      c. Golden State

_____ 11. Utah      d. Gem State

UT

_____ 12. Colorado      e. Equality State

_____ 13. Idaho      f. Silver State

_____ 14. Wyoming      g. Centennial State

WY

MT

**Match each state in Column A with its name's origin in
Column B. Then use a reference book to check your work.**

_____ 15. California      a. Navajo for "upper"

_____ 16. Nevada      b. Spanish for "red"

_____ 17. Montana      c. Invented meaning "gem of the mountains"

_____ 18. Utah      d. Algonquin for "large prairie place"

_____ 19. Colorado      e. Spanish for "mountainous"

_____ 20. Idaho      f. Spanish for "snow-clad"

_____ 21. Wyoming      g. Named for an imaginary island from a Spanish novel

NV

CA

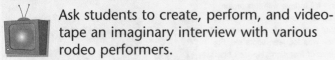

## Interview Rodeo Performers

Ask students to create, perform, and video-tape an imaginary interview with various rodeo performers.

- Have the class generate a list of topics to be researched and covered in the interview, such as the following: events in a rodeo, the differences between events performed by men and women, the relationship between rodeo skills and ranch work (past and present), the qualifications of a rodeo performer, accidents that have been suffered by the performer, highlights and/or awards the performer has received, and so on.

- Have students select an "interviewer", script writers, technical crew, and two or three class members to act as "rodeo performers" to be interviewed. The interviews can be later viewed for the class to identify comparisons and contrasts. Encourage the students to devise simple costumes (a blazer, pants/skirt, and microphone for the interviewer; jeans, lassos, and cowboy hats for the rodeo performers.)

- Remind the "script writers" to include context clues for the audience to understand rodeo terms that may be unfamiliar. The video can be presented to other classes.

## Short Stories of the Gold Rush

Encourage students to use the Internet to research personal accounts of the quest for finding gold in the West. Then have the students compile their research to write short stories of historical fiction that illustrate the development of the West by people determined to "get rich quick." Finally, gather all of the stories together to create one book.

- Guide students to use search engines and web sites such as www.pbs.org and www.historychannel.com to obtain historical facts and read excerpts of personal accounts during the gold rush of 1849–1899 in the West.

- Encourage students to use a word processing program to write their short stories in order to compile all of them into one book. They may also want to include illustrations that they have made or downloaded from the Internet for their stories that can be scanned onto the pages.

- Students should also include the following types of context clues when writing their short stories about the gold rush: experience, compare and contrast, words in a series, and definitions.

- Encourage students to create a display and share the collection of short stories in the school or local library.

## Folksongs of the West

Have students compile and record an audiocassette of folk songs that celebrate the spirit of the West.

- Brainstorm with students a list of folksongs that use the West as a theme or character for example: "Home on the Range," "I've Been Working on the Railroad," "My Darling Clementine," and so on. Then assign groups to ask the school music teacher and librarian to help find the lyrics to these songs. Have them note lyrics that contain the types of context clues that were introduced in the unit, such as definition, words in a series, compare, contrast, etc.

- Encourage each group to practice one song to be performed and recorded on audiocassette. Play the songs for the class to enjoy.

## Introduction to
### Context Clues

#### Objectives

- **To enjoy a nonfiction selection related to the theme the *West***
- **To identify context clues**

### Starting with Literature

- Ask a student to read "Picture This " aloud for the class.

- Write the words **photographer**, **photograph**, **photo** on the board. Ask: *Which word can be both a noun and a verb?* **(photograph)**

#### Critical Thinking

- Ask students to reread the third paragraph to find the answer to the first question.

- Guide students to discuss ways that a photographer or artist might cause people to change the way they view something.

- For question three, ask students to use vivid words to describe how they would feel.

### Introducing the Skill

Have students reread the selection, noting unfamiliar words. Ask them to look at the surrounding text for clues. Explain that they may not be able to determine an exact meaning, but they may be able to form a general idea.

### Practicing the Skill

Have students find the word **mural** in paragraph three. Ask them which surrounding words give clues to the meaning of the word **mural.** Discuss the meaning and then have a volunteer compare it to the definition found in the dictionary. Do the same with the words **inspired** and **magnificent** in paragraph five.

---

# Picture This

Anyone who has ever lived in or visited the West is familiar with its natural beauty. In this unit, you will meet a photographer and many other people who fell in love with this region.

The photographer Ansel Adams first visited Yosemite National Park on a family vacation. It was 1916, and he was fourteen years old. For Adams, it was love at first sight. He took his first pictures of Yosemite on that trip. He would go back there again and again.

Ansel Adams was a fine photographer. In 1941, officials of the United States government asked Adams to go to national parks in the West. They hoped he would photograph wild natural areas for a set of murals. Adams gladly took the job. He wanted Americans to share in the beauty of their country.

The Mural Project lasted for less than a year. The reason: The United States had entered World War II. Fortunately, in that short time, Adams had turned out more than 250 photographs of the West.

Adams' wilderness photos set the tone for the kind of work he would do for the rest of his career. He also worked to protect nature. In fact, his photos inspired artists and conservationists alike. His magnificent pictures opened all our eyes to the beauty of the American land.

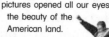

### Critical Thinking

1. What did the U.S. government want Ansel Adams to do? Why?

2. Do you think that photographers and artists can influence the way people see the world? Explain.

3. If you could step into Ansel Adams' photograph of the Grand Tetons at the top of the page, how would you feel?

1. They wanted Adams to photograph wild natural areas in national parks in the West for a set of murals. They wanted Americans to share in the beauty of our country.
2. Answers will vary.
3. Answers will vary.

LESSON 68: Introduction to Context Clues    139

---

# Theme Activity

**VISUAL COMPOSITION OF THE WEST** Invite students to create a collage or mural of the West. Their visual composition should highlight famous people and places (both present-day and historic) of the western states: California, Nevada, Montana, Utah, Colorado, Idaho, and Wyoming.

Encourage students to think of interesting ways to design their collage or mural. For example, their collage might include shapes of the western states with call outs for significant people and places. These call outs might include pictures or photographs accompanied by detailed captions based on students' research.

As students develop their visual compositions, encourage them to apply the context-clues strategies they learn in this unit. Remind students to include information about all of the states in the West.

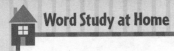

**Visit us at**
**www.sadlier-oxford.com**

## Dear Family,

In Unit 5, your child will learn about the importance of using context clues as a word-study strategy. By using context clues, your child will discover the meaning of unfamiliar words and will become a better reader. The theme of this unit is the *West*, including its people and history.

**Context clues** can help a reader figure out the meaning of an unfamiliar word. By understanding the context (the nearby words in a sentence or paragraph), your child will be able to unlock the meaning of a word.

## Family Focus

- Read together the nonfiction selection on page 139. Look at Adams' wilderness photograph of Grand Teton National Park in Wyoming. Discuss the subject and the composition of the photo. How does the photo make each member of your family feel?

- Together, look at a map of the United States. Identify the states that make up the West: California, Nevada, Montana, Utah, Colorado, Idaho, and Wyoming. Which of these states have you or friends visited? Which would you like to visit? Plan a real or an imagined road trip through the West.

## LINKS TO LEARNING

To extend learning together, you might explore:

**Web Sites**
www.adamsgallery.com
www.nps.gov

**Videos**
*America's Historic Trails*, PBS Home Video, 6 videos.
*Our National Parks*, PBS Home Video.
*The West*, a film by Ken Burns and Stephen Ives, PBS Home Video, 9 videos.

**Literature**
*Ansel Adams: The National Park Service Photographs*, ©1995.
*Justin and the Best Biscuits in the World* by Mildred Pitts Walter, ©1986.

## Word Study at Home

- The Word-Study-at-Home page provides an opportunity for students and their families to work together to further students' language skills.

- On the Word-Study-at-Home page for Unit 5, students and their families will find activities that relate to the theme the *West* focusing on using context clues as a word-study strategy.

- Have students remove page 140 from their books. Direct them to take the page home so that their families may share in the Word-Study-at-Home activities.

- Encourage students to talk about states of the West they have visited or perhaps even lived in. Ask students to compare these states to their home state.

- Invite students to describe specific places of interest in the West that they have visited, heard of, or read about. Encourage students to find out more about these places. Students may wish to research which western cities attract the most visitors and why.

## Multicultural Connection

Many places in the West derive their names from Native American words. For example, the name **Yellowstone** may be traced back to a Native American word referring to the yellow cliffs along the Yellowstone River. Have students research the word history of other western place names, such as **Wyoming**, **Yosemite**, (Lake) **Tahoe**, and **Utah**, to identify words of Native American origin.

## Social Studies Link

Divide students into groups and assign each group a national park in the West to research. Ask each group to create a travel brochure with photographs and illustrations that would entice tourists to visit the area. Have the groups display the brochures for the class.

## Theme-Related Resources

### Books

*National Geographic's Guide to the National Parks of the United States*, by Elizabeth L. Newhouse (Editor), 1997

*Wyoming: Wild and Beautiful*, by Fred Pflughoft, 1999

### Videos

*The Story of Yellowstone National Park*, Questar Inc.

### Web Sites

www.anseladams.com

# Context Clues— Experience

## Objectives

- **To use context clues to determine the meaning of unknown or missing words**
- **To use personal experience to determine the meaning of unknown or missing words**

## Warming Up

- Write the following sentences on the board.

    Gray clouds darken the sky.

    A sudden breeze rustles the leaves.

    I hear a distant rumble.

- Ask a student to read the sentences aloud and explain what might be happening. (A thunderstorm is approaching.) Ask students how they came to this conclusion. (Possible answer: A dark sky can indicate an approaching storm. The distant rumble might be the sound of thunder.)

## Teaching the Lesson

- Explain that context clues are nearby words that help readers determine the meaning of an unfamiliar word in sentences or paragraphs.

- Ask a volunteer to read aloud the Helpful Hints on page 141. Remind students that context clues may come before or after an unfamiliar word.

- Have another student read aloud the Helpful Hint on page 142. Emphasize that readers use context clues in combination with their prior experience. Point out that the reader may not be able to determine the exact meaning, but may be able to form a general idea.

---

Name _____

California sunset

### Helpful Hints

You can use **context clues** to figure out the meaning of an unknown word and to develop a better understanding of what you are reading. By using context clues and your own **experience**, you usually can get the general meaning of a word. Look for context clues *before* or *after* an unfamiliar word to help you unlock meaning that may not be stated directly.

 Read each sentence. Then underline the best answer to the question. On the line, explain your thinking. Use your experience. Look for context clues to help you understand each sentence.

1. The setting sun turns the sky a glorious shade of purple and gold.
   What time of day is it?  morning  noon  <u>early evening</u>

   What context clue(s) helped you? _____ setting sun _____

2. When the alarm sounded, the class quickly filed outside and waited for news.
   What was going on?  wake-up call  <u>fire drill</u>  lunchtime

   What context clue(s) helped you? _____ alarm, class, news _____

3. The group knew that empty canteens would mean serious problems.
   Where might the group be?  <u>in a desert</u>  by a stream  at a movie

   What context clue(s) helped you? _____ empty canteens, problems _____

4. We were out of granola, so we prepared some oatmeal.
   What was going on?
   grocery shopping  packing lunch  <u>making breakfast</u>

   What context clue(s) helped you? _____ granola, oatmeal _____

5. It's lucky that we had on our life jackets when we capsized and that the shore was not far.
   What was going on?
   <u>a boat tipped over</u>  a plane landed  swimmers raced

   What context clue(s) helped you? _____ life jackets, capsized, shore _____

### CHALLENGE

Use your experience to explain to a friend the scene being described in this sentence:

It was bleak outside, but I didn't need to open my umbrella.

---

# UNIVERSAL ACCESS
## Meeting Individual Needs

### Logical Learners

Describe several situational contexts, such as: people laughing in a movie theater, sports fans clapping and cheering, a student reacting with shock while looking at a returned test. Have students analyze each situation and explain how clues plus experience help them to determine what is going on in each situation.

### Auditory Learners

Write several common nouns on index cards, such as: **shoe, basketball, radio,** and **apple.** Have a volunteer choose a card and challenge the class to guess the word by listening to a sentence that the student provides. For example: *I wear it on my foot, but it's not a sock.* The student who guesses correctly chooses the next card. Have students explain the context clues used.

You can use your experience, along with context clues, to figure out a missing word in a sentence. Read carefully. Think about the meaning of the sentence. Here's an example:

I have two _____ cats and three female ones.

Think about what you know. The word **male** makes sense in this sentence.

⭐ Complete each sentence with a word from the box below. Look for context clues to determine the missing word. Write the word on the line. Make sure it makes sense in the sentence.

> dull    floss    jacket    pudding    light

1. I stirred the _pudding_ constantly so that it wouldn't stick to the pot.

2. This knife is too _dull_ for slicing a whole watermelon.

3. Traffic came to a complete halt when the _light_ changed.

4. I always brush my teeth, but I don't always _floss_ them.

5. The _jacket_ didn't fit comfortably, so I tried on the next size.

⭐ Each sentence below is missing a word. Look for context clues to help you figure out what the word should be. Then on the line, write a word that makes sense in the sentence. There may be more than one choice. Answers will vary, but may include the following:

6. I can't _decide_ whether to order a taco or a burrito.

7. When you take the pie out of the oven, be sure to use _pot holders_.

8. It's smart to _water_ your plants before you go away for the weekend.

9. Control the _volume_ on the stereo so that you don't disturb the neighbors.

10. The four _tires_ on the car are worn out, so I'll have to replace them.

11. As you climb high up the mountain, the _air_ feels thinner and cooler.

12. In circus class, I'm learning how to _balance_ a plate on the end of a broomstick.

142    LESSON 69: Context Clues— Experience

**Home Involvement Activity** Find a number of interesting sentences in a newspaper. Take turns reading each sentence aloud, but leave out one word. Challenge your family to suggest a word that makes sense.

---

## Practicing the Skill

- Read aloud the directions on page 141. Ask students to be specific when they explain which context clues helped.

- Read aloud the directions on page 142. Remind students to combine their experience with context clues.

Turn to page 139K for an Intervention Strategy designed to help students who need extra support with this lesson.

## Curriculum Connections

### Spelling Link

Have students listen for context clues as you read aloud the following sentences. Ask students to write the missing word that would make the most sense.

> We felt the earth shake and knew it was an _____. (**earthquake**)
>
> A _____ is a hot, sandy place with little water. (**desert**)
>
> When a boat _____, it turns over. (**capsizes**)
>
> I use dental _____ to clean between my teeth. (**floss**)
>
> If my radio is too loud I lower the _____. (**volume**)

### Writing Link

- Explain that many popular television programs are filmed in Hollywood, California. Ask students to write a description for a program they would like to see on television.

- Remind them to make sure their readers can understand any unfamiliar words by using context clues.

### Observational Assessment

*Check to see that students look for context clues before and after an unfamiliar word.*

---

### English-Language Learners/ESL

Display photographs showing people involved in various activities. Ask students to point out the clues in the pictures that help them determine what is going on. Encourage them to discuss how their own experiences would help them understand the photographs. Write sentences about the pictures on the board and point out the use of context clues.

### Gifted Learners

Provide students with brief articles from a newspaper or magazine. Have students make a mark through every fifth word and then exchange articles with a partner. Challenge students to identify which words are missing.

### Learners with Special Needs

Additional strategies for supporting learners with special needs can be found on page 139L.

# Context Clues—Definitions 1

## Objectives

- **To use context clues to figure out the definitions of words**

- **To use context clues to determine the relevant meaning of multiple-meaning words**

## Warming Up

- Write the following paragraph on the board. Ask a volunteer to read it aloud.

  Thirsty? People in Los Angeles would be very thirsty if the city didn't use **aqueducts**, or large pipes that transport water. Aqueducts carry water over great distances to people.

- Have a volunteer circle the word **aqueducts** and then find the definition within the paragraph.

## Teaching the Lesson

- Have students read the Helpful Hint on page 143. Explain that when a sentence contains an unfamiliar word, the meaning of the word may often be found within the sentence. Explain that the meaning of the word is often more of an explanation, and not the same definition you might find in a dictionary.

- Have a volunteer read aloud the Helpful Hint on page 144. Discuss the use of context when trying to determine the meaning of a multiple-meaning word. Say the following sentence: *The hikers came to a fork in the road.* Ask: *What does* **fork** *mean in the sentence? How do you know?*

---

Name _____

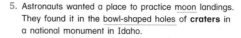

### Helpful Hint

Sometimes, you may not know the meaning of a word in a sentence. Try using **context clues** to help you figure out the definition of the word. One way to do this is by looking for other words in the sentence that may give a **definition**. This definition may differ from what you would find in a dictionary. Yet it can help you unlock the meaning of the unfamiliar word.

**Read the sentences. Underline the word or words that give a definition of the word in bold type.**

1. Bison live on the National Bison Range in Moiese, Montana. This range gives the wild animals a **refuge,** a safe place where they can live free of danger.

2. **Drought,** a long period of dry weather, is always a danger in Western states.

3. A **jackelope** is an imaginary animal that seems to be a cross between a jackrabbit and an antelope.

4. Miners came to the West to search for gold, silver, and copper. **Entrepreneurs,** people who took business risks in order to make profits, soon followed.

Bison on National Bison Range in Montana

5. Astronauts wanted a place to practice moon landings. They found it in the bowl-shaped holes of **craters** in a national monument in Idaho.

6. Montana's rocky **bluffs**—high, steep cliffs—are one feature of the state's interesting landforms.

7. In a **depleted** mine, few minerals are left to dig out.

8. Trout fishers need to lure their trout to bite. Therefore, they cast colorful flies to **entice,** or attract, the hungry fish.

9. Dad collects mining **relics,** displaying some of the precious old objects in his office.

### WORK TOGETHER

Think of a word that you think a partner will not know. Use it in a sentence in which other words define it. Have your partner use the context clues in the sentence to figure out the meaning of the word.

---

# UNIVERSAL ACCESS
# Meeting Individual Needs

### Visual Learners

Have students look through a social studies textbook for words that are defined in context. Explain that these words may appear in bold type. Ask students to make a list with two columns, one labeled **word**, the other labeled **meaning**. As students find unfamiliar words, have them write the word and its meaning in the appropriate columns.

### Auditory Learners

Write several multiple-meaning words on the board, such as: **file, plot,** and **grill.** Direct students to write two sentences for each word, using two different meanings of the word. Ask volunteers to read their sentences aloud. Have students raise their hands as soon as they hear the context clues that let them know the correct meaning.

Study the diagram of the handsaw below. Use the diagram to figure out the meaning of the following words or labels. On the lines below, write a sentence for each word as it relates to the handsaw. Be sure that other words in the sentence define the word.

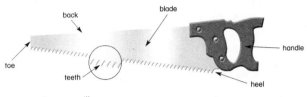

back     blade     handle     toe     teeth     heel

1. toe    Answers will vary. _____

2. back _____

3. blade _____

4. handle _____

5. heel _____

6. teeth  _____

 **Home Involvement Activity** Select a household appliance or a piece of furniture. Choose a word that identifies a part of the item. Use it in a sentence that defines the specific meaning of the word.

## Practicing the Skill

- Read aloud the directions on pages 143–144. Encourage students to reread the sentences on page 143 before selecting an answer.

- For the exercises on page 144, remind students that they must include clues in each sentence that will help define the word.

## Curriculum Connections

### Spelling Link

Write the following sentences on the board. Have students complete each sentence by filling in the appropriate letters for the word in bold type. Remind them to use context clues to figure out the word.

> The archaeologist found an ancient **r_l_c. (relic)**
>
> The rain ended the long **dr_u_ _t. (drought)**
>
> The **cr_ _e_s** on the moon's surface were deep. **(craters)**
>
> We gave food to the birds to **en_i_e** them to return. **(entice)**
>
> The cat found **re_ _ ge** by climbing a tree. **(refuge)**

### Science Link

The type of science that deals with the universe beyond Earth is called astronomy. Have students look in encyclopedias, science textbooks, and nonfiction books for unfamiliar words related to astronomy. Have them make an "Astronomy Glossary" by listing a word and then writing a sentence using the word in context.

### Observational Assessment

*Check to see whether students are able to identify word(s) in context to help them define unfamiliar words.*

### English-Language Learners/ESL

Make picture cards for several multiple-meaning words. Choose words whose meanings are easy to illustrate, such as: **trunk**, **teeth**, **foot**, **bark**, and **play.** Write a sentence for each meaning. Then display the cards and read the sentence aloud. Ask students to match the particular word meaning in the sentence with the correct picture card and then say the word.

### Gifted Learners

Have students look up the etymology of the word **aqueduct.** Then have them research and write a short report about the use of aqueducts in California.

### Learners with Special Needs

Additional strategies for supporting learners with special needs can be found on page 139L.

## LESSON 71 • UNIT 5
## Student Pages 145–146

# Context Clues—Definitions 2

## Objectives

- **To recognize definitions of words in context**
- **To write definitions of words based on contextual information**

## Warming Up

- Write the following paragraph on the board. Ask a student to read it aloud.

  Do you want to visit a real hot spot? The hottest place in the United States is Death Valley, California. This sun-baked region got its name in 1849, when gold-seekers ran out of water and died in the **sweltering** desert.

- Ask a student to circle the word **sweltering** and tell what it means. Discuss context clues that suggest the word's meaning. **(hottest, sun-baked)**

## Teaching the Lesson

- Ask a volunteer to read aloud the Helpful Hint on page 145. Explain that context clues may give a formal definition or may offer an example.

- Write the following sentence on the board and ask if it contains examples that define the word **canine.** (no)

  I have owned many canines.

- Do the same with the following sentence:

  Of all the canines I have ever owned, my favorites were poodles and collies.

- Point out that the clues **poodles** and **collies** help the reader understand that canines are dogs.

**145**

---

Name _____

### Helpful Hint

You know that a word may be defined within the **context** of a sentence. Sometimes, that definition looks formal. Other times, it gives meaning through example.

> Max is the most **mercurial** person I know; one minute he's happy, the next moment he's sad.

Max's mood changes often. His mood is not constant. This is what **mercurial** means in this sentence.

**Daguerreotype** of gold miners in California, 1850

 Read the sentences. Underline the word or words that define the word in bold type. Use the context of the sentence to figure out the meaning of the word.

1. Gold miners often had **daguerreotypes** taken of themselves; this was before modern photography improved upon what early cameras could do.

2. Levi Strauss was a **shrewd** peddler. He knew that the forty-niners needed sturdy pants; he made a fortune by cleverly inventing and selling blue jeans to miners.

3. Gold miners never welcomed **intruders.** The miners did not want uninvited guests snooping around their claims.

4. We knew that the two miners were in **cahoots;** they were always whispering secrets to each other.

5. In the 1850s, a large number of **emigrants** left Europe. These people left their countries to make a new life in the West.

6. They hiked to the top of the largest **butte** in the valley; like the other mounds, it was freestanding and flat on top.

7. One of the diggers at the site was a **curmudgeon;** he was always in a bad mood and ready with a rude remark.

### CHALLENGE

Write one sentence each for three of the words above. Be sure that each sentence shows the meaning of the word.

LESSON 71: Context Clues—Definitions 2 **145**

# UNIVERSAL ACCESS
# Meeting Individual Needs

### Logical Learners

Have students make up a nonsense word and then write a sentence in which the word is defined by example. Model by writing the following on the board:

> I enjoy playing different **galts**, especially soccer and tennis.

Ask a volunteer to define **galts.** Have students read their sentences and ask the class to guess the meaning of the nonsense words.

### Visual Learners

Write the following sentences on the board and discuss the position of the context clues.

> Lisa is a **benevolent** person, always doing good deeds.

> Lisa does so many good deeds because she is a **benevolent** person.

Write several words on the board and have students write two sentences for each, one with context clues before the word, one with the clues after.

145

The sentences below tell about Mesa Verde National Park in Colorado and the Anasazi who moved there about 1,500 years ago. Read each sentence. Figure out the meaning of the word in bold type. Then on the lines, write your own definition of the word.

Mesa Verde National Park in Colorado

1. The Anasazi used to be a **nomadic** people, moving from place to place in search of food and a new home. By the time they got to Mesa Verde, they had settled into farming.

Answers will vary, but may include the following:

wandering from place to place

2. The Anasazi built small villages on the top of **mesas;** these hills were smaller than plateaus but also flat on top.

hills, flat on top

3. These people lived in multiroom pit houses. The Anasazi also built **kivas**—round rooms which were partly underground and were used for religious ceremonies.

round rooms partially underground used for religious ceremonies

4. They built sturdy houses from **adobe** bricks; these bricks were made of sun-dried clay, which kept the inside of the house comfortable in heat or cold.

substance made of sun-dried clay, keeping houses comfortable

5. The population of Mesa Verde grew. By A.D. 1000, the Anasazi began to use **masonry** to build large stone houses.

stonework

LESSON 71: Context Clues— Definitions 2

 **Home Involvement Activity** Discuss the different rooms in a house and their uses. Cut out or draw pictures of these rooms and label each one.

---

- Read aloud the directions for the exercises on page 145 and have students complete the page. Guide students as needed.

- For exercises on pages 145–146, encourage students to be alert for context clues that appear before and after the words in bold type.

## Curriculum Connections

### Spelling Link

- Write the following words on the board.

| | |
|---|---|
| shrewd | intruder |
| adobe | butte |
| mesa | curmudgeon |
| emigrants | masonry |

- Ask students to read and then spell the words aloud. Have volunteers define the words by using each word in a sentence.
- Erase the words from the board and then call out the words, asking students to write the words on paper.

### Social Studies Link

When the gold rush began people wanted a quicker and more efficient way to go out West. By 1858, a new road had been built and stagecoaches left twice a week from Tipton, Missouri, headed for San Francisco. Have students check atlases or other resources to find maps showing the probable route of this stagecoach. Students may make a map showing the beginning and ending points for this trip. Encourage them to include symbols to show topography, such as lakes, rivers, and mountains.

### Observational Assessment

*Check to see that students can identify context clues to figure out the meaning of unfamiliar words.*

---

## English-Language Learners/ESL

Write these sentences on the board and underline as shown.

The village was on the flat top of a <u>mesa</u>. Their houses were made of sun-dried clay bricks, called <u>adobe</u>.

Show photographs that depict **mesa** and **adobe**. Ask students to find clues in the sentences and in the pictures that help them better understand the meanings of the words.

### Gifted Learners

Have students research the "apartment-type" structures that the Anasazi built. Suggest they write an essay about the reasons why the Anasazi may have preferred these dwellings and then compare them to modern-day apartment buildings.

### Learners with Special Needs

Additional strategies for supporting learners with special needs can be found on page 139L.

# Context Clues— Words in a Series 1

## Objectives

- **To use words in a series to determine meaning of unfamiliar words**
- **To use contextual information to write the meanings of words**

## Warming Up

- Write these sentences on the board:

  Nevada, Montana, Utah, and Wyoming are four of the western _____. **(states)**

  San Francisco, Los Angeles, and Sacramento are three major _____ in California. **(cities)**

- Ask volunteers to read and complete the sentences. Explain that the series of words at the beginning of each sentence gave clues about the missing word.

## Teaching the Lesson

- Ask a student to read aloud the Helpful Hint on page 147. Remind students that they used sentence context, along with what they already know about flowers, to figure out the meaning of **hyacinths.**

- Have students create lists with headings such as **Sports**, **Games**, **Tools**. Have students use each series of items in a sentence. For example, students might use items listed under **Tools** to write: "Carpenters use hammers, saws, and screwdrivers to build wooden shelves."

- Challenge students to include a few difficult or unfamiliar words in their lists. Have them write sentences using two familiar words in a series, plus one unfamiliar word.

147

---

Name _____

**Helpful Hint**

Another way to use **context clues** is to look for a list, or **series.** You can often figure out what a word means by thinking about the other words in the same series.

When our garden blooms, I love to see the purple tulips, irises, and **hyacinths.**

You may not know the word **hyacinths,** but you know they bloom in a garden. Your experience should help you realize that **hyacinths** are flowers.

*Craters of the Moon National Monument in Idaho*

⭐ **Read each sentence. Underline the series of words that belong together in the sentence. Then fill in the circle of the choice that tells how the words in the series are linked.**

1. Craters of the Moon National Monument in Idaho is a great place to visit. There you can see scoria, obsidian, pumice, lava bombs, and other volcanic stone.

   This is a series of _____.
   ○ bullets     ● rocks     ○ diamonds

2. Idaho's most famous food crop includes bakers, mashers, russets, and plain old spuds.

   This is a series of _____.
   ○ flowers     ○ cattle     ● potatoes

3. The visitors' center has information about the sage grouse, quail, pheasant, and partridge in the area.

   This is a series of _____.
   ● game birds     ○ fish     ○ insects

4. If you bring the tempera, the oils, and the watercolors, I'll bring the paper and frames.

   This is a series of _____.
   ○ snack foods     ● art supplies     ○ fabrics

**WORD STRATEGY**

You don't always need the exact meaning of a word in order to understand it. A broad meaning may do. Read this sentence:

The menu has New England clam chowder, corn chowder, and **bouillabaisse.**

This French word names a kind of

_____

---

# UNIVERSAL ACCESS
# Meeting Individual Needs

### Tactile Learners

Label four containers with the following: **Mammals, Lenses, Jewels, Berries.** On separate cards, write three examples of each item. For example: **bear, cat,** and **whale** for "Mammals," **telescope, camera,** and **eyeglasses** for "Lenses." Shuffle the cards and have students sort them into the correct containers. Then have them write a sentence using the three words in a series.

### Logical Learners

Have students look through catalogs to find three related items. Have them write a sentence using two of the three items, and leave a blank for the third. For example:

"I need a tent, a backpack, and a _____ for my camping trip." Have students trade papers with a classmate and fill in the blank with a word that makes sense.

★ Look for words in a series. Use these words and other context clues to write a simple meaning for each word in bold type.

1. The cowhands taught us how to tie square knots, **bowlines,** half hitches, and slipknots.

   _a kind of knot_

   _____

2. Horses can be trained to walk, pace, trot, **canter,** and gallop to certain commands.

   _a way that horses move_

3. You may substitute **filberts,** pecans, almonds, or cashews for walnuts in this recipe.

   _a kind of nut_

4. The butternut, **crookneck,** white bush, and acorn are all members of the squash family.

   _a kind of squash_

5. You can walk, stroll, or **shamble**—just arrive at soccer practice on time!

   _a kind of walking pace_

6. I can't tell a sailboat from a canoe or a **schooner,** but I'd love to ride in one.

   _a kind of boat_

7. Is there a grocery, supermarket, or **bodega** around the corner?

   _a kind of store_

8. That specialty shop sells bowlers, Stetsons, berets, and **turbans.**

   _a kind of head covering_

9. We packed the first-aid kit with bandages, tape, cotton, soap, and a **salve.**

   _a first-aid supply_

LESSON 72: Context Clues— Words in a Series 1

 **Home Involvement Activity** Play a listing game. Choose a category, such as animals, vegetables, cities, or athletes. In turn, name something in that category that begins with a, then b, then c, and so on.

---

### English-Language Learners/ESL

Make picture cards for several series of items. For example, make separate cards for roses, daisies, and tulips, and for elephants, zebras, and camels. Label each card. On the board, write the headings **Flowers, Animals.** Mix the cards, and have students come up and place each card under the correct heading. Then have students write sentences using each series of items.

### Gifted Learners

In the mid 1800s many Americans headed West in search of new opportunities. Have students read about this westward expansion and then write a poem about what these adventurers were hoping to find. Ask them to use words in a series.

### Learners with Special Needs

Additional strategies for supporting learners with special needs can be found on page 139L.

---

## Practicing the Skill

● Read aloud the directions on pages 147–148. Make sure students understand what they are to do.

● Explain that on page 148, their definitions may be broad since the sentences contain limited information.

**Intervention Strategy**

Turn to page 139K for an Intervention Strategy designed to help students who need extra help with this lesson.

## Curriculum Connections

### Spelling Link

● Read the following words aloud. For each word, have a volunteer spell the word aloud and then write it on the board. Ask another student the meaning of the word. They may consult a dictionary if necessary.

| | |
|---|---|
| grouse | pumice |
| pheasant | tempera |
| canter | shamble |
| schooner | salve |

● Finally, have students use each word in an original sentence that contains a series.

### Science Link

● Scientists often use classification systems. For example, when grouping and discussing plants and animals scientists use two classifications: the plant kingdom, and the animal kingdom.

● Have students check the library's resources to find plants and animals that are native to the West. Ask them to create a classification chart listing names of the plants and animals. Have them illustrate the examples.

● Then have students write sentences using words in a series to describe what they found.

## Observational Assessment

_Check whether students use items in a series to determine word meaning._

# Context Clues— Words in a Series 2

## Objectives

- **To use context clues to determine the meaning of unfamiliar words**

- **To use context clues to determine missing words in passages**

## Warming Up

- Write the following paragraph on the board. Have a student read it aloud.

  Yellowstone National Park in Wyoming is a popular tourist attraction. Visitors love to watch Yellowstone's **geysers** in action. These hot springs send spurts of water and steam into the air.

- Ask if students can determine the meaning of **geyser** by using context clues. Point out that the clues appear in a different sentence from the word itself.

## Teaching the Lesson

- Have volunteers read aloud the Helpful Hint on page 149. Review how using words in a series can help them define the meanings of unfamiliar words.

- Have a student read aloud the Helpful Hint on page 150. Remind students that context clues may appear before or after an unfamiliar word in the same sentence. Explain that the clues may even appear in other nearby sentences.

- Point out that context clues don't always reveal the exact meaning of a word. Sometimes they provide only a general understanding.

---

Name _____

> **Helpful Hint**
>
> Remember that words in the same **series** as that of an unknown word may give you the **context clues** you need to figure out the meaning of the word.

Star garnet—Idaho's gemstone

⭐ **Read each short passage about Idaho. Then answer the question that follows the passage. Use context clues to help you.**

1. Idaho is nicknamed the Gem State. Rock hounds all over the state have found fine pieces of **beryl,** jade, jasper, opal, and topaz. Idaho's official gemstone is the star garnet. This stone is found only in Idaho and in India.

   What is **beryl?** _____ a kind of gemstone

2. Hagerman Fossil Beds National Monument is a rare spot. It is along the Snake River, across from a high school. This Idaho park is filled with traces of early North American small mammals. Scientists have found fossils of early horses, camels, **peccary,** and beaver. The fossil beds are more than 3.5 million years old.

   What are **peccary?** _____ small mammals

3. Buhl, Idaho, is the rainbow trout capital of the nation. This small town on the Snake River leads the United States in research into trout and other freshwater fish. Huge farms in the area raise trout, as well as catfish, salmon, and **tilapia.**

   What are **tilapia?** _____ fish _____

4. There are many kinds of landforms throughout the West. Some types of tablelands are the mesa, butte, plateau, **hogback,** and cuesta. All are broad regions of higher land that rise from flatter surfaces. Some people think they look like giant tables.

   What is a **hogback?** _____ tableland _____

> **CHALLENGE**
>
> Use a map and context clues to understand this statement:
>
> The Snake River **demarcates** Idaho's border with Washington.
>
> What is the meaning of **demarcates?**

---

# UNIVERSAL ACCESS
## Meeting Individual Needs

### Logical Learners

Direct students to work with a partner. Have students find a word in the dictionary they think their partner won't know. Tell students to write a sentence or two using the word and include context clues that clearly suggest the word's meaning. Then have students exchange papers and try to determine the meaning of each other's words.

### Auditory Learners

Have students complete the following sentence: I went to the _____ and bought _____, _____, and _____. Ask students to make up a nonsense word for the first blank, but include three related items for the last three blanks. As students read their sentences orally, have classmates guess at the meaning of the nonsense word using the three related words as clues.

Student poets at the Cowboy Poetry Gathering

**Each passage below is missing a word. Use context clues to figure out a word that could fill in the blank correctly. Write a word that makes sense. Then explain your choice on the lines below.**

Answers will vary, but may include the following:

1. Each year in January, Elko, Nevada, hosts the Cowboy Poetry Gathering. The goal of this event is to preserve cowboy culture. Programs include

   songs, artwork, tall tales, and, of course, _____poetry_____.

   Explain your choice. ____It's a poetry gathering.____

2. Reno, Nevada, has a fine planetarium. It offers public shows that open our minds to the wonders of the night sky. Programs vary all year long. Shows

   may focus on stars, meteors, _____planets_____, comets, or eclipses, to name a few popular topics.

   Explain your choice. ____You can see planets at a planetarium.____

3. Wide-open spaces lure fans of outdoor activities to the West. Hikers, skiers,

   horseback riders, and _____biking_____ come to play in the great outdoors.

   Explain your choice. ____You could go biking in wide open spaces.____

4. Many animals are able to thrive in areas where other animals might suffer.

   These include the scorpion, _____iguana_____, gecko, and rattlesnake. Such animals adapt to the heat of the Nevada desert by hunting at night.

   Explain your choice. ____Iguanas live in the desert.____

 **Home Involvement Activity** Work together to think of other answers to items 1–4. Use the context clues given. There are many possible choices.

## Practicing the Skill

- Read aloud the directions on pages 149–150. Remind students that the context clues may give a general understanding of the word rather than a precise definition.

- For items 1–4 on page 150, remind students that they must write a word that makes sense and then explain their answers.

## Curriculum Connections

### Spelling Link

- Write the following words on the board and have a volunteer read them aloud:

  | garnet | plateau | peccary |
  | eclipses | activities | planetarium |
  | meteors | gecko | rattlesnake |

- Have students scramble the words and then trade papers with a partner. Have students unscramble the words and write sentences using them in a series.

### Multicultural Connection

- The word **geyser** is derived from Geysir, the name of the largest hot spring in Iceland, which shoots water 200 feet into the air.

- Have students research Iceland's hot springs, the water from which is used to heat many of the country's homes. Ask students to write a paragraph comparing Iceland's geysers to those in the American West.

- As students research, remind them to use context clues to help them determine the meaning of any unfamiliar words.

## Observational Assessment

*Check to see that students are able to find context clues to help them understand unfamiliar words in a passage.*

### English-Language Learners/ESL

Choose short passages from a textbook that explain terms and are accompanied by illustrations. For example, a paragraph describing **photosynthesis** in a science text is typically accompanied by a picture showing the process. Discuss with students how the passage, like the illustration, includes specific clues to meaning.

### Gifted Learners

Have students imagine they are rock hounds in Idaho. Ask them to do research to find out what equipment they would use, where they would go, and what they would see. Have students write a journal entry that describes what one day might be like for them.

### Learners with Special Needs

Additional strategies for supporting learners with special needs can be found on page 139L.

# Connecting Reading and Writing

## Objectives

- To read a nonfiction selection and respond to it in writing
- To use personal experience in relating to reading and to synthesize information
- To write diary entries from another person's point of view

## Warming Up

### Comprehension Skills

- Write the names **Meriwether Lewis** and **William Clark** on the board. Explain that these men were U.S. explorers who led an expedition through the West and Northwest. Their journey took place from 1804 to 1806 and covered more than 8,000 miles.
- Tell students that as they read, they will **synthesize** information—that is, put together information and make sense of it. They will also **relate their reading to their own experiences.**

## Teaching the Lesson

- To answer the first Reader's Response question, remind students to use what they know about context clues.
- Ask students to consider what information gathered by Lewis and Clark would be valuable to the new settlers.
- Have students reflect on any "difficult but exciting" experiences they have had.

## Practicing the Skill

- Read aloud the directions on page 152. Remind students that thinking about their own experiences may help them better relate to these two explorers.
- Encourage students to use the Writer's Tip as they explore point of view.

151

---

Name _____

 Read about the famous explorers, Lewis and Clark. Then answer the questions that follow.

# Catching Up with Lewis and Clark

from a nonfiction article in Time for Kids magazine

Nobody likes a litterbug, but historians wish that Meriwether Lewis and William Clark had left more behind as they traveled across the North American continent 200 years ago. They cleaned up so well after themselves that it's hard to tell exactly where they stopped on their journey from St. Louis, Missouri, to the Pacific Ocean.

But researchers hope to answer age-old questions about these great trailblazers of the West, whose work made it possible for the U.S. government to claim the Oregon territory. This led to pioneers settling the West in the mid-1800s.

In 1803, President Thomas Jefferson asked Lewis to explore the Louisiana Purchase, a huge area of land that the United States was about to buy from France. He hoped to learn of a water route between the Mississippi River and the Pacific Ocean that would help U.S. trade.

Lewis and his best friend, Clark, left St. Louis in May 1804 with a party of 42 men. They never found the water route, but they became the first U.S. citizens to see many of America's wonders—the endless Great Plains, the Rocky Mountains, and the Pacific. They faced many hardships and dangers, including bear attacks and bitter cold. More than 500 days and 4,000 miles after they had set out, Lewis and Clark reached the Pacific.

The explorers kept superb maps and diaries. They were the first to describe 122 kinds of animals and 178 plants, and to meet many native tribes. But they left barely a trace behind. That makes it hard to say "Lewis and Clark were here!"

1. Answers will vary.
2. Their work made it possible for the U.S. government to claim the Oregon territory. This led to pioneers settling the West in the mid-1800s.
3. Answers will vary.

 **Reader's Response**

1. Lewis and Clark were trailblazers. What context clues helped you figure out the meaning of the word?
2. How did the excellent diaries and maps of Lewis and Clark help the pioneers to settle the West?
3. What experience have you had that can help you identify with the difficult but exciting journey of Lewis and Clark?

LESSON 74: Connecting Reading and Writing
Comprehension—Relate Reading to Your Own Experience; Synthesize

151

---

# UNIVERSAL ACCESS
## Meeting Individual Needs

### Visual Learners

Have students make a map tracing the route that Lewis and Clark took on their expedition. Encourage them to draw symbols depicting some of the things that the explorers encountered. Ask students to include a map key.

### Auditory Learners

Have students discuss the differences between reading a diary entry and hearing a television news reporter's account of the same event. Ask students to write several questions that a television reporter might ask Lewis and Clark about their adventure. Have partners pretend to be Lewis and Clark and then perform the "live" television interview for the class.

### Learners with Special Needs

Additional strategies for supporting learners with special needs can be found on page 139L.

Lewis and Clark filled their journals with interesting information. For example, they wrote about Sacajawea, an English-speaking Shoshone woman, who spoke with the Native Americans they met. Clark also described what it felt like to see the Pacific Ocean for the first time. "Ocian in view! O! the joy!" Clark may not have been a good speller, but his diary and Lewis's proved to be the best guidebooks to the West.

⭐ **Imagine that you are Lewis *and* Clark. Write paired diary entries. Choose an exciting event, such as the day you met Sacajawea, the day a bear attacked, or the day you finally reached the Pacific Ocean. Write two diary entries, one from Lewis's point of view, the other from Clark's. Include at least two of these words.**

expedition  travel  journey  explore  guide  arrived  observed  sight
magnificent  helpful  dangerous  hardship  first  next  then  finally

| Lewis | Clark |
|---|---|
| Answers will vary. | |

**Writer's Tip**

Think about how the two men probably were similar, yet different. This will help you present each explorer's point of view about the same event.

**Speaker's Challenge**

Imagine that you are a TV reporter. You are telling the news about a scientist's recent discovery of what may have been one of Lewis and Clark's campsites. Tell about the scientist's "dig" and the items that he or she may have found. Explain how this discovery may prove that Lewis and Clark were there!

*The Guide Sacajawea with Lewis & Clark,* by N. C. Wyeth, 1940.

LESSON 74: Connecting Reading and Writing Comprehension—Relate Reading to Your Own Experience; Synthesize

152

**English-Language Learners/ESL**

Call on volunteers to read aloud the article on page 151. Help students with difficult vocabulary words. Discuss key ideas and details in the article, and help students relate what they read to personal observations and experiences. For example, ask students to describe sights and sounds of a forest or park they have visited.

**Gifted Learners**

The role of Sacajawea, the English-speaking Shoshone woman (whose likeness now appears on a one-dollar coin) is often misunderstood or misrepresented. Have students learn more this young Native American and the part she played in the Lewis and Clark expedition. Then have students write a diary entry from Sacajawea's point of view.

## The Writing Process

Discuss with students the purpose of keeping a diary to record important events. Read aloud the directions on page 152.

**Prewrite** Have students decide on an event and then imagine how Lewis might view it and how Clark might view it. It may help them to make a list of their ideas.

**Write** Tell students to allow for similarities as well as differences in the two men's viewpoints. Suggest that before they start to write, students consider which spelling words might work best.

**Revise** Have students reread their entries and revise them as necessary. Encourage them to exchange papers with a partner and give each other constructive criticism.

**Proofread** Tell students to read their work slowly and to check for errors in spelling, grammar, and punctuation.

**Publish** Have students copy their final drafts onto page 152 or a separate piece of paper. Ask volunteers to read their diary entries aloud.

**Computer Connection** Share the following tip with students who use a word processor to do their writing.

• When creating a document you may want to make note of the date it was created, last printed, or saved. Go to the toolbar and click on "View" then pull down to Header and Footer. Click where you want to insert the date or time. On the Header and Footer toolbar, click on date (a calendar icon). If you also want to insert the time, click on the clock icon.

• This will automatically insert the date and time onto your document. Close the Header and Footer. Each time you open the document to work on it, the date and time will be updated.

**Portfolio** Have students add their finished diary entries to their portfolios.

# Reviewing and Assessing
## Context Clues

### Objective
**To review and assess context clues**

## Warming Up

- Write the following paragraph on the board. Have a student read it aloud.

  As people moved West, the buffalo suffered. Hunters killed the buffalo for food and to sell their hides. Finally **conservationists** stepped in and made efforts to save the buffalo from extinction.

- Ask students to use context clues to determine the meaning of the word **conservationists**.

## Teaching the Lesson

- Review the Helpful Hints on pages 141, 143, 145, and 147.

- Remind students that they can understand the meaning of an unfamiliar word from the context and from their own knowledge and experience.

- For the exercises on pages 153–154, explain that it is important to look for clues both before and after an unfamiliar word. Make sure students read all of the choices for the exercise on page 154.

---

Name _____

Read each passage. Use context clues to answer the question that follows it.

1. Imperial County in California has some of the richest farmland in the world. Its main crops are tomatoes, cotton, melons, lettuce, and beets. Yet this area was once a dry and dusty desert. **Irrigation** changed all that. The new canals and sprinkler systems soon gave the region its lush pastures and fields.

   What is **irrigation**? Answers will vary.
   _____

*Migrant workers in Imperial County*

2. It just wouldn't work—and we were so hot! We turned on two old fans, closed the shades, put on shorts, and drank ice-cold lemonade until the repair person came to fix it.

   What wouldn't work? How do you know? _____
   _____

3. In Spanish, *los gatos* means "the cats." Los Gatos is the name of a small city in California. It was founded in 1868 on part of an old Spanish land grant. Its name **harks back** to past times when mountain lions and wildcats freely roamed the nearby hills.

   What does **harks back** mean? _____
   _____

4. In Long Beach, California, you can visit an old Russian submarine from the Cold War era. Tours take you into many parts of the ship. You can see the torpedo room, the sleeping quarters, the old top-secret command center, and the **galley,** where food was prepared.

   What is a **galley**? _____
   _____

---

# UNIVERSAL ACCESS
## Meeting Individual Needs

### Logical Learners
Remind students to use logic to determine the meaning of multiple-meaning words. For example, discuss the meaning of the word **explosive** and use it in a sentence. Then use the phrase **explosive situation** in a sentence. How does the meaning change? Have students do the same with examples such as **magnetic** and **magnetic personality.**

### Auditory Learners
Have students work in pairs to write riddles that reveal the meaning of two vocabulary words through context. (You may want to provide a list of words for students to choose from.) Ask volunteers to read their riddles aloud. Have the class use context clues to define the words.

### Learners with Special Needs
Additional strategies for supporting learners with special needs can be found on page 139L.

**Read each passage. Circle the letter of the word that means about the same as that of the word in bold type. Use context clues.**

1. If it starts to rain, we may decide to **curtail** our hike. However, I'm willing to get an early start so that we can cover most of the trail while the weather is still fair.
   a. shorten     b. extend     c. film

Hikers in Glacier National Park in Montana

2. Try to oil your baseball glove each week. This will keep the leather **supple**, which may prevent cracks and tears. It makes the glove easier to use, too.
   a. wet     b. clean     c. flexible

3. Our parents are always trying to make ends meet. They try not to spend too much money on most items. Yet they never **scrimp** on food. Mom says that a good diet will ensure a healthy mind in a healthy body.
   a. spend as little as possible     b. complain     c. deposit money

4. The metal smith makes beautiful jewelry from bronze, copper, silver, gold, and **platinum.** Of course, the platinum pieces are the most expensive.
   a. type of rock     b. an earring     c. a precious metal

5. The team whined and complained. They offered every excuse. Yet the coach remained **obstinate**. He refused to change his mind. He would not yield to any of the arguments.
   a. active     b. stubborn     c. flexible

6. Very few women wear fancy hats anymore, so the owner decided to close the **millinery** section of the department store. It just wasn't worth it to keep that department going.
   a. men's shoes     b. children's toys     c. ladies' hats

**Extend & Apply**

**Gaunt** means "very thin and bony, with hollow eyes and a starved look." Use this word in a sentence or a paragraph that gives context clues that suggest its meaning.

# Reteaching Activities

### Context Construction

Review with students the exercises on page 141. Have students work with a partner to create a similar series of sentences and questions. Remind students to make their context as clear as possible. Have student pairs exchange papers and answer each other's questions.

### Mini-Lessons

Write the Helpful Hints in Lessons 69–73 on separate index cards. Have students choose a card and prepare a "mini-lesson" to teach their hint to the class. Encourage the rest of the class to participate actively, ask questions, and give responses as the students present their lessons.

## Assessing the Skill

**Check Up** The exercises on pages 153–154 will help students review the use of context clues to determine word meaning. The exercises will also help you evaluate students' progress toward mastery.

Read aloud the directions on page 153, and have students complete the page. Encourage them to read each passage slowly and carefully and to reread passages as needed. Remind students to consider all answer choices on page 154 before deciding on one. Tell students to reread sentences to ensure understanding.

**Observational Assessment** Watch students for hesitation or confusion as they complete the pages. Note which passages appear to challenge students most. Review your recorded observations from previous lessons in the unit to help you monitor students' progress.

**Student Skills Assessment** Keep track of students' progress in understanding context clues using the checklist on page 139H.

**Writing Conference** Meet with students individually to discuss their written work, such as the diary entries on page 152. Encourage students to recall favorite pieces of writing in their portfolios and share them with the class. Discuss how knowledge of context clues can help students become better readers and, in turn, better writers.

Group together students who need further instruction in context clues, and have them complete the *Reteaching Activities*. Turn to page 139C for alternative assessment methods.

# Context Clues—Comparison

## Objectives

- **To determine the meaning of unfamiliar words by using context clues that show comparison**

- **To use contextual information to write the meanings of words**

## Warming Up

- Write the following sentences on the board. Have volunteers read them aloud.

  The ice skater's body was **lithe** and graceful, just like a dancer's.

- Ask students what two things are being compared in the first sentence. (an ice skater's body and a dancer's) Ask how this comparison helps them to understand what **lithe** means.

## Teaching the Lesson

- Read aloud and discuss the Helpful Hint on page 155. Discuss with students that in a comparison their prior knowledge of one thing helps them to understand another.

- Point out that certain words signal comparisons. Explain that words such as **like**, **as**, **similar**, and **same** often indicate a comparison.

- Ask a student to choose two items in the classroom and compare them using the words **like**, **as**, **similar**, or **same.**

---

Name _____

A pioneer woman in a **pinafore**

**Helpful Hint**

When you **compare** two items, you tell how they are alike.

Like an athlete before a big game, Pat was **apprehensive** before the debate.

You can use the **comparison** *like* as a **context clue** to help figure out how Pat felt before the debate. You know that athletes may worry about performing poorly before a big game. You can guess that in this sentence **apprehensive** means "anxious or fearful."

⭐ Each sentence compares two things. Read the sentence. Answer the questions that follow.

1. Her light, sleeveless dress, which ties in the back, is similar to the **pinafore** that a pioneer woman often wore over her clothes.

   Which words show a comparison? _____similar to_____

   What is a **pinafore**? _____a light, sleeveless dress_____

2. Saying that something is **gaudy** is the same as saying it is flashy and tasteless.

   Which words show a comparison? _____the same as_____

   What does **gaudy** mean? _____flashy and tasteless_____

3. The **piquant** flavor of the sauce is just as sharp as my mom's spiciest tacos.

   Which words show a comparison? _____is just as_____

   What does **piquant** mean? _____sharp_____

4. We **vanquished** the Lions in much the same way that we defeated the Bears.

   Which words show a comparison? _____the same way_____

   What does **vanquished** mean? _____defeated_____

**WORK TOGETHER**

Work in a small group. Brainstorm a list of words or phrases that you might use to signal a comparison between two items.

LESSON 76: Context Clues—Comparison    **155**

---

# U N I V E R S A L   A C C E S S
## Meeting Individual Needs

### Visual Learners

Explain that advertisements often compare two things in order to sell a product. Ask students to invent a name for a new product. For example, a new car called a Road Rocket. Then have them to create an advertisement comparing their product to something else that will help sell it.

### Musical Learners

Have students find examples of popular song lyrics that include comparisons. Have volunteers share their examples with the class. Ask students to explain each comparison and identify the words or phrases that the songwriter uses, such as **like** and **as.** Discuss the qualities that each comparison is meant to emphasize.

★ **Figure out the meaning of the word in bold type. Use words that show a comparison in the sentence as context clues to help you.**

1. People **hastened** to Sutter's Mill when gold was discovered there in the same way that a dog rushes for a juicy bone.

   Hastened means _____ rushed _____.

2. The gate was as **unyielding** to our pushing as a wall of solid rock.

   Unyielding means ____ immovable as a wall of solid rock ____.

3. Her look was as **serene** as the calmest lake I have ever sat by.

   Serene means _____ calm _____.

4. His approach to life is just as **intrepid** as that of the brave heroes he admires.

   Intrepid means _____ courageous or brave _____.

5. Jack London was as **productive** a writer as Babe Ruth was a hitter.

   Productive means _____ able to produce _____.

6. In an earthquake, even sturdy buildings can **topple** like a house of cards.

   Topple means _____ fall like a house of cards _____.

7. Hoover Dam **impounds** the waters of Lake Mead in the same way that a corral holds wild horses.

   Impounds means ___ to confine like a corral ___.

8. Her **melodic** voice sounds as rich as a lark's sweet song.

   Melodic means ___ tuneful, like a sweet song ___.

Hoover Dam

🏠 **Home Involvement Activity** A **simile** is a figure of speech that compares two unlike things by using the words **like, as,** or **than.** *She is as graceful as a swan.* Make up your own similes.

**156** LESSON 76: Context Clues—Comparison

---

**English-Language Learners/ESL**

Display pictures that show comparisons. For example, show a picture of a large mansion. For each picture, say or write a sentence, such as: *This house is as **gigantic** as a castle* or *This **gigantic** house is similar to a castle in size.* Ask students what two things are being compared, (house/castle) and in what way. (size) Explain to students how the comparison helps define the word **gigantic.**

**Gifted Learners**

Explain that metaphors (comparisons made without using **as** or **like**) also provide context clues. For example: *The volcano's **scalding** lava was an ocean of fire.* Have students write other metaphors that make clear the meaning of a word.

**Learners with Special Needs**

Additional strategies for supporting learners with special needs can be found on page 139L.

---

## Practicing the Skill

● Read aloud the directions on page 155. Remind students that for each item they must answer two questions. The first asks them to identify signal words (see *Teaching the Lesson*). The second asks them to use context clues to write the meaning of the word in bold type.

● Have students read the directions on page 156 and complete the page on their own.

● Point out that the sentences on pages 155 and 156 have different kinds of context clues that show comparison. Some sentences contain synonyms for the words in bold type. Other sentences have explanatory phrases.

## Curriculum Connections

### Spelling Link

● Say the following words aloud. For each one, have a volunteer make up a sentence that involves a comparison. For example: *Amy wore such bright colors that she looked as gaudy as a circus clown.*

| | | |
|---|---|---|
| **gaudy** | **melodic** | **vanquish** |
| **unyielding** | **serene** | **intrepid** |
| **productive** | **topple** | **hasten** |

● After the volunteer says the sentence, have another student spell the word and write it on the board.

### Writing Link

A simile is a comparison using **like** or **as.** Poets often use similes for dramatic effect. Have students look through poetry collections to find examples of similes and then share them with the class. Ask students to write a short poem using similes.

### Observational Assessment

*Check whether students recognize words that signal comparisons.*

# Context Clues— Contrast

## Objectives

- **To determine the meaning of unfamiliar words by using context clues that show contrast**
- **To use contextual information to write the meanings of words**

## Warming Up

- Write the following sentence on the board. Ask a student to read it aloud.

  Unlike Montana, which is **frigid** in the winter, California has generally mild temperatures.

- Ask students what is being compared in the sentence. (winter temperatures in Montana and California) Ask whether the climate of the two states is alike or different. What word shows this? **(unlike)**

## Teaching the Lesson

- Have a student read aloud the Helpful Hint on page 157. Explain that as with other context clues, sentences that contrast two things may give only a general understanding of an unfamiliar word rather than a precise meaning.
- Point out that there are certain words that signal contrasts, such as **unlike, although, but, as opposed to,** and **whereas.**
- Ask a student to think of two things that are dissimiliar and make up sentences comparing them.

157

---

Name _____

### Helpful Hint

When you **contrast** two items, you show how they are different. You can get at the meaning of an unfamiliar word by noticing how two things contrast.

Miki says arugula tastes *unlike* other salad greens.

The word *unlike* signals that a contrast is being made. You can use this **context clue** to figure out that arugula is a kind of salad green.

 Each sentence contrasts two things. Read the sentence. Answer the questions that follow.

A butte in Zion National Park, Utah

1. The walls of the butte are **crimson,** whereas few other landforms are red.

   Which word signals a contrast? _____ whereas

   What does **crimson** mean? _____ red

2. Meg is **prosperous,** but in contrast to millionaires, her wealth is modest.

   Which words signal a contrast? _____ but in contrast

   What does **prosperous** mean? _____ wealthy

3. The guard was **vigilant;** otherwise, he would not have spotted the thief.

   Which word signals a contrast? _____ otherwise

   What does **vigilant** mean? _____ observant

4. My sister is often **morose,** as opposed to my brother, who is always cheerful.

   Which words signal a contrast? _____ as opposed to

   What does **morose** mean? _____ sad / gloomy

5. Carlos is **brawny,** although he is no weight lifter.

   Which word signals a contrast? _____ although

   What does **brawny** mean? _____ strong / muscular

 **WORK TOGETHER**

Work in a small group. Write five sentences, each contrasting two items. Then underline the words or phrases that signal a contrast.

LESSON 77: Context Clues—Contrast **157**

---

# UNIVERSAL ACCESS
## Meeting Individual Needs

### Logical Learners

Write the following sentence on the board. Discuss how the contrast word helps explain the meaning of the word **somber.**

Liz had been **cheerful,** but she became **somber** after hearing the news.

Ask students to substitute other adjectives to create contrasts. For example, have students replace **cheerful** with **calm** and **somber** with **apprehensive.**

### Auditory Learners

Read aloud several sentences that contain two contrasting words. For example: *Unlike his* **hostile** *brother, Jim is* **friendly** *toward everyone.* Ask students to call out the two contrasting words. **(hostile/friendly)** Then have students use the contrasting word pairs in their own sentences.

**Figure out the meaning of the word in bold type. Use words that signal a contrast in the sentence as context clues to help you.**

1. Brixton is a **hard-boiled** rodeo star, but he has a soft spot for poetry and flowers.

   **Hard-boiled** means ___tough___ .

A rodeo rider in Wyoming

2. Instead of **gamboling** in the field with the other children, she sat nursing her sore ankle.

   **Gamboling** means ___skipping___ .

3. The others climbed to the **belfry** while I stayed at the foot of the tower, listening for the bells.

   **Belfry** means ___a bell tower___ .

4. He is **insolent**; on the other hand, all his classmates are courteous and respectful.

   **Insolent** means ___disrespectful___ .

5. Unlike Ray, who is a **pessimist,** Courtney sees the brighter side of things.

   **Pessimist** means ___one who sees the gloomy side___ .

6. In contrast to the **robust** lifeguard at West Beach, the one here looks weak and thin.

   **Robust** means ___strong and healthy___ .

7. Danny is honest in his dealings with people, whereas Greg is disloyal and **deceitful.**

   **Deceitful** means ___dishonest___ .

8. Iris tried to **pacify** the baby; however, Rob did nothing to soothe the child.

   **Pacify** means ___soothe___ .

**158** LESSON 77: Context Clues—Contrast

 Home Involvement Activity Use these words to create four sentences, each contrasting two things: **unlike, but, however,** and **while.**

---

## English-Language Learners/ESL

Show students pairs of pictures that contrast two objects or places. For example, show a picture of a large dog and a picture of a small dog. For each pair say or write a sentence, such as: *This dog is **immense**, but this one is small.* Ask students in what way the dogs are being contrasted. (size) Point out how the structure of the sentence helps to define the word **immense.**

## Gifted Learners

Have students write a paragraph in which they contrast two different places in the West. Ask students to use words that signal a contrast.

## Learners with Special Needs

Additional strategies for supporting learners with special needs can be found on page 139L.

---

## Practicing the Skill

• Read aloud the directions for the exercises on pages 157–158. Point out that for page 157, students must answer two questions for each item.

• If students have difficulty with the exercises on page 158 tell them to first identify the signal word and then look for the two contrasting words.

## Curriculum Connections

### Spelling Link

Read aloud each word and sentence, and have students write the words.

| | |
|---|---|
| **vigilant** | The **vigilant** soldier stayed alert for signs of the enemy. |
| **morose** | Three days of rain made Jen feel **morose**. |
| **gambol** | The ponies loved to **gambol** in the field. |
| **insolent** | The boy was punished for his **insolent** remark. |
| **pessimist** | A **pessimist** always thinks the worst will happen. |
| **robust** | The **robust** young man was an outstanding athlete. |
| **deceitful** | Cheating is a **deceitful** act. |

### Multicultural Connection

• At least half of America's fifty states have names derived from Native American words. Many other states' names are of European origin. Have students research the names of the western states.

• Ask them to create a map depicting the state, its name, and a brief description of how each state got its name.

## Observational Assessment

*Check whether the students know which words signal a contrast in a sentence.*

LESSON 78 • UNIT 5
# Student Pages 159–160

# Context Clues—Comparison and Contrast

### Objectives

- **To determine the meaning of unfamiliar words by using context clues that show comparison or contrast**
- **To use contextual information to write the meanings of words**

## Warming Up

- Write the following sentences on the board. Ask volunteers to read them aloud.

  The peaceful town was as **tranquil** as a fairy-tale village.

  Unlike the **tranquil** life of a small town, big-city life is busy and chaotic.

- Ask students which sentence compares two things and which contrasts them. Have students identify the signal words that serve as clues. **(as, unlike)**

## Teaching the Lesson

- Review with students that comparison shows how two things are alike, while contrast shows how two things are different.
- Focus students' attention on the two sentences in the *Warming-Up* exercise. Ask students if both sentences reveal the meaning of **tranquil** in the same way. Point out that the first sentence contains the synonym, **peaceful**, which is an important context clue.

Name ______________________________

**Helpful Hint**

Remember that you use **comparison** to show how two items are *alike*. You use **contrast** to show how two items are *different*.

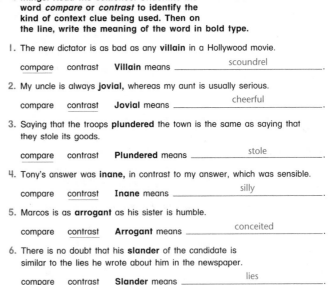

Scene from the movie *The Villain Still Pursued Her*, 1940

**Each sentence compares *or* contrasts two things. Read the sentence. Underline the word *compare* or *contrast* to identify the kind of context clue being used. Then on the line, write the meaning of the word in bold type.**

1. The new dictator is as bad as any **villain** in a Hollywood movie.

   compare   contrast   **Villain** means scoundrel.

2. My uncle is always **jovial**, whereas my aunt is usually serious.

   compare   contrast   **Jovial** means cheerful.

3. Saying that the troops **plundered** the town is the same as saying that they stole its goods.

   compare   contrast   **Plundered** means stole.

4. Tony's answer was **inane,** in contrast to my answer, which was sensible.

   compare   contrast   **Inane** means silly.

5. Marcos is as **arrogant** as his sister is humble.

   compare   contrast   **Arrogant** means conceited.

6. There is no doubt that his **slander** of the candidate is similar to the lies he wrote about him in the newspaper.

   compare   contrast   **Slander** means lies.

7. Dad gives me **subtle** hints, while my mother is much more forceful and direct.

   compare   contrast   **Subtle** means fine and delicate ______________________________.

**CHALLENGE**

Write two sentences that compare **and** two that contrast.





UNIVERSAL ACCESS

# Meeting Individual Needs

### Visual Learners

Write the following chart on the board for students to copy.

| Comparison | Contrast |
|---|---|
| like | unlike |
| as | but |
| similar to | although |
| same as | as opposed to |

Have students use the signal words in sentences that compare or contrast items.

### Kinesthetic Learners

Ask students to hold or touch two items in the classroom and then say two sentences that compare and contrast the items. For example: *This door is closed, but this window is open. Like the door, this window is rectangular.* Ask the other students to identify which sentence compares and which one contrasts.

Salt Lake City, Utah

1. Hatch, Utah, is a **hamlet**; on the other hand, Salt Lake City is a major urban area.

   **Hamlet** means __a small village__.

2. The mayor will try our plan, even though she is usually **skeptical** about new ideas.

   **Skeptical** means __doubtful__.

3. She **flails** her arms about in the same way that people do in the water to attract the lifeguard.

   **Flails** means __wave around__.

4. Karen **garbles** her words, unlike Gabe, who speaks loudly and clearly.

   **Garbles** means __mumbles__.

5. Similarly, her outfit was as **flamboyant** as her flashy new car.

   **Flamboyant** means __flashy__.

6. To say that I am **cynical** is the same as saying that I doubt and sneer at the things people say and do.

   **Cynical** means __doubtful__.

7. Despite the **havoc** usually caused by hurricanes, this storm caused little damage.

   **Havoc** means __disaster__.

8. Some rain would be **beneficial** to our region, whereas too much would ruin the crops.

   **Beneficial** means __helpful__.

9. To spot the **elusive** gray wolf in the wild is equal to finding a four-leaf clover.

   **Elusive** means __hard to get hold of__.

160 | LESSON 78: Context Clues— Comparison and Contrast

 **Home Involvement Activity** Find three hard words in a dictionary. Then use each word in a sentence that has **compare** or **contrast** clues. Challenge family members to figure out the meaning of the three words.

---

### English-Language Learners/ESL

To reinforce the difference between comparison and contrast, display pairs of pictures or actual objects that are similar but different. For example, show a small paintbrush and a very large one. Help students make up appropriate sentences to compare and contrast the items. For example: *Like the large brush, the small one has black **bristles**. Unlike the large brush, the small one has very short **bristles**.*

### Gifted Learners

Explain that poets use simile quite often. Ask students to compile a list of words that fit the following phrase: *as _____ as a _____.* Have students use these comparisons in a series of poems

### Learners with Special Needs

Additional strategies for supporting learners with special needs can be found on page 139L.

---

## Practicing the Skill

● Read aloud the directions on pages 159–160. On page 159 remind students to identify the kind of context clue, in addition to writing the meaning of each word.

● Encourage students to find the signal words in each sentence before using the context clues to define the word.

## Curriculum Connections

### Spelling Link

Write these scrambled words and sentences on the board. Have students unscramble the words and write them in the blanks to complete each sentence.

**ijvola**      Jim is always _____ and funny. **(jovial)**

**enina**      I can't believe I gave such an _____ answer! **(inane)**

**gtanror**    The bragging winner was quite _____. **(arrogant)**

**tfnlaaymob**  I chose a colorful and _____ costume for the play. **(flamboyant)**

**tsleub**     Kate's hints were so _____ I almost missed them. **(subtle)**

### Science Link

Zion National Park in Utah is a spectacular cliff-and-canyon wilderness full of unexpected geological shapes. Have students research the unusual land formations found in the park to determine the scientific causes. Encourage students to use context clues to figure out unfamiliar words they may encounter.

### Observational Assessment

*Check whether students can distinguish between context clues that show comparison and those that indicate contrast.*

# Context Clues— Inference 1

## Objectives

- **To make inferences based on prior knowledge and context clues**
- **To recognize word meaning based on inference**

## Warming Up

- Write the following paragraph on the board and have a student read it aloud.

  "This food is **delectable**!" Mr. Smithers said, smiling as he chewed. He raised his plate. "Please, may I have some more?"

- Ask students how Mr. Smithers feels about what he's eating. Ask what the word **delectable** means.

- Have students discuss how they were able to reach their conclusions.

## Teaching the Lesson

- Focus students' attention on the paragraph in the *Warming-Up* exercise. Ask: *Does the paragraph state that the food was delicious?* (no)

- Explain that students made an inference, or drew a conclusion about how the food tasted based on the clues in the paragraph and what they know. Point out that the fact that Mr. Smithers was smiling, and that he asked for more, are clues that he thought the food was delicious.

- Tell students that the inference is an "educated guess" and that they should examine the guess to make sure it is the correct one.

**161**

---

Name _____

> **Helpful Hint**

When you make an **inference**, you draw a conclusion about something that is not stated directly. To use inference to figure out the meaning of an unfamiliar word, read carefully. Relate ideas to what you know. Then make an "educated guess" about the meaning of the word.

**Read each sentence. Then answer the questions that follow. You will need to make inferences based on context clues in the sentences.**

Possible answers may include:

1. Dad **swerved** off the road to avoid hitting a deer that had suddenly appeared.

   What was Dad doing? _____ steering the car away from the deer

   Therefore, what does it mean to **swerve**? _____ to turn away from, to avoid

2. We want the best **orator** in our school to give the main speech at graduation.

   What traits should someone who gives an important speech have? _____ good public speaking skills

   Therefore, what is an **orator**? _____ someone who speaks publicly

3. We cleared away the **debris** on the beach so that we could have a clean, unspoiled spot for swimming.

   What would make a beach unclean or spoiled? _____ litter or garbage

   Therefore, what is **debris**? _____ the remains of something that is thrown away

> **WORD STRATEGY**
>
> An inference is an "educated guess." After you make an inference, go back to test your guess. Does it work in the sentence? Does it help you understand the meaning of the unfamiliar word? If not, try again.

---

# UNIVERSAL ACCESS
## Meeting Individual Needs

### Auditory Learners

Write ten phrases on cards, such as: **climb a mountain, baby-sit for a young child, walk a dog.** Have a volunteer choose a card and then give clues to help classmates guess the correct phrase. For "climb a mountain," the student might say: *I see a beautiful view from the top of this big hill.* Discuss with students which clues were most useful.

### Logical Learners

Have students write five fill-in sentences that include clear context clues for the missing word. Give the example: *You should always brush and ____ your teeth after eating.*

Ask students to exchange papers with a partner and use their inferential skills to complete each other's sentences.

⭐ **Read each sentence. Choose the word or phrase from the box whose meaning matches the word in bold type. Write that word or phrase on the line.**

| agreement | hate | in spite of | touches | ordered |
|---|---|---|---|---|
| newness | | on time | similar | unplanned |

1. The Montana State Fair in Great Falls attracts 200,000 visitors each year, **regardless of** how far people have to travel to get there.
   _____in spite of_____

2. They wound up playing an **impromptu** game of baseball with a broom and a bag of green apples.
   _____unplanned_____

Great Falls, Montana

3. We **detest** war and will do everything we can to support the United Nations.
   _____hate_____

4. When Grandma **caresses** my face, she always strokes it gently.
   _____touches_____

5. It took hours of discussion and debate, but our group finally came to a **consensus.** _____agreement_____

6. Try to be **punctual** for an interview, even if you think that the other person may be late. _____on time_____

7. He **commanded** his troops to retreat, but one soldier continued to fight.
   _____ordered_____

8. After the **novelty** of the twist wore off, people quickly grew tired of this dance. _____newness_____

9. Ansel Adams and I are **kindred** spirits; we both admire the natural beauty of the West. _____similar_____

LESSON 79: Context Clues— Inference I

 **Home Involvement Activity** Pick a Word of the Day. Family members can take turns introducing this new word and using it in a sentence. Be sure that the meaning of the word can be determined by context clues.

- Read aloud the directions for the exercises on page 161. Remind students to make inferences, or "educated guesses," to figure out the meanings of the words.

- For the exercises on page 162, tell students to use the process of elimination to narrow their choices.

## Curriculum Connections

### Spelling Link

Read aloud the following sentences, emphasizing the words in bold type. Have students write the words on a piece of paper and then check their work as you spell the words aloud.

We picked up **debris** on the roadside.

The **orator** delivered a moving speech.

I like asparagus, but I **detest** broccoli.

Please be **punctual** when you come over to my house.

I went to the parade **regardless** of the rain.

Can we come to a **consensus** about our plans?

### Social Studies Link

An important part of Navajo culture is the singing of songs that tells of their origin. Have students research Native American tribes that lived in the West and write a report describing their customs and beliefs. Ask students to compare and contrast various tribes and discuss the impact that westward expansion had on these native peoples.

### Observational Assessment

*Check whether students use context clues to make appropriate inferences.*

**English-Language Learners/ESL**

To help students make inferences, display several thought-provoking pictures and have students discuss the story behind the scenes or events depicted. You may want to use photographs from newspapers or magazines. Encourage students to look for specific clues in each picture. Ask them to interpret the meaning of the pictures.

**Gifted Learners**

Ask students to think about the statement, "Making inferences is not just a language skill, it is part of daily life." Have students write a paragraph explaining why this statement is true and include some examples.

**Learners with Special Needs**

Additional strategies for supporting learners with special needs can be found on page 139L.

# Context Clues—Inference 2

## Objectives

- **To make inferences based on context clues, prior knowledge, and experience**
- **To use inference to write the meanings of words**

## Warming Up

- Write the following paragraph on the board. Ask a volunteer to read it aloud.

  Copper miners in Montana dig **shafts** into the earth in order to reach buried mineral ore. The miners descend, separate the **ore** from the surrounding rock, and send it up to the surface.

- Discuss clues in the paragraph that helped students infer the meaning of the word **shaft,** such as **dig, buried**, and **descend.** Extend the discussion by asking students to infer the meaning of the word **ore.**

## Teaching the Lesson

- Review the idea that when you draw a conclusion about something not directly stated you are making an inference.

- Discuss how readers combine various context clues with their own knowledge and experience to make sense of what they read. For example, you know that to reach something buried you have to dig a hole. You also know that for miners to descend into a shaft and send up mineral ore, the hole must be large.

- Point out that sometimes inference gives only a general idea of meaning. Students can get a sense of what **ore** is, but they may not be able to determine an exact definition.

---

Name _____

Copyright © by William H. Sadlier, Inc. All rights reserved.

Firefighters in Yellowstone National Park

> ### Helpful Hint
> Use **inference** to figure out the meaning of something not stated directly. This is the most common type of **context clue.**

 Read each sentence. Use inference to guess the meaning of the word in bold type. Then write the word in bold type next to the definition below that most closely matches its meaning.

- A wild **inferno** left behind burned trees.

- Raccoons are **adept** at using their paws, which makes them good backyard thieves!

- Smooth talk may **beguile** you out of your money.

- Unfortunately, politicians don't often give their **candid** opinion about the issues.

- She is so creative that she can **cobble** together junk and make it look like art.

- Some superstars think that their fame lets them break the law without **penalty.**

- Science has **eradicated** some diseases and made others easy to treat.

- She used strength she didn't know she had to escape from the **rubble** caused by the earthquake.

eradicated _____ 1. gotten rid of forever

penalty _____ 2. punishment

candid _____ 3. honest or frank

inferno _____ 4. intense fire with great heat

cobble _____ 5. put together roughly

rubble _____ 6. pieces from ruined buildings

adept _____ 7. highly skilled

beguile _____ 8. trick, cheat, deceive

> ### CHALLENGE
> In an analogy, relationships between words are unstated. Use inference to see the relationship in this analogy:
>
> **Juvenile** is to **mature** as **early** is to **late.**
>
> Tell how the ideas are connected.

---

# UNIVERSAL ACCESS
## Meeting Individual Needs

### Visual Learners

Help students make a flowchart that shows how to use inference to figure out the meaning of an unfamiliar word. The flowchart steps might include the following:

**Read the sentence carefully.**

→**Look for signal words, if any.**

→**Look for context clues.**

→**Use clues and knowledge to reach a conclusion.**

→**Try out your conclusion in the sentence to see if it makes sense.**

### Auditory Learners

Write the states of the West and a related vocabulary word on index cards. Have students choose a card and use their vocabulary word in a sentence about the state without including the state's name. For example, for the card **Idaho** and **irrigation** a student might say, "This state's farmers use **irrigation** to produce almost a third of our country's potatoes." Challenge the class to use inference to name the state and define each word.

⭐ **Read each sentence about an amusing place name in the West. Use context clues, inference, and your own knowledge and experience to guess the meaning of the word in bold type. Then on the line, write a simple definition of the word.**

1. It's fun to **speculate** about how Wisdom, Montana, may have gotten its name.

   speculate: _____ guess _____

2. The naming of Riddle, Idaho, remains an **enigma** to this day.

   enigma: _____ puzzle/riddle _____

3. I'll bet that the post office did not **inform** you that there is a Manhattan in the middle of Nevada!

   inform: _____ notify _____

4. The folks in Utah may know whether you really can hear the **din** of billions of insects in the Cricket Mountains.

   din: _____ noise _____

5. Let's guess why pioneers in Last Chance, Colorado, gave the town its **ominous** name.

   ominous: _____ threatening _____

6. If you wish to grow a lush garden, you might want to **acknowledge** that Weed, California, is not the place to buy land.

   acknowledge: _____ admit _____

7. It's strange that my friend in Plain City, Utah, plans to build an **elaborate** house.

   elaborate: _____ fancy _____

8. A **chronicle** of the life and times of Story, Wyoming, should give you all the historical facts.

   chronicle: _____ story _____

9. Does the county have an **obligation** to build crooked roads in Bent County, Colorado?

   obligation: _____ duty _____

🏠 **Home Involvement Activity** Refer to a map of your state. Make a list of interesting place names. Try to find out how each of these places got its name.

---

## Practicing the Skill

● Read aloud the directions on page 163. Remind students that they can use the process of elimination in order to narrow their choices.

● Some words on page 164 may prove challenging for students to define. Refer students to the Word Strategy on page 161, and tell them to use their inferential skills to make "educated guesses."

 Turn to page 139K for an Intervention Strategy designed to help students who need extra support with this lesson.

## Curriculum Connections

### Spelling Link

● Read each word aloud. Have volunteers spell the words and write them on the board.

| | | |
|---|---|---|
| adept | eradicate | beguile |
| candid | obligation | penalty |
| inform | speculate | ominous |

● Challenge students to write sentences using two of the words together.

### Writing Link

Writers sometimes use **analogies** to explain how things are alike or different. Discuss with students the definitions of synonyms and antonyms. An example of an antonym analogy would be **fiction is to fact as love is to hate.** A synonym analogy would be **right is to correct as terrify is to frighten.** Ask students to think of other antonym and synonym analogies and share them with the class.

### Observational Assessment

*Check to see that students use their knowledge and experience to help them make inferences.*

---

### English-Language Learners/ESL

Display pictures that lend themselves to descriptive or narrative sentences, such as a busy city street or a diver going off a high board. For each picture, say a sentence, but leave out a key noun or verb. Have students use their inferential skills to choose a word to complete the sentence.

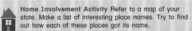

### Gifted Learners

When students read, they make inferences to understand the character and his or her motives. Have students choose a character from a story and write a description based only on what they are able to infer.

### Learners with Special Needs

Additional strategies for supporting learners with special needs can be found on page 139L.

# Context Clues— Mixed Strategies

## Objectives

- **To recognize word meaning based on context clues**
- **To use contextual information to understand the meanings of words**

## Warming Up

- Write the following paragraph on the board and have a student read it aloud.

  Utah attracts visitors throughout the year. In summer, people come to the state's beautiful parks. In winter, sports **enthusiasts flock** to Utah's ski resorts.

- Ask students to explain the meaning of the word **enthusiasts**. Discuss how prior knowledge of the word **enthusiasm** may help define the word **enthusiast**.

- Extend the discussion by asking students how they can infer the meaning of the word **flock** when it is used as a verb if they know its meaning when it is used as a noun.

## Teaching the Lesson

- Explain that readers apply many different strategies in order to figure out the meaning of words and sentences. Point out that if students know that a "flock" of birds means a group, then they can infer that people who "flock" to a ski resort come as a group, or in large numbers.

- Have a student read aloud the Helpful Hints on page 165. Ask volunteers to explain in their own words each of the strategies mentioned and how they may have used them.

Name _____

**Helpful Hints**

You know that you can use context clues to unlock the meaning of words you don't know. There are several ways to do this:

Use your **experience**.
Look for a **definition** in the sentence.
Look for related **words in a series**.
Use clues to **compare** or **contrast**.
Make **inferences**.

James Beckwourth (1798–1867?)

**Read each passage. Fill in the circle of the word or words that have the same meaning as that of the word in bold type. Use context clues.**

1. Before the pioneers settled in the West, mountain men like Jim Bridger and James Beckwourth came. These trappers lived and hunted alone. Life in the wilderness was hard and dangerous. The trappers had to be tough. They had to show great **fortitude** in order to survive.
   ○ wealth    ○ eagerness    ● strength

2. Fort Laramie, Wyoming, was only a fur-trading post in 1834. Yet when the arrival of wagon trains was **imminent,** the fort took on a new role. It soon provided food, shelter, and protection to the pioneers.
   ● close at hand    ○ traveling    ○ far away

3. The restaurant featured singing waiters. The food cost money, but the entertainment was **gratis.**
   ○ cheap    ● free    ○ colorful

4. It is warm and sunny by the beaches in California. The salt air feels good, but it **corrodes** the metal on cars. The metal can gradually wear away.
   ○ paints    ○ covers up    ● eats away

5. Bo teaches in an elementary school in Billings, Montana. Most of his students live in the city. Unlike them, Bo lives in a **rural** area outside the city limits.
   ○ urban    ● country    ○ suburban

Explain to a partner the type of context clue you used to arrive at each correct answer.

# UNIVERSAL ACCESS
# Meeting Individual Needs

## Auditory Learners

Have students listen as you read aloud a paragraph from a nonfiction piece that includes several challenging words. Ask students to use context clues to figure out the meanings. Discuss which strategies they have learned that helped them understand the unfamiliar words. Also discuss where the context clues appeared in relation to each unfamiliar word.

## Logical Learners

Have students work in pairs. Ask them to find a word in a science or social studies textbook they think will be unfamiliar to their partner. Ask students to write sentences using the word in a context that will enable their partner to infer the word's meaning. Then have students trade papers and apply the strategies they have learned to figure out the meaning of the unfamiliar word.

★ **Figure out the meaning of the word in bold type. Use context clues to help you. Write the meaning of the word on the line.**

1. After the **demise** of the mine, the people in the town lost their jobs. However, a group of them set up an old miner's museum to attract visitors.

   **Demise** means _____downfall_____.

2. The science museum displayed the **shale**, sandstone, and limestone found in the canyon walls and in the landforms of the area.

   **Shale** is a kind of _____rock_____.

3. The **belligerent** old prospector loved to quarrel with the other miners. He would pick a fight with anyone who crossed his path.

   **Belligerent** means _____argumentative; quarrelsome_____.

4. We did a **superb** job on that science project. In our opinion, it was similar in quality to the outstanding work that real scientists do.

   **Superb** means _____outstanding_____.

5. When Lin decided to become a scientist, she knew she had found her **niche**; on the other hand, Suki has not yet found a career that suits her.

   A **niche** is a _____a place for which a person is well-suited_____.

6. We tried several experiments to keep the cat away from our food, but our cat is very **persistent**. She keeps trying until she gets her way.

   **Persistent** means _____stubborn_____.

7. My nephew is a **bungler**. He botches up everything he does.

   A **bungler** is a _____incompetent person_____.

8. The work that people did to build the first railroad across the nation was hard. It was boring, too. The work was pure **drudgery**.

   **Drudgery** is _____hard/boring work_____.

Workers on the transcontinental railroad, 1865

LESSON 81: Context Clues—
Mixed Strategies

 **Home Involvement Activity** Today, most cities boast excellent science museums. What would you see in such a museum? What would you like to see? Talk about it. Then plan a family outing to a science museum in your area.

---

## Practicing the Skill

● Read aloud the directions for pages 165–166. Tell students to use any of the strategies they have learned from previous lessons.

● Remind students that context clues may appear in a different sentence than the word itself.

● Encourage students to request help as they work on the pages.

## Curriculum Connections

### Spelling Link

● Say the following words aloud. Have students spell each word orally then write it on the board.

| | | |
|---|---|---|
| **suburban** | **drudgery** | **rural** |
| **fortitude** | **pugnacious** | **demise** |
| **corrode** | **imminent** | **superb** |

● Have students work with a partner to write sentences that illustrate how to use the context clues strategies listed in the Helpful Hints on page 165.

### Social Studies Link

● Divide the class into teams and ask each team to write ten trivia questions about the West. For example: *Where is Hoover Dam located?* (at the Nevada-Arizona border)

● Let each team take turns asking a question while the other team races to find the correct answer in encyclopedias, textbooks, or other reference sources.

### Observational Assessment

*Check to see whether students apply appropriate context clues strategies to determine word meaning.*

---

**English-Language Learners/ESL**

Pantomime several occupations and ask students to guess who you are. For example, pantomime a photographer shooting pictures. Explain to students that they can infer by your actions, even though you aren't directly stating, the occupation. Then write sentences on the board that tell what you were doing. Ask students to point out the context clues.

**Gifted Learners**

Reading poetry often requires students to use context clues. Have students look through a poetry collection and choose a poem to analyze for the different types of context-clues strategies included in this unit.

**Learners with Special Needs**

Additional strategies for supporting learners with special needs can be found on page 139L.

# Connecting Spelling and Writing

## Objectives

- **To say, spell, sort, and write words that signal comparison and contrast**
- **To write a comparison-contrast paragraph using spelling words**

## Warming Up

- Write the following paragraph on the board and ask a student to read it aloud.

  **Like** Montana, Idaho borders Canada. **However,** Idaho's shared border with Canada is short, **while** Montana's is extensive.

- Ask students which sentence makes a comparison and which shows a contrast. Have students identify signal words that serve as clues. **(like, however, while)**

## Teaching the Lesson

- Have students rewrite the first sentence in *Warming Up* using different comparison signal words. For example: Montana and Idaho are **alike** in that both states border Canada.

- Ask students to rewrite the second sentence using different contrast signal words. For example: Idaho's shared border with Canada is short. **By contrast**, Montana's is extensive.

## Practicing the Skill

- Read the directions for page 167 together. Have students read the phrases and spell the words in bold type. Then have students complete the page.
- Extend the activity by having the class use each word or phrase in a sentence.

---

Read each group of words. Say and spell each word or phrase in bold type. Repeat the word or words. Then sort them by whether they signal a comparison or a contrast. Write the word or phrase in the correct box below.

- so many **likenesses**
- a few **differences**
- **while** we aren't sure
- **despite** its differences
- **share** many features
- **although** it can't
- **alike** in several ways
- **compare** with mine
- **similar to** that fruit
- **instead of** buying
- behaves **similarly**

- **equal to** this
- **unlike** that
- **yet** they may not
- **both** seem to be
- **on the other hand**
- **by comparison**
- **by contrast**

San Francisco's Chinatown

| Words That Signal a Comparison | Words That Signal a Contrast |
| --- | --- |
| likenesses | differences |
| share | while |
| alike | despite |
| compare | although |
| similar to | instead |
| similarly | unlike |
| equal | yet |
| both | on the other hand |
| by comparison | by contrast |

---

# UNIVERSAL ACCESS
## Meeting Individual Needs

### Visual Learners

Divide the class into seven groups. Assign each group one of the states of the West: California, Nevada, Montana, Utah, Colorado, Idaho, and Wyoming. Using reference materials, ask students to compare and contrast two cities in their state. Have students first note similarities, then differences. Then have them combine both into a wall chart.

### Musical Learners

Challenge students to find the words to the western states' songs. Ask them to choose two state songs to compare and contrast. Model questions they might ask themselves as they research. For example: *Are both songs about the natural beauty of the states? I see this song mentions a founding father. Does that one?*

### Learners with Special Needs

Additional strategies for supporting learners with special needs can be found on page 139L.

Chinatown is a part of San Francisco. However, unlike the large Marina District, San Francisco's Chinatown is only seven blocks long and three blocks wide. Still, it attracts many visitors. More tourists come to this busy area than to the Marina. They like to visit the unusual restaurants and stores. Even the phone booths in Chinatown have a style all their own!

**Choose two places to compare and contrast. Complete the chart below. List the features of each place in the outside boxes. In the middle box, list how the two places are alike. Later, use at least four of these words or phrases to write a comparison-contrast paragraph.**

| likenesses | differences | while | despite |
| share | although | alike | compare |
| similar to | instead of | | similarly |
| equal to | unlike | yet | both |
| on the other hand | by comparison | | by contrast |

### Writer's Tip

You can organize your paragraph **point-by-point.** This lets you move back and forth between the two places, comparing one place then the other as you go.

**Place #1**
Answers will vary.

**Both Places**

**Place #2**

### Writer's Challenge

Now compare your two places in a paragraph that compares and contrasts. Organize your writing in a way that makes sense. Use your spelling words to help you compare and contrast.

### English-Language Learners/ESL

Display pictures of scenic places in the West. Help students form sentences comparing or contrasting the pictures. For example, you might show pictures of two cities and ask students to explain how they are alike. Or, you might show photos of the Nevada desert and California farmlands and ask how the two scenes differ. Encourage students to use specific language.

### Gifted Learners

A common type of comparison is the before-and-after comparison. Have students identify a before-and-after situation and write a descriptive or explanatory paragraph about it. Possible examples include: dry land before and after irrigation; California before and after the 1849 gold rush.

## The Writing Process

Tell students that on page 168 they will write a paragraph comparing and contrasting two places. Read aloud the directions. Ask a volunteer to read the signal words and phrases in the box and remind students to use at least four of them.

**Prewrite** Have students choose two places they know well. Suggest they make a list of significant features and descriptive details of each place. Guide students in completing the chart on page 168 and using it to organize their paragraph.

**Write** Encourage students to use specific details when they write. Remind them that their paragraph should compare and contrast and should include signal words.

**Revise** Tell students to reread their work and make any improvements they can. Suggest they exchange papers with a partner, share feedback, and then revise further.

**Proofread** Direct students to check for errors in spelling, grammar, and punctuation.

**Publish** Have students copy their final drafts onto page 168 or a separate piece of paper. Ask volunteers to read their paragraphs aloud.

**Computer Connection**

Share the following tip with students who use a word processor to do their writing.

• If you use a computer regularly, you'll soon accumulate a large number of document files. It's important to save each document under a specific file name that distinguishes it from other documents. By doing so, you'll make it easier to find the document you want at a later time.

• You can abbreviate words in file names, but you generally cannot use these characters: / \ > < * . ? " | : ; .

**Portfolio** Suggest that students add their finished paragraphs to their portfolios.

# Connecting Reading and Writing

## Objectives

- **To read a selection and respond to it in writing**
- **To practice comparing and contrasting information and making inferences**
- **To write a compare-and-contrast essay**

## Warming Up

### Comprehension Skills

- Remind students that **comparing** shows how things are alike, and **contrasting** shows how they are different.

- Give a brief description of two vacations to different places, for example a summer trip to a California beach and a ski trip to Lake Tahoe. Ask students to compare and contrast these two vacations.

- Remind them that they can **make inferences** based on context clues and their prior experience or knowledge.

## ★ Teaching the Lesson

- To answer the first Reader's Response question, ask students to make a Venn diagram. Have them use their knowledge and experience to infer what the park is like in the summer.

- For question two, remind students that context clues may appear either before or after the word.

- For the third item, encourage students to suggest thoughtful questions.

## Practicing the Skill

Have students read the directions and the Writer's Tip on page 170. Make sure students understand how to create a chart that organizes their information.

---

Name _____

★ Read about an exciting adventure through Yellowstone National Park. Then answer the questions that follow.

## Snowmobile Safari!

by W. E. Butterworth IV

Eagle Scout Peter Ivie gripped the snowmobile's passenger safety handles with all his strength. He leaned as the driver, Eagle Scout J.R. Fillmore, steered the machine into a snow-packed turn. The snowmobile's front skis found and followed an easy path.

"Go, go, go!" Peter encouraged, shouting to be heard over the engine and wind noises.

But just then, J.R. quickly throttled to idle. The snowmobile slid to a stop. Stepping onto the roadside—and into the boys' path—were a half-dozen bison.

J.R. and Peter looked at the mighty animals. One curious beast ambled toward their snowmobile. The boys turned to each other, exchanging wide-eyed expressions.

"Go, go, go!" both boys cried as J.R. turned the snowmobile in the opposite direction.

"We've run into a lot of wildlife," said Peter. "Well, not *run* into, but we've seen amazing animals."

"And scenery," J.R. added. "I've driven snowmobiles before, but never in such a beautiful wilderness area. I've never seen Yellowstone in winter. It's a whole different place."

Yellowstone National Park covers 2.2 million acres in Wyoming, Montana, and Idaho. Giant columns of hot water and steam, called "geysers," shoot up hundreds of feet. It's considered the world's greatest geyser area. And Old Faithful is Yellowstone's most famous geyser.

The Explorers were not sure if Old Faithful had been the trip highlight. Already the bison were getting bigger with each telling of the story!

Old Faithful geyser erupting in Yellowstone National Park

### ★ Reader's Response

1. The boys are impressed by the beauty of Yellowstone in the winter. How is it different from the park in the summer?

2. The writer says that one of the bison "ambled toward their snowmobile." What context clues helped you figure out what ambled means?

3. Imagine that you could speak with the boys in the story. What would you ask them? What would they say?

1. In the winter it is covered in snow.
2. The bison was "stepping...into the boy's path", toward their snowmobile.
3. Answers will vary.

LESSON 83: Connecting Reading and Writing
Comprehension—Compare and Contrast; Make Inferences

**169**

---

# UNIVERSAL ACCESS
# Meeting Individual Needs

### Visual Learners

Have students choose two states of the West they have visited or would like to visit. First, have students list similarities and differences. Then help students use the information in their lists to create a Venn diagram that they could use in an oral presentation to tell others about these states.

### Auditory Learners

Give a pair of students two photographs that lend themselves to comparing and contrasting, for example, a snow-covered field and a flower-filled meadow. Ask the students to sit across from each other and take turns calling out similarities and differences.

### Learners with Special Needs

Additional strategies for supporting learners with special needs can be found on page 139L.

Bison, elk, moose, deer, antelope, coyote—these are just some of the animals that the boys encountered on their snowmobile safari through Yellowstone National Park.

**Now it's your turn.** Choose two similar animals—such as an elk and a moose. Write a comparison-contrast essay showing how these two animals are similar, yet different. You can begin by making a chart to organize your essay. Include at least two of these words in your essay to show how your two animals are like and unlike each other.

| Similarities: | like | alike | both | also | similar |
| | in the same way | | | by comparison | |
| Differences: | unlike | different | although | while | |
| | but | yet | however | by contrast | |

Answers will vary.

_____

_____

_____

_____

_____

_____

_____

_____

**Writer's Tip**

You can organize your details **item-by-item**. This means presenting all the features of your first animal and then showing how your second animal is similar, yet different.

Bison in Yellowstone National Park

**Writer's Challenge**

Use "Snowmobile Safari!" for inspiration to create an observation chart of an animal you enjoy watching. Make a chart with two columns, labeled *Actions* and *Reasons*. First, observe and list the animal's actions. Then make inferences to guess why the animal responds in that way.

LESSON 83: Connecting Reading and Writing
Comprehension—Compare and Contrast; Make Inferences

## English-Language Learners/ESL

Select three students to read aloud "Snowmobile Safari!" as if it were a play. Have one student read the part of Peter Ivie, another student read the part of J.R. Fillmore, and a third student read the narrative portions of the text. Help students with challenging vocabulary and where possible show or draw pictures for further explanation. Pause every few paragraphs to discuss important ideas and details.

## Gifted Learners

Have students write a sequel to "Snowmobile Safari!" In the sequel, the two scouts return to Yellowstone National Park during the summer for a camping trip. Tell students to be creative as they describe the experience through a blend of narrative text and dialogue. Encourage students to do research to find details about Yellowstone to include in their writing.

# The Writing Process

Explain to students that on page 170 they will write an essay comparing and contrasting two similar animals. Read aloud the directions. Remind students to include at least two signal words in their essays.

**Prewrite** Encourage students to consider various pairs of animals, such as butterflies and moths, frogs and toads, alligators and crocodiles, crows and ravens. Guide students in creating a chart to organize their essay.

**Write** Tell students to look for subtle similarities and differences between the animals in addition to obvious ones. Remind them to use vivid words when describing these similarities and differences.

**Revise** Have students reread their work and make necessary changes. Encourage them to trade papers with a writing partner and offer each other useful suggestions for improving their essays.

**Proofread** Tell students to read their work slowly to check for mistakes in spelling, grammar, and punctuation.

**Publish** Have students copy their final drafts onto page 170 or a separate piece of paper. Ask volunteers to read their essays aloud.

**Computer Connection** Share the following tip with students who use a word processor to do their writing.

● The Find feature lets you quickly search for text. The Find and Replace feature lets you search for text and also change it automatically.

● With Find and Replace, you can substitute different letters, numbers, words, or symbols throughout a document. Be careful, though. Make sure that you really want every word replaced before using Find and Replace. It's a good idea to read through your document after using this feature.

**Portfolio** Suggest that students add their compare-contrast essays to their portfolios.

# Reviewing and Assessing
## Context Clues

### Objective

To review and assess context clues

## Warming Up

- Write the following paragraph on the board and ask a student to read it aloud.

  Can you imagine Los Angeles as a small farming community? That's what it was in 1781. Over time it grew, so that by its **bicentennial** year in 1981, it was the nation's second largest city.

- Ask students what context clues help them to determine the meaning of the word **bicentennial.** Challenge them to use their inferential skills to define the word **tricentennial**.

## Teaching the Lesson

- Review key points about context clues highlighted in the Helpful Hints from preceding lessons.

- Remind students that you can usually understand a general meaning of a word using context clues, and that the clues may appear either before or after an unfamiliar word. Point out to students that combining their prior experience with context clues is another useful strategy for determining word meanings.

- For the exercise on page 171, suggest that students try each possible answer to see which word's meaning best fits the surrounding context.

---

Name _____

Read each passage about northern California. Fill in the circle of the word that has the same meaning as that of the word in bold type. Use context clues to help you.

1. Sequoia trees, named for the Cherokee Sequoyah, grow in northern California. Some of the mature trees are more than 2,000 years old. These strong trees **thrive** in foggy areas where they can collect moisture on their needles.
   - ● do well
   - ○ weaken
   - ○ rot

2. Point Arena is a busy port town on the Pacific Coast. Fishing is its main source of income. The **wealthiest** merchants do well selling sea urchin, or *uni.* Japanese clients pay high prices for this salty treat.
   - ○ most unusual
   - ○ smartest
   - ● richest

3. Blue Lake might consider changing its name. The Mad River, which once fed Blue Lake, changed its direction. Now there is no more lake; instead, there is a squishy **bog** where the lake once was.
   - ● marsh
   - ○ beach
   - ○ forest

4. Have you been to the annual Slug Fest in Guerneville? This festival honors a local **inhabitant,** the banana slug. Banana slugs live in redwood forests. These slimy creatures look like bright yellow snails without shells.
   - ○ hero
   - ● resident
   - ○ festival

5. Some Native Americans honored Mount Shasta as a holy place. They believed that it was the home of the Great Spirit. To show respect, they never **ascended** higher than the tree line. This way, they would never disturb the Great Spirit's rest.
   - ○ sang
   - ○ looked
   - ● climbed

6. The llama is used as a pack animal for hikes in wilderness areas. Llamas are strong, calm, sure-footed, and do little to harm nature. They can nibble leaves and grasses as they **descend** a hiking trail. Northern California has several llama ranches.
   - ● go down
   - ○ go up
   - ○ move sideways

7. New York is called The Big Apple. Sacramento residents call their city The Big Tomato. This nickname **recalls** Sacramento's roots in farming.
   - ○ excites
   - ● brings back to mind
   - ○ removes

---

# UNIVERSAL ACCESS
## Meeting Individual Needs

### Visual Learners

In small groups have students create a wall chart summarizing what they have learned about context clues in this unit. Tell them to think about how to make the charts useful to students studying context clues for the first time. Encourage them to make their charts as eye-catching as possible.

### Auditory Learners

Write several challenging words from the preceding lessons on index cards. Have each student choose a card and give clues as to the word's meaning without directly stating either the word, or its meaning. Ask the other students to use context clues and inference to make "educated guesses" about the word.

### Learners with Special Needs

Additional strategies for supporting learners with special needs can be found on page 139L.

**REVIEW & ASSESS**

Read the passage. Fill in the circle of the answer to each question below.

Nellie Tayloe Ross
(1876–1977)

Wyoming has two nicknames—the Cowboy State and the Equality State. It is easy to guess how it got its first name. But do you know why it is called the Equality State?

In 1869, Wyoming wasn't a state yet. It was called the Wyoming Territory. Yet it was the first place in North America where women could legally vote. In those days, people had different ideas about women's rights than they do now. Back then, most men thought that women were unfit to vote. Yet Wyoming lawmakers did not agree with this **viewpoint.** They gave women full equality at the ballot box for local elections.

Wyoming became a state in 1890. Happily, its women kept their **suffrage.** Wyoming was a **model** for other Western states. Not long after, women **obtained** the right to vote in Utah, Colorado, Idaho, Montana, and Nevada. Wyoming is proud of its reputation as the Equality State. In fact, Nellie Tayloe Ross of Wyoming became the first female governor in the United States.

1. **Viewpoint** means ⚪ lesson ⚪ sight ⬤ position
2. **Suffrage** is the right to ⬤ vote ⚪ drive ⚪ marry
3. **Model** means ⬤ example ⚪ fashion ⚪ shape
4. **Obtained** means ⚪ fought ⚪ bought ⬤ got

Read the passage again. Circle the letter of the correct answer.

5. How did Wyoming lead other states?
   a. It had more cowboys.
   b. It had more people.
   c. Its land was richer.
   ⓓ Its women could vote.

6. The ballot box is where
   a. farmers bale hay.
   ⓑ people vote.
   c. judges live.
   d. the capital is.

**Extend & Apply**

You know what *divide* means in math. Yet you may not know what the *Continental Divide* is. Do research and then write an encyclopedia entry about the Continental Divide. Hint: You can see it in Yellowstone National Park.

# Reteaching Activities

## Group Mini-Lessons

Divide the class into five or more small groups. Assign each group one of the context-clues strategies studied in this unit: definition, series, compare, contrast, and inference. Have the groups use their own words and examples to prepare a mini-lesson to teach their strategy to the class. Encourage class participation as each group presents its lesson.

## Strategies in Action

Select several passages from sources such as encyclopedias, popular magazines, novels, and scientific articles. Make sure the passages contain several challenging words. Have students work independently to determine the meaning of the words from the context. Then, as a class, compare their conclusions and discuss which strategy or combination of strategies proved most useful.

## Assessing the Skill

**Check Up** The exercises on pages 171–172 will help students review the use of context clues. The exercises will also help you evaluate students' ability to determine word meaning from context.

On page 172, encourage students to reread all or part of the passage as needed in order to answer the questions.

**Observational Assessment** As students do the exercises, try to identify any areas of difficulty or confusion. Review your notes from preceding lessons in this unit to help you determine whether previously observed weaknesses have improved. Also watch for reading difficulties. Evaluate both individual student improvement and overall class progress.

**Student Skills Assessment** Record each student's progress in using context clues on the checklist on page 139H.

**Writing Conference** As you complete Unit 5, meet with students individually to discuss their writing progress. Review portfolio samples and other written work, offer encouragement, and make constructive suggestions. Remind students that by developing their ability to use context clues and inferential skills, they will become better readers and writers.

Group together students who need further instruction in context clues, and have them complete the *Reteaching Activities.* Turn to page 139C for alternative assessment methods.

# UNIT 6 PLANNING RESOURCE

# Dictionary and Thesaurus Skills; Vocabulary Skills

## Theme: Northwest and Hawaii

### STANDARDS

- ✪ Read grade-appropriate expository text and understand its content
- ✪ Develop and strengthen vocabulary
- ✪ Use dictionary and thesaurus skills
- ✪ Identify synonyms, antonyms, homonyms; and clipped, blended, and borrowed words
- ✪ Understand idioms and analogies

### OBJECTIVES

- ▶ To appreciate theme-related articles
- ▶ To use dictionary and thesaurus skills
- ▶ To identify and distinguish between synonyms, antonyms, homonyms; and clipped, blended, and borrowed words
- ▶ To identify idiomatic expressions
- ▶ To complete word analogies

### LESSONS

Lesson 85 . . . . Introduction to Dictionary and Thesaurus Skills; Vocabulary Skills

Lesson 86 . . . . ABC Order

Lesson 87 . . . . Guide Words 1

Lesson 88 . . . . Guide Words 2

Lesson 89 . . . . Entry Words 1

Lesson 90 . . . . Entry Words 2

Lesson 91 . . . . Pronunciation Key

Lesson 92 . . . . Accent Marks

Lesson 93 . . . . Connecting Spelling and Writing

Lesson 94 . . . . Connecting Reading and Writing—Comprehension: Compare and Contrast, Synthesize

Lesson 95 . . . . Review and Assess

Lesson 96 . . . . Synonyms

Lesson 97 . . . . Antonyms

Lesson 98 . . . . Homonyms

Lesson 99 . . . . Multiple-Meaning Words and Homographs

Lesson 100 . . . Thesaurus 1

Lesson 101 . . . Thesaurus 2

Lesson 102 . . . Review and Assess

Lesson 103 . . . Clipped Words and Blended Words

Lesson 104 . . . Borrowed Words

Lesson 105 . . . Eponyms and Collective Nouns

Lesson 106 . . . Connecting Spelling and Writing

Lesson 107 . . . Idiomatic Expressions

Lesson 108 . . . Word Analogies

Lesson 109 . . . Connecting Reading and Writing—Comprehension: Distinguish Between Fact and Fiction, Synthesize

Lesson 110 . . . Review and Assess

### Assessment Strategies

An overview of assessment strategies appears on page **173C**. It offers suggestions for using unit-specific assessment tools, including **Pretests** and **Post Tests** (pages **173D–173G**), the **Activity Master** (page **173M**), and the **Assessment Checklist** (page **173H**).

# Thematic Teaching

In Unit 6 students will learn about dictionary and thesaurus skills and vocabulary skills. Students practice these skills in the context of nonfiction selections and exercises related to the theme the *Northwest and Hawaii.*

Students begin their investigation of this theme by creating a word wall for the region. The resource list below provides titles of books, videos, and other materials that can help students focus their study of the regions. Many of the Teacher's Edition lessons in this unit open with theme-related poems or riddles. These "hooks" can spark students' interest in the theme and in the play of words.

# Curriculum Integration

### Writing

Students write sentences on page **178**, replace words on page **204**, write a story on page **214**, and write dialogues on pages **206** and **218**.

### Art

Students create a cartoon on page **200**.

### Science

Students research volcanoes on page **180** and look for clipped words on page **210**.

### Literature

Students discuss word connotations on page **196**.

### Social Studies

Students create a map on page **174**, list cities on page **176**, research democracy on page **182**, research places on page **186**, look up homographs on page **202**, and examine local terms on page **212**.

### Math

Students write math abbreviations on page **184** and devise proportions on page **220**.

### Drama

Students perform a skit on page **198**.

# Optional Learning Activities

### Meeting Individual Needs

Most of the Teacher's Edition lessons offer activities for students with distinct learning styles or particular intellectual or sensory strengths. The activities are labeled for learners with the following "styles": **Visual, Kinesthetic, Auditory, Logical, Musical,** and **Tactile.**

### Multicultural Connections

Students research the Inuit people on page **174** and look for accent marks on page **188.**

### Word Study Strategies

Pages **173I–173J** offer activities that give students practice with word study strategies. Students sort words, build words, and define words in context.

### Universal Access

Exercises tailored to meet the needs of **English-Language Learners** and **Gifted Learners** can be found in almost every Teacher's Edition lesson. Strategies designed to help **Learners with Special Needs,** such as students with Visual/Perceptual Deficits, are on page **173L.**

### Intervention

Page **173K** offers **Intervention Strategies** designed to help students performing below grade level understand the concepts taught in **Lessons 89, 91,** and **92.**

### Reteaching

Students hunt for respellings and match words on page **194**, identify word pairs and search for words on page **208,** and find missing words on page **224.**

### Technology

Page **173N** offers activities for students who enjoy working with technology. In addition, **Computer Connections**—tips designed for students who use a word processor—can be found on pages **190, 192, 216,** and **222.**

## RESOURCES

**Books**
Linnea, Sharon. *Princess Ka'iulani: Hope of a Nation, Heart of a People,* NY: Wm. B. Eerdmans Publishing, 1999.
Shepherd, Donna. *Alaska (America the Beautiful. Second Series),* NY: Children's Press, 1999.

**Videos**
*Alaska: Spirit of the Wild,* IMAX, 1996.
*Hawaii—Strangers in Paradise,* National Geographic Video, 1991.

**CDs**
*Hawaiian Steel Guitar Classics,* Folk Lyric, 1993.

# 6 ✓ ASSESSMENT

In Unit 6 students learn dictionary and thesaurus skills; synonyms, antonyms, and homonyms; word origins and development. To evaluate students' mastery of these skills, use any or all of the assessment methods suggested below.

## Pretests and Post Tests

The tests on pages **173D–173G** objectively assess how well students understand the use of dictionary and thesaurus skills; synonyms, antonyms, and homonyms; clipped, blended, and borrowed words; eponyms and collective nouns; idioms and analogies. These tests may be used at the beginning of the unit as an informal diagnostic tool or at the end of the unit as a more formal measure of students' progress.

## Observational Assessment

Each lesson includes a reminder to observe students as they apply lesson-specific skills. Check students' written work on a regular basis to see whether they continue to apply what they learn successfully.

## Using Technology

The Technology activities on page **173N** may also help evaluate students who language skills are best shown when using computers or audio/video equipment.

## Performance Assessment

Select six pairs of words from the lessons that have any of the following relationships: **synonyms, antonyms, homonyms, clipped, blended,** and **borrowed words**. Have students write each pair of words and label them as follows: **S** (synonyms), **A** (antonyms), **H,** homonyms, **CL** (clipped words), **BL** (blended words), or **BR** (borrowed words). Have students find a pair of words for each type from the lessons and label them accordingly.

## Portfolio Assessment

The portfolio icon in the lesson plans indicates an opportunity for students to add to the growing body of work in their portfolios. Each student's portfolio will be different and should contain pieces that the student feels good about. You may wish to give students additional opportunities to add to their portfolios.

### Rubric for Writing

| | Always | Sometimes | Never |
|---|---|---|---|
| Uses capitalization, punctuation, spelling, and grammar appropriately | | | |
| Creates a variety of sentences containing synonyms, antonyms, homonyms, idioms; clipped, blended, and borrowed words; eponyms and collective nouns | | | |
| Develops a clear dialogue to explain ideas and purpose | | | |
| Uses a dictionary and thesaurus | | | |
| Conveys purpose and meaning through writing | | | |

### Answer Key

**Page 173D**
1. attack, attic, author
2. comb, company, compile
3. (flō)
4. (hâr)
5. (īs)
6. mile
7. will not
8. pound
9. did not
10. antonym
11. synonym
12. homonym
13. 2
14. 1
15. borrowed
16. clipped
17. blended
18. cause/effect
19. antonyms
20. object/use

**Page 173E**
1. shed, sheep, shelf, shell
2. roar, roll, roof, rope
3. season, secret, seem, self
4. abbreviations
5. blended
6. antonyms
7. clipped
8. homonyms
9. contractions
10. borrowed
11. synonyms
12. brother
13. smile
14. tree
15. sweet
16. candy
17. crumb
18. honey
19. measure
20. sign
21. attic
22. liquid
23. ocean
24. buy
25. highlight

**Page 173F**
1. furious, furnace, further
2. order, organ, orphan
3. (grā′ ve)
4. (lĭt)
5. (sel)
6. let us
7. dozen
8. I am
9. feet
10. antonym
11. homonym
12. synonym
13. 2
14. 1
15. blended
16. borrowed
17. clipped
18. object/use
19. synonym
20. cause/effect

**Page 173G**
1. wife, wild, wind, wish
2. null, number, nurse, nut
3. trouble, trough, trousers, trout
4. abbreviations
5. synonyms
6. antonyms
7. contractions
8. borrowed
9. homonyms
10. clipped
11. blended
12. peace
13. piano
14. bottom
15. sing
16. fault
17. pledge
18. comic
19. nice
20. browse
21. flimsy
22. knight
23. rhyme
24. chute
25. review

Name _____

**Fill in the circle next to the column that is in ABC order.**

| 1. ○ attic ○ attack ○ author | 2. ○ compile ○ company ○ comb |
|---|---|
| author attic attic | comb compile company |
| attack author attack | company comb compile |

**Fill in the circle next to the correct respelling of the word in bold type.**

**3. flow**          **4. hair**         **5. ice**

○ (flo)   ○ (flô)   ○ (flō)     ○ (har)   ○ (hār)   ○ (hâr)     ○ (ise)   ○ (īc)   ○ (īs)

**Write the word(s) that each abbreviation or contraction stands for.**

**6. mi.** _____    **7. won't** _____    **8. lb.** _____    **9. didn't** _____

**Fill in the circle next to the term that identifies each word pair.**

| 10. awkward/graceful | ○ synonym | ○ antonym | ○ homonym |
|---|---|---|---|
| 11. name/title | ○ synonym | ○ antonym | ○ homonym |
| 12. throne/thrown | ○ synonym | ○ antonym | ○ homonym |

**Write the number of the definition that is used in each sentence.**

bark¹ outer covering of a tree; bark² sharp cry

**13.** My dog will **bark** if he hears the doorbell ring. _____

**14.** The **bark** on the old tree is dry and brittle. _____

**Fill in the circle next to the term that identifies each word.**

| 15. aloha | ○ clipped | ○ blended | ○ borrowed |
|---|---|---|---|
| 16. champ | ○ clipped | ○ blended | ○ borrowed |
| 17. moped | ○ clipped | ○ blended | ○ borrowed |

**Fill in the circle next to the choice that identifies each analogy.**

| 18. wash : clean :: fertilize : grow | ○ antonyms | ○ cause/effect | ○ object/use |
|---|---|---|---|
| 19. true : false :: cheery : gloomy | ○ antonyms | ○ cause/effect | ○ object/use |
| 20. stove : cook :: nose : breathe | ○ antonyms | ○ cause/effect | ○ object/use |

Possible score on Unit 6 Pretest 1 is 20. Score _____

Name _____

**Write the following words in ABC order.**

| | | | |
|---|---|---|
| **1.** sheep _____ | **2.** rope _____ | **3.** secret _____ |
| shell _____ | roof _____ | self _____ |
| shelf _____ | roll _____ | season _____ |
| shed _____ | roar _____ | seem _____ |

**Choose a word from the box to describe each word pair.**

| | | | |
|---|---|---|---|
| abbreviations | synonyms | clipped words | homonyms |
| blended words | antonyms | borrowed words | contractions |

**4.** in./ft. _____        **5.** smog/glare _____

**6.** dawn/sunset _____        **7.** tux/lab _____

**8.** groan/grown _____        **9.** can't/won't _____

**10.** noodle/coffee _____        **11.** error/mistake _____

**Write a word to complete each word analogy.**

**12. girl : sister :: boy :** _____        **13. sad : cry :: happy:** _____

**14. page : book :: branch :** _____        **15. right : wrong :: bitter :** _____

**Match each word from the box with its respelling.**

| | | | | |
|---|---|---|---|---|
| ocean | liquid | honey | sign | crumb |
| measure | buy | candy | attic | highlight |

**16.** (kan′ dē) _____        **17.** (krum) _____

**18.** (hun′ ē) _____        **19.** (mezh′ ər) _____

**20.** (sīn) _____        **21.** (at′ ik) _____

**22.** (lik′ wid) _____        **23.** (ō′ shən) _____

**24.** (bī) _____        **25.** (hī′ līt) _____

Possible score on Unit 6 Pretest 2 is 25. Score _____

Name _____

**Fill in the circle next to the column that is in ABC order.**

| 1. | ○ further | ○ furious | ○ furnace |
|---|---|---|---|
| | furious | furnace | furious |
| | furnace | further | furnace |

| 2. | ○ order | ○ orphan | ○ orphan |
|---|---|---|---|
| | organ | organ | order |
| | orphan | order | organ |

**Fill in the circle next to the correct respelling of the word in bold type.**

**3. gravy**
○ (gra ve') ○ (grā' vē) ○ (grā vē')

**4. light**
○ (līt) ○ (lit) ○ (līgt)

**5. cell**
○ (sēl) ○ (kel) ○ (sel)

**Write the word(s) that each abbreviation or contraction stands for.**

6. let's _____  7. doz. _____  8. I'm _____  9. ft. _____

**Fill in the circle next to the term that identifies each word pair.**

| 10. above/below | ○ synonym | ○ antonym | ○ homonym |
|---|---|---|---|
| 11. hall/haul | ○ synonym | ○ antonym | ○ homonym |
| 12. allow/permit | ○ synonym | ○ antonym | ○ homonym |

**Write the number of the definition that is used in each sentence.**

**fan**¹ a device used to circulate air; **fan**² a devoted supporter

13. Tom is a true **fan**; he came to every game. _____

14. Tom bought a **fan** to keep the living room cool. _____

**Fill in the circle next to the term that identifies each word.**

| 15. brunch | ○ clipped | ○ blended | ○ borrowed |
|---|---|---|---|
| 16. khaki | ○ clipped | ○ blended | ○ borrowed |
| 17. memo | ○ clipped | ○ blended | ○ borrowed |

**Fill in the circle next to the choice that identifies each analogy.**

| 18. ax : chop :: pen : write | ○ antonyms | ○ cause/effect | ○ object/use |
|---|---|---|---|
| 19. easy : simple :: hard : difficult | ○ synonyms | ○ cause/effect | ○ object/use |
| 20. heat : melt :: cold : freeze | ○ antonyms | ○ cause/effect | ○ object/use |

Possible score on Unit 6 Post Test 1 is 20. Score _____

Name _____

**Write the following words in ABC order.**

1. wish _____  2. nurse _____  3. trout _____

   wind _____     null _____     trough _____

   wife _____     nut _____     trousers _____

   wild _____     number _____     trouble _____

**Choose a word from the box to describe each word pair.**

| | | | |
|---|---|---|---|
| abbreviations | synonyms | clipped words | homonyms |
| blended words | antonyms | borrowed words | contractions |

4. mi./km. _____  5. try/attempt _____

6. early/late _____  7. shouldn't/we'll _____

8. banana/khaki _____  9. peace/piece _____

10. lab/memo _____  11. glimmer/motel _____

**Write a word to complete each word analogy.**

12. friend : enemy :: war : _____  13. finger : hand :: key: _____

14. right : left :: top : _____  15. story : read :: song : _____

**Match each word from the box with its respelling.**

| | | | | |
|---|---|---|---|---|
| review | browse | chute | pledge | nice |
| knight | flimsy | comic | fault | rhyme |

16. (fôlt) _____  17. (plej) _____

18. (kom' ik) _____  19. (nīs) _____

20. (brouz) _____  21. (flim' zē) _____

22. (nīt) _____  23. (rīm) _____

24. (shüt) _____  25. (ri vū') _____

Possible score on Unit 6 Post Test 2 is 25. Score _____

# UNIT 6 STUDENT PROGRESS CHECKLIST

Student Name ____________________

## UNIT SIX
## STUDENT SKILLS ASSESSMENT CHECKLIST

◪ Assessed ☒ Retaught ■ Mastered

- ❑ ABC Order
- ❑ Guide Words 1
- ❑ Guide Words 2
- ❑ Entry Words 1
- ❑ Entry Words 2
- ❑ Pronunciation Key
- ❑ Accent Marks
- ❑ Synonyms
- ❑ Antonyms
- ❑ Homonyms
- ❑ Multiple-Meaning Words and Homographs
- ❑ Thesaurus 1
- ❑ Thesaurus 2
- ❑ Blended and Clipped Words
- ❑ Borrowed Words
- ❑ Eponyms and Collective Nouns
- ❑ Idiomatic Expressions
- ❑ Word Analogies

## TEACHER COMMENTS

In Unit 6 students study dictionary and thesaurus skills: synonyms, antonyms, and homonyms; word origin and development: blended, clipped, and borrowed words; idioms and word analogies. To give students opportunities to master word study strategies, use any or all of the activities suggested below.

## Word Order

Circle the three entry words that would appear on the same dictionary page as the guide words. Then write the circled words in ABC order on the lines.

1. **hare/harvest**

   harden    harm    have    harsh    harp

   _____  _____  _____

2. **coverage/cozy**

   coward    crazy    covet    coyote    cover

   _____  _____  _____

3. **earring/eastward**

   easy    earth    easel    ease    ear

   _____  _____  _____

4. **shield/shingle**

   shimmer    shift    shirt    shiny    shine

   _____  _____  _____

5. **fin/finger**

   film    final    fingernail    finch    finesse

   _____  _____  _____

## Multiple Meanings

Circle the letter of the definition that fits the meaning of the word in bold type in each sentence.

1. I hope something different happens on this **routine** day.

   a. not special    b. usual procedure

   c. program performed regularly

2. Please **prop** the chair under the doorknob to keep the door shut.

   a. support    b. lean    c. stage item

3. The **composition** of cement includes lime and iron oxide.

   a. musical work    b. short story    c. make-up

4. Young children can **digest** picture books with simple words.

   a. written summary    b. understand

   c. body absorption of food

5. We hung the wire **mobile** from the ceiling.

   a. moveable    b. showing moods easily

   c. sculpture

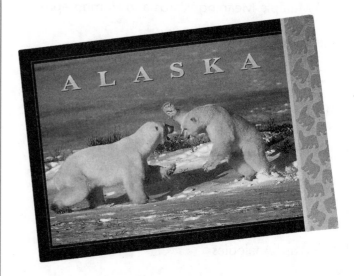

ALASKA

## Language Building

Use the words in the box to complete the sentences below.

| | | |
|---|---|---|
| lasso | flurry | garage |
| grad | camcorder | champ |

1. It is a blended word of **camera** and **recorder**.

   _____

2. It is a clipped word for **graduate.**

   _____

3. It is a French word for a **place to keep a car.**

   _____

4. It is a Spanish word for a **rope with a noose.**

   _____

5. It is a clipped word for **champion.**

   _____

6. It is a blended word of **flutter** and **hurry.**

   _____

## Meaningful Idioms

Write a word or phrase from the box that means the same as the underlined idiom in each sentence.

| | |
|---|---|
| something to complain about | keep still |
| common knowledge | worried |
| spoke quickly and at length | big trouble |

1. The speaker <u>talked a blue streak</u> while the audience yawned.

   _____

2. I was <u>on pins and needles</u> while I waited for the test results.

   _____

3. Dad has a <u>bone to pick</u> with whoever broke the window.

   _____

4. You are <u>in hot water</u> because you were late again this week.

   _____

5. <u>Hold your tongue</u> if you can't say something nice about your guest.

   _____

6. The movie star's life was <u>an open book.</u>

   _____

## Word Analogies

Write a word from the box to complete each analogy. Then circle how the words in the analogy are related.

| | | |
|---|---|---|
| dry | west | sweep |
| glad | plant | eat |

1. pen : write :: broom : _____

   **synonyms**    **antonyms**    **object/use**

2. joke: laugh :: hungry : _____

   **part/whole**    **synonyms**    **cause/effect**

3. north: south :: east : _____

   **antonyms**    **synonyms**    **part/whole**

4. page : book :: flower : _____

   **part/whole**    **object/use**    **cause/effect**

5. straw : sip :: towel : _____

   **cause/effect**    **antonyms**    **object/use**

6. unhappy : sad :: happy : _____

   **part/whole**    **antonyms**    **synonyms**

# INTERVENTION STRATEGIES

| **LESSONS** | **89** Entry Words 1 | **91** Pronunciation Key | **92** Accent Marks |
|---|---|---|---|
| **Problem** | Student has difficulty identifying the entry word in a word that contains a prefix and/or a suffix. | Student is confused by the symbols in the pronunciation key. | Student has difficulty selecting the appropriate word when the pronunciation differs by the accented syllable. |
| **Intervention Strategies** | • Remind the student that not all forms of words are listed as entry words in a dictionary.<br><br>• Encourage the student to recall the lessons in Unit 4 that explained prefixes and suffixes. Remind the student that he/she identified prefixes, roots, suffixes, and base words. Identifying an entry word in Lesson 89 is the same as identifying a base word in Unit 4.<br><br>• List the following words: **coldness, pardonable, sadden,** and **scroll-like.** Have the student identify each base word (entry word), then find each entry word in a dictionary. Have them read the definitions and note other forms of each entry word that are included. | • Make sure that the student understands that each symbol represents a different sound.<br><br>• Provide photocopies of a pronunciation key. Have the student suggest examples of words that include each sound.<br><br>• Then have him/her write two versions of each word beside the appropriate symbols—one using phonetic spelling and one using the actual spelling.<br><br>• Encourage the student to refer to this personal pronunciation key when necessary. | • Brainstorm with student a list of words that are spelled the same but are pronounced differently, also known as **heteronyms,** such as: **compact, content,** and **entrance.**<br><br>• Have the student list each word two times and use a dictionary to write the pronunciations for each word.<br><br>• Encourage the student to highlight the syllable that contains an accent mark, and is therefore "stressed."<br><br>• Have the student write the appropriate definition and a contextual sentence for each pronunciation.<br><br>• Encourage the student to repeat this activity when completing items 1-10 on page 188. |

*Hawaii*

**T**he following activities offer strategies for helping students with special needs to participate in selected exercises in Unit 6.

## Auditory/Oral Discrimination
### Pronunciation Key

Students who have difficulty detecting differences in sounds may find the activities that require using a pronunciation key to be troublesome. Creating "flash cards" that correspond to an audiocassette may provide assistance for these students.

- Write each sound symbol that is listed on page 186 on individual index cards. On the other side of the card, draw and label a picture of the word that contains the same sound. For example, one card may have the sound symbol **ôr** on one side of the card, and a labeled picture of **fork** is on the other side.

- Record the sounds and corresponding words to match the labeled index cards on an audiocassette to be used by the students.

- Encourage the students to review each side of the "flash cards." Then have them place the cards on a desk with the sound symbol in view. Have students take turns listening to the audiocassette that contains the corresponding picture words. When the student hears the word **fork** from the audiocassette, he or she should point the sound symbol **ôr.**

- When the audiocassette is complete and the cards have been matched, encourage the student to listen to the audiocassette again and write an additional word that contains the sound, for example: **ôr, horse.**

## Visual-Perceptual Deficits
### ABC Order

Students who experience letter-sequencing problems may have difficulties with the activities in lessons 86–88. Provide these students with "hands on" assistance for these activities.

- Laminate a horizontal copy of the alphabet for each student. Provide students with tissues and markers that can be easily wiped off the laminated alphabet strip.

- Encourage the students to use the markers and alphabet strips for the activity on page 175. First, have them find the letter **X** on the strip and circle it with the marker. Next, have them look at the letter that comes before the circled letter. Then have them write the answer **W** in the appropriate box. Finally, the student wipes off the strip with a tissue and continues with the activity.

## Conceptual Deficits
### Idiomatic Expressions

Students with conceptual deficits may have difficulty comprehending idiomatic expressions. Teaching idiomatic expressions in the same manner as teaching vocabulary may be beneficial for these students.

- List on the board the following sentences that contain idioms: *John **coughed up ten dollars** to buy the gift. Jen always gets **butterflies in her stomach** before a test. Brian has a large garden, he must **have a green thumb.***

- Encourage students to visualize each sentence. Invite them to pantomime their ideas about the literal meaning of the words in the idiomatic expression in each sentence or draw their ideas on the board or on a sheet of paper. Then discuss the sentences and their "true" meanings. Remind students that idiomatic expressions are words that do not use their literal meaning. Guide the students to visualize each sentence literally when completing the exercises on pages 217 and 218. Encourage them to pantomime or draw their ideas and then select the appropriate answer.

GAMES

| | | | | |
|---|---|---|---|---|
| Seward | Fairbanks | Tacoma | Springfield | Nome |
| Yakima | Seattle | Spokane | Honolulu | Hilo |
| Olympia | Eugene | Kapaa | Kamuela | Kailua |
| Salem | Medford | Juneau | Fort Yukon | Portland |

**Use an atlas to identify the cities that belong in each state. Then write the cities' names in ABC order in the correct state's outline.**

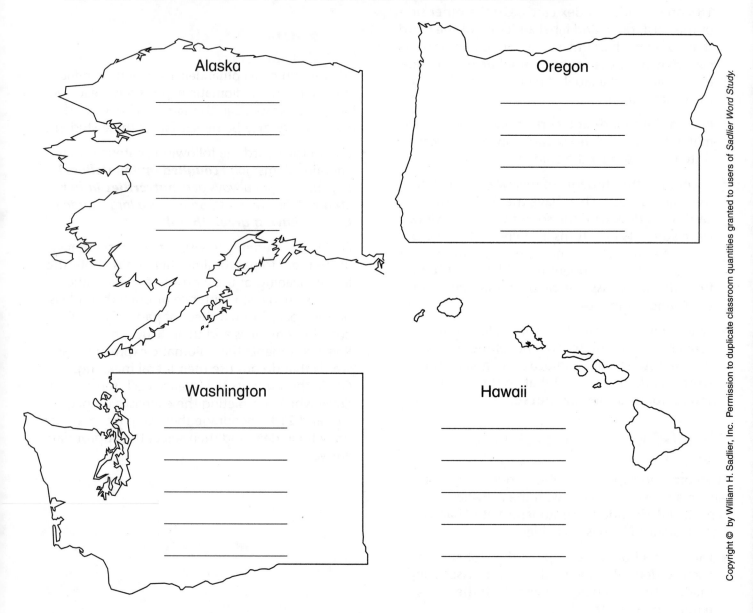

Alaska

Oregon

Washington

Hawaii

## Create a Hawaiian Dictionary

Invite students to use the Internet to research words and phrases in the Hawaiian language in order to create a Hawaiian dictionary.

- Brainstorm with students a list of common words that were borrowed from the Hawaiian language such as: **aloha, hula, lei, luau,** and **ukulele.**

- Encourage students to use the Internet to research other words in the Hawaiian language to include in the phrasebook. They may want to use search engines to find web site matches about the Hawaiian language.

- Remind students that the Hawaiian alphabet contains only 12 letters—**a, e, i, o, u, h, k, l, m, n, p,** and **w**. Divide students into small groups with each group focusing on finding words for two to three specific letters.

- Have each student note the word, its sound respelling, and the definition. Remind students to include accent marks in the sound respelling to aid in pronunciation. For example, **lei (lā)—a wreath of flowers or leaves worn around the neck**

- Then have the members of each group combine their words, pronunciations, and definitions alphabetically. Next, the groups will combine their lists together alphabetically. Finally, guide students to enter their Hawaiian words, pronunciations, and definitions using a word processing program on the computer.

- Have students create a pronunciation key with example words to aid in pronouncing the Hawaiian words and a cover for the dictionary.

## Create a "How-to" Video

Invite students to create a video that demonstrates how to make an Alaskan totem pole.

- Have students research the origins of totem pole carving that was popular among the native people of southeastern Alaska. Have them note the significance of animals that were depicted in the carvings. Students may want to use reference books about Alaska and Alaskan totem poles or the Internet to aid them in their research.

- Provide students will art materials such as: cardboard boxes, cardboard tubes (from paper towels or wrapping paper), construction paper, papier-maché, paint, markers, scissors, glue, feathers, etc. Have them develop their own way of creating a miniature Alaskan totem pole using the materials provided.

- Encourage students to list the steps involved in creating their finished product. Have them include words with multiple meanings, synonyms, pronunciations of Alaskan words, or analogies in their presentation. Remind students that the totem poles will be presented in a "How-to" format, so their instructions must be clear and concise.

- Volunteers can assist with the video camera. Show the finished video to the class and/or share the video with another class.

## Create a Northwestern Postcard

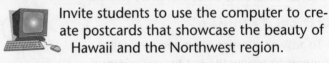

Invite students to use the computer to create postcards that showcase the beauty of Hawaii and the Northwest region.

- Have students clip images of the natural beauty of Hawaii, Oregon, Washington, and Alaska. These images can come from magazines, photos from the Internet, other postcards, etc.

- Have students create a postcard with an image on one side and an area for writing on the other. The images can be scanned on the computer or downloaded and printed.

- Have students write messages to another class member on the postcards that describe their "vacation" to the area pictured on their postcard. Their messages should include skills that were taught in Unit 6.

- Have students read "their mail" to the class, and have them identify the skills from Unit 6 in the messages. Display the postcards in the classroom.

## Introduction to
## Dictionary and Thesaurus Skills; Vocabulary Skills

### Objectives

- **To enjoy a nonfiction piece about Alaska**
- **To develop dictionary and thesaurus skills**
- **To learn about synonyms, antonyms, homonyms, and multiple-meaning words; blended, clipped, and borrowed words; eponyms and collective nouns; idioms and analogies**

### Starting with Literature

- Read "The Great Land" to the class. List words from the selection and their synonyms and antonyms.

| last | final | first |
| huge | large | small |
| gorgeous | beautiful | ugly |

- Ask students how these words are related.

### Critical Thinking

- To answer questions one and two, tell students to review the last two paragraphs.
- For question three, encourage students to use their imagination.

### Introducing the Skill

Explain that words with similar meanings, such as **last/final, gorgeous/beautiful,** and **huge/large** are called synonyms. Words with opposite meanings, such as **last/first, huge/small, gorgeous/ugly** are called antonyms. Tell students that they will learn about these and other word study strategies in this unit.

### Practicing the Skill

Have students work in small groups to list pairs of synonyms and antonyms.

173

# "The Great Land"

Alaska and Hawaii were the last two United States territories to become states. Alaska became the forty-ninth state in 1959. A year later, Hawaii became the fiftieth state. In this unit, you will discover the natural beauty of our country's Pacific Northwest. You will also learn about Alaska and Hawaii, our nation's two youngest states.

The native people of Alaska were right when they called it *Alyeska,* which means "the great land." Alaska is twice the size of Texas. Within its 586,400 acres of wilderness there are 3 million lakes and 1,800 islands. There are 100,000 glaciers, 9 national parks, and 2 national forests.

The United States bought Alaska from Russia in 1867 for just two cents an acre. At the time, many thought that Secretary of State William Seward had made a bad deal. In fact, the Alaska purchase was called "Seward's Folly." Yet with this deal, the country gained a gorgeous frontier land, rich in oil, gold, fish, and timber.

Today, Alaska remains a feast for the eyes. Look up and you can see Mount McKinley, the tallest peak in North America. Look up even higher, to the night sky. There you may see dancing ribbons of red, white, blue, and green. These are the northern lights.

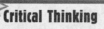

### ? Critical Thinking

1. **How is Alaska a feast for the eyes?**
2. **Why was Seward's purchase called "Seward's Folly"? Was it foolish? Explain.**
3. **Close your eyes. What do you see when you think of Alaska? Draw a picture and write a caption.**

1. Alaska contains Mount McKinley, the tallest peak in North America, as well as the beautiful northern lights.
2. Seward's purchase was called "Seward's Folly" because in 1897 people thought he had paid too much.
3. Answers will vary.

LESSON 85: Introduction to Dictionary and Thesaurus Skills; Synonyms, Antonyms, and Homonyms; Word Origin and Language Development

173

## Theme Activity

**WORD WALL FOR THE NORTHWEST AND HAWAII**

Create a large wall chart divided into four sections, each one for a different state: **Oregon, Washington, Hawaii, Alaska.** Have students add to each section of the chart, index cards containing words that relate to that state. For example, **huge** would apply to Alaska, **island** would relate to Hawaii.

As students work through the unit, have them develop their index cards into dictionary entries. That is, have them add syllable breaks and phonetic respellings, definitions and parts-of-speech labels, word histories, and example sentences. When applicable, also have them include synonyms and antonyms. Then have students arrange the cards in each section alphabetically.

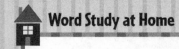
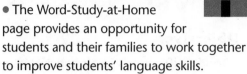
Visit us at
www.sadlier-oxford.com

## Dear Family,

Your child has begun Unit 6. Lessons in this unit focus on dictionary and thesaurus skills; on synonyms, antonyms, and homonyms; on clipped, blended, and borrowed words; on eponyms and collective nouns; on idioms and analogies. The theme of this unit is the *Pacific Northwest, Alaska, and Hawaii*, including their people and history.

**Synonyms** are words that have the same or nearly the same meaning (**small** and **tiny**).

**Antonyms** are words that have opposite meanings (**small** and **large**).

**Homonyms** are words that sound the same but have a different meaning and a different spelling (**wood** and **would**).

**Word analogies** show how words and ideas are related. (**High** is to **low** as **big** is to **small**.)

## Family Focus

• Read the nonfiction selection on page 173 and talk about it together. Have you ever been to Alaska? Would you like to visit the "Last Frontier"? If so, what would you want to see and do there?

• Obtain travel brochures for destinations in Hawaii and the Northwest, including Alaska. Plan a real or an imagined family trip.

• Keep a dictionary at hand. Make a list of the words you look up as you discover more about the people, history, and natural wonders of the places in this unit.

### LINKS TO LEARNING

**Web Sites**
www.state.ak.us
www.everythingalaska.com

**Videos**
*Denali: Alaska's Great Wilderness,* part of *The Living Edens* series, PBS Home Video.

*Explore Alaska: The Last Frontier,* National Geographic Video, 3 videos.

*Mount St. Helen's Fury,* TLC Video.

**Literature**
*A Day in the Life of Hawaii* by David Cohen and Rick Smolan, 1984.

*My Denali* by Kimberly Coral, ©1995.

LESSON 85: Introduction to Dictionary and Thesaurus Skills; Synonyms, Antonyms, and Homonyms; Word Origin and Language Development—Word Study at Home

---

• The Word-Study-at-Home page provides an opportunity for students and their families to work together to improve students' language skills.

• On the Word-Study-at-Home page for Unit 6, students and their families will find activities that relate to the theme the *Northwest and Hawaii* and focus on dictionary and vocabulary skills.

• Have students remove page 174 from their books. Direct them to take the page home so that their families may share in the Word-Study-at-Home activities.

• Invite students to share their thoughts about what they would like to see and do in Alaska. You may also want to have students do research to learn more about Alaska and its people, and then share their findings with the class. Students are likely to discover that their image of Alaska is rather different from the reality.

• As students gather their travel brochures, encourage them to make comparisons between different destinations. Ask questions such as *How would you dress?* and *How would you travel there?*

## Multicultural Connection

The Inuit people are native to northern North America, living in parts of Alaska, Canada, and Greenland. (Although the term **Eskimo** is still commonly used in Alaska, **Inuit** is the preferred name.) Inuit make up more than 8 percent of Alaska's population. Have students research the Inuit people to learn more about their customs, culture, and way of life. Encourage students to find out how Inuit ways have changed in recent decades.

## Social Studies Link

Divide the class into four groups. Assign each group one of the states linked to this unit: Oregon, Washington, Alaska, and Hawaii. Have students in each group work together to create a large resources map of their state, including symbols and a map key. Display maps around the classroom. Extend the activity by having students add a time line beneath the map depicting important events in their state's history.

### Theme-Related Resources
**Books**

*Alaska*, by Art Wolfe and Nick Jans, Sasquatch Books, 2000

*Ghost Canoe*, by Will Hobbs, William Morrow & Company, 1997 (also available as an audiocassette from Bantam Books)

*Woodsong* by Gary Paulsen, Puffin, 1991

### Videos

*AAA Travel Video Series: Pacific Northwest*, AAA Travel Video Series, 1991

# ABC Order

## Objectives

- **To identify words in alphabetical order**
- **To alphabetize words using the second and third letters**

## Warming Up

- On the board, write the names of these Alaskan cities and read them aloud.

  **Fairbanks   Barrow   Nome**

  **Anchorage   Valdez   Sitka**

- Ask a volunteer to circle the first letter of each city's name. Then have him or her list the cities in alphabetical order. You may wish to extend the lesson by working with students to locate the cities on a map.

## Teaching the Lesson

- Remind students that words in a dictionary are arranged in alphabetical order. Use a dictionary with students to verify that the cities in the *Warming-Up* exercise are listed correctly.

- Have a student explain how words are arranged alphabetically when their first letters are the same. For example, in what order would you find **Anchorage, Atka,** and **Amchitka** listed in a dictionary? **(Amchitka, Anchorage, Atka)**

- Discuss what happens when the first two letters of words are the same. Write these cities' names on the board: **Walla Walla, Wahiawa,** and **Waipahu.** Have students put the words in alphabetical order, using the third letter in each word as their guide.

- Read aloud the Helpful Hint on page 175 and discuss the examples with students.

---

Name _____

### Helpful Hint

Words in a dictionary are arranged in **ABC order,** or **alphabetical order.** To put words in ABC order, look at the first letter of each word. If the first letter is the same in each word, look at the next letter or letters to decide the ABC order of the words.

Read the names of these cities in Alaska, Hawaii, Washington, and Oregon. The names are arranged in ABC order.

Honolulu  Juneau  Pearl City  Portland  Salem  Seattle  Sitka  Tacoma

**Write each group of words in ABC order.**

1. admire — acre
   advance — admire
   artist — advance
   acre — arid
   arid — artist

2. rhythm — reunion
   reunion — rhyme
   sweatshirt — rhythm
   suitable — suitable
   rhyme — sweatshirt

**Figure out this riddle. In each box, write the letter of the alphabet that comes *before* the letter given in the box. Then write the riddle's question and answer on the lines below. The first letter is given.**

| W | H | A | T | | D | O | | P | E | O | P | L | E | | D | O |
|---|---|---|---|---|---|---|---|---|---|---|---|---|---|---|---|---|
| X | I | B | U | | E | P | | Q | F | P | Q | M | F | | E | P |

| I | N | | O | R | E | G | O | N | | W | H | E | N | | I | T |
|---|---|---|---|---|---|---|---|---|---|---|---|---|---|---|---|---|
| J | O | | P | S | F | H | P | O | | X | I | F | O | | J | U |

| R | A | I | N | S | ? | | L | E | T | | I | T | | R | A | I | N |
|---|---|---|---|---|---|---|---|---|---|---|---|---|---|---|---|---|---|
| S | B | J | O | T | | | M | F | U | | J | U | | S | B | J | O |

**Question:** __What do people in Oregon do when it rains?__

**Answer:** _____ Let it rain. _____

### CHALLENGE

Teresa tasted many green grapes is a sentence with words in *reverse* **ABC order.** Create a similar sentence of your own. Make it as long as you can.

LESSON 86: ABC Order   **175**

---

## UNIVERSAL ACCESS
# Meeting Individual Needs

### Tactile Learners

Have students work in pairs. Give each pair a set of letter tiles or magnetic letters to spell and alphabetize groups of words. Include word groups that require students to refer to second and third letters. Students who need support may wish to remove or separate initial letters until they come to a letter that is different.

### Visual Learners

Direct students to write their first names on the board, listing them in random groups of four or five. Then have students rearrange each group of names into alphabetical order. Next, have the class combine two groups, and arrange the names alphabetically. Continue in this way until students have created an alphabetized master list of all the students' names.

**Write each group of words in ABC order.**

1.  ingredient    _illustrate_
    indefinite    _indefinite_
    illustrate    _ingredient_
    kennel    _kennel_
    kernel    _kernel_

2.  distort    _discourage_
    discourage    _distort_
    divine    _diver_
    diver    _divine_
    dodge    _dodge_

3.  warp    _wage_
    wary    _wanderer_
    wanderer    _warp_
    wage    _warrior_
    warrior    _wary_

4.  past    _outcry_
    overcoat    _overcoat_
    password    _partial_
    partial    _password_
    outcry    _past_

**All of these towns are in Alaska. Write their names in ABC order.**

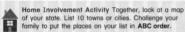

| Kasigluk | Kwethluk | Kotzebue | Kiana | Kipnuk | Togiak |
| King Salmon | Kenai | Ketchikan | King Cove | Kasilof |
| Kotlik | Kodiak | Nulato | Kiawok | Hoonah |

5.  _Hoonah_
6.  _Kasigluk_
7.  _Kasilof_
8.  _Kenai_
9.  _Ketchikan_
10. _Kiana_
11. _Kiawok_
12. _King Cove_
13. _King Salmon_
14. _Kipnuk_
15. _Kodiak_
16. _Kotlik_
17. _Kotzebue_
18. _Kwethluk_
19. _Nulato_
20. _Togiak_

**176**    LESSON 86: ABC Order

**Home Involvement Activity** Together, look at a map of your state. List 10 towns or cities. Challenge your family to put the places on your list in **ABC order.**

---

## Practicing the Skill

● Read and discuss the directions for pages 175 and 176. Be sure students understand that for the second exercise on page 175 they should write the preceding letters of the alphabet.

● For the exercises requiring students to alphabetize words, suggest that students cross out matching letters one by one until they come to a different letter.

## Curriculum Connections

### Spelling Link

Read aloud the following sentences. Have students spell each pair of words in bold type and write the words on the board. Then have students tell which word in the pair comes first in alphabetical order.

> Sarah's family moved from **Salem,** Oregon to **Seattle,** Washington.
>
> Which way would you travel to get from **Nome** to **Nulato?**
>
> How long does it take to drive from **Kotlik** to **Kodiak?**
>
> Jason would rather live in **Honolulu** than **Hoonah.**
>
> **Kenai** is northwest of **Ketchikan.**
>
> We drove through **King Salmon** and **King Cove.**

### Social Studies Link

Display a map of the Pacific Northwest. Have students list the names of six or seven cities in Oregon. Then have students rewrite the names in alphabetical order. Repeat the activity with cities in Washington, Alaska, and Hawaii.

### Observational Assessment

*Note whether students know alphabetical order and can alphabetize words to the third letter.*

---

### English-Language Learners/ESL

Ask students to list names of objects they see in the classroom. Then help them follow the guidelines in this lesson to rearrange the words on their list in alphabetical order. Repeat the activity using other lists that students create, such as names of foods, animals, or sports.

### Gifted Learners

Have students work in groups to list the fifty states that make up our country. Then challenge the groups to put their lists in alphabetical order. The first group to list the states in the correct order wins.

### Learners with Special Needs

Additional strategies for supporting learners with special needs can be found on page 173L.

# Guide Words 1

## Objectives

- **To identify guide words**
- **To use guide words to locate entry words in a dictionary**

## Warming Up

- Write this rhyme on the board and read it aloud with students.

  On every dictionary page
  Are two words that set the stage.
  They are the first and last entries
  Of words arranged by ABC's.

- Tell students that this lesson focuses on dictionary guide words and how to use them to locate other words in a dictionary.

## Teaching the Lesson

- Tell students that the words found in a dictionary are called entry words. Remind them that entry words are arranged in alphabetical order.

- Explain that each dictionary page is headed by the first and last entry words found on the page. These words are the guide words. Readers use the guide words to determine whether the entry word they seek would be found on a particular page.

- Write sample pairs of guide words on the board. Have students use their dictionaries to list five words that might appear on the pages headed by each pair of guide words.

---

Name _____

> **Helpful Hint**
>
> Two **guide words** appear at the top of every dictionary page. They show the first and last **entry words** given on that page. The other words on the dictionary page appear in alphabetical order between those two guide words.

Narwhals

**Read the guide words in bold type. Cross out two words on the list that would *not* be on the same dictionary page as the guide words. Then write the three other words in ABC order.**

**1  nap / natural**
narwhal
~~nautical~~
napkin
nation
~~nameless~~

napkin
narwhal
nation

**2  praise / precise**
prank
~~prince~~
prance
present
prayer

prance
prank
prayer

**3  shack / shake**
~~shaky~~
shag
shaft
~~shark~~
shadow

shadow
shaft
shag

**4  current / curve**
cursor
curry
~~currency~~
~~cushion~~
curtain

curry
cursor
curtain

**5  bristle / broaden**
~~brood~~
broach
~~broadtail~~
brittle
broad

brittle
broach
broad

> **WORK TOGETHER**
>
> Choose a partner. Ask each other riddles, such as: *I am a word found on a page with the guide words* **honk / hope**. *I am the sound that an owl makes. What am I?* Check your answer in a dictionary.

---

# UNIVERSAL ACCESS
## Meeting Individual Needs

### Visual Learners

Display pairs of guide words on a bulletin board. On index cards, print words that would appear on dictionary pages showing the guide words displayed. Make two cards for each student. Have students post their cards under the matching guide words. When all the words have been posted, have students alphabetize each set.

### Kinesthetic Learners

Write pairs of guide words on colored cards. On white cards, write entry words that fall between the guide words. There should be only one entry word per guide-word pair. Mix the cards and place them face down. Have students take turns trying to match entry words with guide words. Play until all cards have been matched.

☆ Write each word from the box under the correct guide words below.

| shift | shallow | serve | serious |
| shimmer | shark | shatter | sesame | shield |

| 1 series/session | 2 shale/shawl | 3 shell/shine |
|---|---|---|
| serious | shallow | shield |
| serve | shark | shift |
| sesame | shatter | shimmer |

☆ Read each sentence. Underline the word that would appear in a dictionary between the two guide words given at the left.

frenzy/friend    4. Salmon are born in <u>fresh</u> water and then find their way to the ocean to grow.

saline/samba    5. Years later, mature <u>salmon</u> swim upstream to get back to their birthplace.

news/nibble    6. There, they spawn to begin the <u>next</u> new generation.

fire/five    7. A few dams along natural salmon runs have blocked the <u>fishways</u>.

button/byway    8. One solution is to build a "fish ladder" to help salmon <u>bypass</u> the dams.

laundry/lead    9. A fish ladder is a series of pools in a step-by-step <u>layout</u>.

omit/ooze    10. The salmon can leap from <u>one</u> pool to the next in order to get over the dam.

tinsel/toad    11. Eddies provide rest areas for the <u>tired</u> fish.

Fish ladder

 Home Involvement Activity How many pages does your dictionary have? How many guide words? About how many entry words are there on a page? Do the math together. Use estimation.

---

● Read aloud the directions for page 177 and complete the first item with students.

● Read aloud and discuss the directions for the exercises on page 178. For items 4–10, explain that only one word in the sentence would be found between the guide words.

## Curriculum Connections

### Spelling Link

● Have students write the following lists of words as you read them aloud.

| prince | curtain | shaft |
| prank | cursor | shag |
| prance | currency | shaky |
| prayer | curry | shadow |
| present | cushion | shark |

● Ask students to rearrange each list in alphabetical order.

● Once students have alphabetized the words, have them circle the two words in each list that could serve as guide words.

### Writing Link

Some of the words that appear on pages 177–178 are likely to be new to students, such as **narwhal**, **curry**, **shale**, and **byway**. Have students look up the meaning of any unfamiliar words in a dictionary, using guide words to help them find the entries. Then have them write an original sentence for each word.

## Observational Assessment

*Check to see that students understand how to use guide words to find word entries in a dictionary.*

---

### English-Language Learners/ESL

Display a dictionary page. Point out the guide words at the top of the page, the same words as entry words, and the other entry words arranged in alphabetical order. Have students identify these same features on another page. Then write words on the board and help students use guide words to find the words in the dictionary.

### Gifted Learners

Challenge students to open to any page in the dictionary and write either a short poem or a tongue twister using the two guide words at the top of the page. Ask volunteers to share their work with the class.

### Learners with Special Needs

Additional strategies for supporting learners with special needs can be found on page 173L.

# Guide Words 2

## Objectives

- **To use a dictionary by dividing it into three parts**
- **To determine whether an entry word would be found in the beginning, middle, or end of a dictionary**
- **To identify the guide words that can help locate an entry word**

## Warming Up

- Write this sentence on the board, and have a student read it aloud:

  Three of Washington's main cities are **Olympia**, **Seattle**, and **Bellevue**.

- Have students visualize a dictionary split into three parts: the beginning, the middle, and the end. Ask in which part the name of each city would appear.

- Explain that thinking of the dictionary as having three parts can help students locate words quickly.

## Teaching the Lesson

- Explain that the dictionary may be divided into three parts as follows:

  Beginning:   letters **A–I**
  Middle:      letters **J–Q**
  End:         letters **R–Z**

- Make a chart on the board, using the three parts of the dictionary as headings. Say words such as **brilliance**, **occupy**, and **transparent** and have students tell whether each word is located in the beginning, middle, or end of the dictionary. List the words in the chart.

- Have students look up the words in a dictionary by opening to the appropriate part of the dictionary.

---

Name _____

> **Helpful Hint**
>
> Think of the dictionary as having three parts.
>
> The words in the **beginning** part start with the letters A–I.
> The words in the **middle** part start with the letters J–Q.
> The words in the **end** part start with the letters R–Z.
>
> Turn to the beginning, the middle, or the end of the dictionary to locate words quickly.

Aerial view of Crater Lake

 Each sentence below has a word in bold type. Write *beginning*, *middle*, or *end* to tell in which part of the dictionary you would find that word.

1. Crater Lake in Oregon is the deepest **lake** in the country.          middle

2. It was formed about 7,700 years ago in a violent **volcanic** eruption.          end

3. The top 5,000 **feet** of what was once Mount Mazama collapsed.          beginning

4. Lava flow formed a sealed-off bowl called a **caldera**.          beginning

5. Rain and melted **snow** eventually filled the deep bowl, forming the lake.          end

Sort the words about Crater Lake according to the part of the dictionary in which you would find them. Write each word in the correct column below.

> peak   lava   depth   ridge   crater   volcano   plateau   eruption   summit

| 6 **Beginning: A–I** | 7 **Middle: J–Q** | 8 **End: R–Z** |
|---|---|---|
| crater | lava | ridge |
| depth | peak | summit |
| eruption | plateau | volcano |

 **CHALLENGE**

Read the first activity again. Find another word in each sentence that would appear in the same part of the dictionary as that of the word in bold type.

---

# UNIVERSAL ACCESS
## Meeting Individual Needs

### Logical Learners

Have students read articles in an encyclopedia about the Pacific Northwest, Alaska, and Hawaii. Ask them to list unfamiliar words, look them up in a dictionary, and write down their meanings. Tell students to open to the appropriate part of the dictionary and use guide words to help locate the words.

### Visual Learners

Write these words on the board: **volcanic, depth, lava, scenery, exhibit, kilometer, university, dignified, plateau, eruption.** Say each word aloud, and have students find it in a dictionary as quickly as they can. Stress that students should open to the appropriate part of the dictionary and then use guide words to help them locate the word. Discuss the definition of each word.

180

Write *Beginning, Middle,* or *End* to tell in which part of the dictionary you would find each numbered word. Use A–I for the beginning part, J–Q for the middle part, or R–Z for the end part. Then underline the pair of guide words that would be on the same page as that of the numbered word.

1. exhibit — Beginning
   exhibitor/exotic | <u>exempt/exist</u> | excite/exhaust

2. settlement — End
   self/seminar | set/shade | <u>slug/smear</u>

3. scenery — End
   school/schwa | <u>scare/scavenger</u> | scene/scholar

4. dignified — Beginning
   dignity/dime | <u>diner/diorama</u> | digital/dilute

5. university — End
   unity/unkindly | union/universe | <u>unique/universal</u>

6. kilometer — Middle
   kick/kiln | <u>kidney/kimono</u> | key/kilogram

7. mountain — Middle
   motor/mourn | <u>mouth/Mozart</u> | motel/mound

8. summit — End
   sultan/summarize | <u>summary/sun</u> | sunburn/super

9. climb — Beginning
   climber/clock | <u>clever/cliff</u> | click/cling

 Read the words in the box. Imagine that they are on one page of a dictionary and that two of them are guide words. Which would be the first guide word? Which would be the second?

> lanyard land lanky landscape language

10. First guide word — land
11. Second guide word — lanyard

Climber near top of Mount Hood, Oregon

 **Home Involvement Activity** Do a simple dictionary study. Which letter has the greatest number of entry words? The fewest? First, take a guess. Then find out together. Did anyone guess correctly?

180    LESSON 88: Guide Words 2

---

## Practicing the Skill

● Read the directions for page 179. You may wish to extend the activities on this page by discussing the definition of words such as **summit** and **caldera**.

● Read and discuss the directions for page 180. Encourage students to ask questions if they are uncertain how to proceed.

## Curriculum Connections

### Spelling Link

Read aloud the sentences below. Have students spell the words in bold and write them on the board. Ask students to say whether each word would be found in the beginning, middle, or end of a dictionary.

> The **peak** of the **mountain** was only one **kilometer** above us.
>
> From the mountain **summit**, we looked down into the **crater**.
>
> We **climbed** to a **settlement** that was on a **plateau**.
>
> The museum had a beautiful **exhibit** of the surrounding **scenery**.

### Science Link

A number of words in this lesson relate to volcanoes, including **volcanic, caldera, lava,** and **eruption.** Have students research and write brief reports about volcanoes. Assign a variety of topics, such as the causes of eruptions, famous volcanoes, and notable eruptions of the past. Encourage students to use words from the lesson, checking their definitions in a dictionary as needed. Have volunteers share their reports with the class.

## Observational Assessment

*Check to see that students open to the correct part of the dictionary when looking up words.*

---

### English-Language Learners/ESL

Display on the board these three parts of a dictionary:

**A–I (beginning)  J–Q (middle)  R–Z (end)**

Have students list all the letters of the alphabet that would appear in each part. Then write simple words on the board, such as **cat** and **up.** Say the words aloud and help students find them in the dictionary.

### Gifted Learners

Ask students to debate how best to divide the dictionary. They can favor three parts (thirds), two parts (halves), or four parts (quarters). Encourage students to develop reasoned, specific arguments for their viewpoints.

### Learners with Special Needs

Additional strategies for supporting learners with special needs can be found on page 173L.

# Entry Words 1

## Objectives

- To look up the correct base word to find the meaning of another word
- To match entry words with context clues
- To use entry words in sentences

## Warming Up

- Write this rhyme on the board, and ask a volunteer to read it aloud.

  Dictionaries list their words,
  Arranged from **A** to **Z**.
  Ones in **bold** are **entry words**—
  The info's the **entry**.

- Ask a volunteer to explain what entry words are. (the words that appear in bold type in a dictionary)

## Teaching the Lesson

- Read aloud the Helpful Hints on page 181. Review each term discussed and ask students for examples of each.

- Write several entry words on the board. Help students suggest related forms of each that would not appear as separate entries. For example, the entry word **graceful** would include meanings for the words **gracefully** and **gracefulness**.

- Ask why dictionaries do not list every form of every word separately. Discuss how doing so would make a dictionary too long, repetitious, and cumbersome.

---

Name _____

Surfer in Hawaii

### Helpful Hints

Words given in a dictionary are called **entry words**. Entry words appear in bold type in **ABC order**. The information about an entry word (its syllables, pronunciation, part of speech, definition, word history, and other forms of the word) is called the **entry**.

Many words that have **endings**, **prefixes**, or **suffixes** will not appear as separate entry words. You need to figure out the **base word** to know which entry word to look up.

surfer → **surf**      greatness → **great**
cleverly → **clever**   unshaken → **shake**

 Read each word below. Write the entry word you would look up in the dictionary in order to find the word. Use a dictionary to help you.

1. cleverness — clever
2. generously — generous
3. countries — country
4. gliding — glide
5. clearer — clear
6. forceful — force
7. independent — independent
8. sprains — sprain
9. nonhuman — human
10. sharpness — sharp
11. reappear — appear
12. carpenter — carpenter
13. fulfillment — fulfill
14. nicest — nice
15. northern — north
16. silliness — silly
17. debated — debate
18. forgave — forgive
19. carelessness — careless
20. unidentified — identify

### CHALLENGE

Write the **entry word** you would look up in the dictionary in order to find each of these words:

gratefully
inaccurately
nationalities

---

# UNIVERSAL ACCESS
## Meeting Individual Needs

### Visual Learners

List on the board ten words that have prefixes, suffixes, and/or inflected endings. Have volunteers use four different colored chalks to underline base words, prefixes, suffixes, and inflected endings. Then discuss what entry word students would look up in the dictionary to learn the meaning of each word.

### Kinesthetic Learners

Write on separate index cards approximately 20 words, half of which are entry words and half of which are not. Mix up the cards and have students sort them into two piles: "Entry Word" and "Not an Entry Word." Then have students identify base words, prefixes, suffixes, and inflected endings in the latter pile. Urge students to consult a dictionary as needed.

**democracy** A government in which the people rule directly, as through town meetings, or indirectly, through elected representatives.
**de•moc•ra•cy** (di mok´rə sē) *noun, plural* **democracies.**

**demolish** To tear down, destroy, or ruin completely. The workers will *demolish* the old library to make way for the new one.
**de•mol•ish** (di mol´ish) *verb.*

**forsake** To give up or desert completely. Do not *forsake* your old friends. [Old English *forsacan,* to give up.]
**for•sake** (fôr sāk´) **-sook** (-sùk´), **-sak•en, -sak•ing** *verb.*

**island** A body of land completely surrounded by water.
**is•land** (ī´lənd) *noun.*

**murky** Dark or gloomy. The waters of the muddy river were *murky.*
**murk•y** (mûr´kē) **murk•i•er, murk•i•est** *adjective.* —**murk•i•ness** *noun.*

 **Read the dictionary entries for the five entry words above. Then write the entry word for each clue below.**

1. This is what you do if you decide to give up or leave. ____forsake____

2. This is the fairest form of government. ____democracy____

3. Vancouver, British Columbia, which is off the southwestern coast of the mainland, is one of these. ____island____

4. This is how cloudy, thick pond water might look. ____murky____

5. This is what you do if you destroy something completely. ____demolish____

⭐ **Write your own sentence for each of the five entry words above.**

6. ____Answers will vary._____

7. _____

8. _____

9. _____

10. _____

**182** LESSON 89: Entry Words I

 **Home Involvement Activity** Suppose that the name of your street, county, and city or town appeared in a dictionary. Which entry word would appear just before? Just after? Look in a dictionary to find out.

---

**English-Language Learners/ESL**

On cards, write simple base words that can be illustrated (such as **drink)** and word endings (for example, drink + **ing)**. Have students read each base word aloud. Then help them match it with an ending and read the new word aloud. Finally, have students look up the base word in a dictionary.

**Gifted Learners**

Explain that state names have related noun and adjective forms, such as **Oregonian** for **Oregon**. Have students look up the related forms for **Washington** and **Alaska**. Then have them look up the form for **Hawaii**. Ask: *Why is **Hawaiian** listed as a separate entry word?*

**Learners with Special Needs**

Additional strategies for supporting learners with special needs can be found on page 173L.

---

## Practicing the Skill

● Read and discuss the directions for the exercises on pages 181–182.

● Encourage students to use their imagination when writing the sentences for items 6–10 on page 182. You may also wish to challenge students to use more than one word in the same sentence.

 Turn to page 173K for an Intervention Strategy designed to help students who need extra support with this lesson.

## Curriculum Connections

### Spelling Link

Read aloud the sentences below. Have students spell each pair of words in bold type and write them on the board. Then have students identify base words, prefixes, suffixes, and inflected endings.

> The sky in **northern** Washington is **clearer** today than yesterday.
>
> A flock of birds was **gliding** on the **forceful** wind.
>
> We **debated** whether the defeated candidate would **reappear**.
>
> **Carelessness** weakens the government of **countries**.

### Social Studies Link

Page 182 shows a sample dictionary entry for **democracy** and **democracies**. Have students research the word history of **democracy**. Then have them identify and define as many other words as they can that start with the letters **democra**. Note which words are entry words and which are not. Extend the activity by having students identify prefix combinations (**un**democratic, **pro**democratic).

### Observational Assessment

*Check that students can identify the different parts of a dictionary entry.*

# Entry Words 2

## Objectives

- To recognize contractions, abbreviations, and acronyms as entry words

- To identify the words that contractions, abbreviations, and acronyms stand for

## Warming Up

- Write the following rhyme on the board. Ask a student to read it aloud.

  **Isn't** and **wouldn't**,

  **They'll** and **she'll**,

  **Can't** and **couldn't**,

  **We'll** and **he'll**.

  Some numbers are fractions—

  Some words are contractions!

- Have students circle the contractions and tell what two words each one stands for.

- Ask what the punctuation mark is called (apostrophe) and what it shows (where letters are omitted).

## Teaching the Lesson

- Read aloud the Helpful Hints on page 183. Have students look up the abbreviations in a dictionary.

- Discuss the Helpful Hint on page 184. Elicit or provide a few additional examples, such as **radar** and **UFO**.

- Ask how an acronym is different from a contraction or an abbreviation. Explain that a contraction combines words, an abbreviation is a shortened form of a word, and an acronym is a word formed from the first or first few letters of a series of words.

---

Name _____

### Helpful Hints

Many dictionaries have **entry words** for **contractions** and **abbreviations**. These entry words are listed in alphabetical order as if they were entire words.

All contractions have an **apostrophe** ('). But *not* all abbreviations have a **period** (.). Standard abbreviations may use all upper-case letters, all lower-case letters, or a combination of the two.

HI → Hawaii   mi. → mile   km → kilometer   Dr. → Doctor or Drive

Write the two words that each contraction stands for. Use a dictionary, if needed.

1. we've — we have
2. who'll — who will
3. you're — you are
4. doesn't — does not
5. I'm — I am
6. didn't — did not
7. let's — let us
8. wouldn't — would not
9. they're — they are
10. won't — will not

Write the word or words that each abbreviation stands for. Use a dictionary, if needed.

11. OR — Oregon
12. AK — Alaska
13. WA — Washington
14. lb. — pound
15. P.S. — Post Script
16. Mr. — Mister
17. doz. — dozen
18. pkwy. — parkway

### WORK TOGETHER

Choose a partner. Write the **entry word** for each of these common abbreviations:

in.     oz.
pkg.    mph

---

# UNIVERSAL ACCESS
## Meeting Individual Needs

### Visual Learners

Copy these columns on the board. Have students draw a line connecting each item in the first column with its match in the second column.

| | |
|---|---|
| we are | it's |
| Oregon | doesn't |
| let us | haven't |
| she is | WA |
| pound | we're |
| it is | let's |
| have not | lb. |
| Washington | OR |
| does not | she's |

### Tactile Learners

Use letter tiles to spell the acronyms below, but scramble the letters. Challenge students to rearrange the tiles to spell the words correctly. Then have students look up each word and explain its meaning.

| | |
|---|---|
| sonar | PTA |
| UFO | COD |
| radar | TLC |
| ZIP | laser |
| scuba | ASAP |

Many dictionaries include entry words for acronyms. An **acronym** is a word formed from the first or first few letters of a series of words. Acronyms are listed in **ABC order** just as regular words are. Here are two acronyms:

NASA = National Aeronautics and Space Administration
scuba = self-contained underwater breathing apparatus

Read each sentence. On the line below it, write the word or words that the abbreviation or acronym in bold type stands for. Use a dictionary to help you. Many abbreviations and acronyms are listed as entry words in the dictionary.

1. **NASA** maintains a large infrared telescope in Hawaii, called the Keck.
   National Aeronautics and Space Administration

2. Hawaii has two official languages: **Eng.** and Hawaiian.
   English

3. Hawaii has many fine spots that attract **scuba** divers.
   self-contained underwater breathing apparatus

4. Popular beaches get very crowded on **Sat.** afternoons.
   Saturday

5. My **ZIP** code in Honolulu is 96814.
   Zone Improvement Program

6. Haleakala, Hawaii's largest volcano, rises more than 10,000 **ft.** above sea level.
   feet

7. We measured the Hawaiian flag in **in.**
   inches

8. Submarines in Hawaii use **sonar** to detect underwater objects.
   sound navigation ranging

Keck Telescope in Hawaii

**Home Involvement Activity** Each state has an official 2-letter postal abbreviation. For example, HI stands for Hawaii. How many of the post office abbreviations for the states do you know? Work together to try to list all fifty.

## English-Language Learners/ESL

Make pairs of cards for contractions. On one card, write the contraction; write the corresponding phrase on the other. Give the contraction cards to one set of students and the phrase cards to another. Have the groups take turns holding up a card for the other group to match. Students should read each card aloud.

## Gifted Learners

Many groups use acronyms for names, such as **MADD**: **M**others **A**gainst **D**runk **D**riving and **NOW**: **N**ational **O**rganization for **W**omen. Challenge students to make up their own acronyms for imaginary groups, such as **SOBS**: **S**tudents **O**pposing **B**russels **S**prouts.

## Learners with Special Needs

Additional strategies for supporting learners with special needs can be found on page 173L.

## Practicing the Skill

- Suggest that students review the Helpful Hints before doing the exercises. Answer any questions students may have.

- Read and discuss the directions for the exercises on pages 183–184.

- Point out that the word **won't** (item 10 on page 183) is an exception to the typical way in which contractions are usually formed.

## Curriculum Connections

### Spelling Link

Read aloud the following questions. Have students write their answers, being careful to punctuate and capitalize correctly.

What contraction means "who will"?
How do you abbreviate **dozen**?
What equipment do divers use to breathe underwater?
What is the contraction for "they are"?
What are the abbreviations for **Hawaii** and **Alaska**?
What contraction means "will not"?
How do you abbreviate the word **kilometer?**

### Math Link

Have students look through a mathematics textbook and list as many abbreviations as they can find. Next to each one, ask students to write its meaning, using a dictionary if needed. Then have the class create a master list of all their abbreviations. Extend the activity by having students sort the abbreviations (For example: weight, distance, time).

## Observational Assessment

*Check that students correctly punctuate and capitalize contractions, abbreviations, and acronyms.*

# Pronunciation Key

## Objectives

- To use a dictionary pronunciation key
- To use phonetic respelling as an aid to pronunciation

## Warming Up

- Write the following poem on the board. Read it aloud to the class.

  Some say **Ôr′ i g ə n**

  Is the jewel of the Northwest.

  Others prefer **Wosh′ ing t ə n**

  Above all the rest.

  I like **ə las′kə**

  But **Hə wä′ē** is the best!

- Ask the class why the words in bold type are written the way they are. (They are spelled phonetically.)

- Have volunteers write the four state names the way they are normally spelled. Then have students refer to a pronunciation key as you help them sound out the phonetically respelled names.

## Teaching the Lesson

- Tell students that the pronunciation key shows how to say the phonetic respellings given in dictionary entries. Display a large pronunciation key, or have students refer to the key in their books.

- Explain how the key uses letters, symbols, and example words to model pronunciation. Begin by focusing on the phonetic respelling of a few simple one-syllable words, such as **say**, **rule**, and **far**. Then move on to more challenging words of two and more syllables.

- Point out that one symbol is not an actual letter: the symbol ə (called a **schwa**). Explain that this symbol represents an unstressed vowel sound.

185

---

Name _____

### Helpful Hints

Every dictionary has a **pronunciation key**. This key appears at the beginning of the dictionary and usually at the bottom of each right-hand page. The pronunciation key uses letters, symbols, and sample words to guide you to say the sounds of the entry words.

Each dictionary entry gives a **respelling** of the entry word, usually inside **parentheses** ( ). The respelling uses the pronunciation key to show you how to say the word.

bear (bâr)    book (bük)    honey (hun′ē)

A caribou in Alaska's Denali National Park

**Pronunciation Key—Bottom of Dictionary Page**

at; āpe; fär; câre; end; mē; it; īce; pîerce; hot; ōld; sông, fôrk; oil; out; up; ūse; rüle; pull; tûrn; chin; sing; shop; thin; this; hw in white; zh in treasure. The symbol ə stands for the unstressed vowel sound in about, taken, pencil, lemon, and circus.

Use the pronunciation key above to help you say each respelled word in parentheses. Then write each word in the way it is usually spelled. Use the words in the box below to help you.

| lounge | diary | enjoy | soar |
|---|---|---|---|

1. If you **(en joi′)** seeing wildlife, then a trip to Alaska may be for you.     enjoy

2. Be sure to take binoculars and a **(dī′ə rē)** for writing notes.     diary

3. Watch the barking sea lions **(lounj)** on the beaches.     lounge

4. See the falcons **(sôr)** above you.     soar

### CHALLENGE

Here are respellings of the names of three places. Write the standard spelling for each of the names:

ə las′kə

ē′gəl

kō′dē ak′

---

# UNIVERSAL ACCESS
# Meeting Individual Needs

### Auditory Learners

Make flash cards showing the respelling of several words. Include words with a range of sounds. Hold up one card at a time. Have a student pronounce the word and then write it on the board as it is normally spelled. Ask the student to explain how she or he figured out the pronunciation of the word. Display a pronunciation key for reference.

### Visual Learners

Divide the class into six groups. Assign each group a specific sound segment of the pronunciation key on page 186 (**a, e, i, o, u**, and **ə**). Assign one group all sounds with the letter **a**, another group all sounds with the letter **e**, and so on. Have each group make a display chart using examples different from those in the key. Display students' charts around the room.

185

The **pronunciation key** in the front of a dictionary shows the sound of each vowel and some consonants. Look at the pronunciation key below. It gives the sound of each vowel and sample words that have that vowel sound.

A humpback whale flapping its tail

Read each respelling below. Next to it, write the words from the pronunciation key that have the same vowel sound. Then give the usual spelling for the word. The first one has been done for you.

| | Respelling | Example Words with Same Vowel Sound | Usual Spelling |
|---|---|---|---|
| 1 | (cou) | out, now | cow |
| 2 | (tāl) | ape, pain, day, break | tail |
| 3 | (stôr) | order, fork, horse, story, pour | store |
| 4 | (fôl) | coffee, all, taught, law, fought | fall |
| 5 | (kůk) | put, wood, should | cook |
| 6 | (spâr) | care, pair, bear, their, where | spare |
| 7 | (noiz) | oil, toy | noise |
| 8 | (nit) | it, big, English, hymn | knit |
| 9 | (fŕr) | burn, hurry, term, bird, word, courage | fur |
| 10 | (spül) | rule, true, food | spool |
| 11 | (stûr) | burn, hurry, term bird, word, courage | stir |
| 12 | (fîrs) | ear, deer, here, pierce | fierce |
| 13 | (rēth) | equal, me, feet team, piece, key | wreath |

**Pronunciation Key— Front of Dictionary**

| | |
|---|---|
| a | at, bad |
| ā | ape, pain, day, break |
| ä | father, car, heart |
| âr | care, pair, bear, their, where |
| e | end, pet, said, heaven, friend |
| ē | equal, me, feet, team, piece, key |
| i | it, big, English, hymn |
| ī | ice, fine, lie, my |
| îr | ear, deer, here, pierce |
| o | odd, hot, watch |
| ō | old, oat, toe, low |
| ô | coffee, all, taught, law, fought |
| ôr | order, fork, horse, story, pour |
| oi | oil, toy |
| ou | out, now |
| u | up, mud, love, double |
| ū | use, mule, cue, feud, few |
| ü | rule, true, food |
| ů | put, wood, should |
| ûr | burn, hurry, term, bird, word, courage |
| ə | about, taken, pencil, lemon, circus |

**Home Involvement Activity** You can hear the **schwa** sound (ə) in many words. Work together to underline the vowel that makes the schwa sound in these words: **around, shaken, stencil, melon, custom.**

## English-Language Learners/ESL

Display a pronunciation key like the one on page 186. Help students read it aloud, carefully guiding their pronunciation of each sound. As students become comfortable with a sound, work with them to say and write words that rhyme with the sample words, such as **bat** and **cat** for **at**.

## Gifted Learners

Assign students two sounds from the pronunciation key. Challenge them to write a rhyme using the sounds, as in this example:

Joe has a new **car**
That will not go **far**.
It's really no **fun**,
Because it won't **run**.

Have volunteers read their poems aloud to the class.

## Learners with Special Needs

Additional strategies for supporting learners with special needs can be found on page 173L.

## Practicing the Skill

● Read and discuss the directions on page 185. Point out that the pronunciation key on page 185 is a shorter version of the key that appears at the front of a dictionary.

● Read aloud the directions on page 186. Discuss the example (item 1), and if necessary, do the next item with students. Once students understand the task, have them complete the page on their own.

**Intervention Strategy** Turn to page 173K for an Intervention Strategy designed to help students who need extra support with this lesson.

## Curriculum Connections

### Spelling Link

Read aloud the following sentences. Have students write the words in bold type. Then have them look up each word in a dictionary, make any necessary spelling corrections, and compare the respelling to the normal spelling.

I hope you **enjoy** your trip to Oregon.

Write about it in your **diary**.

You'll see birds **soar** through the air.

You may also see **fierce** animals.

They make a lot of **noise**.

Take along a **spool** of thread.

You can buy one at the **store**.

### Social Studies Link

**Tacoma, Spokane, Puget Sound, Mount Rainier,** and **Grand Coulee Dam** are all places in Washington. Have students look up each one and use a pronunciation key to learn how to say its name correctly. Extend the activity by having students locate the places on a map.

## Observational Assessment

*Check whether students are able to use a pronunciation key and respellings to say words correctly.*

# Accent Marks

## Objectives

- To recognize that accent marks show syllable stress in dictionary entries
- To use accent marks as an aid to pronouncing words and understanding word meaning

## Warming Up

- Write the following rhymes on the board. Read them aloud.

    Farm workers are loading
    fresh **produce** into crates,
    While workers in factories
    **produce** dinner plates.

    I strongly **object**
    to your charges, you see.
    This **object** was broken—
    but not by me!

- Ask volunteers to circle the words that appear twice in each rhyme.

- Have students compare the meanings of the circled words, using a dictionary if needed.

## Teaching the Lesson

- Have students look up the respellings of **produce** and **object**. Call attention to the accent marks. Have students underline the accented syllable in the circled words.

- Ask students in what three ways the circled words differ. (in meaning, pronunciation, and part of speech)

- Have volunteers read aloud the Helpful Hints on page 187. Discuss the examples. Extend the discussion to three-syllable words by comparing the respellings and pronunciation of **nation** and **national** and **fulfill** and **fulfillment**. Point out the accent mark in each word.

---

Name _____

### Helpful Hints

When a word has two or more syllables, one syllable is **accented** more than the other syllable or syllables. You say the accented syllable with greater force, or stress.

In a dictionary respelling, look for an **accent mark** (′) *after* the accented syllable. This will help you say the word.

nation (nā′shən)    cascade (kas kād′)

Cascade at Olympic National Park in Washington State

⭐ **Read each entry word. Then read the respelling in parentheses. Add an accent mark after the syllable you say with the greater or greatest force. Check a dictionary, as needed.**

1. achieve  (ə chēv)      2. enemy    (en′ ə mē)
3. careful  (kâr′ fəl)     4. visible  (viz ə bəl)
5. vertical (vûr′ ti kəl)  6. mountain (moun′ tən)

### Helpful Hint

The same word may be pronounced in different ways, depending on its meaning or part of speech. The accent mark may shift to another syllable.

desert (dez′ ərt) → a dry, sandy region
desert (di zûrt′) → to leave someone or something

### CHALLENGE

Check a dictionary. Find two meanings and pronunciations for **address**. Write a sentence using both meanings and pronunciations.

⭐ **Read each sentence below. Underline the respelling of the word that best fits the meaning of the sentence.**

7. I plan to _____ my Spanish on our trip.  (pûr′ fikt)  (pər fekt′)
8. Our class won the math _____ easily.  (kon′ test)  (kən test′)
9. Are you making _____ in class.  (prog′ res)  (prə gres′)

---

# UNIVERSAL ACCESS
## Meeting Individual Needs

### Auditory Learners

Write these words on the board: **content, suspect, upset, project, defect, incline.** Tell students to use a dictionary to help them identify two different pronunciations and meanings for each word. Have volunteers say the words aloud and explain their meanings. Then ask students to use the words in oral sentences.

### Kinesthetic Learners

Write two different respellings of ten words on separate index cards. Choose words that have noun, adjective, and/or verb meanings, such as **minute, present, perfect, contract.** Mix up the cards and direct students to sort them according to part of speech, using a dictionary as needed.

**Complete each sentence with a word from the box. Some words will be used more than once. Then underline the respelling of the word in parentheses that matches the meaning of the sentence.**

| entrance | perfect | present |
|----------|---------|---------|
| record | refuse | subject |

Hoh Rainforest in Olympic National Park

1. The ___subject___ of my paper is the Hoh Rainforest in Washington's Olympic Park.　　(sub′ jikt)　(səb jekt′)

2. I took a trip there with my class. I kept a written ___record___ of everything I saw.　　(rek′ ərd)　(ri kôrd′)

3. I used a pocket-sized notebook to ___record___ my observations.　　(rek′ ərd)　(ri kôrd′)

4. The Hoh is a place that will ___entrance___ you. Nearly every bit of space is taken up with plants.　　(en′ trəns)　(en trans′)

5. Let me ___present___ this fact. More than 12 feet of rain falls in the Hoh each year!　　(prez′ ənt)　(pri zent′)

6. If people leave the trails, they may ___subject___ the delicate environment to damage.　　(sub′ jikt)　(səb jekt′)

7. Naturally, all visitors should take out with them any ___refuse___ that they may have brought in.　　(ref′ ūs)　(ri fūz′)

8. Who could ___refuse___ to do that?　　(ref′ ūs)　(ri fūz′)

9. I fully enjoyed my visit to the Hoh. I thought it was the ___perfect___ trip.　　(pûr′ fikt)　(pər fekt′)

10. At the ___entrance___ to the Hoh, another tour group eagerly waited to begin its visit.　　(en′ trəns)　(en trans′)

**188**　LESSON 92: Accent Marks

**Home Involvement Activity** Make a list of ten places in your community that you and your family visit each week. Use the pronunciation key and accent marks from a dictionary to respell the names of these places.

---

## Practicing the Skill

- Read aloud the directions on pages 187–188. Do the first items with students.
- Point out that for items 7–9 on page 187, students are choosing between words that differ in meaning, pronunciation, and part of speech.

**Intervention Strategy**

Turn to page 173K for an Intervention Strategy designed to help students who need extra support with this lesson.

## Curriculum Connections

### Spelling Link

Read aloud the sentences below. Have students write the words in bold type. Then have them add an accent mark to show pronunciation. Finally, ask students to identify each word's part of speech.

Rainfall in Seattle today set a **record**.
Hawaii is the **perfect** vacation spot.
At **present**, highway traffic is light.
Visitors lined up at the **entrance**.
I hope you won't **refuse** my request.
The **contest** winner gave a speech.
A real friend will never **desert** you.

### Multicultural Connection

- Explain that some words from other languages are written with accent marks when used in English. For example, **résumé**, **consommé**, and **Nez Percé** come from French. **San José**, which comes from Spanish, has an accent mark when referring to the capital of Costa Rica but not when referring to the California city.
- Have students look up the meaning, pronunciation, and history of these words.

### Observational Assessment

*Check to see that students can correctly distinguish between words that are spelled the same but have different pronunciations and meanings.*

---

### English-Language Learners/ESL

Display objects named by simple two-syllable words, such as **pencil** and **flower.** Hold up each object, write its name on the board, and say the word. Ask which syllable is stressed. Help students identify the correct syllable and have a volunteer add an accent mark.

### Gifted Learners

Explain why many respellings show both a heavy (primary) accent mark and a light (secondary) accent mark. Then have students find examples of two-, three-, and four-syllable words having both kinds of accent marks.

### Learners with Special Needs

Additional strategies for supporting learners with special needs can be found on page 173L.

# Connecting Spelling and Writing

## Objectives

- **To say, spell, sort, and write words relating to dictionary use**
- **To write an article for a children's encyclopedia**

## Warming Up

- Write the following rhyme on the board. Read it aloud to the class.

  **Oregon**'s capital is the city of **Salem**.
  **Hawaii**'s is **Honolulu,** as you know.
  **Olympia** is the capital of **Washington**,
  And the capital of **Alaska** is **Juneau**.

- Direct students to arrange the names of the states and their capitals alphabetically.
- Have students sort the words by their location in the beginning (**A-I**), middle (**J-Q**), or end (**R-Z**) of the dictionary.

## Teaching the Lesson

- Make a three-column chart on the board with these headings: **Beginning: A-I, Middle: J-Q, End: R-Z.**
- Have a volunteer write a word in the first column. Then have other students write words in the second and third columns. Continue in this way until all students have added words to the chart.
- Ask students to name the guide words that could appear at the top of pages containing words that you call out.

## Practicing the Skill

- Discuss the directions for page 189. Have students read each phrase aloud.
- Have students complete the page. Provide extra support to help them remember the correct spelling of **abbreviate, separate**, and **visualize**.

189

---

Name _____

Read each of the phrases below. Say and spell each word in bold type. Repeat the word. Then sort the words according to where you would find them in a dictionary. Write each word in the correct column below.

- gave a helpful **example**
- some **knowledge** of Japanese
- **research** its meaning
- the **standard** spelling
- help **pronounce** the word
- in **alphabetical** order
- an **unusual** word history
- longest **entries** in the book
- **abbreviate** the title
- forming a **contraction**
- **separate** into syllables
- learn a new **language**
- in the middle **section**
- **capitalize** your name
- the **origin** of the word
- so easy to **misspell**
- to **visualize** the word
- the **meaning** of the phrase

| Beginning: A–I | Middle: J–Q | End: R–Z |
|---|---|---|
| example | knowledge | research |
| alphabetical | pronounce | standard |
| entries | language | unusual |
| abbreviate | origin | separate |
| contraction | misspell | section |
| capitalize | meaning | visualize |

---

# UNIVERSAL ACCESS
## Meeting Individual Needs

### Kinesthetic Learners

Say a series of spelling words as you write them on the board. After each word, have students do one of the following: clap their hands if the word appears in the beginning part of the dictionary (**A–I**); snap their fingers if the word appears in the middle (**J–Q**); raise both arms if the word appears in the end part (**R–Z**).

### Visual Learners

List these terms in a column: **guide words, entry, respelling**. In a second column, list the following items in random order: **number of syllables, accents, vowel sounds, location of word, part of speech, definition.** Have volunteers draw lines connecting items in the two columns and explain their reasoning.

### Learners with Special Needs

Additional strategies for supporting learners with special needs can be found on page 173L.

You know that like a dictionary, an encyclopedia is a reference work. You have probably used a print or an on-line encyclopedia to do research. Encyclopedias have general articles, or entries, on many subjects. Like a dictionary, these articles appear in ABC order. A few encyclopedias are on special subjects, such as baseball. Some encyclopedias are just for children.

**Write an article for a children's encyclopedia. Your topic is the *dictionary*. Give the key facts. Imagine that students in a younger grade will be reading your article to learn what a dictionary is and how to use it. Include a sample dictionary entry. Use at least two of these spelling words in your encyclopedia article.**

| | | | | |
|---|---|---|---|---|
| example | knowledge | research | standard | pronounce |
| alphabetical | unusual | entries | abbreviate | contraction | separate |
| language | section | capitalize | origin | misspell | visualize | meaning |

Answers will vary.

_____
_____
_____
_____
_____
_____
_____
_____
_____
_____

**Writer's Tips**

• When you revise your writing, cross out any unimportant details.

• Add any important information that you may have left out.

### Speaker's Challenge

Look up the word **research** in two different dictionaries. Compare and contrast the definitions. How are they alike? How are they different? Which meaning is easier to understand? Discuss your findings with a group.

190  LESSON 93: Connecting Spelling and Writing

---

## The Writing Process

Tell students that on page 190 they will write an article for a children's encyclopedia. Discuss the directions and spelling words at the top of the page.

**Prewrite** Discuss with students how they would go about explaining to younger students what a dictionary is and how to use it. Encourage them to plan what information they will include and how best to organize it.

**Write** Tell students to keep in mind that they are writing for children in a younger grade. Encourage them to present information clearly and simply.

**Revise** Have students reread what they've written and revise as needed. Call attention to the Writer's Tips on page 190.

**Proofread** Have students check for errors in spelling, grammar, and punctuation.

**Publish** Have students copy their final drafts onto page 190 or onto a sheet of paper. Then have them exchange papers with a partner and offer each other constructive feedback.

**Computer Connection** Share the following tip with students who use a word processor to do their writing.

• It's easy to "cut and paste" words, sentences, or even whole paragraphs from one place in a document to another or from one document to another. The commands you'll need typically appear on the toolbar and/or on the "Edit" menu.

• First, highlight the text. Then use either the "Copy" command or the "Cut" command. Next, position your cursor where you want to copy or move the text. Give the "Paste" command.

**Portfolio** Have students add their completed encyclopedia articles to their portfolios.

---

### English-Language Learners/ESL

Read a passage from a children's encyclopedia with students. Choose simple words from the passage for students to look up in a dictionary. Discuss the meaning and pronunciation of each word. Finally, have students use each word in an oral sentence.

### Gifted Learners

Challenge students to make up a word and create their own dictionary entry. Have them include a respelling and a few definitions. Ask volunteers to share their words with the class.

# Connecting Reading and Writing

## Objectives

- **To read a nonfiction selection and respond to it in writing**
- **To practice comparing, contrasting, and synthesizing information**
- **To write a then-and-now paragraph**

## Warming Up

### Comprehension Skills

- Display "then" and "now" photographs of a familiar scene or object. Have students **compare** and **contrast** the photos. List the similarities and differences students find on the board.

- Remind students that **synthesizing** information during reading means to put together the most important ideas in the selection and make sense of them.

## Teaching the Lesson

- Tell students to read the selection more than once and to think carefully about the ideas and details presented.

- Point out that the second Reader's Response question calls on students to contrast the Hawaii of yesterday and today.

- For the third question, encourage students to think over their answer carefully and explain their reasoning.

## Practicing the Skill

- Read aloud and discuss the directions on page 192. Call students' attention to the Writer's Tips.

- Encourage students to include a variety of specific examples in their writing.

---

Name _____

Read about the Hawaii of yesterday and today. Then answer the questions that follow.

# Hawaii—Then and Now

by Marcie and Rick Carroll

**THEN**

Thousands of years ago, people sailed across the Pacific Ocean to see what they could find. They found Hawaii—a string of islands in the middle of nowhere. This new place had erupting volcanoes, roaring shorelines, lots of birds, beautiful flowers, and thick tropical forests. Early settlers made themselves at home in the new territory and soon created their own language, customs, and traditions. Historians don't really know what island life was like in the beginning, because most ancient Hawaiian history is told either in old chants (sung in the Hawaiian language), or in unusual symbols and drawings that were carved into rocks long ago.

**NOW**

Today you'll find 1.1 million people living on the islands of Hawaii. You'll find cars, computers, film crews, and even the largest telescope in the world! Visit the city of Honolulu and you'll spot high-rise buildings, hotels, and hundreds of tourists arriving every day to check out the island life. Today, Hawaii may look a lot different than it did when the first settlers arrived, but many things haven't really changed. The air still smells like tropical flowers, the volcanoes are still erupting, the beaches are still golden, and the islands are still full of nooks and crannies to explore. Even ancient traditions—like hula, leis, and luaus—are still a big part of Hawaii. Aloha!

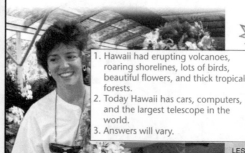

1. Hawaii had erupting volcanoes, roaring shorelines, lots of birds, beautiful flowers, and thick tropical forests.
2. Today Hawaii has cars, computers, and the largest telescope in the world.
3. Answers will vary.

### Reader's Response

1. What was Hawaii like when the first settlers arrived thousands of years ago?
2. How has Hawaii changed? Give three examples.
3. What do you think is the one most important thing that hasn't changed in Hawaii? Explain your choice.

LESSON 94: Connecting Reading and Writing
Comprehension—Compare and Contrast;
Synthesize

191

---

# UNIVERSAL ACCESS
# Meeting Individual Needs

### Visual Learners

To help jog students' memories, suggest that they look at photographs of themselves taken five years earlier. Ask: *How have you changed in appearance? In other ways? Are there some things about you that are the same as when that picture was taken?* Have students make a "Then" and "Now" chart, listing similarities and differences.

### Musical Learners

Have students listen to two different recordings of a well-known song. For example, you might play a modern, jazzy version of "The Star-Spangled Banner" and a more stately, traditional version. Have students compare and contrast the two recordings. Extend the discussion by asking to whom each version would most likely appeal, and why.

### Learners with Special Needs

Additional strategies for supporting learners with special needs can be found on page 173L.

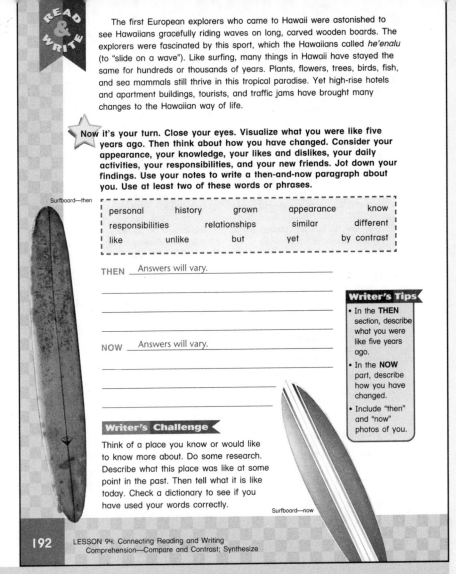

The first European explorers who came to Hawaii were astonished to see Hawaiians gracefully riding waves on long, carved wooden boards. The explorers were fascinated by this sport, which the Hawaiians called *he'enalu* (to "slide on a wave"). Like surfing, many things in Hawaii have stayed the same for hundreds or thousands of years. Plants, flowers, trees, birds, fish, and sea mammals still thrive in this tropical paradise. Yet high-rise hotels and apartment buildings, tourists, and traffic jams have brought many changes to the Hawaiian way of life.

**Now it's your turn. Close your eyes. Visualize what you were like five years ago. Then think about how you have changed. Consider your appearance, your knowledge, your likes and dislikes, your daily activities, your responsibilities, and your new friends. Jot down your findings. Use your notes to write a then-and-now paragraph about you. Use at least two of these words or phrases.**

Surfboard—then

| personal | history | grown | appearance | know |
|---|---|---|---|---|
| responsibilities | relationships | similar | different | |
| like | unlike | but | yet | by contrast |

THEN   Answers will vary.

_____

_____

NOW   Answers will vary.

_____

_____

**Writer's Tips**
• In the **THEN** section, describe what you were like five years ago.
• In the **NOW** part, describe how you have changed.
• Include "then" and "now" photos of you.

**Writer's Challenge**

Think of a place you know or would like to know more about. Do some research. Describe what this place was like at some point in the past. Then tell what it is like today. Check a dictionary to see if you have used your words correctly.

Surfboard—now

192   LESSON 94: Connecting Reading and Writing
Comprehension—Compare and Contrast; Synthesize

### English-Language Learners/ESL

Help students read aloud the "Then" and "Now" sections of the article on page 191. Pause frequently to focus on important ideas and details. Write key words on the board, discuss their meaning, and have students say the words aloud. Guide students in identifying similarities and differences between Hawaii's past and present.

### Gifted Learners

The Hawaiian language has the world's shortest alphabet: five vowels and seven consonants. Invite teams of students to debate whether having such a short alphabet is good or bad. Urge students to support their views with reasons. After teams debate, have the class vote on the issue.

## The Writing Process

Read aloud the introduction and directions on page 192. Discuss other kinds of changes, such as seasonal changes. Let students practice visualizing these changes. Review the words in the box, and remind students to include at least two in their then-and-now paragraphs.

**Prewrite** Explain to students that planning before writing makes writing easier. Encourage them to list specific then-and-now details and to plan the most logical order in which to present them.

**Write** Point out that students need not use every detail they write down, just those that best support their main idea. Suggest, too, that students focus on significant changes in their lives.

**Revise** Have students reread their paragraph and revise it as needed. Encourage them to trade papers with a partner and offer constructive feedback.

**Proofread** Have students check for spelling, grammar, and punctuation errors.

**Publish** Students can copy their final drafts onto page 192 or a sheet of paper. Have volunteers read their work aloud.

**Computer Connection**  Share the following tip with students who use a word processor to do their writing.

• Word processing software usually offers a choice of fonts, or typefaces. Some fonts have a more formal look than others, and some are easier to read than others.

• You can change font appearance or size of an entire document or just the headings. One way to do this is to highlight the text and click the desired font in the "Font" box on the formatting toolbar.

**Portfolio**  Suggest that students add their completed then-and-now paragraphs to their portfolios.

## LESSON 95 • UNIT 6
## Student Pages 193–194

# Reviewing and Assessing
### Dictionary Skills

**Objective**

To review and assess dictionary skills

## Warming Up

- Write the following poem on the board. Ask a volunteer to read it aloud.

  The Pacific <u>region</u> offers <u>fishing</u> and <u>farming.</u>

  Its <u>land</u> and its <u>waters</u> are really quite charming.

  <u>Minerals</u> and <u>lumber</u> are noted <u>resources,</u>

  And <u>tourists</u> visit to hike and ride horses.

- Ask students whether each underlined word would appear in the beginning part of a dictionary (**A–I**), the middle (**J–Q**), or the end (**R–Z**).

- Have students arrange the underlined words in alphabetical order. Extend the activity by having students identify guide words that might appear on the dictionary page that contains each entry word.

## Teaching the Lesson

- Lessons 86–92 (pages 175–188) include Helpful Hints relating to dictionary skills. Ask volunteers to review each hint with the class, using their own words and examples to explain them.

- On the board, write the terms **guide words, entry word, entry, pronunciation key, respelling, accent mark**. Have students explain each term.

- Review the pronunciation key. Remind students that the **schwa** symbol ə stands for an unstressed vowel sound.

---

Name _____

 Read each group of words. Fill in the circle of the words that appear in ABC order.

1. ● break freeze Greece juice
   ○ hornet horse husband hurry
   ○ west wrist willow zero

2. ○ crush brush plush thrush
   ○ gnome gorgon dragon flagon
   ● cracker crockery crook crystal

3. ○ dawn morning midday sunset
   ○ although after afterward shortly
   ● gargle giggle gurgle jangle

4. ○ draft drain drift drench
   ● frown laugh smirk snarl
   ○ iron immature inning itchy

5. ○ imitate initial invitation interest
   ● lavender lettuce licorice lotus
   ○ spend scream steam stream

6. ○ Oregon oregano organ orange
   ○ hawk Hawaii hawthorn hayseed
   ● quack quarter question quicken

7. ● phase phrase praise prance
   ○ tickle ticklish ticket tidy
   ○ over overlook overtake oven

8. ● unbuckle uncle unclear undergo
   ○ value valley valiant vanquish
   ○ yearly yeast yellow yawn

9. ● ocean o'clock October octopus
   ○ point poem poet palm
   ○ weather whether whale wail

10. ○ mast mist misty mistletoe
    ● lead leaky lei luau
    ○ ukulele uncle ulcer under

 Each of the entry words in bold type is a fruit that grows in Hawaii. Read each entry word. Underline the pair of guide words that would appear on the same dictionary page as that of the entry word.

| 11. **coconut** | cobble/cocoa | <u>cobbler/cocoon</u> | code/coffee |
| 12. **banana** | <u>ball/band</u> | bandit/bangle | bank/bark |
| 13. **papaya** | papyrus/parakeet | <u>palm/papa</u> | pantry/paper |
| 14. **pineapple** | <u>pile/pinch</u> | pilot/pinto | pink/pipe |
| 15. **mango** | <u>mane/manicure</u> | mandolin/mangle | mangy/manner |

Rewrite the five entry words above in alphabetical order.

16. <u>banana.</u>  <u>coconut</u>  <u>mango</u>  <u>papaya</u>  <u>pineapple</u>

LESSON 95: Review and Assess   **193**

Copyright © by William H. Sadlier, Inc. All rights reserved.

---

# UNIVERSAL ACCESS
# Meeting Individual Needs

**Kinesthetic Learners**

Ask each student to list three entry words from the same dictionary page on a card. On a second card, have each student write guide words for that page. Repeat the process four more times, so that each student has five entry-word cards and five guide-word cards. Then have pairs of students swap cards and match entry words with guide words.

**Visual Learners**

Make a three-column chart on the board with these headings: **Beginning: A–I, Middle: J–Q, End: R–Z**. Read aloud a series of words, including entry words and words that would not appear as separate entries. As you read each word, have a student write it in the correct column. When the columns are full, have students alphabetize the words and then identify the nonentry words.

**Learners with Special Needs**

Additional strategies for supporting students with special needs can be found on page 173L.

**193**

The words below name some of Oregon's important crops and products. Underline *beginning*, *middle*, or *end* to tell in which part of the dictionary you would find each word. Use A–I for the beginning, J–Q for the middle, or R–Z for the end.

1. lumber — beginning — <u>middle</u> — end
2. semiconductor — beginning — end — <u>middle</u>
3. paper — beginning — <u>middle</u> — end
4. hay — <u>beginning</u> — middle — end
5. electronics — <u>beginning</u> — middle — end
6. onion — beginning — <u>middle</u> — end
7. mint — beginning — <u>middle</u> — end
8. cement — <u>beginning</u> — middle — end
9. wheat — beginning — middle — <u>end</u>
10. pear — beginning — <u>middle</u> — end

Columbia River Gorge in Oregon

Read each sentence. Underline the respelling that fits the meaning of the word in bold type.

11. Oregon's nickname is the **Beaver** State. — (bē′ vər) — <u>(bē vər′)</u>

12. Its moderate **climate** makes it a popular place in which to live. — (klī mit′) — <u>(klī′ mət)</u>

13. Mount Hood is the **perfect** spot for outdoor activities. — (pûr′ fikt) — <u>(pər fekt′)</u>

14. I live **close** enough to the sea to hear the whales. — <u>(klōz)</u> — (klōs)

15. The Columbia River **Gorge** is deep. — <u>(jôrj)</u> — (gôrj)

### Extend & Apply

Use a dictionary to look up the meanings of these words: **canyon, gorge,** and **valley.** How are the meanings of these words the same? How are they different? Write your answer.

Answers will vary.

# Reteaching Activities

## Sound Search

Select ten words from the preceding lessons and write them on the board. Have students look up the respelling of each word. Then have them identify other words that contain the same vowel sound(s), but not the words shown in the pronunciation key. For example, the sound of **e** in **frenzy** is the same as the sound of **e** in s**e**nd and regr**e**t.

## Word Match-up

Write pairs of phrases on the board containing words that have different respellings depending on meaning or part of speech, such as:

one **minute** left in the game

a **minute** spot of dirt

Distribute dictionaries. Have students identify the guide words on the dictionary page that contains each word and match the word as used in each sentence with its definition.

## Assessing the Skill

**Check Up** Have students complete the exercises on pages 193–194 to review alphabetical order, guide words, respellings, and using a dictionary. The exercises can also be used to help you assess students' progress.

Read aloud the directions for the exercises. For items 11–15 on page 193, remind students that guide words show the first and last entry words on a page. For items 11–14 on page 194, suggest that students say the respellings softly to themselves.

**Observational Assessment** Observe students as they work, looking for signs of confusion. For example, are students having trouble placing entry words between guide words? Pay extra attention to how students complete the second exercise on page 194. Students can often benefit from additional instruction in respellings and use of the dictionary pronunciation key.

**Student Skills Assessment** Keep track of each student's progress with dictionary skills using the checklist on page 173H.

**Writing Conference** Meet with students individually to discuss their writing progress. Review how dictionary skills relate to writing. For example, point out that students can look up the definition of a word they want to use, to make sure it means what they think it means. When students proofread their work, they can use a dictionary to check the spelling of both entry words and nonentry words.

Group together students who need further instruction in dictionary skills and have them complete the *Reteaching Activities.* Turn to page 173C for alternative assessment methods.

# Synonyms

## Objectives

- **To recognize and identify synonyms**
- **To use synonyms in context**

## Warming Up

- Write the following poem on the board. Ask a volunteer to read it aloud.

  The Pacific Northwest

  has trails to explore.

  Through the dense woods

  you can **roam** and **hike**.

  **Walk** through the greenery;

  **stroll** the hills o'er.

  **Amble** along

  as long as you like.

- Ask students to name words in the poem that mean "to move on foot." List the words on the board as students say them aloud.

- Ask what words with a similar meaning are called. (synonyms) Then ask students if they can suggest other synonyms to add to the list. Some possible answers are **march**, **wander**, and **trudge**.

## Teaching the Lesson

- Have students read the Helpful Hint on page 195. Discuss the examples and have students use them in sentences.

- Point out that synonyms are not identical in meaning. This means that the synonym a writer chooses affects sentence meaning.

- On the board, write general words such as **happy, cry, say**. Have students write a sentence for each. Ask students to list synonyms for the words. Then have them substitute each of their synonyms in the sentence and discuss its effect on sentence meaning.

---

Name _____

> **Helpful Hint**
>
> **Synonyms** are words that have the same or nearly the same meaning.
>
> make—create    worth—value    high—lofty

 In each box, match the words in the first column with their synonyms in the second column.

| 1 | | 2 | |
|---|---|---|---|
| love | demonstrate | dwell | conceal |
| show | adore | hide | live |
| frank | honest | mend | heal |

| 3 | | 4 | |
|---|---|---|---|
| error | respond | couple | provide |
| answer | yell | supply | frequently |
| shout | mistake | often | pair |

Totem pole in Alaska

In each group of words below, one word does not belong. Cross out that word. Then explain on the lines why the word does not belong in the group.

5. say       state
   rejoice    remark

   _____Answers will vary._____

   _____

6. thief      detective
   crook      robber

   _____Answers will vary._____

   _____

7. attack     terrify
   frighten   alarm

   _____Answers will vary._____

   _____

8. omit       restore
   delete     remove

   _____Answers will vary._____

   _____

9. idea       thought
   concept    energy

   _____Answers will vary._____

   _____

10. fragile    delicate
    hazardous  breakable

    _____Answers will vary._____

    _____

> **WORK TOGETHER**
>
> Form a small group. Work together to list as many **synonyms** for **big** and **small** as you can. Take 5 minutes. Compare your lists with those of another group.

---

# UNIVERSAL ACCESS
## Meeting Individual Needs

### Auditory Learners

On the board, write a sentence such as: *The thick fog caused drivers to slow down.* Read it aloud. Ask a volunteer to say a similar sentence, substituting a synonym for any word in the first sentence. For example, the student might substitute **dense** for **thick**. Have students create additional sentence pairs in which the second sentence has a synonym in place of a word in the first sentence.

### Kinesthetic Learners

Write approximately two dozen pairs of synonyms on separate index cards and divide the pairs into two sets of cards. Distribute one set to students. Display the other set of cards on a large bulletin board. Have students come up one by one and match the word on their card with the correct synonym.

**Read the sentences below. Replace each word in bold type with a synonym from the box. Write the synonym on the line.**

| reside | provide | summit | visitors | active | numerous |

1. Thousands of **tourists** explore Mount Rainier National Park each year. _____ visitors

2. The **peak** of Mount Rainier is always covered in snow. _____ summit

3. People who **live** in the city of Tacoma are only a short drive from Mount Rainier National Park. _____ reside

4. Each day, **many** ferries leave Seattle, Washington, for the San Juan Islands. _____ numerous

5. People in the city of Seattle may spend several hours at the **lively** Pike Place Market. _____ active

6. One of the uses of the Grand Coulee Dam in Washington State is to **supply** power. The dam is also used for irrigation and flood control. _____ provide

**Each scrambled word is a synonym for the word next to it. First, read the word. Then unscramble the letters in bold type. Write the unscrambled word on the line.**

7. injure **downu** _____ wound
8. slim **redslne** _____ slender
9. empty **vactan** _____ vacant
10. beginner **earnrel** _____ learner
11. income **gniaersn** _____ earnings
12. victor **napoimhc** _____ champion
13. agree **contnes** _____ consent
14. reduce **snelse** _____ lessen

Grand Coulee Dam

**Home Involvement Activity** Parts of the Pacific Northwest get a great deal of rainfall. Therefore, plants and trees grow very tall in this region. Work together to list as many synonyms as you can for the word **tall**.

---

### English-Language Learners/ESL

On the board, list these pairs of synonyms in two columns, mixing up their order: **pants/trousers, hat/cap, car/automobile, road/street, woods/forest, rock/stone, steps/stairs**. Read the words aloud. Then display pictures illustrating each word pair. Have students draw a line connecting the two words suggested by the picture.

### Gifted Learners

Explain the difference between **connotation** and **denotation**. Then have students examine newspaper headlines to find examples of words that have an implied meaning.

### Learners with Special Needs

Additional strategies for supporting learners with special needs can be found on page 173L.

---

● Have students read the directions for page 195. If necessary, do item 5 together. Then have students complete the page on their own.

● Read and discuss the directions for page 196. You may want to have students work in pairs to do items 1–6.

● After students finish the exercises, ask how using synonyms can help them as writers. Discuss how synonyms add variety and precision to writing.

## Curriculum Connections

### Spelling Link

● Read aloud the following words and have students list them: **frequently, terrify, delicate, conceal, reside, summit, numerous,** and **thief.**

● Next, read aloud these words in random order, and have students write each one next to its synonym: **many, peak, fragile, frighten, hide, robber, often, live.**

### Literature Link

● Explain that authors choose their words carefully to create a positive or negative impression. For example, **brave** is a positive descriptive word, while **reckless** is negative.

● Have students find examples of positive and negative words in their reading. Then discuss what synonyms the author might have used in each instance to create a different impression.

## Observational Assessment

*Check to see that students can recognize pairs of synonyms.*

# Antonyms

## Objectives

- To identify antonyms
- To use antonyms in context

## Warming Up

- Write the following rhyme on the board. Have a student read it aloud.

  **Upward** and **downward**,

  **Wet** and **dry**,

  **Forget** and **remember**,

  **Laugh** and **cry**,

  **Expensive** and **cheap**,

  **Different** and **same**.

  How many pairs of such words

  Can you name?

- Ask students what the pairs of words have in common. (The words in each pair have opposite meanings.) Ask what words with opposite meanings are called. (antonyms) Then have students suggest pairs of antonyms.

## Teaching the Lesson

- Have students read the Helpful Hint on page 197. Discuss the pairs of antonyms given as examples, and have students use them in sentences.
- Point out that antonyms may be nouns, verbs, adjectives, or adverbs. Give examples of different kinds of antonym pairs and write them on the board. Have students sort them by part of speech.
- Ask students to include their own suggestions for antonym pairs and list them on the board.

---

Name _____

> **Helpful Hint**
>
> **Antonyms** are words that have the opposite or nearly the opposite meaning.
>
> powerful—weak          gain—lose          many—few

⭐ Each row has three antonyms for each numbered word. Underline the three antonyms in each row.

1. **give**        receive        grant        take        get
2. **healthy**     unhealthy      ill          fit         sick
3. **permanent**   unstable       short-lived  temporary   everlasting
4. **funny**       gloomy         depressing   amusing     sad
5. **polite**      courteous      discourteous impolite    rude

⭐ Read each sentence. Replace the word in bold type with its antonym from the box. Write the word on the line.

> dull   saved   closed   left   raised

_raised_  6. You can see the **sunken** hull of the USS *ARIZONA* in Pearl Harbor.

_saved_   7. The battleship *Arizona* was **destroyed** during World War II.

_left_    8. The United States **entered** the war after the ship was sunk.

_closed_  9. Today, the *Arizona* Memorial in Hawaii is **open** to tourists.

_dull_    10. A helicopter ride over Pearl Harbor can be a **thrilling** experience.

*Arizona Memorial in Hawaii's Pearl Harbor*

> **WORK TOGETHER**
>
> Form a small group. Work together to list all the **antonyms** you can think of for the words **wet** and **dry**. Which list will be greater?

LESSON 97: Antonyms   **197**

---

# UNIVERSAL ACCESS
# Meeting Individual Needs

## Visual Learners

Write ten pairs of antonyms on the board. Then write each word on a card, making a total of twenty cards. Mix the cards and place them in rows, face down. Have students turn over two cards at a time to try and match a word with its antonym. Play until students have paired all the cards. Extend the activity by having students use each pair of words in a sentence.

## Kinesthetic Learners

Write each of these words on a card: **hot, weak, sad, boring, brave, quick.** Have volunteers draw a card and pantomime an antonym for the word. Ask students to guess the word and its antonym. As each antonym pair is identified, write it on the board. Point out that some words may have more than one possible antonym.

★ **Write an antonym from the box for each numbered clue below. Write one letter in each space. Then read down the shaded column to answer the question at the bottom.**

| begin | rude | healthy | asleep | seldom | major | quiet |
| uneven | forgive | front | most | hero | straight |

1. sick      h e a l t h y
2. minor      m a j o r
3. noisy      q u i e t
4. awake      a s l e e p
5. blame      f o r g i v e
6. least      m o s t
7. back      f r o n t
8. crooked      s t r a i g h t
9. coward      h e r o
10. level      u n e v e n
11. often      s e l d o m
12. polite      r u d e
13. finish      b e g i n

**Question:** Haleakala National Park is in the eastern part of the Hawaiian island of Maui. It is named for the awesome Haleakala volcano. From the edge of the volcano's crater you can see several other islands. This special park has a nickname. What is it?

**Answer:** _____ House of the sun

Haleakala Crater

 **Home Involvement Activity** Mauna Kea is the highest point in Hawaii. Alaska's highest point is Mt. McKinley. Find out the highest point in your state. How does it compare with the tallest peaks in Alaska and Hawaii?

**198**    LESSON 97: Antonyms

---

# Homonyms

## Objectives

- **To understand that homonyms are words that sound alike but have different meanings and different spellings**
- **To identify pairs of homonyms**
- **To use homonyms correctly**

## Warming Up

- Write the following riddles on the board and help students answer them. Explain that each answer will be a pair of words that sound alike but have different meanings and different spellings.

  Which fruit comes in two's?
  (**pairs** of **pears**)

  What are letters sent to men and boys?
  (**male mail**)

  What is a large grizzly animal without its fur? (a **bare bear**)

  Where might you buy parts of boats?
  (a **sail sale**)

- Write the answers on the board and point out the different spellings of the words in each pair.

## Teaching the Lesson

- Tell students that the answers to the above riddles are homonyms—words that sound alike but have different meanings and spellings. Point out that when homonyms are used for comic effect, as in the riddles above, they are sometimes called puns. A pun is the humorous use of words that sound alike but have different meanings.

- Have a student read the Helpful Hint aloud. Then ask *What is a strategy for figuring out the correct meaning of a homonym?* (using context clues)

---

Name _____

> **Helpful Hint**
>
> **Homonyms** are words that sound alike but have different meanings and different spellings.
>
> dear—deer    pause—paws    flower—flour

**Write the homonym from the box for each numbered word below.**

| doe | tacks | beat | principle | crews | reel |
|-----|-------|------|-----------|-------|------|
| steak | aloud | towed | boar | ceiling | passed |

1. tax _____tacks_____    2. beet _____beat_____
3. bore _____boar_____    4. sealing _____ceiling_____
5. cruise _____crews_____    6. dough _____doe_____
7. allowed _____aloud_____    8. real _____reel_____
9. past _____passed_____    10. principal _____principle_____
11. toad _____towed_____    12. stake _____steak_____

### CHALLENGE

**I'll**, **isle**, and **aisle** are a set of *three* homonyms. How many other sets of three homonyms can you think of? Make a list.

**Choose the homonym in parentheses that completes each sentence. Write the word on the line.**

13. Our (tour, tore) group was welcomed at the airport. _____tour_____

14. We will hike up Diamond Head (whether, weather) or not you join us. _____whether_____

15. Try to guess how much a humpback whale (ways, weighs). _____weighs_____

16. It is an honor to be a (guessed, guest) at Iolani Palace, the only palace in the United States. _____guest_____

17. They (threw, through) a party on King Kamehameha Day. _____threw_____

18. I snorkeled along a (choral, coral) reef. _____coral_____

19. Will you (surf, serf) at Sunset Beach tomorrow? _____surf_____

LESSON 98: Homonyms    **199**

---

# UNIVERSAL ACCESS
## Meeting Individual Needs

### Visual Learners

Have students make picture cards for the words **tacks, doe, boar, steak, beet, toad, ceiling.** Then have them make word cards for the homonyms **tax, dough, bore, stake, beat, towed, sealing.** Tell students to shuffle all the cards and place them face down. Have them take turns trying to pair each picture card with its matching homonym word card.

### Auditory Learners

Discuss how comedians might use homonyms in their acts. Have students write several riddles, jokes, or comedy sketches using homonyms from the lesson. Invite students to take turns doing their own "Homonym Stand-Up" routines for the rest of the class.

★ **Underline the pair of homonyms in each sentence. Then write a definition of each homonym. Use a dictionary, if needed.**

1. It is eerie to hear the <u>wail</u> of a lonely <u>whale</u> in the harbor.

   wail – a sad, crying sound

   whale – a large sea mammal

2. The meeting of the tenants' <u>board</u> <u>bored</u> me to tears.

   board – group

   bored – wearied

3. Please do not <u>meddle</u> in our plans for the <u>medal</u> ceremony.

   meddle – interfere

   medal – award

4. Among the <u>loot</u> the thieves took from the music shop were a trumpet and a <u>lute</u>.

   loot – stolen goods

   lute – instrument like a guitar

5. I hope that <u>our</u> meeting won't last longer than an <u>hour</u>.

   our – possessive case of **we**

   hour – 60 minutes

6. The messy child smeared grape <u>jam</u> on the door <u>jamb</u> near the kitchen.

   jam – fruit preserves

   jamb – side opening of a doorway

7. At the <u>war</u> memorial, Uncle Joe <u>wore</u> his old Army uniform.

   war – armed conflict

   wore – past tense of **wear**

8. <u>I</u> have told you many times not to rub your <u>eye</u>.

   I – first person singular pronoun

   eye – the organ of sight

 **Home Involvement Activity** *Did you know the gnu that Drew knew?* is a funny sentence that uses a pair of homonyms. Create at least five funny sentences with homonym pairs.

---

## Practicing the Skill

● Read aloud the directions on pages 199–200. Complete the first item in each exercise with students.

● Remind students to use context clues to help them choose the right word in exercises 13–19 on page 199.

● Encourage students to work in pairs if they feel it would be helpful.

## Curriculum Connections

### Spelling Link

● Write the following homonym pairs on the board:

| | |
|---|---|
| **board/bored** | **meddle/medal** |
| **loot/lute** | **principal/principle** |
| **choral/coral** | **jam/jamb** |
| **isle/aisle** | **threw/through** |

● Then have students write sentences to help them remember the difference between the spellings of the homonyms above. For example: **The thief put the loot in the boot.**

### Art Link

● Write the following homonym pairs on the board:

| | |
|---|---|
| **chili/chilly** | **fowl/foul** |
| **bore/boar** | **chews/choose** |
| **band/banned** | **need/knead** |

● Ask students to create a cartoon about a misunderstanding caused by a homonym pair. For example, they might show a scene in a restaurant. Smoke is coming out of the diner's mouth and ears. He or she is saying to the waiter, "I thought you said this dish was **chilly!**"

## Observational Assessment

*Check to see that students use context clues to determine which homonym belongs in a sentence.*

---

### English-Language Learners/ESL

Make picture/word cards for the following homonym pairs: **toe/tow, plain/plane, knight/night,** and **meet/meat.** Display each card and say the words. Have students repeat them. Ask volunteers to use the homonym pairs in sentences.

### Gifted Learners

Invite students to write a skit in which mistaking one word in a homonym pair for the other causes a comedy of errors. For example, mistaking the word **flower** for **flour** might lead to a comic situation. Have students perform their skits for the class.

### Learners with Special Needs

Additional strategies for supporting learners with special needs can be found on page 173L.

# Multiple-Meaning Words and Homographs

## Objectives

- **To identify multiple-meaning words and distinguish between their different meanings**

- **To identify homographs and distinguish between their different meanings**

## Warming Up

- Write the following rhyme on the board and read it aloud with students.

  A word with several meanings

  But only one entry, I've heard,

  Like **issue** and **endure** is

  A multiple-meaning word.

  A word with more than one entry

  Followed by numbers in bold

  Like **dove** and **down** and **date** is

  A homograph, I'm told.

- Have a student identify the words used as examples of multiple-meaning words and homographs in the rhyme. (shown in bold)

## Teaching the Lesson

- Have students find the words **issue** and **endure** in the dictionary. Ask what the entries for these words (multiple-meaning words) have in common. (Both entries have only one entry word and the different meanings that follow are numbered.)

- Then ask students to find the words **dove, down,** and **date** in the dictionary. Explain that the different meanings for these words (homographs) are listed as separate entries, and the entry words are followed by small raised numbers. Point out that the word **dove** is pronounced two ways: **dŭv** (as in the bird) and **dōv** (as in the past tense of **dive**).

201

---

Name _____

> **Helpful Hint**
>
> An **entry word** with more than one meaning is called a **multiple-meaning word.** Each of the different meanings for that entry word is numbered.

 Read each dictionary entry. Then read the sentences below it. On the line, write the number of the definition that fits the meaning of the word as it is used in the sentence.

> **clumsy 1.** Awkward; not skillful or graceful. She is too *clumsy* to be a good gymnast. **2.** Awkwardly made or shaped. The *clumsy* gate kept hitting the bushes. **3.** Said or done without skill. His *clumsy* sentences were all the same length.

___2___ 1. We need a piece of wood to prop the **clumsy** window open.

___3___ 2. Don't use **clumsy** phrases in a poem!

___1___ 3. Their routine is too **clumsy** to be chosen for the dance solo.

> **endure 1.** To undergo and survive; stand; bear. The first European explorers to come to the Americas had to *endure* many hardships. **2.** To continue to be; last. Mozart's music will *endure* forever.

___2___ 4. A beloved film like *The Wizard of Oz* will **endure** for generations to come.

___1___ 5. Grandpa told us of the many dangers he had to **endure** when he was a soldier.

> **issue 1.** The act of sending or giving out. I was in charge of the *issue* of supplies to all the students. **2.** Something that is sent or given out. Do you have this month's *issue* of the magazine? **3.** A matter that is under discussion or consideration. The council debated the *issue* of raising local taxes.

___2___ 6. Pictures of Eugene, Oregon, appear in this month's **issue** of *Pacific* magazine.

___3___ 7. Recycling was the **issue** under debate.

___1___ 8. That librarian is in charge of the **issue** of new library cards.

 **WORD STRATEGY**

**Multiple-meaning words** may act as different parts of speech. What does each word mean as a noun? As a verb?

back

level

slump

---

# UNIVERSAL ACCESS
## Meeting Individual Needs

### Kinesthetic Learners

Write the following homographs on the board: **file, blow, ball, jam, spell.** Have students pair up with a classmate. Have each team choose a homograph from the board and pantomime two different meanings. Have the rest of the class guess which pair of homographs is being demonstrated.

### Visual Learners

Invite students to draw two pictures illustrating the different meanings of one or more of these words: **press, vault, pen, bark.** Tell them not to label or identify the pictures. Let students exchange pictures with a classmate and figure out which homograph pair is represented.

**Homographs** are words that have more than one dictionary entry. Homographs are spelled the same but have different meanings. They may or may not sound alike. You can identify homographs in a dictionary by the small raised number that follows them. Here is a pair of homographs:

**dove¹** Any small bird belonging to the pigeon family. A white *dove* is a symbol of peace.

**dove²** A past tense of **dive**. The swimmer *dove* from the cliff into the lake.

★ **Read the list of homographs and their meanings. Then decide which word to use to complete each sentence below. Write the word and its number on the line.**

Cliff diver at Waimea Falls in Hawaii

| | | | |
|---|---|---|---|
| **down¹** | From a higher to a lower place. | **mole¹** | A small brown spot on the skin. |
| **down²** | Fine, soft feathers. | **mole²** | A small animal with fur and long claws that burrows holes underground. |
| **grate¹** | Framework of bars set in or over an opening. | **spell¹** | To write or say the letters of a word in order. |
| **grate²** | To make a scraping sound by rubbing. | **spell²** | State of being enchanted or fascinated. |
| | | **spell³** | A period of time. |

1. "Don't ___grate²___ your teeth," the dentist warned.

2. That region had a hot, dry ___spell³___ last summer.

3. A jacket filled with goose ___down²___ will be warm and lightweight.

4. The ___mole²___ that lives in our backyard has ruined our lawn.

5. I can't resist the ___spell²___ of Italy—its music and art are enchanting.

6. We took the dusty stairs ___down¹___ to the storage room in the basement.

7. At night a ___grate¹___ goes over the door to prevent looting.

8. Dad grew a beard to cover up the ___mole¹___ on his chin.

9. Some people find long Hawaiian words and names hard to ___spell¹___.

**202**  LESSON 99: Multiple-Meaning Words and Homographs

 **Home Involvement Activity** Write two sentences for each of these homographs: **rock, slide, pitcher,** and **handle.** Then compare how you used these multiple-meaning words.

### English-Language Learners/ESL

Have students choose one of these homographs: **desert, down, dove,** or **mole.** Have them draw pictures to illustrate the different meanings. Then have them exchange papers with another student and write sentences using the homographs that are illustrated.

### Gifted Learners

Invite students to create a crossword puzzle using puns as definitions. Have them make a list of homographs and their meanings. The clues for the puzzle should combine two meanings in a funny way: **a wooden club found in a cave (bat).**

### Learners with Special Needs

Additional strategies for supporting learners with special needs can be found on page 173L.

## Practicing the Skill

● Read aloud the direction lines on pages 201–202. Complete the first item in each exercise with students.

● Remind students to use context clues to help them decide which definition to use.

## Curriculum Connections

### Spelling Link

Read the following sentences aloud and repeat the word in bold type. Ask a student to spell the word and say whether it is a multiple-meaning word or a homograph.

A white **dove** flew out of the magician's coat pocket.

Have you read the latest **issue** of this magazine?

Neil was a fast runner but was **clumsy** when playing soccer or basketball.

Shortly after hatching, a chick's **down** dries to become soft and fluffy.

### Social Studies Link

● Tell students that many homographs have different histories or come from different languages despite the fact that they are spelled alike. Here is an example: The word **bongo,** meaning a set of connected drums played with the hands, is of American Spanish origin. The word **bongo,** meaning an African antelope, is Bantu (an African language) in origin.

● Have students use the dictionary to research the histories of the following homographs: **mole, date, refrain, dock, duck, go, pit,** and **pitch.**

### Observational Assessment

*Check to see that students pronounce homographs correctly depending on their meaning.*

# Thesaurus 1

## Objective

- **To understand the purpose of a thesaurus**
- **To use a thesaurus to find synonyms that express more precise meanings**

## Warming Up

- Write these sentences on the board:

  The little girl _____ at the monkey's tricks. (giggled)

  The witch _____ as she turned the prince into a frog. (cackled)

  The giant _____ at the snarling mouse. (snickered)

- Ask students to fill in the blanks with synonyms for the verb **laughed**. Give them the following list of synonyms to choose from: **snickered**, **cackled**, and **giggled**. Ask them to choose the synonym that best fits each sentence.

## Teaching the Lesson

- Tell students that using a thesaurus to find synonyms can help them improve their writing.

- Explain that using precise synonyms enables writers to vary their language, to explore different shades of meaning, and to make their descriptions more accurate.

- Have a volunteer read aloud the Helpful Hint on page 203 as others follow along silently. Then ask *How could it be helpful to know an antonym for a word?*

---

Name _____

> **Helpful Hint**
>
> In a dictionary, you look up a word to learn its meaning. In a **thesaurus**, you look up a word you already know to find other words with the same or a similar meaning. A thesaurus lists **synonyms**. Sometimes, a thesaurus also gives **antonyms** for a word. Use a thesaurus to find the exact word you need to make your writing clearer and more interesting.

**Choose a synonym for the word *throw* that best fits the movement shown in each picture. Use the words from the thesaurus entry below. Do not use a word more than once.**

**throw** [v] cast, chuck, flick, fling, heave, hurl, launch, lob, pelt, pitch, scatter, shower, thrust, toss, volley
**Ant** catch, receive

1. toss
2. pitch
3. heave
4. cast
5. shower
6. hurl

> **WORD STRATEGY**
>
> Use a **thesaurus** to find the exact word to use in your writing. For example, would you **launch**, **pelt**, **scatter**, or **toss** a log into the fire? Write a sentence for each word you did *not* choose.

# UNIVERSAL ACCESS
## Meeting Individual Needs

### Logical Learners

Write these pairs of synonyms on the board: **skillful/crafty**, **charming/polite**, **showy/conceited**. Tell students to make a compare-and-contrast chart showing how the synonyms in each pair are alike and how they are different. Then have them write sentences that show the different meanings of the words in each synonym pair.

### Kinesthetic Learners

Write each of the following synonyms on a slip of paper: **amble, hike, lumber, plod, shuffle, march, strut, stroll, tramp, trudge, prance,** and **prowl**. Place the slips of paper in a box. Have a student choose a slip of paper and act out the word for classmates to guess. The student who correctly guesses the word chooses the next slip of paper and acts out the word on it.

⭐ **Read the synonyms for each of the three entry words below. Then read each sentence. Choose the best synonym for the word given in parentheses. Write the synonym on the line.**

**walk** [v] amble, hike, lumber, plod, roam, shuffle, stalk, stride, tramp, wander

**harm** [v] bruise, damage, mangle, ruin, sabotage, shatter, spoil, trample

**rest** [v] ease up, idle, loaf, lounge, nap, recline, relax, sleep

1. I put the milk in the refrigerator so that it wouldn't __spoil__. (harm)

2. We began to __hike__ up the steep mountain trail. (walk)

3. The sly cat began to __stalk__ the unsuspecting mouse. (walk)

4. To __relax__ after studying, I went for a swim in the lake. (rest)

5. If you drop a glass onto the sidewalk, it will probably __shatter__. (harm)

6. One more poor performance could temporarily __damage__ the athlete's career. (harm)

7. The holiday crowds __trample__ the grass and the flower beds. (harm)

8. The spies worked to __ruin__ the enemy's plans. (harm)

9. I plan to __nap__ for about ten minutes; please don't wake me. (rest)

10. We watched the clumsy old bear __lumber__ across the gravel. (walk)

11. Some nomads __roam__ the desert in search of food and a temporary home. (walk)

12. After years of dry weather, the land was in a state of __ruin__. (harm)

13. You will __mangle__ your hand if you're not careful with that machine. (harm)

14. Only a giant could __stride__ through the forest like that. (walk)

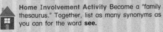

🏠 **Home Involvement Activity** Become a "family thesaurus." Together, list as many synonyms as you can for the word **see**.

---

## English-Language Learners/ESL

Pair fluent speakers with English-language learners. Ask them to find synonyms for **run** in a thesaurus, selecting only those for the meaning "to move swiftly on foot." Then have partners work together to write a sentence for each synonym. Have them share their sentences with the rest of the class by reading them aloud.

## Gifted Learners

Invite students to write an objective description of an acquaintance. Then have them substitute subjective synonyms for objective words or phrases. For example, they might substitute **performs brilliantly** for **gets the highest grades.**

## Learners with Special Needs

Additional strategies for supporting learners with special needs can be found on page 173L.

---

## Practicing the Skill

● Read aloud the directions on pages 203–204. Complete the first item in each exercise with students.

● Ask students to write sentences for each synonym for the word **throw** shown on page 203.

● In the exercise on page 204, help students use context clues to help them choose the correct synonym.

## Curriculum Connections

### Spelling Link

Read aloud the words listed below. Have students write the words in their notebooks as you read them. Then ask students to sort the words according to whether they are synonyms for **walk, harm, rest,** or **throw.**

| | | |
|---|---|---|
| **spoil** | **hike** | **sabotage** |
| **wander** | **toss** | **relax** |
| **lumber** | **nap** | **pitch** |
| **fling** | **stalk** | **damage** |
| **shatter** | **cast** | **lounge** |

### Writing Link

● Write the following paragraph on the board:

Mandy came home feeling **hungry.** Her mother had made some **good** cookies. They looked **nice** as they cooled on the counter. Mandy ate one, then another, then another. When she finally stopped, she was **surprised** to see that she had eaten them all!

● Ask students to replace the words **hungry, good, nice,** and **surprised** with more precise synonyms.

## Observational Assessment

*Check to see that students understand the distinctions between synonyms in order to use them effectively in sentences.*

## Student Pages 205–206

# Thesaurus 2

## Objectives

- **To sort synonyms by meaning**
- **To replace words in context with more precise synonyms**

## Warming Up

- Write these pairs of sentences on the board and read them aloud.

  The detective <u>looked</u> at the evidence.

  The detective _____ the evidence.

  Jasmine <u>walked</u> through the meadow.

  Jasmine _____ through the meadow.

- Have students read the sentence pairs. Then ask them to replace the underlined words with synonyms that express the action more precisely.

- Encourage students to look up the underlined words in a thesaurus and compare their replacements with the synonyms given there.

## Teaching the Lesson

- Review synonyms and antonyms with students. Remind students that they can find them in a thesaurus.

- Use the following activity to help students understand how a dictionary and a thesaurus complement each other. Ask students to look up the word **apologetic** in a thesaurus. Then have them write sentences that demonstrate the difference between the synonyms **apologetic** and **contrite**. Encourage them to use the dictionary to find the exact meanings of these words.

- Have a volunteer read aloud the Helpful Hint on page 205 as others follow along silently.

---

Name _____

### Helpful Hint

A **thesaurus** lists synonyms and antonyms. Entry words in a thesaurus are arranged in **ABC order,** just as they are in a dictionary.

The box below has synonyms from a thesaurus for the words *slow, heavy,* and *fast.* Sort the words by their meaning. Write each word in the correct column below.

| brisk | bulky | hefty | sluggish | snaillike | huge |
| dull | quick | overweight | swift | massive | hasty | gradual |
| unhurried | burdensome | accelerated | rapid | slack |

| 1   slow | 2   heavy | 3   fast |
|---|---|---|
| sluggish | bulky | brisk |
| snaillike | hefty | quick |
| dull | huge | swift |
| gradual | overweight | hasty |
| unhurried | massive | accelerated |
| slack | burdensome | rapid |

**Rank** each set of words from *least* to *most.* Write the words in the correct order on the line.

4. from *least* happy to *most* happy: pleased, elated, cheerful

   _____ pleased cheerful elated _____

5. from *least* sad to *most* sad: sorrowful, gloomy, heartbroken

   _____ gloomy sorrowful heartbroken _____

6. from *least* cold to *most* cold: frosty, crisp, cool

   _____ cool crisp frosty _____

### WORK TOGETHER

Get together with a partner. Write one more synonym for each word in items 4–6. Where would you rank your word in the list? Explain your decision.

---

# UNIVERSAL ACCESS
# Meeting Individual Needs

### Visual Learners

On the board, write these pairs of synonyms: **eat/devour, hold/clutch, old/ancient.** Ask students to draw pictures showing the difference between the synonyms in each pair. Have students give their unlabeled pairs of pictures to a classmate and ask him or her to label them with the synonyms.

### Auditory Learners

Have students work in pairs. Give each pair a timer. Read a list of words—for example: **work, get, big, fast, conscientious, angry,** and **hurry.** Partners can take turns saying as many synonyms for each word as they can in one minute. Repeat the activity, having students list antonyms for the words.

⭐ **Replace each word in bold type with a more exact word from the box. Use a word only *once*.**

| snaillike | overweight | brisk | swift | accelerated |
|---|---|---|---|---|
| massive | rough | hasty | bulky | slack |

1. The very bright student was placed in a(n) **fast** class. _accelerated_

2. A **heavy** boulder blocked the road, so we couldn't pass. _massive_

3. The sleek and **fast** cheetah can run faster than almost any other animal. _swift_

4. Business was **slow;** we had no customers at all after two o'clock. _slack_

5. The **fast** decision we made may come back to haunt us. _hasty_

6. The **heavy** dieter was shedding 10 pounds a week! _overweight_

7. Business was **fast** in the first month. It slowed down after that. _brisk_

8. The committee moves at a **slow** pace. _snaillike_

9. It was awkward to carry the **heavy** package up the stairs. _bulky_

10. You can get from Seattle to Vancouver, Canada, by ferry if the sea is not too **heavy.** _rough_

⭐ **Choose any three words from the box above. Use each word in a sentence that makes the meaning of the word clear.**

11. _Answers will vary._ _____

12. _____

13. _____

Passengers aboard a Seattle ferry

🏠 **Home Involvement Activity** Use three words from the box at the top of the page to describe doing chores at your house. Give everyone a chance to contribute. Choose one person to write the description.

### English-Language Learners/ESL

Ask English learners to make a list of words in their language that mean **walk**. Have volunteers read the words to the class and explain or pantomime the shades of meaning these synonyms express. Then ask fluent speakers to suggest equivalent English words.

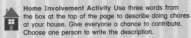

### Gifted Learners

Ask students to write two descriptions of a vacation spot: one that would reassure parents and one that would appeal to their classmates. Students can write either description first and then change it by replacing, for example, words that would reassure parents, with synonyms that would appeal to younger people.

### Learners with Special Needs

Additional strategies for supporting learners with special needs can be found on page 173L.

---

## Practicing the Skill

Read aloud the directions on pages 205 and 206. Complete the first item in each exercise with students. For items 4–6 on page 205, have students use a dictionary and a thesaurus to check the meanings of the three synonyms in each item.

## Curriculum Connections

### Spelling Link

● Read aloud the following sentences, repeating the words in bold type.

> Hannah was impatient with the **snakelike** pace of the mail.
>
> The postal worker carried the **bulky** package to the front door.
>
> Hannah was **elated** to receive her gift at long last.
>
> She wrote her aunt a **cheerful** thank-you note.
>
> In one **brisk** movement, she tossed her letter into the mailbox.

● Call on students to spell each word in bold as you write it on the board. Have students suggest a synonym for each word.

### Writing Link

Have students write down as much as they can remember of a conversation they had with a friend. Then ask them what they might do to change the dialogue so that it sounds more interesting. Encourage students to replace vague words with more precise synonyms. Have volunteers read both versions of their dialogues to the class when they have finished.

## Observational Assessment

*Note whether students use synonyms to vary their vocabulary and to express themselves more precisely.*

# Reviewing and Assessing

## Synonyms, Antonyms, Homonyms, and Thesaurus Skills

### Objective

To review and assess synonyms, antonyms, homonyms, and thesaurus skills

## Warming Up

- Write the following list of word pairs on the board: **bear/bare, brave/courageous, fast/speedy, right/wrong, right/left, careful/cautious, lead/led, hare/hair,** and **increase/reduce.**

- Have volunteers identify each pair as homonyms, antonyms, or synonyms. Ask students to write sentences using both words in each pair. Then invite volunteers to read their sentences aloud.

## Teaching the Lesson

- Have students reread the Helpful Hints in Lessons 96–101 (pages 195–206). Then ask volunteers to define and give examples of synonyms, antonyms, homonyms, and words with multiple meanings.

- Make sure students can distinguish between the different kinds of multiple-meaning words by having them identify and sort these examples: **wind/wind, bow/bow, content/content, live/live, read/read, bass/bass,** and **lead/lead.**

- Ask students to explain the difference between a dictionary and a thesaurus. Have them give examples of times when they would use a dictionary and times when they would use a thesaurus.

- Ask why it is a good idea to check a dictionary for the meanings of words found in a thesaurus.

207

---

Name _____

★ Read each pair of words. Write S if the words are *synonyms*. Write A if the words are *antonyms*. Write H if the words are *homonyms*.

| | | | | | |
|---|---|---|---|---|---|
| 1. | dwell—live | S | 2. | mist—missed | H |
| 3. | bore—boar | H | 4. | omit—delete | S |
| 5. | supply—provide | S | 6. | conceal—hide | S |
| 7. | gain—lose | A | 8. | polite—rude | A |
| 9. | strong—weak | A | 10. | ceiling—sealing | H |
| 11. | aisle—I'll | H | 12. | partial—complete | A |
| 13. | slender—thin | S | 14. | lessen—reduce | S |
| 15. | paws—pause | H | 16. | pedal—peddle | H |
| 17. | annoy—bother | S | 18. | distant—nearby | A |
| 19. | week—weak | H | 20. | crooked—straight | A |
| 21. | tacks—tax | H | 22. | often—frequently | S |

★ The box below has words from a thesaurus. Sort the words by their meaning. Write each word in the correct column below.

| | | | |
|---|---|---|---|
| bake | boil | bound | broil |
| consider | decide | grill | spring |
| leap | ponder | reason | vault |

| 23 Words for **jump** | 24 Words for **cook** | 25 Words for **think** |
|---|---|---|
| bound | bake | consider |
| spring | boil | decide |
| leap | broil | ponder |
| vault | grill | reason |

**CHALLENGE**

Replace the word in bold type with both a **synonym** and an **antonym**. All phrases should make sense.

**skinny** clown
loud **laugh**
**damp** weather

---

# UNIVERSAL ACCESS
## Meeting Individual Needs

### Logical Learners

Ask students to design charts to help them review the material taught in Lessons 96–101. For example, they might create a Venn diagram to demonstrate how thesauruses and dictionaries and the different kinds of words featured in these lessons are alike and different.

**bass**
(short **a**)
type of
fish

spelled
alike

**bass**
(long **a**)
low-pitched
musical tone

### Visual Learners

Ask students to find or draw pictures that illustrate the different kinds of words featured in Lessons 96–101. Visual puns, such as a fir tree covered in fur, might represent homonyms. The likenesses and differences in then-and-now pictures might be labeled with synonyms and antonyms. Have students write captions for their pictures and then display them in the classroom.

### Learners with Special Needs

Additional strategies for supporting learners with special needs can be found on page 173L.

Underline the synonym for each word in bold type.

| | | | |
|---|---|---|---|
| 1. made too many **errors** | <u>mistakes</u> | calls | excuses |
| 2. **grateful** for your kindness | angry | bored | <u>thankful</u> |
| 3. **frighten** the audience | entertain | charge | <u>scare</u> |
| 4. the newest **champion** | <u>victor</u> | loser | player |
| 5. **numerous** activities for kids | <u>many</u> | few | math |

Underline the antonym for each word in bold type.

| | | | |
|---|---|---|---|
| 6. **receive** birthday cards | <u>send</u> | get | buy |
| 7. too **sweet** for my taste | crunchy | sugary | <u>sour</u> |
| 8. **east** of the lake | north | <u>west</u> | outside |
| 9. plays in the **major** leagues | <u>minor</u> | soccer | student |
| 10. **seldom** has dessert | never | <u>often</u> | rarely |

The sentences below are about the Oregon Trail. The pioneers traveled this trail on their way to the West. Choose the homonym that makes sense in the sentence. Write the word on the line.

| | | |
|---|---|---|
| 11. There was no easy __route__ to the West. | root | route |
| 12. The trip took months in all kinds of __weather__. | weather | whether |
| 13. The Oregon Trail was once a main __road__ west. | rowed | road |
| 14. It went __through__ Wyoming and Idaho. | threw | through |

**Extend & Apply**

Use a thesaurus to revise sentences 11–14. Change one word in each sentence. Choose a word that is more interesting or exact, but do *not* change the meaning of the sentence.

The Oregon Trail
- City
- Fort
- Trail
- Pass

Ft. Vancouver  Washington
Oregon City
Ft. Boise
Oregon  Idaho
South Pass  Ft. Laramie
Wyoming  Nebraska
Ft. Bridger  Ft. Kearny
Kansas
Independence, Missouri

## Reteaching Activities

**Think Tank**

Have students identify the word pairs described below.

- These words are pronounced the same but have different spellings and meanings.
- These words are spelled the same, can be pronounced the same or differently, and have different meanings.
- These words have opposite meanings.
- These words have similar meanings.

**Thesaurus Safari**

Students can go on a "Thesaurus Safari." Give them a list of words from Lessons 96–101. Have them use a thesaurus to find two synonyms for each word. Then have students choose one of the sets of three synonyms and write a sentence for each synonym. Ask them to explain how the synonyms they chose are similar in meaning and how they are different.

## Assessing the Skill

**Check Up** Have students complete the exercises on pages 207–208. Suggest that they refrain from checking the Helpful Hints until all items in these exercises are completed. Point out that correcting their own errors afterward will reinforce the reviewing process and improve their retention of the material they have learned.

**Observational Assessment** Encourage students to share with you the results of the self-testing described above. Note specific areas of weakness and strength. Review notes made during previous observations and assess students' progress.

**Student Skills Assessment** Keep track of each student's progress using the checklist on page 173H.

**Writing Conference** Meet with students individually to discuss their written work. Review portfolio samples and favorite pieces from their Home Portfolios. Point out ways in which using the dictionary and the thesaurus as they write can help students become better writers.

Group together students who need further instruction in identifying synonyms, antonyms, and homonyms, and in using a thesaurus. Have them complete the *Reteaching Activities*. Turn to page 173C for alternative assessment methods.

# Clipped Words and Blended Words

## Objectives

- **To identify and form clipped words**
- **To identify and form blended words**

## Warming Up

- Write these rhymes on the board and read them aloud.

  My car just died—refused to go.
  And here is why: I did not know
  That **gas** and **gasoline** were one.
  So fill 'er up and watch 'er run.

  Too late for **breakfast?**
  Too soon for **lunch?**
  Just combine them—
  Bring on the **brunch!**

- Underline the words shown in bold in the rhymes above. Draw students' attention to the first rhyme. Ask them how they think the words **gas** and **gasoline** are related. (Lead them to understand that **gas** is a shortened form of **gasoline.**)
- Then have students look at the second rhyme. Ask them what two words have been blended together to form the word **brunch. (breakfast** and **lunch)**

## Teaching the Lesson

- Explain to students that words sometimes get shortened as people use them over time. Such words are called clipped words. For example, **gym** is a shortened form of the word **gymnasium.**
- Point out that words are also invented by combining parts of other words. These are called blended words. For example, **smog** is a combination of **smoke** and **fog.**

---

Name _____

### Helpful Hint

Language changes all the time as people use it. Sometimes, long words get shortened so that they are easier to say and spell. These shorter forms are called **clipped words.** Here are some clipped words:

gymnasium → gym    automobile → auto    photograph → photo

Match each clipped word in Column A with the long form of the word in Column B. Write the long form of the word on the line.

| | A | B |
|---|---|---|
| gasoline | 1. gas | a. limousine |
| champion | 2. champ | b. teenager |
| hamburger | 3. burger | c. gasoline |
| omnibus | 4. bus | d. referee |
| tuxedo | 5. tux | e. laboratory |
| laboratory | 6. lab | f. champion |
| referee | 7. ref | g. hamburger |
| limousine | 8. limo | h. omnibus |
| teenager | 9. teen | i. tuxedo |

gymnasium → gym

Read the sentences. Replace each word in bold type with the clipped form of the word in the box. Write the clipped word on the line.

| vet | ad | taxi | grad |

10. I cut out an **advertisement** from the newspaper. — ad
11. My cousin is a recent **graduate** of that university. — grad
12. Dawn took her cat to see the **veterinarian.** — vet
13. They rode home in a **taxicab.** — taxi

### CHALLENGE

What are the long forms of these clipped words? Use a dictionary to help you find and spell your answers.

flu
memo
sax

LESSON 103: Clipped Words and Blended Words    **209**

---

# UNIVERSAL ACCESS
## Meeting Individual Needs

### Kinesthetic Learners

Write clipped words and parts of blended words on cards. Mark various areas of the room and hide a card in each area. When students find a clipped word, they must identify the longer word from which it was formed. When they find part of a blended word, they must guess the other part. The player to identify the most words correctly wins the game.

### Auditory Learners

Have students work in pairs. Ask both partners in each pair to write a list of clipped words and blended words. Have partners take turns reading their lists to each other. Ask the reader to pause after each item so that the listener can supply the longer form of the clipped word or the two words that were combined to form the blended word.

motor + pedal → moped

## Helpful Hint

Language also changes when new words are added. A **blended word** is a new word that is formed by combining two words. As a result, some letters are dropped.

motor + hotel → motel
television + marathon → telethon

 **Complete each sentence. Combine the letters in bold type in the two words to form one blended word.**

1. If you blend **mot**or + p**ed**al, you get _____ moped _____.

2. If you blend **br**eakfast + l**unch**, you get _____ brunch _____.

3. If you blend **fl**utter + h**urry**, you get _____ flurry _____.

4. If you blend **sm**oke + f**og**, you get _____ smog _____.

5. If you blend **fla**me + g**lare**, you get _____ flare _____.

6. If you blend **cam**era + re**corder**, you get _____ camcorder _____.

7. If you blend **gl**eam + sh**immer**, you get _____ glimmer _____.

8. If you blend **info**rmation + com**mercial**, you get _____ infomercial _____.

 **Write one of the blended words from above to complete each sentence.**

9. We saw the first _____ glimmer _____ of light on the horizon at 5:00 A.M.

10. They served eggs, sausages, muffins, and fruit for _____ brunch _____.

11. A _____ flurry _____ of wind upset the small boat.

12. We took our new _____ camcorder _____ to film our vacation.

13. The city in the valley was always wrapped in _____ smog _____.

14. The ship sent up a _____ flare _____ to signal other vessels.

15. Julia always rides her red _____ moped _____ to school.

16. Have you ever watched that _____ infomercial _____ on how to exercise.

210    LESSON 103: Clipped Words and Blended Words

 **Home Involvement Activity** Many products, such as health and beauty aids, have names that are clipped or blended words. How many of these words can you name? List them. Look in magazines or flyers for examples.

---

### English-Language Learners/ESL

Help students make a list of clipped words that are used in everyday conversation (**photo, bus,** etc.). Ask students to write the long form of each word beside the clipped word. Then have students mask part of the long form of each word so that only the clipped word is showing.

### Gifted Learners

Have students invent creatures that have selected traits of real animals. The creature's name can be a blend of the animals' names. For example, a **horbit** might have qualities of both a **rabbit** and a **horse.** Invite students to draw and describe their creatures.

### Learners with Special Needs

Additional strategies for supporting learners with special needs can be found on page 173L.

---

## Practicing the Skill

● Read aloud the directions on pages 209–210. Complete the first item in each exercise with students.

● Ask students to define **infomercial, moped,** and **camcorder** in their own words. Then have them write sentences that clarify their definitions.

## Curriculum Connections

### Spelling Link

Display the exercise below for students to copy. Have them write a clipped word or a blended word in the blanks, as appropriate. Ask them to check their spelling.

| | |
|---|---|
| **photograph** | _____ |
| **champion** | _____ |
| **hamburger** | _____ |
| **limousine** | _____ |
| **flutter + hurry =** | _____ |
| **gleam + shimmer =** | _____ |
| **flame + glare =** | _____ |
| **motor + hotel =** | _____ |

### Science Link

Tell students that scientific terms are good candidates for becoming "clipped" words as a result of their tendency to be long. Examples from this lesson include **veterinarian** and **laboratory.** Have students look through a dictionary or a science textbook to find other examples. (Suggestions include **ab** for **abdominal, temp** for **temperature,** and **rehab** for **rehabilitation.**)

## Observational Assessment

*Note whether students can correctly identify the longer forms of clipped and blended words.*

210

# Borrowed Words

## Objective

To recognize and use words borrowed from other languages

## Warming Up

- Read this rhyme aloud for students.

  Some words come to English

  From places far away

  Like **sapphire** and **safari**,

  And **episode** and **lei**.

  Like **ketchup** and **coyote**,

  **Paprika** and **poodle**,

  Like **khaki** and **karate**,

  **Igloo**, **gum** and **noodle**.

- Ask students to identify the words in this rhyme that originated in a language other than English. (the words in bold type)

- Explain that most languages borrow words from other languages. Some words change their spelling in the process, while others retain their original spelling.

## Teaching the Lesson

- Identify the languages from which the words in the *Warming-Up* exercise were borrowed. (**Sapphire** is Hindi, **safari** is Swahili, **episode** is Greek, **lei** is Hawaiian, **ketchup** is Chinese, **coyote** is Nahuatl, **paprika** is Hungarian, **poodle** is German, **khaki** is Hindi, **karate** is Japanese, **igloo** is Inuit, **gum** is Egyptian, **noodle** is German.)

- Lead a discussion about the ways in which these words may have become part of the English language. Help students understand that words, like people and goods, move from place to place as a result of trade, colonization, and tourism.

**211**

---

Name _____

Copyright © by William H. Sadlier, Inc. All rights reserved.

> **Helpful Hint**
>
> Language is always changing. English borrows words from many other languages. Some words stay the same. Other words change a little. Here are some **borrowed words**:
>
> **lasso** (from Spanish)  **pretzel** (from German)
> **karate** (from Japanese)  **menu** (from French)

BIENVENUE EN PARTIE FRANÇAISE WELCOME TO THE FRENCH SIDE

 Each word in the box below has been borrowed from another language. On the line, write the word from the box that fits each clue.

| aloha | garage | gymnastics | honcho | khaki | plaza |
|---|---|---|---|---|---|
| noodle | opossum | parka | piano | percent | coffee |

1. French word for a place to keep a car — garage

2. Aleut word for a hooded jacket — parka

3. German word for a flat strip of dry dough, served in soup — noodle

4. Algonquian word for a small animal with a ratlike tail — opossum

5. Hawaiian word for *hello* and *good-by* — aloha

6. Arabic word for a dark-brown drink — coffee

7. Hindi word for a dull yellowish-brown color or cloth — khaki

8. Japanese word for the person in charge — honcho

9. Latin word meaning "a hundredth part" — percent

10. Spanish word for a public square — plaza

11. Italian word for a musical instrument — piano

12. Greek word for the sport of exercising — gynmastics

>  **CHALLENGE**
>
> Match the name of each invention with the language it came from. Use a dictionary to help you.
>
> robot     Latin
> wheel     Czech
> tractor   Greek

---

# UNIVERSAL ACCESS
# Meeting Individual Needs

## Kinesthetic Learners

Have students play "Charades" with borrowed words. Write the words **piano, lasso, menu, coffee, karate, mirror, gum**, and **shampoo** on slips of paper and place them in a box. Have each player choose a slip of paper and try to convey the word's meaning to classmates using pantomime. The student who guesses the word correctly becomes the next player.

## Logical Learners

On the board, write the words **curry, sauerkraut, boutique, bronco, gondola**, and **kangaroo**. Ask students to discuss what they know about each word. Then have them guess the language that each word comes from. Invite volunteers to share their guesses with the class, giving reasons to support their ideas. Finally, look up each word in a dictionary to find out its language of origin.

⭐ Solve this puzzle that uses borrowed words. Write one letter in each space. Then copy the letters in the shaded column, from top to bottom, to answer the question below. Each answer appears in the Word Bank, along with the language from which it was borrowed.

1. opening in a wall to let in light    w i n d o w
2. temporary house made of ice    i g l o o
3. African trip for photographing animals    s a f a r i
4. fastener for clothes    b u t t o n
5. sparkling blue gemstone    s a p p h i r e
6. Hawaiian wreath of flowers    l e i
7. pepper that makes a red spice    p a p r i k a
8. highest singing voice    s o p r a n o
9. something sticky you chew    g u m
10. soap for washing your hair    s h a m p o o
11. part of a story or series    e p i s o d e
12. a food made from milk    y o g u r t
13. Western farm for horses    r a n c h
14. glass showing your reflection    m i r r o r
15. popular red sauce for hamburgers    k e t c h u p
16. wild animal like a thin, small wolf    c o y o t e

**Question:** What is so special about Barrow, Alaska?

**Answer:** It is the _____ northernmost city _____ in the United States.

**Word Bank**

| | | | |
|---|---|---|---|
| *Chinese:* ketchup | *Greek:* episode | *Icelandic:* window | *Sanskrit:* sapphire |
| *Egyptian:* gum | *Hawaiian:* lei | *Italian:* soprano | *Spanish:* ranch |
| *Eskimo:* igloo | *Hindi:* shampoo | *Latin:* mirror | *Swahili:* safari |
| *French:* button | *Hungarian:* paprika | *Nahuatl:* coyote | *Turkish:* yogurt |

 **Home Involvement Activity** Many food names, such as **ravioli, tortilla, sushi,** and **sauerkraut,** are borrowed from other languages. Work together to list foods that you eat whose names are borrowed words.

## Practicing the Skill

● Read aloud the directions on pages 211–212 and complete the first item in each exercise with students.

● Point out that some borrowed words, such as **button, mirror,** and **window,** have been part of the English language for so long that they do not seem foreign.

## Curriculum Connections

### Spelling Link

Have students unscramble the following words so that they are spelled correctly.

**phisprea    doleno    afrisa**
**spoomsu    oglio    dopesei**
**aparkip    groytu    treencp**

(Answers are as follows: **sapphire, noodle, safari, opossum, igloo, episode, paprika, yogurt, percent.**)

### Social Studies Link

● Inhabitants of different areas in the United States still use words from the languages of the region's European settlers. For example, many New Yorkers call the steps in front of their buildings **stoops.** This word comes from the Dutch word **stoep** and reminds us that New York City was once a Dutch colony.

● Have students research local expressions that come from other languages. Invite them to share their findings with the class.

## Observational Assessment

*Note whether students can use and spell borrowed words correctly.*

### English-Language Learners/ESL

Ask English-language learners to name any English words that were borrowed from their home language. Have volunteers tell what they know about these words regarding their history, spelling, and meaning. Encourage fluent speakers to talk about borrowed words that their relatives use or have passed down to them.

### Gifted Learners

Remind students that many roots of English words come from Greek or Latin. Ask students to research the roots **-aud-, -chron-, -cred-, -photo-, -pend-.** Then have them make a chart showing whether each root is Greek or Latin, the root's meaning, and English words that include it.

### Learners with Special Needs

Additional strategies for supporting learners with special needs can be found on page 173L.

# Eponyms and Collective Nouns

## Objectives

● **To recognize and use words that come from proper names**

● **To recognize and use collective nouns**

## Warming Up

● Write the following rhyme on the board and read it aloud with students.

The inventor of the **saxophone**

Was Belgian Adolphe Sax

And buttoned **cardigans** were worn

On English people's backs.

● Draw students' attention to the word **saxophone.** Ask them what they notice about the word and the name of the instrument's inventor. (The man's name is included in the word.) Point out that the root **-phon-** means "sound." Then ask volunteers to explain their ideas about the origin of the word **cardigan.** Ask a student to look up the word in the dictionary and tell the class the word's origin.

## Teaching the Lesson

● Tell students that a word based on a person's name is called an eponym.

● Ask a volunteer to read aloud the Helpful Hint on page 213. Encourage students to discuss how eponyms suggest the history of the things or ideas they name.

● Ask a volunteer to read the Helpful Hint on page 214. Explain that collective nouns make it easier to talk about a group of things, people, or animals that have some kind of relationship to one another. Ask volunteers to explain what the word **deck** tells you about the cards that comprise it. (The word **deck** implies that it is made up of a complete set of fifty-two cards—not just a random collection of cards.)

213

---

Name _____

> **Helpful Hint**
>
> An **eponym** is a word that came from the name of a person. English contains many eponyms. Each eponym has a story behind it. Here are two eponyms you may know:
>
> **sandwich**—named after John Montagu, 4th Earl of Sandwich
> **Braille**—named for Louis Braille, a French teacher who invented this system of printing and writing for the blind

A student learning **Braille**

 **Read the list of words or names in the box. Match each word with the clue that tells how the word got its name. Write the word from the box on the line. Use a dictionary, if needed.**

| cardigan | Georgia | Pennsylvania | saxophone | silhouette |

1. ___Pennsylvania___ is one of the 13 original colonies. William Penn (1644–1718) founded the colony and gave it his name.

2. A ___silhouette___ is an outline drawing cut from black paper. French leader Etienne de— (1709–1767) liked this cheap way to do portraits.

3. ___Georgia___ is a Southern state and one of the 13 original colonies. This state was named after King George II of England, who gave money to make it a colony.

4. A ___cardigan___ is a knitted sweater or jacket that buttons down the front. English general James Brudenell, 7th Earl of— (1797–1868), wore this style.

5. A ___saxophone___ is a brass wind instrument with valves, from Belgium. Inventor Adolphe Sax made this musical instrument more than a century ago.

 **CHALLENGE**

Many scientific words are eponyms. Use a dictionary to discover where the following names came from and what they mean:

| diesel | volt |
| hertz | curium |

---

# UNIVERSAL ACCESS
## Meeting Individual Needs

### Visual Learners

Invite students to draw pictures that will help them and their classmates remember that certain things are named after people. For example, they might sketch a nineteenth-century officer knitting a sweater during a battle or an earl ruling over an area on a map shaped like a sandwich. Display the finished products on the bulletin board.

### Logical Learners

Ask students to identify which animals congregate in groups called **herds** or **flocks** and which animals gather in groups called **prides** or **packs.** Then have students write a brief comparison of the "herd/flock" animals and the "pride/pack" animals, contrasting the animal's choice of food and methods of obtaining it.

**Helpful Hint**

Some nouns name a group of people, nations, animals, or things. This special naming word is called a **collective noun**. Here are two collective nouns:

a **flock** of sheep    a **galaxy** of stars

The Milky Way **Galaxy**

 **Each phrase below contains a collective noun. Underline the group of people, animals, or things that are named in this way. Then write the word on the line.**

1. a **deck** of ___cards___    boats    <u>cards</u>    ducks
2. a **company** of ___soldiers___    <u>soldiers</u>    water    geese
3. a **crew** of ___sailors___    tar    dogs    <u>sailors</u>
4. a **grove** of ___trees___    <u>trees</u>    graves    tables
5. a **mound** of ___dirt___    air    teachers    <u>dirt</u>
6. a **herd** of ___cattle___    <u>cattle</u>    cars    violins
7. a **pride** of ___lions___    mice    <u>lions</u>    babies
8. a **school** of ___fish___    <u>fish</u>    books    grades
9. a **swarm** of ___bees___    money    <u>bees</u>    sandwiches
10. a **fleet** of ___ships___    checkers    <u>ships</u>    papers

 **Choose the collective noun from the box below that best completes each sentence. Write the word on the line.**

| committee | nest | troop | team |
|---|---|---|---|

11. Have you seen the ___nest___ of sparrows by the chimney?
12. You have to be at least eight years old to join a Scout ___troop___.
13. The audience applauded the ___team___ of gymnasts.
14. A ___committee___ of senators will vote on the issue of raising taxes.

214    LESSON 105: Eponyms and Collective Nouns

 **Home Involvement Activity** Work together to find out the history of these fashion words. For whom was each named: **mackintosh, Levi's, raglan sleeve, chesterfield?** Then clip and label an example of each from a catalog.

## English-Language Learners/ESL

Give English-language learners pictures that illustrate some of the words in this lesson. Number the pictures and have students list the numbers. Then ask students to write the word naming the object beside the number of the picture in which it appears.

## Gifted Learners

Tell students that a collective noun can be used to create a metaphor. For example, the phrase **a galaxy of actors** suggests that the actors are all stars. Ask students to create metaphors using the words **gaggle** and **pride** by applying them to persons or items that are not usually associated with them.

### Learners with Special Needs

Additional strategies for supporting learners with special needs can be found on page 173L.

## Practicing the Skill

● Read aloud the directions on page 213 and help students complete the first item. Have students underline the phrases in the rest of the items that provide clues to the answers.

● Point out to students that they already know and use many of the collective nouns on page 214. Silently saying the phrases to themselves may help them as they complete the exercise.

## Curriculum Connections

### Spelling Link

Read the following sentences aloud. Repeat the word in bold type for students to write in their notebooks. Work together to check students' spelling of the words.

Lou's favorite **sandwich** is a BLT.

The **silhouette** of the bare tree against the sky is beautiful.

Jenna prefers **cardigans** to pullovers.

Dan's **saxophone** lesson is at 3:30.

Wendy opened a new **deck** of cards.

A **herd** of cattle grazed in the field.

Little Bo Peep lost a **flock** of sheep.

Out of the nest rose a **swarm** of bees.

### Writing Link

● Invite students to write brief stories giving their own imaginary versions of why the Earls of Cardigan and Sandwich invented the things that were named after them.

● Extend the activity by asking students to think of something to invent, and then to give it their name.

### Observational Assessment

*Note whether students can use and spell eponyms and collective nouns correctly.*

214

# Connecting Spelling and Writing

## Objectives

- **To recognize, spell, and use synonyms, antonyms, homonyms, eponyms, and collective nouns**
- **To write a report to explain how a place got its name**

## Warming Up

Write the following sentences on the board. As you point to each one, have students fill in the blanks.

1. The term for words that come from proper names is _____. (eponyms)

2. The term for pairs of words that have the same spelling but different meanings is _____. (multiple-meaning words or homographs)

3. The term for pairs of words that have the same pronunciation but different spellings and meanings is _____. (homonyms)

4. Synonyms and antonyms can be found in a _____. (thesaurus)

5. The term for words that refer to groups of things, animals, and people is _____. (collective nouns)

## Teaching the Lesson

- List on the board all the kinds of words to be reviewed. Have volunteers come to the board and write examples of each kind of word beside its name. Ask the class if the examples are spelled correctly.

- Ask students to write sentences using the examples. Have them take turns reading their sentences.

---

Name _____

 Read each phrase below. Say and spell each word in bold type. Repeat the word. Then sort the words. Look for pairs of synonyms, antonyms, and homonyms. Find the eponyms and the collective nouns. Write each word in the correct box below.

- **sealing** a package
- **seldom** hear music
- wore a **cardigan**
- **often** eat pasta
- a **temporary** shelter
- repeat your **response**
- left a **permanent** stain
- play the **saxophone**
- an **accelerated** pace

- watch a **whale** in Alaska
- hear the wind **wail**
- cut out a **silhouette**
- the correct **answer**
- painting the **ceiling**
- take a **brisk** walk
- a **herd** of buffalo
- a **pride** of lions
- a **swarm** of bees

A humpback **whale** breaching

| Synonyms | Antonyms | Homonyms |
|---|---|---|
| response | seldom | sealing |
| answer | often | ceiling |
| accelerated | temporary | whale |
| brisk | permanent | wail |

| Eponyms | Collective Nouns |
|---|---|
| cardigan | swarm |
| saxophone | herd |
| silhouette | pride |

---

# UNIVERSAL ACCESS
## Meeting Individual Needs

### Kinesthetic Learners

Have students make their own flash cards. On one side of each card, they can write the term for a special kind of word, such as homonym. On the other side, they can write a word or pair of words that exemplify the term. Have students find partners and quiz each other with the flash cards.

### Learners with Special Needs

Additional strategies for supporting learners with special needs can be found on page 173L.

### Auditory Learners

Have students play this game: One student gives a clue as to the identity of a kind of word, for example: *These words are not spelled alike.* A classmate asks for more information: *Do these words mean the same thing?* The student answers the question and gives more information: *No. These words sound alike.* The student who correctly identifies the kind of word (homonym) then gives the clues.

Many place names are eponyms. These places were named for the people who founded, conquered, or ruled them. For example, the city of Alexandria, in Egypt, was named for Alexander the Great. This young king conquered Egypt in 332 B.C. He then founded the great city of Alexandria and gave it his name.

★ With a small group of classmates, brainstorm a list of places, such as Alexandria, Pennsylvania, or New York, that were named after people. First, choose a place. Next, look in a print or an on-line encyclopedia to find out all that you can. Take notes. Then write a brief research report to explain how the place got its name. Use at least two of these spelling words.

| | | | | | |
|---|---|---|---|---|---|
| sealing | seldom | cardigan | often | temporary | response |
| permanent | saxophone | accelerated | whale | wail | silhouette |
| answer | ceiling | brisk | herd | pride | swarm |

Alexander the Great

Answers will vary.

_____

_____

_____

_____

_____

_____

**Writer's Tip**

State your topic in the **introduction**. Develop it in the **body** of your report. Summarize your information in the **conclusion**.

### ▶ Speaker's Challenge ◀

Present your report to the class. First, make an outline of your main points. Next, write your outline on note cards. Then, practice speaking from your cards. Use a strong voice.

Alexandria, Egypt, today

## The Writing Process

Tell students that on page 216 they will write a report about how a place got its name. Read aloud the introduction, directions, and spelling words at the top of the page.

**Prewrite** Discuss with students how to use both a printed encyclopedia and an on-line encyclopedia for research. Review with students how to take notes effectively.

**Write** Call students' attention to the Writer's Tip on page 216. Remind students to include at least two spelling words and to use their notes.

**Revise** Have students exchange their reports with a partner. Tell them to ask *Is this report clear? Do I understand how this place got its name?* Students should revise accordingly.

**Proofread** Have students check for errors in spelling, grammar, and punctuation.

**Publish** Students may copy their final drafts onto page 216 or a sheet of paper. Display the reports on a bulletin board.

**Computer Connection**

Share the following tips with students who use a word processor to do their writing.

● If a word includes an accent or a symbol such as **Á,** you can include it in your document file.

● Put your cursor on the place in the word where the symbol belongs. Go to the menu bar and click on "Insert." Click on "Symbol" from the list of options in the window you have opened. This will open a dialogue box with various symbols. Highlight the appropriate symbol and click on "Insert" to place it where it belongs in the document.

**Portfolio** Have students add their completed reports to their portfolios.

### English-Language Learners/ESL

Write the spelling words on the board. With students, pronounce each word and spell it aloud. Ask volunteers to define the words. Write each definition beside the word it defines. Then erase the word. Ask students to write each word on a sheet of paper as you point to its definition. Have students check their spelling in a dictionary.

### Gifted Learners

Invite students to write a composition about an imaginary place that they have "discovered" and named after themselves. Ask them to use synonyms and antonyms to compare and contrast this place with the actual place where they live. Challenge them to use homonyms in a creative way.

# Student Pages 217–218

## Idiomatic Expressions

### Objectives

- **To recognize the meaning of idioms**
- **To write sentences using idioms**

### Warming Up

- Write the following rhyme on the board and read it aloud for students.

  Idiomatic expressions

  Are made up of two or more words.

  Examples include to be **a snap**,

  **On the house**, and **for the birds**.

- Have students identify the idioms shown in bold type above. Ask volunteers to explain what they mean. (Something that's **a snap** is easy. Something that's **on the house** is free. Something that's **for the birds** is not very good.)

### Teaching the Lesson

- Tell students the phrases they identified in the *Warming-Up* exercise are called idioms, or idiomatic expressions. Explain that the meaning of an idiom is different from the literal meaning of the words that make it up. For example, to have a meal **on the house** does not mean to eat a meal on a housetop. It is a way of saying that the meal was free, or paid for by the restaurant (the house, in this case).

- Point out that students can sometimes figure out the meaning of unfamiliar idioms by using common sense and context clues. Use the examples in the Helpful Hint to demonstrate this strategy.

---

Name _____

> **Helpful Hint**
>
> An **idiomatic expression** (or **idiom**) is a phrase that means something different from what it seems to mean. Idiomatic expressions are part of everyday speech.
>
> Our dinner was **on the house.** *means* Our dinner was *free.*
> I **hit it off** with her parents. *means* I *got along well* with her parents.
> This lesson is **over his head.** *means* This lesson is *too hard for him.*

Each numbered sentence has an idiom in bold type. Circle the letter of the answer that means the same thing.

1. We decided to **clear the air.**
   a. We decided to drive only electric cars to reduce air pollution.
   b. We decided to buy room freshener to sweeten the air.
   c. We decided to say what was on our minds to get rid of the tension.

2. The science test was **a snap.**
   a. The science test was a surprise quiz.
   b. The science test was very easy.
   c. The science test was very hard.

3. I thought that the new movie was **for the birds.**
   a. I thought that the new movie was terrible.
   b. I thought that the new movie was about crows.
   c. I thought that the new movie had too much singing in it.

4. Cory's grade is **up in the air.**
   a. Cory's grade is an *A.*
   b. Cory's grade flew away.
   c. Cory's teacher has not yet decided Cory's grade.

**Danny's Diner**

**GUEST CHECK**
04847

Roast Fresh Turkey  16.95
Vegetable Platter  13.95
2 Iced Tea  4.50

FREE

$35.40
TAX  2.83
TOTAL: $38.23

> **CHALLENGE**
>
> Draw a funny cartoon to illustrate one of these **idiomatic expressions** or another one you know. Ask a classmate to guess the idiom you have drawn.

---

# UNIVERSAL ACCESS
## Meeting Individual Needs

### Kinesthetic Learners

Ask students to select three idioms and pantomime first the idioms' literal meanings and then the feelings or actions that they express. Help students select idioms that are easy to act out, such as the following: *They **rolled out the red carpet** for me. The miser **coughed up** a quarter for the waiter's tip. When Jim got into trouble, his friend **went to bat** for him.*

### Visual Learners

Give students pictures of objects mentioned in some common idioms—a piece of cake, a cup of tea, and a frozen pond with a sign saying "Danger—Thin Ice." Ask students to write a sentence using the idiom that each picture suggests.

**Each sentence at the left has an idiom in bold type. Draw a line to match the sentence at the left with the sentence at the right that means the same thing.**

1. They **put their heads together.**  a. They got the most attention.
2. They **talked my ear off.**  b. They thought about it together.
3. They **stole the spotlight.**  c. They chatted endlessly.

4. He's **up to his ears** in homework.  a. He is in trouble.
5. He **calls the shots.**  b. He is overwhelmed.
6. He's **in hot water.**  c. He is in charge.

7. We were still **in the running.**  a. We were running away from something.
8. We were **on the run.**  b. We had a chance to win the contest.
9. We were **running rings around** them.  c. We were beating them.

10. She was **hot under the collar.**  a. She felt very angry.
11. She could not make **head or tail of** it.  b. She realized what might happen.
12. She saw **the handwriting on the wall.**  c. She could not understand.

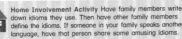

**Choose four idioms from above. Write a sentence for each one.**

13. Answers will vary.

_____

14. _____

_____

15. _____

_____

16. _____

_____

 **Home Involvement Activity** Have family members write down idioms they use. Then have other family members define the idioms. If someone in your family speaks another language, have that person share some amusing idioms.

## Practicing the Skill

● Read aloud the directions for pages 217 and 218, and complete the first item in each exercise with the students. Remind students to reread the Helpful Hint when completing the exercises.

● Point out to students that they already know and use many idioms. Ask volunteers to suggest idioms that have not been included in this lesson. Encourage the rest of the class to guess what these idioms mean.

## Curriculum Connections

### Spelling Link

Most idiomatic expressions contain fairly common words, so students should not have much trouble with their spellings. However, the terms **idiomatic expression** and **idiom** may be new to students. Encourage them to use a dictionary to check the spellings, pronunciations, and meanings of the words **idiom, idiomatic,** and **expression.**

### Writing Link

● Tell students that idioms often provide good clues about character in a piece of writing. Writers often use idioms in dialogue, or a conversation between two or more people.

● Invite students to write two dialogues about the same subject. One conversation should be spoken by people their own age and one by adults. Suggest that the type of idioms the speakers use should hint at whether they are younger or older.

● Ask students to exchange papers and have a partner guess which conversation took place between adults and which between young people.

### English-Language Learners/ESL

Make picture cards for the following images: a plate of food on top of a house, two heads together, and handwriting on a wall. Have students take turns choosing a card, acting out the idiom's meaning and using the idiom in a sentence.

### Gifted Learners

Give students a list of idioms and ask them to use them in sentences. Then challenge students to replace them with fresh metaphors or similes that convey the same feeling in a more original way.

### Learners with Special Needs

Additional strategies for supporting learners with special needs can be found on page 173L.

## Observational Assessment

*Make sure students are able to use context clues to help them distinguish between literal and figurative meanings of idioms.*

**218**

# Student Pages 219–220

## Word Analogies

### Objectives

- To recognize relationships between words and pairs of words in word analogies
- To complete word analogies

## Warming Up

- Write these word pairs on the board.

| | |
|---|---|
| thick : dense | rain : wet |
| sun : dry | tame : wild |
| sad : happy | bad : wicked |

- Ask volunteers to draw lines connecting the word pairs whose words are related in the same way. Suggest that students identify the ideas that connect the words in the first column and then look for word pairs in the second column that are similarly related. Students should look for three different relationships.

- Explain that each set of two word pairs is called a word analogy. The words in both pairs of a word analogy are related to each other in the same way.

## Teaching the Lesson

- Have a volunteer read aloud the Helpful Hints on page 219. Ask other volunteers to identify the relationships that were used in the *Warming-Up* exercise.

- Discuss all the relationships covered in the Helpful Hints. Have students give at least one word pair as an example of each relationship.

- Point out that the order of the word pairs in a word analogy may be reversed without changing the analogy.

---

Name _____

### Helpful Hints

Analogy questions often appear on standardized tests. **Word analogies** test your ability to understand how words and ideas relate. Read this:

**Up** is to **down** as **fast** is to **slow**.

THINK: **Up** and **down** are *opposites*. **Fast** and **slow** are *opposites*.

The words in both pairs relate in exactly the same way. Both are **antonyms**.

You can also write the analogy like this:   **up : down :: fast : slow**

Here are some other ways that pairs of words and ideas are related:

| | |
|---|---|
| They are *synonyms*. | **Fix** is to **repair** as **sew** is to **mend**. |
| They show *cause and effect*. | **Tired** is to **rest** as **happy** is to **smile**. |
| They show *parts of a whole*. | **room : house :: page : book** |
| They show *how objects are used*. | **pen : write :: crayon : draw** |
| They show *how products are produced*. | **milk : cow :: honey : bee** |

 **Read each word analogy. Write the correct description from the box below to show how the words in both pairs are related. The first answer is given.**

| word : antonym | object : use | product : producer |
|---|---|---|
| word : synonym | cause : effect | part : whole |

1. *Axe* is to *chop* as *scissors* is to *cut*. — **object : use**
2. *Toe* is to *foot* as *branch* is to *tree*. — part: whole
3. *Heat* is to *melt* as *cold* is to *freeze*. — cause: effect
4. *Top* is to *bottom* as *left* is to *right*. — word: antonym
5. cheese : goat :: feathers : chicken — product: producer
6. fast : speedy :: heavy : weighty — word: synonym
7. knife : slice :: strainer : drain — object: use
8. tall : short :: narrow : wide — word: antonym

 CHALLENGE

Make up three word analogies. Leave out the last word in each. Challenge a classmate to complete your analogies.

---

# UNIVERSAL ACCESS
## Meeting Individual Needs

### Logical Learners

Have students design charts and other graphics to express the different relationships used in word analogies. For example, they might show a **cause : effect** relationship with a flow chart or a **part : whole** relationship with a pie chart. For synonyms and antonyms that express degrees of intensity or measurement, students might use a scale that shows the most neutral word on the middle line, with synonyms above and antonyms below.

### Kinesthetic Learners

Give students a list of objects that can be found in the classroom. Invite them to find each object and demonstrate its relationship, either with another object or with an action. Then ask students to find two other objects, or an object and an action, that share the same relationship. Have students identify the relationship. For example, **finger : point :: toe : tap.** They would identify this relationship as **object : use.**

☆ **Circle the letter of the word that completes each analogy. Then write the word on the line.**

1. *Foot* is to *leg* as *mouth* is to ___face___.
   a. teeth
   b. lips
   c. ear
   (d.) face

2. *Rope* is to *mountain climbing* as *racket* is to ___tennis___.
   a. football
   b. volleyball
   (c.) tennis
   d. ice hockey

3. *Bat* is to *hit* as *glove* is to ___catch___.
   a. mitten
   b. buy
   c. uniform
   (d.) catch

4. *Hungry* is to *eat* as *study* is to ___learn___.
   a. student
   (b.) learn
   c. write
   d. lesson

5. *Easy* is to *simple* as *hard* is to ___difficult___.
   (a.) difficult
   b. harder
   c. soft
   d. rock

6. *Book* is to *library* as *dish* is to ___cupboard___.
   a. eating
   b. silverware
   c. dinner
   (d.) cupboard

7. Bad : good :: fat : ___thin___.
   (a.) thin
   b. eat
   c. hungry
   d. pork

8. thin : slender :: injury : ___wound___.
   a. thick
   (b.) wound
   c. slim
   d. doctor

9. Wool : sheep :: feathers : ___goose___.
   a. fur
   (b.) goose
   c. cotton
   d. whale

10. tickle : giggle :: embarrass : ___blush___.
    a. run
    (b.) blush
    c. laugh
    d. smile

**Home Involvement Activity** Solve this word analogy: *Composer* is to *symphony* as *carpenter* is to _____. Explain your answer. Make up other analogies to solve together.

---

**English-Language Learners/ESL**

Introduce word analogies by using pictures, real objects, and pantomime. Once students have grasped the concept, ask them to create their own word analogies using the pictures, real objects, and/or pantomime. Have fluent speakers name the relationship shared by the words in each pair of the word analogy.

**Gifted Learners**

Write an analogy such as the following on the board: **purple : lavender :: red : pink.** Help students identify the relationship between the items (from greater intensity to lesser intensity). Ask them to make up their own analogies based on relationships not mentioned in Lesson 108.

**Learners with Special Needs**

Additional strategies for supporting learners with special needs can be found on page 173L.

---

**Practicing the Skill**

● Read aloud the directions on pages 219–220, and help students complete the first item on each page.

● After students have finished the exercise on page 220, ask them to identify the relationship between the word pairs in each analogy.

**Curriculum Connections**

**Spelling Link**

● Give students a quiz to assess their ability to spell the terms—**synonym**, **antonym**, **relationship**, **product**, and **producer**—from Lesson 108.

● After the quiz, help students learn the words they missed by pointing out common suffixes, prefixes, and roots. Give a follow-up quiz and ask students to use each word in a sentence.

**Math Link**

● Tell students that mathematical proportions show relationships between numbers just as word analogies show relationships between words. Use this example to demonstrate: **100 : 50 :: 40 : 20.** Help students see that the relationship between the numbers in each pair is based on division. The second number in each pair is half of the first number.

● Invite students to make up their own proportions based on addition, subtraction, and multiplication. Have them tell how the number pairs are related.

**Observational Assessment**

*Check to see that students can complete word analogies correctly.*

# Connecting Reading and Writing

## Objectives

- **To read a nonfiction piece and respond to it in writing**
- **To distinguish between factual and fictional explanations of a natural event**
- **To synthesize ideas**
- **To write a myth**

## Warming Up

### Comprehension Skills

- Tell students that an article about a natural event often includes myths that were invented to explain the event before people came to understand the scientific reasons for it. As students read the article about the northern lights, they will need to **distinguish between fact and fiction.**

- Remind students that **synthesizing** ideas as they read means putting the ideas together and making sense of them.

## Teaching the Lesson

- For the first Reader's Response question, have students reread the article and take notes about the stories people invented.
- Have students focus on the information given in the third paragraph of the article to answer the second question.
- Encourage students to give reasons for their answers to the third question.

## Practicing the Skill

Invite volunteers to read the introduction, directions, and words in the box on page 222. Provide myths for students to use as models for their own writing.

---

Name _____

 Read about the dazzling northern lights that you can sometimes see in Alaska's night sky. Then answer the questions that follow.

# Fire in the Sky
### by David Foster

It's a shivering-cold night in Alaska—a good night to stay in by the fire. So why are people standing outside in the snow, hooting and hollering? Follow their gaze upward and you'll see. Ghostly, glowing ribbons of green, white, blue, and red are moving across the sky. It's the best fireworks show in the sky—the northern lights.

The northern lights' shimmering dance has mystified people for thousands of years. Ancient Eskimos believed the lights were spirits playing ball with a walrus head. Some gold-rush prospectors thought the lights were vapors rising from a hidden mine.

Today's scientists are more factual. They say the northern lights, also called the *aurora borealis,* occur when tiny particles from the sun hit Earth's atmosphere. The sun gives off not only heat and light but solar wind—a stream of electrically charged atomic particles. As they approach Earth, the particles are guided by our planet's magnetic field toward the North and South poles. Sixty to 200 miles above the ground, the particles collide with air molecules and make them glow like a neon sign.

Sometimes the aurora is a broad sheet of light. At other times, it looks like wavy ribbons. Big displays can last hours, with rays of light darting across the sky 100 times faster than a jet airplane! They also make a crackling noise.

1. Ancient Eskimos believed the lights were spirits playing ball with a walrus head; prospectors thought the lights were vapors rising from a hidden mine.
2. They say the lights occur when tiny particles from the sun hit Earth's atmosphere.
3. Answers will vary.

Usually the northern lights appear only in the Far North. But sometimes solar flares whip up big magnetic storms around Earth and create auroras that spread farther south. These rare southern appearances can cause quite a stir!

### Reader's Response

1. What are some stories that people have made up about the northern lights?
2. How do scientists explain the northern lights?
3. If you were looking at the northern lights, how do you think you would feel?

LESSON 109: Connecting Reading and Writing
Comprehension—Distinguish Between Fact and Fiction; Synthesize

221

---

# UNIVERSAL ACCESS
# Meeting Individual Needs

### Auditory Learners

Play taped readings or dramatizations of myths and legends for students. Then have pairs work together to prepare an oral presentation of their own myths. One student might pretend that he is trying to explain the strange and beautiful lights in the sky to someone who has never seen them. Tape-record their stories so they can share them with the class.

### Visual Learners

Show students several pictures of the northern lights. Ask them to use the pictures as inspiration for their stories. Encourage them to create watercolor, pastel, or crayon illustrations based on their stories. Provide a "gallery" space in the classroom for students to display their illustrated stories for their classmates to enjoy.

### Learners with Special Needs

Additional strategies for supporting learners with special needs can be found on page 173L.

**READ & WRITE**

For thousands of years, the people in what is now Alaska have been watching the dazzling displays of the northern lights. As with other natural events, ancient peoples made up stories to try to explain this grand fireworks display. Today, scientists know that the appearance of the northern lights is based on solar activity. Yet the old myths still entertain us.

⭐ **Make up your own myth about the northern lights. You could begin by reading some "how" or "why" stories. Native American myths are filled with stories that explain *how* or *why* something happens in nature. Then write your own myth. Explain why the northern lights occur. Use your imagination. Include at least two of these words.**

> beginning later meanwhile now when while therefore but yet
> before after although create observe first next then finally

Answers will vary.

_____

_____

_____

_____

_____

_____

_____

_____

**Writer's Tips**

- Include a strong sequence of events in your myth.
- Use transition words, such as *first*, *next*, and *then*, to connect your ideas and make them flow.

**Writer's Challenge**

Use science and facts to explain why another natural event occurs. For example, tell why earthquakes happen. Do some research. Then write a paragraph to explain this natural event.

The northern lights in Alaska

**222**

LESSON 109: Connecting Reading and Writing Comprehension—Distinguish Between Fact and Fiction; Synthesize

---

## The Writing Process

Have students visit the library to locate collections of myths told by Native Americans of the Northwest. Read examples of "how" or "why" stories with students.

**Prewrite** Have students make a web of words that express their feelings about the northern lights. Ask students if the words suggest a situation and a main character. After deciding on a situation and main character, have students outline their story.

**Write** Call students' attention to the Writer's Tips on page 222. Point out that the transition words listed will help them write their story using a clear time sequence.

**Revise** Ask students to read their stories with a partner and exchange feedback. Tell students to ask *Does this myth explain how or why the northern lights occurred?* Have partners revise accordingly.

**Proofread** Have students check for errors in spelling, grammar, and punctuation.

**Publish** Have students copy their final drafts onto page 222 or a sheet of paper.

**Computer Connection** Share the following tip with students who use a word processor to do their writing.

- Most word processing programs offer a Help feature on the menu bar. To get help while you are working on a document, go to the Help menu and then click on "Contents and Index." Look for the topic that you need help with.

- You may also be given the option to print the help topic. In the Help topic window, click "Options" and then "Print Topic."

**Portfolio** Have students add their completed myths to their portfolios.

---

### English-Language Learners/ESL

Invite students to create panels of pictures that show myths from their home cultures. Have them use pictures from magazines or original drawings. Invite students to act out their myths for the class, using their illustrations as graphic aids.

### Gifted Learners

Myths tell us much about other cultures. Through these tales, we can learn how people from ancient cultures interacted with their environment and how they tried to make sense of their world. Ask students to find a myth from another culture and explore what can be learned about the people who once told the tale. Encourage students to practice telling the tale orally. Offer a time when students can share the myth with the class.

# Reviewing and Assessing

## Clipped Words, Blended Words, Idioms, Word Analogies, Synonyms, Antonyms, and Dictionary Skills

### Objective

**To review and assess clipped words, blended words, idioms, word analogies, synonyms, antonyms, and dictionary skills.**

## Warming Up

Write these sentences on the board and have volunteers complete them.

1. Guide words show the first and last _____ _____ on a dictionary page. (entry words)

2. **Ad** is a _____word. (clipped)

3. The phrase **walking on air** is a(n) _____. (idiom)

4. The word _____ is a blend of **breakfast** and **lunch**. (brunch)

5. The word analogy **needle : sew :: axe : chop** shows a(n) _____ : _____ relationship. (object : use)

6. **Bad** is a(n) _____ for **evil**. (synonym)

## Teaching the Lesson

- Ask students to review the material from the *Warming-Up* exercise by rereading the Helpful Hints in Lessons 88, 96, 97, 103, 107, and 108.

- Have students find the word **smooth** in the dictionary and identify the guide words on the page on which the word is listed.

- Ask students to read any synonyms and antonyms given under the dictionary definition for **smooth**. Then ask them to compare these with the synonyms and antonyms given for **smooth** in a thesaurus.

223

---

Name _____

Is it a clipped word or a blended word? Underline your answer. Then on the line, write the word or words that make up the clipped or blended word.

1. gas          <u>clipped word</u>   blended word    gasoline
2. telethon     clipped word   <u>blended word</u>   telephone marathon
3. champ        <u>clipped word</u>   blended word    champion
4. smog         clipped word   <u>blended word</u>   smoke fog
5. grad         <u>clipped word</u>   blended word    graduate
6. moped        clipped word   <u>blended word</u>   motor pedal
7. flu          <u>clipped word</u>   blended word    influenza
8. brunch       clipped word   <u>blended word</u>   breakfast lunch

Each sentence below has an idiom in bold type. Circle the letter of the answer that means the same thing.

9. Our dinner was **on the house.**
   a. Our dinner tasted like wallpaper paste.
   (b.) Our dinner was free.
   c. Our dinner came from an old family recipe.

10. We are **in hot water.**
   a. We are all old sailors.
   b. We are going to take a bath.
   (c.) We are in big trouble.

Circle the letter of the word that best completes each analogy. Then write the word on the line.

11. Sleepy : yawn :: unhappy : ____frown____
   a. happy
   b. frown
   c. laugh
   d. gloomy

12. Much : little :: late : ____early____
   a. soon
   b. morning
   c. few
   d. early

# UNIVERSAL ACCESS
## Meeting Individual Needs

### Logical Learners

Have students outline the material reviewed in Lesson 110. Ask them to create a heading for each exercise and list the words or concepts reviewed in each. For example, the first heading would be: **A. Clipped Words and Blended Words.** Under that head the words **gas, telethon,** and so on would be listed. Have students continue in this manner for all the exercises in the lesson.

### Learners with Special Needs

Additional strategies for supporting learners with special needs can be found on page 173L.

### Visual Learners

Have students think of creative ways to convey the meaning of the terms **clipped words, blended words, antonyms,** and **synonyms,** using the terms themselves. For example, students might print **CLIPPED WORD** on an index card and then cut off everything but the word **CLIP.** Ask students to demonstrate their "graphic definitions" for the class.

**Read the passage. Then circle the letter of the answers below.**

Fairbanks, Alaska, hosts the World Eskimo-Indian Olympics (WEIO) each year. Contestants come from all over the state. Each year sees record-breaking crowds and more participants than the year before.

The events at the WEIO are not like those you may know. Yet all WEIO events have a common origin. They test the strength, agility, balance, and endurance needed to live in the harsh climate of the frozen north. The competitors show survival skills in events such as the knuckle hop, kneel jump, stick pull, ear weight, one-hand reach, and toe kick.

The blanket toss, or *nalakatuk*, is a popular WEIO event. It echoes a survival skill—the ability to spot game far off in the distance. The blanket is a walrus skin. A group of people hold it and stretch it like a trampoline. One person gets on the skin. That person gets tossed into the air. Judges look for the best height, balance, and air movements.

1. **WEIO** is the abbreviation for
   a. World Eskimo-Inuit Olympics.
   b. Weight Endurance International Open.
   c. World Eskimo-Indian Olympics.
   d. World Eskimo International Olympics.

2. You will find the word **state** on a dictionary page with the guide words
   a. staple – startle.
   b. starve – station.
   c. statue – steady.
   d. standard – star.

3. The best *antonym* for **harsh** is
   a. gentle.     b. changing.
   c. severe.     d. cool.

4. A *synonym* for **tossed** is
   a. thrown.     b. waved.
   c. caught.     d. lowered.

**Extend & Apply**

Visit the Web site at **www.weio.org** to find out more about the blanket toss and other events at the WEIO Olympics. Which do you think would be the most fun to see?

224     LESSON 110: Review and Assess

---

# Reteaching Activities

### Missing Links

Give students word analogies, each of which has one item missing. They can find the missing word by identifying the relationship between the words in the first pair. Model this example: *Open is to close as up is to ____.* State the relationship: **Open** is the opposite of **close.** Then have students identify the opposite of **up. (down)** Ask volunteers to supply the missing words in the rest of the word analogies.

### Idioms, Literally!

List idioms from Lesson 107 on the board. Have students think about how the literal meaning of each one could be related to its common use. For example, when your **feet get cold**, you slow down and stop moving until they warm up. Have students suggest a situation in which they would stop in the middle of what they were doing. Ask them to write a sentence about the situation using the idiom **to get cold feet.** Have them repeat the process for each idiom.

---

## Assessing the Skill

**Check Up** If you have not yet assigned the exercises on page 223 as outlined in *Teaching the Lesson,* do so now. Page 224 will help you assess students' mastery of abbreviations, antonyms, synonyms, and guide words. Read the directions aloud.

**Observational Assessment** Observe students as they work. Review your notes from previous lessons. Evaluate specific improvements as well as overall progress by comparing your earlier observations with current ones.

**Student Skills Assessment** Keep track of each student's progress in understanding clipped words and blended words, idioms, word analogies, synonyms, antonyms, and dictionary skills using the checklist on page 173H.

**Writing Conference** Meet with students individually to discuss their written work. Review portfolio samples and any other written work from earlier lessons in the unit. Have students look at earlier writing assignments, such as their dialogues on page 218. Have students review the myths they wrote on page 222 and discuss how their writing has improved. Ask students to recall a favorite piece of writing in their Home Portfolios and invite them to share it with the class.

Group together students who need further help with this material and have them complete the *Reteaching Activities.* Turn to page 173C for alternate methods of assessment.

# References for Word Study Research Base

Adams, M. J., R. Treiman, and M. Pressley. 1996. "Reading, Writing, and Literacy." In *Handbook of Child Psychology.* Edited by I. Sigel and A. Renninger, vol. 4, Child Psychology in Practice. New York: Wiley.

Braunger, J. and J. P. Lewis. 1997. *Building a Knowledge Base in Reading.* Portland, OR: Northwest Regional Educational Laboratory's Curriculum and Instruction Services.

Gaskins, I. W. and L. C. Ehri, et al. 1996/1997. "Procedures for Word Learning: Making Discoveries About Words." *The Reading Teacher* 50: 312–336.

Hennings, D. G. 2000. "Contextually Relevant Word Study: Adolescent Vocabulary Development Across the Curriculum." *Journal of Adolescent & Adult Literacy* 44: 268–279.

Morrow, L. M. 1997. *The Literacy Center: Contexts for Reading and Writing.* York, ME: Stenhouse Publishers.

_____. 2001. *Literacy Development in the Early Years: Helping Children Read and Write.* 4th ed. Needham Heights, MA: Allyn & Bacon.

Morrow, L. M. and D. Tracey. 1997. "Strategies Used for Phonics Instruction in Early Childhood Classrooms." *The Reading Teacher* 50: 644–653.

National Institute of Child Health and Human Development. 2000. *Report of the National Reading Panel: Teaching Children to Read and Evidence-Based Assessment of the Scientific Research and Literature on Reading and Its Implications for Reading Instruction.* Washington, DC: National Institute of Child Health and Human Development.

Pearson, D. P., L. R. Roehler, J. A. Dole, and G. G. Duffy. 1992. "Developing Expertise in Reading Comprehension." *In What Research Has to Say About Reading Instruction.* Edited by J. S. Samuels and A. E. Farstrup. Newark, DE: International Reading Association.

Texas Education Agency. 1997. *Beginning Reading Instruction: Components and Features of a Research-Based Reading Program.* Austin, TX: Texas Education Agency.

Vacca, J. L., R.T. Vacca, and M. K. Gove. 2000. *Reading and Learning to Read.* New York: Addison Wesley Longman.

Vacca, R. T. 2000. "Word Study Strategies at the Middle Grades." New York: William H. Sadlier, Inc.

Vacca, R. T and J. L. Vacca. 1999. *Content Area Reading: Literacy and Learning Across the Curriculum.* New York: Addison Wesley Longman.

Wong Fillmore, L. 1991. "When Learning a Second Language Means Losing the First." *Early Childhood Research Quarterly* 6: 323–346.